Too Scared to Learn
Women, Violence, and Education

Too Scared to Learn
Women, Violence, and Education

Jenny Horsman

Spiral Community Resource Group,
Toronto, Ontario, Canada

2000

LAWRENCE ERLBAUM ASSOCIATES, PUBLISHERS
Mahwah, New Jersey   London

Cover photo: The Women's Success Course, Parkdale
Project Read. Photo courtesy of Marsha Sfeir.

Lawrence Erlbaum Associates, Inc., Publishers
10 Industrial Avenue
Mahwah, NJ 07430

Cover design by Kathryn Houghtaling Lacey

Library of Congress Cataloging-in-Publication Data

Horsman, Jenny.
Too scared to learn : women, violence, and education /
   Jenny Horsman.
         p. cm.
      Includes bibliographical references and index.
ISBN 0-8058-3658-6 (cloth : alk. paper) —
   ISBN 0-8058-3659-4 (pbk. : alk. paper)
1. Abused women—Education. 2. Language arts.
   3. Literacy—Social aspects. I. Title.
LC1481 . H67 2000
371.822—dc21   99-058536
                                                      CIP

Books published by Lawrence Erlbaum Associates are printed on
acid-free paper, and their bindings are chosen for strength and
durability.

Printed in the United States of America
10 9 8 7 6 5 4 3 2 1

For Catherine Garrity,
who set me on this road;

For every woman
who is learning in the aftermath of violence;

In memory of Lois Heitner, Marie Barton, and Pat MacNeil,
who offered wisdom along the way;

And in memory of Mary Kernohan

But we must not be silent,
or we, too, will share the blame.

I think about the swallows
and I think about the time
when the miners used canaries
to give warning in the mine
and if the birds fell dead
the miners knew to get away.
The swallows are all dead,
my God, how can they make us stay?

Swallows in the rafters,
canaries in the mine
tell us we've been poisoned,
we're running out of time.

Linda Allen[1]

[1]Written by Linda Allen, from "Canaries in the Mine" (1991). Audio recording on *Washington Notebook: New Songs of the Northwest Sung by Northwest Musicians*. Published by Victory Music. Produced by Linda Allen and Cary Black. Used by permission.

Contents

Part II: Learning in the Context of Trauma

Part III: Bearing Witness

Part IV: Pulling It All Together

Preface

Too Scared to Learn is directed primarily at educators. It is based on my belief that educators and the education system must recognize the impact of women's and girls' experience of violence on their attempts to learn. This belief comes out of many years of work—as a practitioner and researcher/writer—in the field of adult literacy and job training. Although the research and practice that inform this book are drawn primarily from work with adult literacy learners, the implications are much broader—extending to girls' experiences of learning and all other settings in which adult women endeavor to learn.

Extensive research forms the basis of this book. I interviewed counselors and therapists, literacy learners, and educators working in different situations and read a wide range of theoretical and experiential publications. My purpose was to begin to build a bridge between therapeutic and educational discourses to encourage greater exchange of knowledge between the two fields and to contribute to the development of new discourses and practices that reconceptualize the intersection between violence and learning. Reconceptualization is crucial because previous understandings have pathologized learners and minimized the problem, rather than recognize the need to develop educational practices that facilitate learning for all.

I talked to an enormous number of people in each region of Canada, yet know that learners, practitioners, and counselors in other locations could have added further insights. I continued the research through conversations, in person and on e-mail, with practitioners based in Canada, the United States, and Australia sparked by an online seminar, workshops, presentations, and my requests for permission to quote. All these interactions

have contributed to the analysis presented here. It has been difficult to stop
adding new insights and send this book out into the world.

Although many of those quoted clarified and strengthened their meaning (and often mine too) when I checked with them later, I encouraged them
to keep the style of spoken interview or online chat. Where possible, I have
named each person whose words I am quoting or who provided me with information. Although as a reader you may wonder why names are included, I
believe the wonderful breadth of people whose wisdom informed this book
must be visible. For many women, the acknowledgment of their contribu-
tion to the book was an important reminder of the value of their words and
ideas and affirmed their status as *knowers*.

Too Scared to Learn was written for literacy and adult upgrading practitioners, as well as teachers of English to speakers of other languages. I imagined myself speaking to others, like me, who worry about how to help their
students learn successfully and struggle to respond adequately to direct disclosures of violence and the myriad other ways that violence and its aftermath are a daily presence in the classroom. Encouraged by Susan Heald, reviewer and critical reader, as well as other educators, I have increasingly
begun to imagine a wider audience that includes not only those involved in
adult basic education, but also in other areas of adult and children's education. I believe many educators hold pieces of the puzzle of how to teach in
ways that recognize the impacts of violence on learning. I hope that this
work, by bringing together so much of this wisdom, provides a key to new
understandings and analysis.

In my life and in my work, I believe in bridging the divides between theory
and practice. This book is no exception. Here I rethink conceptualizations
of violence in society and connections between violence and learning. I interweave a wealth of practical ideas, possibilities, and thoughts about what
practitioners might *do* differently in classrooms and educational institutions
if we begin to *think* differently about violence. I hope that this book is also
read by those interested in theory—academics, activists, and
policymakers—so that theoretical and systemic change might result and
broaden the possibilities for societal and educational change.

I encourage practitioners to read with highlighters and post-it notes in
hand so that they are able to locate again the ideas threaded throughout the
book that they want to try out in their own setting. This book is not intended
to be a how-to or offer prescriptions. However, it is hoped that the detailed
practical ideas spark educators to notice new things in the classroom and try

out new strategies. Through this book, I want to shift thinking and provide clues to new practices that could be developed.

The book is divided into four parts. The first part is called *Canaries in the Mine* to highlight a shift from seeing those who have experienced violence as *damaged goods*, to recognizing that they provide an early warning system that current levels of violence are not healthy. This part contains three chapters that together provide the backdrop for looking at violence and learning. Chapter 1 introduces the book, provides more information about the research that led to it, and firmly places the stance of the book as beyond deficit thinking. Chapter 2 provides the theoretical background to support the questioning of common conceptions of violence. Many forms of violence and the ways they impact on education are introduced briefly in chapter 3. This is done so that we can recognize the presence of trauma in education, particularly in adult literacy settings.

Part II addresses in-depth *Learning in the Context of Trauma*. Three lengthy chapters (chaps. 4, 5, and 6) allow the space to explore the complex ways the aftermath of violence might be present in the classroom and suggest approaches to enhance learning for all learners in the face of that.

Part III focuses on *Bearing Witness*. Chapter 7 looks at a myriad of ways in which connections between literacy and counseling can be created to support current and new program models. In chapter 8, I look at the experience of bearing witness and the burden it places on educators, arguing for a recognition, both of the value of bearing witness and the importance of creating a range of supports to ensure that practitioners do not become depleted and burned out. Part IV, *Pulling It All Together*, contains the concluding chapter, which confirms the changes needed in education and society more broadly and stresses the urgency with which policymakers and educators must begin to instigate change.

As I complete this book, I am preparing to return to the classroom to try out many of the ideas presented here while working with women learners in a small urban community program. I am also starting another stage of research, together with Susan Heald, to look at what happens when literacy practitioners try to make violence more visible in their programs and respond to the impacts of violence on learning through exploring new possibilities for practice. Exploring the process of change, examining barriers and enablers to creating trauma-sensitive practice, will provide more information about the possibilities for creating fundamental change in education practice. As practitioners in a range of programs try out the ideas proposed here, clarity about what does and does not work in a variety of settings—community college, small community agency, large urban center, rural outpost, northern community, one-person program, large institution, and so on—can provide support for more practitioners to explore change in their own settings.

This continuing blend of theory, research, and practice means that the conversations that have led to the writing of this book will continue. I invite you to join in. Write to me via my Web page (www.jennyhorsman.com) and tell me about your reactions to this work. What happens when you rethink violence or break the silences in your program and put ideas presented here, or new possibilities you envisage, into practice? Your perspective may help inform the next book, or you might want to write about your approach. It is my hope that, as the talk and writing continues, the silences about the presence of violence in society and its impact on learning will be diminished and understandings of educators about how to support learning for all students will be enhanced. I dream that such change can ultimately contribute to a reduction in violence in society.

Acknowledgments

I wrote this book to honor all women who know from their own experience that violence against women and girls, both overt and subtle, is far too prevalent. I contribute my voice as one among many who speak out against all violence. I hope to make visible what this violence means for education, and for literacy learning in particular, and suggest ways to help women learn.

I wrote too for my father, who tells me often that he does not believe there is still violence against women, and for all those who deny the evidence of violence and think that it only happens somewhere else. I have had arguments in the past, insisting that he recognize what I knew from my work, from a friend's murder, from the disclosures I have heard, from altogether too much evidence. Instead of arguing, I now write.

I am fortunate to have had enormous numbers of people around me who believed in this work and helped make it possible. I thank and acknowledge their contributions in chronological order:

- Catherine Garrity for what I learned from our work together.

- Wendy Wildfong, my therapist for many years, for her support as I work through my own issues and questions about the possibility of violence in my life and the impact of researching and writing such hard material.

- Kathleen Rockhill for helping me rethink my research plans and reconceive the funding proposal when it looked as if it would not be funded.

- The National Literacy Secretariat of Human Resources Development Canada for funding both the initial research and the writing and publishing (in Canada); Marla Waltman Daschko, and Margaret Robinson, the human face of the institution, who helped me through the process. Margaret, my ongoing contact, was steady and reliable in her interest and support of the work.

• Canadian Congress for Learning Opportunities for Women (CCLOW) board and literacy committee for sponsoring the projects. Bernnitta Hawkins, executive director during the research process, gave wonderful support and gave me hope to continue the work, helping me even after she left CCLOW.

• Evelyn Battell, Mary Norton, Cate Sills, and Catherine O'Bryan who helped me set up interviews, each in their own region. Without Cate Sills' support, I would have missed the opportunity to learn from many wonderful people in the North West Territories. Sally Gellard, Sylvia Provenski, and Maureen Doherty who helped locally with contacts and interview groups.

• Everyone who participated in interviews. There are too many to name here, but those willing to be named are listed at the end of this book. I thank them all for their generosity and wisdom. Their knowledge makes up the heart of this book. Some are named in connection with their words. Others, interviewed in groups, or whom I was unable to contact, I could not name. They also contributed immensely to this work.

• The advisory committee from across the country who participated in the initial research project: Jeanette Austin Odina, Evelyn Battell, Mary J. Breen, Nancy Cooper, Jane Field, Susan Goodfellow, Susan Heald, Moon Joyce, Michele Kuhlmann, Mary Norton, Kathleen O'Connell, Kathleen Rockhill, Linda Shohet, Cate Sills, Denyse Stewart, Aisla Thomson, Tracy Westell, and Helen Woodrow. They helped shape this work, each in their own way, responding to e-mails, bouncing ideas, and helping to ground me.

• Carrying out interviews, the enormity of the issue I had taken on, led my back to seize up. The discovery of yoga and Alex Krivicich, an outstandingly sensitive teacher, helped me connect with and heal my body.

• Haley Gaber-Katz and Nicole Ysabet-Scott scoured libraries for articles, photocopied, transcribed endless interview tapes, and generally supported this work with skill and enthusiasm. Keri O'Measa picked up the support tasks in the final stages, patiently typing in an elusive and chaotic pile of references.

• Susan Heald and Evelyn Battell believed in this study from the first, tirelessly bounced ideas, and supported me to hold to the knowledge that it is important work.

• The participants in workshops where I checked out my thinking helping to develop this analysis. Carolyn Medel-Añonuevo, Linda Shohet,

Sue Shore, and Daphne Greenberg gave me key opportunities to present or lead workshops and test out my ideas.

• Participants in the online seminar on Alphacom (now Alphaplus) discussed an early paper, giving me more insights and ideas. Betsy Trumpener publicized it efficiently and helped everyone to participate, contributing to the success.

• Linzi Manicom and Tracy Westell read an early draft and helped me see that I really did have a book and had better look for funding to sink into further analysis.

• Evelyn Battell, Priscilla George, Susan Goodfellow, Susan Heald, and Mary Norton, critical readers, and Elsa Auerbach, publisher's reviewer, read the close-to-final manuscript and gave me excellent feedback.

• Sharon Rosenberg and Tanya Lewis let me join their writing group, offered me encouragement, helped me clarify my ideas and find references, *and*, through their own writing on violence—challenging the concept of normalcy—helped me discover the ground I needed to explore.

• Ann Decter, editor, writing coach, and much more. Without her unfailing encouragement, careful edits, and suggestions to strengthen the manuscript at every stage, there would be no book. Naomi Silverman, editor at Lawrence Erlbaum Associates, enthusiastically recommended the manuscript for publishing and shared my belief in the importance of this work. Renata Butera, production editor, checked every last detail with a grace and humor that made it a pleasure to work with her. Barbara Schon generously created wonderful indexes, committed to helping readers use the book with ease.

• Alice de Wolff met with me in staff meetings throughout, helped me strategize how to do the work I wanted to do and write funding proposals, read drafts, and generally kept me on track with this project from start to finish.

• Moon Joyce, bore the brunt of much of my anxiety—my swings from elation to despair as I worked on this research and writing. Talking through ideas when I was blocked, reading drafts when I did not know what came next, finding impossible references, encouraging me, cooking meals—her support, encouragement, and firm belief that I could do this thing and that it *will* prove valuable is precious beyond words.

Although this may sound like an endless list of names, I still wake in the night worrying that there are ideas in the book that I have not credited and people who helped me whom I have not thanked. I nearly forgot family and friends especially my mother, sister, and friend Elaine

Gaber-Katz who encouraged me throughout! I have talked to so many friends and colleagues during the last few years whose thoughts, insights, and comments have encouraged me, enhanced my analysis, or provided examples to support an argument. I know I have not credited or thanked them all. When I had hoped to quote but could not find the person to ask permission, I paraphrased their idea or suggestion. If you recognize your input to this work, I thank you and apologize for my failure to add your name to the text.

This work holds enormous importance to me. When I began, I was tired. I had been working in literacy for more than 20 years and was wondering whether I should leave the field. The research connected me to many wise women in literacy and the therapeutic field and renewed my belief in literacy work. Now I see my next steps and have faith that recognizing the impact of trauma on learning can make learning more possible for those who otherwise judge themselves harshly. I developed the analysis presented here based on the insights and ideas of an enormous number of people. I take full responsibility for all errors of fact or interpretation. I offer heartfelt thanks to everyone mentioned here and all others who played a role, however tiny, in making it possible for me to complete this stage of the work. Thank you!

I

CANARIES IN THE MINE

1

Introduction

I'm just realizing that the violence is so big and the situation is so great that if it were happening to some other group, if it were happening in some other country, it would be called genocide. . . . If it was an occasional thing it would be terrible. But because it happens every day to so many women it's ordinary. And I just keep getting struck by the sense that people aren't paying any attention to it because it's so ordinary. I keep thinking, "Well, I just have to tell them, because if I tell them they'll do something about it."
    —Evelyn Battell, literacy instructor from British Columbia[1]

I used to teach a class for welfare women, 98% of whom had either been in abusive relationships and gotten out, or were still in them.
    The figures for the women in my class that had come from a background of childhood violence or abuse were horrifying—100% (there were 20 women in my class).
    —Beth Crowther, coordinator, ESOL project, Texas

In 1986, when I interviewed women in Nova Scotia about their experience of limited illiteracy, many of the women talked about experiences of violence in their lives.[2] I am ashamed to admit that initially I saw this information as irrelevant to my study. When time was short, I would en-

---

[1]Quotes are from interviews and input to an online seminar. Interview data are verbatim except for the omission of words such as *I think, sort of,* and *um.* More substantial omissions are indicated with three dots (...). I have tried to identify the names and locations of people interviewed. However, because most literacy interviews were in groups, there are many occasions when I can only indicate the group, not an individual. In contrast, I interviewed most therapists and counselors in individual sessions so I can identify individuals by name. All quotes are used with permission.

3

courage women to *move on* from these stories to speak about the experience of literacy practices in their lives. Later, as I listened to the
interview tapes and heard over and over again about experiences of violence, I began to question the connections between these experiences of
violence and their literacy learning as children and adults. The women in
Nova Scotia spoke of childhood violence at home and in school and of
violence as adults living with violent men. In the context of that study, I
began to see a broad range of violence as the backdrop against which I
was examining the promise of literacy. Ten years after interviewing
women for that research, I shifted to a direct focus on these issues—moving the issue of violence to the foreground and examining learning in
light of it.

I have been particularly influenced in this shift by my experience tutoring one literacy student. I began working with her in 1990 and have
previously described the beginnings of this tutoring:

> Several years ago, when a woman from the women's literacy group I was
> facilitating called me to apologize for speaking about her unhappy child-
> hood in our last group session, I said she had no need to apologize. This
> was the beginning of a relationship I had no experience to handle. This
> woman had never told anybody else about her childhood. This telling, and
> my acknowledgement that it was fine that she spoke of it, led to a difficult
> process where she at first wanted to tell me the horrors of her childhood
> and wanted more and more of my time and my support. I kept backing off
> and then feeling bad—scared that she was asking more of me than I could
> give, but unwilling to let her down. Finally I suggested that I could try to
> give her support through a regular meeting where she could speak, read
> and write about her memories of childhood and the abuse she experienced
> then. She decided to meet with me and we began a long process of negoti-
> ating how we would work together, which evolved into a special kind of
> tutoring situation. (Horsman, 1994a, p. 56)

Working closely with this learner—I call her Mary in my writings (1994a,
1995, 1996)—I noticed many features of her literacy learning and participation in a literacy program; I began to question to what extent these features resulted from her experiences of violence. Observing Mary also led
me to observe similarities in the learning and participation of other learners, and to question whether programs and instructors should be working
differently with learners, taking into account impacts of violence on
learning and participation. The more I have talked and written about

---

²I have written about this research in full in the original thesis (1989a), in an adaptation
as a book (1990), and in several articles (1988, 1989b, 1994b).

these issues, the more I have found that other literacy workers are also asking similar questions.[3]

Increasingly, conversations have also included teachers and trainers in other settings—from elementary school to university—all talking about difficulties they recognize and questioning what they might do differently if they, and the institutions they work within, acknowledged the impact of violence on learning. Educators expressed doubts about how to respond to learners whom they know, or suspect, may have experienced violence in their lives. This research was directly prompted by my desire to collect information so that I, and other literacy workers, can learn how to work more effectively with Mary and learners like her. With the study completed, I realize we need to radically change literacy practice and apply these understandings to education at all levels and in all settings.

LITERACY, BUT NOT ONLY LITERACY . . .

It is particularly important to look at the impact of violence on learning in the area of literacy, not simply because there may be extremely large numbers of adult literacy learners who have experienced violence, but also because literacy learning is likely to work as a particularly strong trigger for memories of violence for many women. However, the effects of violence are not confined to literacy learning. Education at all levels is profoundly affected. Because literacy takes learners back to their failure to learn to read well as children, it may also take them back to memories of being a child—to memories of violence at home or school. Literacy learning may be the first return to a schoollike situation for many learners, and that, in itself, may be terrifying and lead to panic. Learning something that many assume should have been learned in childhood may pose a challenge to anyone—more so for a person struggling with their sense of self and low self-esteem—who may also have experienced violence or trauma.[4]

In the face of trauma, literacy learning is complex work. Literacy learners who have experienced violence in childhood—in the home or at school—find the horrors of their childhood brought back to the present

---

[3]I have led workshops and made presentations on these issues throughout Canada, in many places in the United States and Australia, and to an international audience in Hamburg, Germany. In all these settings, my focus on violence has resonated with many literacy workers (and where they were present also with literacy learners). They have talked about their experiences and the issues in their contexts, confirming for me the importance of examining impacts of violence.

[4]The term *trauma* focuses on the person's response to violence. Traumatic events "overwhelm the ordinary human adaptations to life" (Herman, 1992, p. 33). The term *trauma* is discussed further in chap. 2.

when they return to the classroom and try to improve their reading—a task they first approached in childhood. Learners who have experienced violence as adults may have difficulty concentrating on learning. Deaf students and those with intellectual or physical disabilities are particularly vulnerable to abuse by those on whom they depend. Even those learners who have tried to escape the violence in their lives and see learning as a means to move forward may find that the cycle of violence continues. First Nation students bring the legacy of residential schooling with them to their learning, even those who did not experience it directly. Students who seek to escape violent relationships often find the violence escalates when they begin to attend school. For some, the classroom may be the only safe place they experience. For others, that too may be dangerous, as they are exposed to harassment and put-downs by other students and even teachers. The whole range of violence in learners' lives is vividly present in the classroom, affecting the possibilities of successful learning for large numbers of students.

Literacy learning is an acute example of problems that occur whenever people try to learn and teach; it is not the only learning where the experience of violence creates an impact. My research included also Adult Basic Education (ABE), upgrading and job-readiness teachers, teachers of English to speakers of other languages, and, unintentionally, university and college instructors and staff. During an online seminar, Mary J. Breen described the demands on all instructors:

> . . . all teachers deal with violence in their work because violence is an issue for everyone in this culture. For many people, a teacher is the only outside person they can talk with. I think of a good friend of mine who teaches in a community college. In any typical week, he hears stories such as these: a student misses classes because she was assaulted by her relative at a wedding; a male student misses weeks of classes because of a violent beating outside a bar by strangers; a young woman is always on edge because she has been stalked for a long time by an ex-partner; another student doesn't finish his assignment because he spent days in court with his father. . . . My reason for stressing [this]is that I often hear people speak of the poor in terms of the violent, disruptive lives they lead—as if domestic assault and sexual abuse were issues only pertinent to "them" not "us". . . . (Alphaplus Literacy & Violence Online Seminar,[5] February–April 1998)

---

[5]Alphaplus Centre was created from the merger of Alphacom, an electronic communications network for literacy practitioners, and AlphaOntario a resource library, which distributes literacy and language materials throughout Ontario. Alphacom hosted an 8-week seminar on Trauma and literacy in 1998. I facilitated the seminar focused on a discussion paper based on my research study. The paper is posted at www.Alphaplus.ca (Horsman, 1997).

Unless the everyday presence of violence is acknowledged, teachers can only question how to teach and respond adequately. A university professor explained that the content of courses can bring students' memories of their own experiences front and center, leading to disclosures she feels ill-equipped to cope with:

> What happens usually is that students will come and talk to me, so there's usually an increase in disclosures after a classroom discussion or lecture dealing with a topic such as colonization, structural violence, patriarchy etc. I'm not a counsellor. I can listen and I can suggest where people can go for help, but beyond that I can't counsel. I often end up wondering how I can best deal with this. (personal correspondence, July 1999)

Not all instructors experience disclosures in this way; many may not be perceived as trustworthy or approachable and may never know why students do poorly in their course, leave a class quietly perhaps holding back tears, miss classes, or drop out. One college librarian spoke of numerous students who tell her their stories when they retreat to the library fleeing a class that disturbs them and leaves them unable to stay in class.[6]

Another online participant, Kathryn Alexander, a university tutor, explained:

> I feel that the trajectory of violence and literacy has been a theme in many students' lives—even if they are able to succeed and go on to university—it still affects them—mainly I have heard and experienced stories from women who are searching for means to make sense of their experience of abuse and survival in their own education—choosing certain areas for study—and then struggling with the institutional structures that may in fact mirror back the violence disrespect/control/or discrimination they have survived. (Alphaplus Literacy & Violence Online Seminar, February–April 1998)

Unless education at all levels acknowledges the violence in the lives of women and children, along with its impact on learning, many students will not only fail to learn, but may also experience the educational setting as a silencing place or another site of violence, where they are controlled and diminished by institutional structures or classroom interactions and shamed by their failure to learn.

---

[6]Many autobiographical writings provide vivid accounts of women's experiences in school or college classrooms when past or present violence impinges on learning (e.g., Helfield, 1996/1997; Littman, 1993; Nyquist, 1998; Rundle & Ysabet-Scott, 1995). Two special issues of *Women's Education* also contain many articles (1992, 1994).

BACKGROUND TO THE RESEARCH

A study carried out by the Canadian Congress for Learning Opportunities for Women (Lloyd, Ennis, & Atkinson, 1994a, 1994b, 1994c) identified violence as a major barrier to women's literacy learning. Women involved in this research talked "about the pervasiveness and magnitude of violence against women" (Lloyd et al., 1994a, p. 107). Three women involved in the research taught literacy classes where every woman present had been sexually abused. One *woman-positive*[7] activity, carried out as part of the study, involved a house-to-house survey in rural Newfoundland. As they conducted the survey, men sometimes refused to let the women even answer the survey questions. In a reflection at the end of the study, one interviewer summed up what they had learned:

> On every page of every questionnaire we see violence, poverty, and loneliness. The despair in the young women especially is loud and clear. They are in situations that make life seem hopeless. They either don't know they have choices or they don't want to leave the situation—we don't really know. Or do they really have choices? (Ennis et al., 1994, p. 81)

For the most part, little is written or said about links between violence and literacy. Some have suggested that, as a first step to changing this, a study is needed to look at whether there are higher statistics of violence in the lives of adult literacy learners than in the general population. Accounts of literacy workers who have discovered that all, or most, of the students in a class have experienced sexual or physical abuse as children certainly suggest that such a study might reveal that horrifyingly high numbers of adults, both women and men, in literacy programs experienced abuse as children. In an earlier article, I speculated that children dealing with abuse might be expected to have had difficulty concentrating on learning to read:

> If she was being severely abused as a child, either sexually, emotionally or physically, what was her experience of trying to learn to read? An enormous amount of energy would have been needed to survive, to bury what was happening to her even from her own consciousness, to cry out for help in a myriad of direct or indirect ways, to continually monitor her world for her safety. For some, the experience of abuse may have led to them working even harder at school work, but for others the erosion of sense of self, self-esteem and self-confidence may all have interfered with the process of becoming a successful learner. (Horsman, 1995, p. 207)

---

[7]*Woman-positive* was the term used for activities intended to benefit women in the program.

Although people often ask me about the statistics, I decided not to focus on that issue. For me, the most pressing question is not how *many* literacy learners have experienced trauma, but *how* literacy programs can teach most effectively. Even if the number of women in literacy programs is no higher than the general population, we still need to know how to carry out literacy work and other education in ways that are effective for women and children who have survived trauma.

Statistics for the general population are high, and all evidence suggests that these figures minimize the problems. In 1982, Diana Russel reported statistics learned from her research "that 38 percent of all women are sexually abused by an adult before the age of 18" (Cited in Dinsmore, 1991, p. 2). The *Badgley Report* (1984, p. 3) concluded "approximately 54 percent of the females under the age of 18 have been sexually assaulted. The definition of sexual assault used here is sexual activity ranging from unwanted touching and threats of unwanted touching to rape causing bodily harm . . . Badgley shows that about 31 percent of the males of all ages have been sexually assaulted. The majority of these males were under 21 when the first assault took place" (cited in Mitchell, 1985, p. 88). Recent statistics obtained by Statistics Canada found that 29% of ever-married women have experienced wife assault. The report stated that "Over half of these women experienced serious assaults" (Statistics Canada, 1998, p. 3). Although no statistics separate out literacy learners, we can only assume that these rates are a minimum that applies to literacy learners and acknowledge that anecdotal evidence indicates the figures might actually be much higher.

A project writing curriculum for women in literacy and English as Another Language (EAL) programs made me aware of the need for systematized information about the issue from outside the literacy field and for collected information about the range of approaches within the literacy community. I wanted to know how other literacy workers were addressing issues of violence. What did they do? What tensions and contradictions were they struggling with? I also began to wonder what we could learn in the literacy community from therapists and counselors who address women's experiences of violence directly.

The research study for this book was borne of my desire to begin the process of expanding awareness of and resources for literacy workers so that new approaches, strategies, and programs can be developed to allow more learners the chance to learn and participate effectively in literacy programs. In my proposal for funding, I argued:

If the impacts of violence are not adequately addressed in literacy programs there is a cost for learners, as they face barriers to successful learning; a cost to literacy workers, as they are frustrated by lack of knowledge about how best to support survivors in overcoming barriers to learning; and a cost to programs as a whole, as learners struggle to participate effectively as leaders sharing in running their programs. (CCLOW, 1996, p. 3)

As I talked to learners and workers, that frustration—learners who felt that their failure to learn proves they are stupid and workers who struggled with feeling incompetent as they question what they could do better—confirmed the need for the study and for changes in literacy work to follow from it.

This research[8] looked at the impact of violence on women's literacy learning and program participation to develop approaches to literacy work that will assist women to learn. It included interviews with literacy workers, literacy learners, therapists, counselors, and staff of various organizations in focus group sessions, individual interviews in person, and through computer networks. I concentrated on two key questions: (a) What impacts of abuse do you see in your literacy program/your work? and (b) How can/should literacy programs address these impacts of violence?

I interviewed in five regions of Canada—British Columbia, the Prairies, Central Canada, Atlantic Canada, and the North. Interviewees were those involved in literacy as well as therapists and counselors whose work focused particularly on issues of violence—whether they worked in shelters, health centers, or private practice. My main question for these women was: You have worked with many survivors.[9] If I told you that several of the members of my literacy group are survivors, what could you tell me about them—what to expect, what to do, what to avoid doing. The stories and descriptions collected from all the interviews weave through this book, connecting with threads of my analysis drawn from their words and from my theoretical reading. Discussions during workshops and an online seminar, where educators from across North America and a few from Australia and elsewhere commented on my first writing and thinking, adds to the depth of voices.

---

[8]The research was funded by the National Literacy Secretariat of Human Resources Development Canada and sponsored by the Canadian Congress for Learning Opportunities for Women (CCLOW).

[9]Although I use the term *survivor* in this book, I recognize that it is problematic—part of a discourse that demands women move from victim to survivor and return to *normal*. Problems with the concept of *normal* are discussed in chap. 2. Lewis (1999) provided an excellent critique of the term *survivor*. (p. 27).

GATHERING INFORMATION

To carry out this research, I searched for a methodology that would (a) support my desire to challenge some fundamental assumptions underlying literacy theory, (b) facilitate my commitment to contributing to the skills development of literacy learners and practitioners, and (c) not restrict my need to respectfully and carefully broach delicate and difficult aspects of the lives of those who would participate in this project. Although not satisfied with an epistemology that simply accepted what people told me as truth, I was also not willing to take on the superior and often oppressive position allocated to those who would use others as subjects for their own research. I wanted to begin with workers' and learners' descriptions of the problem and, through a collaborative process, wherever possible tease out the complex picture from a variety of sources.

As I traveled, I met an outpouring of mixed desires to participate in this project and to see its results.[10] I took what I learned in one place and brought it to discussions in the next, developing a national network engaged in asking a similar set of questions and exploring responses. The object of the research did not stand still: Each group I spoke to or conducted a workshop with had the full benefit of whatever knowledge the research had produced to date, including my tentative analysis. Each group helped in the process of pushing the analysis further, sometimes sending me back to rethink, sometimes confirming a direction and adding new insights. Although unwieldy, this led to exciting results, drawing theory and practice closer together. Many people became actively engaged in the research analysis; they continued to develop their own thinking and try out new ideas in their own literacy work. Overall, I wanted the research process to be educational for everyone involved. I hoped gatherings of literacy workers and learners would be valuable for busy, overstretched workers and learners prepared to give up their time to meet with me.

This approach, as the foundation of my research planning, meant that I had no rigid specifications for exactly what an interview would look like or whom I wanted to talk to. I asked a large, diverse group of experienced literacy workers interested in the issues of violence and located across the country to form an advisory group.[11] The advisory group helped me establish directions for the research where possible, pull together groups of literacy workers and learners, and identify individual therapists and coun-

---

[10]See appendix for a brief description of the research journey.
[11]Advisory group members are named and, of course, thanked in the acknowledgments.

selors for me to interview. This process led to many people choosing to participate in the research. Overall, I talked to approximately 150 people, mostly women, in various groupings.[12] Group sessions were as short as an hour and as long as a full weekend, and everything in between, depending on how much time people felt they could free up. Early sessions looked more like interviews, whereas later sessions became more like workshops. As I had more information to share with participants and use to spark their thinking, the sessions became more interactive.

Sometimes this gradually evolving process made me anxious; I often wanted to spend more time with people than was possible. I worried that workers who spent a whole weekend talking would have a stronger voice than those who only met for an evening and could not stay late because of an impending blizzard. When we met over dinner and workers dived enthusiastically into chatting about their workplaces, I agonized about when to bring them back to my agenda. Sessions that took place in local restaurants made it enticing for workers to attend, but taping became impossible. I had to rely solely on notes.

Frequently, I felt that when women agreed to meet with me, they were unclear about what they had agreed to. Sometimes those coming together hoped for a workshop that would provide them with answers on whether they were *doing it right* and tell them what else they could do in response to the range of ways that issues of violence surfaced in the classroom. When I had no substantial information to share, but simply wanted to learn about their experiences and thoughts, I experienced a continual tension and tried to balance the different aspects. In later sessions, I had more and more information that I wanted to check group reactions to, and I wanted to leave enough time for the current group to share all it knew. My anxiety over the balancing act and the certainty that there was not enough time in a session to cover all the ground I hoped for grew greater.

Despite such tensions, the process was incredibly exciting. The layering of information was rich, continually shifting my analysis and adding new insights. When I began the research, I wondered whether the discourses of literacy work, and of education more generally, might obscure

---

[12]I interviewed nine groups of literacy workers (some groups also included counselors and people from other organizations) and met with some workers individually or in twos or threes along with learners from one program. I also interviewed five groups of literacy learners. I interviewed 10 counselors and therapists individually, but a few more participated in groups with literacy workers. See appendix for a list of interviewees who chose to be named. For reasons of confidentiality for themselves or for others, some are unnamed or named by first names only.

impacts of violence and whether therapeutic discourses might help reveal impacts that had previously been obscured. The process—bringing information from interviews with therapists and counselors to sessions with literacy workers and learners—allowed me to check out much of what I had learned from the therapeutic world with the workers and learners, prompt their thinking, and see if this new information led to further insights or shifts in their thinking. I was able to see ways in which discourses—around learner motivation and the question of who is a serious student—obscure impacts of violence on learning. Insights from therapists about all or nothing behavior gave instructors a new lens though which to look at the behavior of some students.[13]

For many literacy workers and learners, participating in the research did—as I had hoped—prove to be valuable. Workers and learners valued the confirmation that they were not the only person struggling with the issues of violence and how they impact on teaching and learning. Workers, in particular, were relieved to speak about what they had seen in their classrooms and their concerns and anxieties about what they should do. Workers discussed their concerns and frustrations, as well as the practical approaches they had tried.

To ensure that interviewees gained something, as well as to collect the information, I usually ended sessions with literacy worker groups by asking them how they take care of themselves when they so often hear about unspeakable violence or see its aftermath in their classrooms. This sharing helped many workers to recognize how little they were doing to look after themselves. It clearly prompted some to recognize that they could set limits and take care of themselves, rather than giving until they were burned out and had no more to give.

Although I worried about the extent to which I was meeting participants' needs, interviewees often spoke about what they had gained by participating. One of the instructors said it was a comfort to talk about her experience in her class and have others know about it. In one preemployment group, when I asked for last words about what would help them deal with the blocks from experiences of abuse, one of the students spoke about how valuable she found just talking to me:

You coming here. . . . You coming makes me look at it, I've been dying for a smoke for the last hour or whatever, but I haven't left because I don't want to miss anything. It makes me look at it. . . . It makes me look at abuse issues and how I was raised and everything. I denied being an abused

---

[13]These issues are described in detail in chap. 3.

child up to about two years ago, we had the perfect family, we were not
dysfunctional, I was never abused, dammit. So I got nowhere, it was just all
fantasy. . . . It's yucky, but I'm glad I'm doing it. (interview, Horizons, British Columbia, November 1996)

Workers suggested that, in the future, they would open up discussions
more in their classes, with their colleagues, and in their local literacy as-
sociations, and would also simply look at their work differently. One
group of staff reassured me that they would not be waiting for my report
to initiate more talk about the issues of violence in their own programs
and in the provincial association.

Experienced literacy instructors who devoted an entire weekend to
discussing the issues ended the weekend talking about how valuable it
had been to have the opportunity to get together with like-minded people. They discussed the possibilities for creating support groups in their
own settings. One participant said, it "helped me sort out what my role
might be" in relation to that ongoing tension between the literacy teaching and the other social issues in a woman's life. Joyce Cameron sent me
a message to tell me what the weekend sparked for her:

I thought I would let you know that your research has had some results already. After our weekend at Salt Spring I felt that my response to violence
in my students' lives was more protective of me than it was helpful to
them. My inability to deal with it in the classroom meant that it was not
getting dealt with at school. Arriving back at work filled with our weekend's discussion, I talked . . . about the possibility of setting up a group to
which we could refer women who had violence in their background or
foreground. Because of provincial government initiatives to get single
mothers off of welfare and back to work, there is a bit of money around for
"access" programs. . . . What we came up with was a seven week course
called "Women's Success" to which we referred women who we felt
needed more support to succeed in school than we could give them in the
classroom. The kind of woman we had spent that weekend talking about.
It was a small group of about seven. One woman dropped out, but the
other women stayed, bonded, and grew very much stronger. The group is
not for therapy, but looks at issues like personal boundaries, unlearning old
views of themselves, assertiveness, etc. Exciting things have happened like
a woman placing a restraining order on her abusive husband for the first
time. It is running again beginning next week, for another seven weeks.
The same women are continuing but they have a very inclusive attitude
and want other women to join so the group will be slightly larger this time.
We hope to make it an ongoing course, jointly sponsored by our department, Counseling and the Women's Center.

So . . . thank you for the work and thought that you have done on this issue. You have been a catalyst in enabling these women to change their lives. (Cameron, personal correspondence, May 1997)

In a workshop I held to begin to share findings from the research project, one literacy worker interrupted me to tell me how frustrated she was. I wondered initially what was frustrating her, but she clarified that her problem was not with what I was saying, but with the silence in literacy about such issues. She thought the field had to recognize that we cannot talk about doing adequate literacy work without recognizing the needs of women who are survivors. Another literacy worker I interviewed, Deborah Morgan (formerly Martin), eagerly handed me an article she had written earlier about her program. She, too, argued for the importance of a recognition of the violence experienced by literacy learners. She wrote: "The word "abuse" makes many people uncomfortable, and so it should. But as literacy workers, we need to get past that discomfort; we need to talk about abuse." (Martin, 1994, p. 26). She also pointed to some of the clues to violence in women's lives:

I remember when I was working as a literacy co-ordinator, hearing little pieces of stories I knew at the time were part of something much bigger than I could see. Students talked vaguely in their interviews about not remembering parts of their schooling, acting out in class, hating school, being told that education wasn't as important as helping out with the chores at home. (Martin, 1994, p. 27)

Literacy discourse needs to encompass experiences of violence to contribute to revealing the bigger picture. This book is another step in the process of stimulating further talk about violence and the broad range of barriers to learning that experiences of violence can create. Hopefully further changes in literacy practice will be a consequence of increased awareness of the issues.[14]

WHAT ABOUT THE MEN?

The main focus of this research was women's experiences of violence. The implication that men do not also experience violence is not intended. In literacy work, I have often heard stories of men's childhood

---

[14]I am also carrying out further research and practical work to explore the process of making substantial change in literacy programs.

experiences and think that, as we begin to open up more talk about the impact of violent experiences on learning, we will hear a lot more. I suspect that the numbers of men, as well as the numbers of women, who have experienced childhood violence and abuse and who, as adults, are trying to improve literacy skills is enormous.

My research looked at issues in women's experiences for a variety of reasons, including the practical one that the research was sponsored by a woman's organization. Women's experiences include many instances of violence by men as adults, so looking at men and women together is problematic. The key reason is that I believe different issues will arise when we begin to look at men's experiences; it may be more useful, at least initially, and easier to look separately at men and women. Research on men's issues is also crucially needed. Such research might be best carried out by a man or at least a team that includes a male. For men, the silence about this issue is different and more profound than for women. The risks are also different. Women have spent two decades breaking silences.

There is overwhelming evidence that men who have been abused frequently become abusive. Once we open up to include the area of men's experiences of violence, we have to be prepared to hear the stories about men who are, or have been, abusive. Although I do not want to imply that women are not also sometimes the abusers, I do want to recognize that much violence is perpetrated by men. This whole area of research—to elicit experiences from men and hear the stories of men who are abusive—waits to be addressed by appropriate researchers.

WHAT ABOUT THE WORKERS?

I also want to recognize that literacy workers as well as learners are survivors of trauma. Such experiences impact on their work and teaching, just as learners' experiences impact on their learning. Although workers' experience of violence is not the central focus of this work, it forms part of the backdrop for thinking about how the impacts of violence on learning can be addressed.

One literacy worker I interviewed—a survivor—speculated that there may be particularly large numbers of women who have experienced violence working and volunteering in literacy. This worker argued that gaining a sense of self-worth through helping others might lead many who have experienced trauma to work or volunteer their time to help those worse off than themselves. The Women's Research Center (1989) in Vancouver explained this tendency precisely:

Being helpful is a trait which our culture encourages in female children, valuing it as a useful skill for women in adult relationships. Women are often expected to take care of the emotional well-being of others. Survivors of childhood abuse learn this role particularly well: Their emotional safety depends on everything and everyone around them being all right. Their thoughts, of necessity, often centre upon taking care of others. Sometimes that is the source of their only sense of personal value. One way to escape from the "bad" feeling inside is to "be good" on the outside. The child picks up clues from those around her to determine what is and is not acceptable behaviour. (p. 145)

It may also be that the love of reading that draws many into literacy—eager to pass on such pleasure—was, for some, learned as part of an escape into the mind and away from the realities of violence. The experience of trauma might mean that workers and volunteers have great sensitivity to the needs of learners, but it might also mean that they are struggling with many of the same issues as learners. That being the case, interactions between learner and volunteer or paid worker may be correspondingly complex.

That same worker also suggested that workers involved in literacy who have not "dealt with their own stuff" may contribute to the silence about the issue. Workers and volunteers who have buried their own pain may not be comfortable speaking about issues of violence with learners, finding it far too scary to open up issues that are so close to home. This could have a significant impact on learners who tentatively try to speak about their experiences of violence. Many learners, as they build trust that the literacy program is a place to take risks and embark on the scary task of learning to read, will test whether they can also speak about the realities of their lives. Literacy workers are often the first people to seem trustworthy enough to be told. The tensions around listening and being heard are discussed further in later chapters.

POINT OF VIEW

I come to this research as an insider to the literacy field, not as an external researcher. I have worked in literacy in some form or other since I was an undergraduate student in the early 1970s and volunteered for my local literacy program in England. Travel to Sierra Leone gave me the opportunity to teach English to Speakers of Other Languages (ESOL) and volunteer in adult literacy. Volunteering led to a job as the coordinator of a large literacy program in Sierra Leone. That experience drew me to

Canada to study more about literacy and development issues. Since the early 1980s, I have carried out a wide variety of projects in adult literacy and ESOL in Canada. I have worked in a community literacy program, run a women's group, designed and led training courses, written curricula, spoken at conferences, facilitated meetings, and continued to study, research, and write about literacy issues. For the last 8 years, I have also been a volunteer, tutoring Mary. As noted, questions and insights from that interaction are central to this book. Although I do not currently live the day-to-day tensions of facilitating a group, teaching a class, or running a program, when I refer to the literacy field or literacy community, I use *we* to reflect my commitment to and involvement in the field.

My own experience of, and the value I have found in, the therapeutic journey forms part of my knowledge of the therapy field. For whatever reason, this work connecting trauma and learning feels like the work I must do. It offers me a valuable exploration for myself both as a teacher and a learner. One literacy worker whose experience of growing up in a violent, alcoholic home shaped her desire to work in literacy and her sensitivities to learners told me that she would not be able to do this research—it would open too many wounds. However, she believes that it is crucial that such work take place and that we begin to open up talk among literacy workers about how our own experiences shape our teaching, as well as how those of learners shape their attempts to learn.

As I write this book, committed to be true to all the different voices I heard from during the research and hoping that I have not missed hearing the voices that differ most strongly from my own, I recognize that my knowledge is always partial—shaped by my own social location and multiple identities. Although I resist defining myself through a series of labels, I recognize that being a white woman not only shapes my experience, but also what I perceive as a researcher and how I am seen by others. My English middle-class background is written on my body and heard in my speech. My lesbian identity might also have been recognized by some of those I interviewed, but my nondisabled and hearing status would go unnoticed by many—as simply normal. Only literacy workers in the Deaf community would find significance in the fact that I am not Deaf, and am an outsider to their community. My lack of knowledge of American Sign Language (ASL) meant that, rather than take part in an interview group, most chose to talk to me in writing through the literacy computer network, Alphaplus (formerly called *Alphacom*). Although my level of education may be taken for granted as a researcher in literacy circles, being a person with *big papers* makes me suspect, marking the distance that separates me from literacy learners, but also increasing the weight of my judgment. Throughout this study, I have tried to listen to a diverse range of voices and represent them fairly here. Yet as I write, I am aware that there are voices less well represented and that my vigilance may not always save me from sliding into setting up white experience as norm and all other experiences as different—an error I do not wish to perpetuate.

Throughout this study, I have tried to keep a balance between theory and application, believing that practitioners are interested in theoretical analysis that shifts the frame for practice and academics in the practical implications of theory. I hope to speak to a range of people—those who theorize educational issues *and* those who engage in day-to-day teaching. It is crucial that we lessen the divide between theory and practice.

BEYOND THE DEFICIT MODEL

As I carried out this study, I was challenged to think about the common ground and differences between experiences of violence and illiteracy. Two educators from the Department of Education in Prince Edward Island mused about their sense that issues of low literacy and violence are both hidden. Neither have a public face, both are unspeakable, and to experience either is seen as shameful. They felt that there were stereotypes about victims of violence and about those labeled *illiterate* and were cautious about making connections between low literacy skills and violence to avoid any suggestion that people are violent, or violated, because they are *illiterate*.

There is a common tendency in literacy work to slide into a deficit model. In societies where literacy is highly valued and part of schooling, it is easy to frame the learner as the problem, with a deficit of skills, and to lose awareness of the learners' strengths and knowledge and of the socially framed nature of the problem. In the North West Territories, for example, several workers said that the common assumption that everyone could have learned to read as children if they were not too lazy to bother led to a sense that literacy learning did not need to be offered to adults who already had their opportunity and failed to make use of it. The lack of literacy education, they argued, will mean that people with low literacy levels, especially women, will be left out of the change to self-government happening in the region.

In the deficit model, only the individual literacy learner needs to change to acquire the lacking—hence, deficit—skills. Society can be left unaltered. Analogies of literacy as a sickness or disease to be eradicated often signal this deficit approach. It is an approach that suggests that the learner simply needs to improve her literacy skills to fit into society; the problems will be solved and she will have access to social mobility in the meritocracy. In the deficit model, the literacy learner's lack of skills is often described as a drain on the economy, and the costs to the literate members of society are frequently detailed. Through this approach, the social practices that create literacy and illiteracy are obscured.

In contrast to the deficit approach, some literacy researchers and theorists argue that schools teach and value only certain forms of literacy. Schools validate the forms of literacy practiced and taught within white, middle-class families and devalue and even obscure awareness of the diverse literacy practices and multitude of different ways of knowing practiced within other cultures and communities. This leads many students to learn through the school system that they are stupid and cannot learn—a legacy that haunts their adult learning attempts. A simple deficit approach does not serve literacy learners well. Instead, it continues to construct them as other to the norm; it preserves the concept that there is only one form of literacy and that it is normal to be literate in that form.

Many workers in adult literacy are attracted to the field as a place to address social inequalities. Those who are categorized as *illiterate*, or *functionally illiterate*, are marginalized by low education levels, poverty, violence, and racist and ableist stereotypes. Many want to question the category of *illiteracy* and the focus on deficiency that positions the illiterate as other. Yet a basic contradiction in much adult literacy work involves the desire to question the categories and privileging of literacy, and particular forms of literacy in society, while also working within these categories to offer critical literacy practices that seek to offer possibilities for change.

Within a society that values literacy highly, it is enormously difficult for literacy workers to hold onto an awareness of the equality of learners as they try to teach the form of reading that literacy learners do not know well. Instructors struggle to maintain a belief in the value of the many other forms of knowledge and reading that learners *do* know well from their life experiences. It is hard to recognize the value of such knowledge when it is devalued in society and even by learners themselves. It is not enough to treat literacy learners as they expect to be treated because learners are often too well steeped in the value system of a society that sees them as ignorant, inadequate, and inferior.

A society that values only one form of reading—the reading of print— discounts all other forms of reading. First Nation educator Priscilla George talked about how she stresses the value of the traditional reading of the environment (e.g., the weather, tracks, etc.)—skills that many

First Nation people know well and that are often now discounted. Other First Nation instructors also stressed the importance of books by First Nation writers and more recognition of Aboriginal knowledge. Recognition of this parallel knowledge, they argued, is empowering for First Nation students. They talked about "fanning the fire within people," recognizing that fire has been dimmed by school and life experiences that have not recognized or validated their identity or their traditional knowledge. They argued for the value of drawing on what people know and helping them see what they know, rather than assuming that they are stupid or lacking.

Literacy workers of all backgrounds seek to teach in ways that recognize that learners are knowledgeable and help them build on their existing knowledge to which they seek to add literacy skills. More and more literacy programs introduce learners and tutors to concepts of learning styles. Although this can become a simplistic process of labeling the particular style of a learner, it can also be a way of helping learners to recognize that not everyone learns in the same way and of supporting the transfer of aptitudes for learning other types of skills to literacy learning. Several learners I interviewed talked about work on learning styles as key to allowing them to see that they did possess knowledge of how to learn and that they had successfully learned many different types of things through learning in ways which worked for them. Such approaches can be crucial in shifting away from a deficit approach to literacy learning. Nevertheless, avoiding sliding into approaches that frame the learner as the problem, and keeping the deficit framework at bay, remains an ongoing challenge.

One potential gain of grappling with questions about the impact of violence on learning is that it may help the literacy field to move away from the deficit model. It is easy to feel frustrated when people do not react as we expect; or when someone does not seem to be learning, it is easy to see the problem as his or her inadequacy. Looking at the impact of violence gives us somewhere else to go besides frustration. It provides a more complete explanation for a learner's difficulties with learning, offering more to think about and observe. It also offers new insights to aid in addressing the problems well and contribute to successful literacy learning.

Looking at the impact of violence on learning creates the danger of another type of deficit or sickness model. Focusing on impacts of trauma can lead to the suggestion that a learner needs to go away and *heal* these impacts and should return to class only when she is better. A focus only on referrals for those struggling with impacts of abuse reinforces this message and offers another trap for educators. Tanya Lewis' work, which challenges the idea that we can return to normal after trauma and offers the image of living beside violation rather than leaving it behind, may help us to side-step this medical version of deficit. Therapist Clarissa Chandler argues that it is important to focus on a person's strengths, noting that a person survives trauma because of what she did receive that was beneficial in her childhood, rather than fails because of the extent of her victimization.

During the process of this study, I was enthralled by what I learned from the therapeutic field and how it could help us to work differently in literacy. However, I also struggled to avoid the ways in which the therapeutic discourse could be a slippery slope to new deficit models for literacy work with those who have experienced violence. The therapeutic focus on individual healing implies that the person is sick and can be well. Ora Avni (1995), speaking of survivors of the holocaust, critiques this approach:

> Yes, we want to "heal." Society wants to heal; history wants to heal. But, no, a simple "life goes on," "tell your story," "come to terms with your pain," or "sort out your ghosts" will not do. It will not do, because the problem lies not in the individual—survivor or not—but in his or her interaction with society. (p. 216)

As Beth Sauerhaft stated online, "simplistic notions of 'healing' and returning to 'normal' negate the broader social and political context in which trauma happens." Sandra Butler (1992) has also eloquently critiqued "individualized, de-contextualized, and de-politicized healing." First Nation holistic approaches also stress the importance of understanding the self in relation to the family, community, nation, and universe (George, personal correspondence, August/September 1998). These approaches from different traditions can all support understandings that move away from a focus on individual deficit.

Survivors of trauma can easily be judged harshly. Judith Herman (1992) spoke of some of the factors that may contribute to a negative judgment:

> Most people have no knowledge or understanding of the psychological changes of captivity. Social judgment of chronically traumatized people therefore tends to be extremely harsh. The chronically abused person's apparent helplessness and passivity, her entrapment in the past, her intractable depression and somatic complaints, and her smoldering anger often frustrate the people closest to her. (p. 115)

Such a picture may be a valid description of many survivors, but it can feed into negative stereotypes. Survivors have encouraged me to recognize skills—gains in "sensitivity" and ability to "read" social dynamics of a situation—they have learned as a consequence of the trauma they have experienced.

Rather than dwelling on individual harm or seeing the aftermath of violence as an individual problem, educators must recognize violence against women as a social inequity. Healing is not an individual problem. Statistically and experientially, it may not even be abnormal in this society for women to have experienced trauma. The goal of education with those who have experienced trauma should not be simply to support their healing—to help them become *normal*. The task is not to encourage educators to believe that they must learn to diagnose who has been traumatized and then treat them differently from other learners. The responsibility of educators, funders, and others in the field is to recognize that *all learning must be carried out in recognition of the needs of trauma survivors*. It is needs of trauma survivors that should be normalized as an everyday part of education. What those needs look like and how they could influence literacy work, as well as how addressing them can lead to broader educational and societal change, is explored in detail in the rest of this book.

2

What Is "Normal" in a Violent Society?

Society deals with violence through silencing the extent and limiting the nuances of the stories that can be told about it. Medical responses encourage survivors of violence, and educators in general, to regard the myriad aspects of the aftermath of violence as private health problems to be faced by individuals. The public injustice that violence represents and the centrality of impacts of violence on learning become obscured in the medical model. These conceptualizations work to individualize responses to violence and prevent violence from being addressed in the day-to-day practice of educational work. The conceptualization of violence is crucial to whether its impact on learning is recognized as a matter for educators to address and, if so, how it is taken up.

DEFINING VIOLENCE

Violence is widespread throughout society. It is not a minority issue experienced by a few women, with impact only on the rare educational interaction. Although there is no general agreement on the correct statistic, and varied figures are offered to assess the numbers of adults—both men and women—who have experienced sexual, physical, or emotional abuse in childhood or as adults, there is increasing acceptance that, whatever the numbers, the problem is widespread. Anecdotal evidence—collected during this study and previously through my work from wide numbers of literacy workers and learners—suggests that the incidence of women in adult literacy programs who have experienced trauma may be far higher than in the general population. Frequently literacy workers speak of working with groups in which every member has experienced major trauma. Experiencing trauma as a child may well have contributed to difficulties with learning to read in the first place. Experiences of violence and control as an adult may contribute to the urgent desire to improve literacy skills to enhance the possibility of making further life changes. English as a Second Language (ESL) literacy learners are often in Canada because they had to leave situations of war, oppression, imprisonment, or torture. Instructors and literacy workers regularly talk of working with groups where most, if not all, learners have experienced major violence in their lives. Violetta Ilkiw, a worker at a Toronto program serving youth on the street, said: "Violence in students' lives is not something we have to guess at here. Building trust and coping with constant disclosure are big issues." (Alphaplus Literacy & Violence Online Seminar, January–April 1998). Deborah Morgan (previously Martin), a literacy educator in rural Alberta, wrote:

> I don't think it's a coincidence that every one of the women who has passed through the doors of the Chapters Program has been seriously abused in her life. Some have been able to escape (at least physically) from the abuse they've suffered, others are still coping with abusive relationships and situations. (Martin, 1994, p. 26)

Cate Sills, a literacy educator in the North West Territories, wrote: "Many of the women participating in literacy and ABE programs in the NWT have experienced extreme levels of violence and dysfunction . . . they are the majority. . ." (personal correspondence). In each region of the country, I heard again and again that violence was particularly widespread and that its effects were intensely present in classrooms. Finally, I could only believe that violence is widespread everywhere in Canada, among all peoples, and speculate that patterns of violence are equally pervasive elsewhere.

Linking Violences

When I first began thinking about what I wanted to explore through this research, I knew I wanted to think broadly about violence. In addition to instances of individual experiences of abuse or battering, few adults who have limited literacy skills will not have experienced the violence of oppression and the marginalization around issues of poverty, class, race, ability, and language. Most will have experienced daily put-downs and erasures that oppress and contribute to a well of anger and frustration.

Through many years of tutoring a white woman who grew up in poverty, I was particularly aware of the impact of her experience of childhood sexual, physical, and emotional abuse. Eventually I also began to see how that childhood experience translated into continued violence and abuse as an adult. The more I looked at the violence experienced by a broad range of women, the more I saw the intertwining contexts of racism, ableism, classism, homophobia, and ageism as integral to how individual abuse is experienced, as well as the ways in which these systemic injustices create specific forms of violence that add to the oppression of sexual, physical, and emotional abuse for many women. Therapist Clarissa Chandler spoke about this weight of oppressions:

> I look at how did they experience race? How did they experience class? How did they experience all those other pieces? Those pieces are as debilitating as being assaulted by a parent or family member and people have a tendency to give that merit in a way that they don't give merit to systemic experiences that are not contextualized . . . and they are not any different—the impact on people physically, emotionally is all the same. (interview, Toronto, November 1996)

Fundamental historical violence, such as slavery, colonialism, and genocide, continue their legacy into the present, providing a backdrop to further violence.

Sociologist Debi Brock (1993) critiqued *feminist popular discourse* for interpreting sexual abuse as key to shaping *who we are* without a recognition of the interweaving of other factors:

> Finally, emotional trauma need not be the direct result of physical and sexual abuse or even of the abuse of male power. Everyday conditions like poverty, racism, or neglect, or traumatic events like the early death of a parent also shape who we are. These cannot be simply dismissed as separate issues. Any of these factors may do more to shape our identity (and our pain) than the experience of sexual abuse. We need to be more aware of how all of our experiences intersect and merge. Sexual abuse cannot be considered in isolation. (p. 112)

Dorothy Allison (1994) depicted the effect of poverty, childhood abuse, and identifying as a lesbian as robbing her of any sense of entitlement. Entitlement, she says, "is a matter of feeling like we rather than they." She continued:

I have known I was a lesbian since I was a teenager, and I have spent a good twenty years making peace with the effects of incest and physical abuse. But what may be the central fact of my life is that I was born in 1949 in Greenville, South Carolina, the bastard daughter of a white woman from a desperately poor family, a girl who had left the seventh grade the year before, worked as a waitress, and was just a month past fifteen when she had me. That fact, the inescapable impact of being born in a condition of poverty that this society finds shameful, contemptible, and somehow deserved, has had dominion over me to such an extent that I have spent my life trying to overcome or deny it. I have learned with great difficulty that the vast majority of people believe that poverty is a voluntary condition. (pp. 14–15)

When I refer to violence, I want to encapsulate the complex interconnection of all types of violence and include a recognition of the power of systemic violence to shame, silence, and exclude.

During this study, I experienced a tension between wanting to reveal the enormity of the violence experienced by many women in literacy programs and wanting to make the impact of the subtle ways women are diminished and put down—particularly those who are poor, racialized, disabled, elderly, or experience any combination of such oppressions—visible. In interview sessions, when I spoke of including a broad range of everyday violence, I found that, rather than leading to more visibility of everyday violence, there was a danger of diluting attention to violence—"all learners have experienced violence, we already know that"—and of literacy teaching continuing as usual. Yet when I focused on major or extreme incidents of violence, it was possible for some workers to assume that the issues did not apply to their students. This tension of denial remained active, one way or the other, throughout the study. The sleight of hand that makes violence both a normal everyday occurrence for women *and* outside normal experience contributes to this tension.

VIOLENCE AND SILENCE

Despite overwhelming evidence about the frequency of violent incidents in Canada, conceptualizations of violence as not normal and silences about the extent of violence in society make it possible to assume that violence is an uncommon event. Tal (1996) suggested that there are three modes by which society diminishes attention to the issues of violence—mythologizing, medicalization, and disappearance:

Mythologization works by reducing a traumatic event to a set of standard-
ized narratives (twice- and thrice-told tales that come to represent "the
story" of the trauma) turning it from a frightening and uncontrollable
event into a contained and predictable narrative. Medicalization focuses
our gaze upon the victims of trauma, positing that they suffer from an "illness" that can be "cured" within existing or slightly modified structures of
institutionalized medicine and psychiatry. Disappearance—a refusal to
admit to the existence of a particular kind of trauma—is usually accomplished by undermining the credibility of the victim. . . . these strategies work in combination to effect the cultural codification of the trauma.
(p. 6)

Both mythologizing and disappearance are part of silence. By *silence*, I
mean a societal reaction that denies or minimizes the existence of violence. The myth takes the place of the true horrors of violence, and disappearance makes it impossible to speak about the extent of the horror
and be believed.

As I became more aware of the staggering and horrifying range of violence in society, I struggled with a sense that society does not want to
know—that "we" cannot bear to see the extent of violence or its impact
on life and learning. As Elly Danica (1996) said, silence is insidious:

I now see that I and numerous colleagues over the years have been breaking the silence over and over again, only to have it subsequently swallow
us up again moments after we speak. The abuse of children, especially of
girls, remains normal, invisible and silenced. (p. 141)

I have struggled with a sense of urgency—a sense that we must stop and
change literacy programs and, more urgently, society. I have wondered
why there is so little reaction to the levels of violence. A recent newspaper article expressed that same view. Columnist Michele Landsberg
(1997) argued that when the enormity of violence against children was
revealed it should have led to immediate action:

The news was so disturbing that it should have stopped us in our tracks.
If we were a sane society, all other public undertakings would have been
suspended temporarily. The legislature would have been called back to
work, party ideologies set aside and dramatic action taken at once to confront the findings of the major Ontario child abuse study reported last
week. (p. L1)

The following words from Judith Herman (1992), perhaps explain the
division between society's knowledge of violence and the failure to ad-

dress it in dramatic or even adequate way.[1] Herman suggested that ordinary life goes on, including enormous numbers of girls and women living through *unspeakable* violence:

> The ordinary response to atrocities is to banish them from consciousness. Certain violations of the social compact are too terrible to utter aloud: this is the meaning of the word *unspeakable*. Atrocities, however, refuse to be buried. Equally as powerful as the desire to deny atrocities is the conviction that denial does not work. Folk wisdom is filled with ghosts who refuse to rest in their graves until their stories are told. Murder will out. Remembering and telling the truth about terrible events are prerequisites both for the restoration of the social order and for the healing of individual victims. (p. 1)

Although I disagree with her implications that truth is a simple matter or that "the restoration of the social order" or "healing" are unproblematic concepts, nevertheless, she named the contradiction I observed—that violence is both hidden and well known and repeatedly revealed and obscured.

Silencing Tactics

The battle over memory—repressed memory or false memory depending on your point of view—provides a vivid example of the tensions between silence and revelations of ghosts. The entire debate has tended to remove the person who experienced the violence from view and to draw attention to, and incite compassion for, those accused of carrying out the violence. Recent newspaper headlines demonstrate that process, in which the victims have shifted: "False memory's victims languish in jail, 'Recovered memory' losing its value" (Makin, 1998, pp. A1, A12). If the memories are a myth, then there is no major problem and society is not required to change:

> It appears that as long as men were found to suffer from delayed recall of atrocities committed either by a clearly identifiable enemy or by themselves, this issue was not controversial. However, when similar memory problems started to be documented in girls and women in the context of domestic abuse, the news was unbearable; when female victims started to

---

[1]Although there is now a wide variety of services for women who have experienced violence, these services are consistently underfunded, and rather than leading to dramatic change, can more accurately be seen as Band-Aids that preserve the status quo.

seek justice against their alleged perpetrators, the issue moved from science into politics. (van der Kolk, McFarlane, & Weisaeth, 1996, p. 566)

Sylvia Fraser (1994) asserted that the denial of women's accounts began as early as Freud's own recanting of his initial paper, which argued that hysterical symptoms arose from experiences of sexual abuse. She quoted his response to the "icy reception" to his 1896 paper, where he stated: "I believe this to be a momentous revelation, the discovery of a source of the Nile of neuropathology." Later he replaced his seduction theory with the concept of an Oedipus complex, arguing that too many women patients said their fathers had seduced them, thus their accounts simply could not be true. She argued that Freud was "too far ahead of his time," but that as experiences of violence become increasingly visible, approximately 100 years later, society may be ready to address the issue: "The bright side of all this is that no culture allows into consciousness a major social problem until it is ready to address it" (Fraser, 1994, p. 59). I want to believe that she is right.

Yet the tension over keeping the issue in the public consciousness continues as memories of abuse are increasingly dismissed. As Fraser (1997) explained in an article reviewing a book on trauma (Freyd, 1997):

Whatever the truth or falsity of any individual case, this group and their spin lawyers have so effectively muddied the scientific waters that many confused members of the public, along with a cynical press, have been persuaded to believe that all recovered memories are bogus. (p. D14)

I found it disturbing that the week following this review, a columnist revealed further sleight of hand, shifting the problem, saying it is not violence that wrecks families and damages children's lives, but abuse literature:

The irony of abuse literature such as Sylvia Fraser's is very great. There's no doubt it's done some good, by validating the experience of genuine victims and encouraging them to deal openly with their past. There's also no doubt that it's done plenty of harm, by encouraging troubled young women to believe Ms Fraser's account of her experience is theirs too. It is time to ask if the harm outweighs the good. The evidence of wrecked lives and shattered families suggests the answer is yes. (Wente, 1997, p. D9)

The irony for me is that the book by Jennifer Freyd, which began this particular exchange, focused on betrayal as an important factor in loss of memory of the abuse. Freyd (1997) asserted:

> In order to survive in cases of core betrayals (abuse by a trusted caregiver on a dependent victim) some amount of information blockage is likely to be required. The probability of amnesia is a function of the degree of betrayal. (p. 75)

I wonder about the continued betrayal of the victims of abuse as their accounts of their experiences are denied. Jennifer Freyd is the daughter of the founders of the False Memory Syndrome Foundation, who continue to attack her credibility and seek to discredit her authority as a researcher. Perhaps this need to discredit their daughter's claim to knowledge is connected to their desire to cast doubt on their daughter's own recovered memories of abuse by her alcoholic father. The battle between burying or remembering the horrors of violence against women and children remains hard fought. Educators play a role when they make violence visible in ways that reveal the full extent of the horror, rather than participating in the complex processes that deny the existence of atrocities and banish them from consciousness.

Telling Tales

Despite this pressure not to see violence or its aftermath, I have felt that many women, particularly those working in literacy programs, do know and do see the violence. There is a body of autobiographical literature—much about experiences of child abuse, some also about violence as adults (e.g., Alleyne, 1997; Bass & Thornton, 1983; Danica, 1988; Fraser, 1987; Green, 1992; Spring, 1987). There are a lot of titles from which to choose. Some written by literacy students (e.g., Battell & Nonesuch, 1996; Byrnes, 1977; Doiron, 1987; Dueno, Santiago, & De Simone, 1993; Fay, 1989; Green, 1990; Roa, Jaber, & Ramirez, n.d.) describe diverse experiences in simple language, yet I must question what has been achieved broadly by such autobiographical literature.

The growing range of studies that focus on this *testimonial* literature explore why hopes that breaking the silence would have a broad social impact have not been fulfilled (e.g., Alcoff & Gray, 1993; Tal, 1996; Williamson, 1994). Janice Williamson included a quote from Louise Armstrong to draw attention to that frustration:

> At least we're talking about it now. . . . Yes. But it was not our intention merely to start a long conversation. Nor did we intend simply to offer up one more topic for talk shows, or one more plot option for ongoing dramatic series. What we raised, it would seem, was discourse. And a sizeable

problem-management industry . . . It was not in our minds, . . . ten years ago, that incest would become a career option. (Armstrong, 1987, p. ix)

Williamson (1994) asked the crucial question about what has been achieved: "Is the speaking over and over and over a substitute for transformation, or a precursor for change?" (p. 225). Have all the autobiographies about abuse merely created "contained and predictable narratives" that lessen, rather than increase, the response that actually addresses the problem? It is crucial that educators not simply create a space for the individual autobiography of abuse, but participate in reconceptualizing violence in ways that support broad social change.

MEDICALIZING VIOLENCE

Medicalizing violence shapes popular understanding of violence and trauma. Medical terms such as *trauma* and even *posttraumatic stress disorder* (PTSD) have become common in everyday language. Medical approaches show trauma as creating individual health problems that need to be addressed through medical and therapeutic means. The demands that the violent nature of society must be changed and the revelation of the presence of the aftermath of violence as a public issue in educational settings are silenced by an emphasis on medical approaches to trauma. Although medical categories can reveal impacts of violence, they also conceal. This contradictory potential creates pitfalls for educators who, as they draw on medical conceptions that support their process of recognizing the impacts of trauma on learning, may become complicit in the mechanisms that frame trauma as an individual health problem and obscure an issue that must also be addressed by social change.

Violence or Trauma?

I use the term *violence* and the more medical term *trauma*, although I do not equate the two. I use both because neither is entirely unproblematic. When I described the study as being about the impact of violence or abuse on women's literacy learning, people I talked to kept asking what I meant or simply assumed I was only including a particular form of abuse. I became interested in trauma because it avoids some of the debates about what counts as violence. Trauma emphasizes the person's response to the event. Judith Herman (1992) provided a description of trauma:

> Traumatic events overwhelm the ordinary systems of care that give people a sense of control, connection and meaning. . . . Traumatic events are extraordinary, not because they occur rarely, but rather because they overwhelm the ordinary human adaptations to life. . . . They confront human beings with the extremities of helplessness and terror and evoke the responses of catastrophe. (p. 33)

In drawing attention to the response of the person experiencing trauma, the nature of these traumatic events can easily disappear from view. Traumatic events include natural disasters where there is no agent, but this inclusion should not lure our attention away from the individual and social agents of trauma—persons who are violent or social systems that are violent. Societally, we need to focus on who and what violates and on who is traumatized. Yet Herman's description is useful for the attention it draws to concepts of control, connection, and meaning—relevant concepts for the literacy classroom.

Although I have concerns about what this medical concept of trauma conceals, I believe it also helps reveal some important awarenesses. As Tal (1996) suggested: "The naming of PTSD as an illness acknowledges the often-traumatic nature of women's experience. It provides us with a new analytical tool for the study of women's psychology and history" (p. 136). The study of trauma has revealed that there is no absolute measure for how traumatic an event is; rather, the judge is the person who experiences it. Much therapeutic literature draws attention to the impact of trauma, which leads a person to experience subsequent violence as also traumatic. For example:

> People with PTSD tend to move immediately from stimulus to response without actually realizing what makes them so upset. They tend to experience intense negative emotions (fear, anxiety, anger, and panic) in response to even minor stimuli; as a result they either overreact and threaten others, or shut down and freeze. . . . Perhaps the most distressing aspect of this hyperarousal is the generalization of threat. The world increasingly becomes an unsafe place. . . . (van der Kolk et al., 1996, p. 3)

> They have an elevated baseline of arousal: their bodies are always on the alert for danger. They also have an extreme startle response to unexpected stimuli, as well as an intense reaction to specific stimuli associated with the traumatic event. (Herman, 1992, p. 36)

This awareness seems valuable for literacy workers and learners. For example, it can help workers and other learners realize that loud and ag-

gressive talk in the classroom might evoke extreme terror in some learners. Also, put-downs or humor that might seem trivial to the person
speaking may be experienced as traumatic by the recipient. One student,
in a book of self-portraits of adult students, described the powerful effect
of a "minor" comment on her:

> And then I decided to go to a college near my home. I took a reading test.
> And I was just waiting for my score when the man happened to come to
> the door. He said, "This is your first time?" I said, "Yeah." He says, "Well,
> when you come here, you gotta make sure you work, work? Okay, you
> have to know what you're doing because otherwise you get out." Forget it.
> That sent me out. Right out of the damn room and down to the street. He
> scared the hell out of me, and I ran out. I said, "Oh, oh, I don't belong
> here." (City University of New York, n.d., p. 32)

An awareness of trauma and PTSD helps explain why many learners
told me that they experience the inadequacy of welfare or government
pressure to get into the workforce as controlling and terrifying. Learners
described how it brought back earlier experiences of being abusively controlled, using the phrases "like punishment", and like "further abuse."
Many women described the way they experience further violence and
control as traumatic. One group of learners talked about having been
provided with support for their literacy learning, but feeling blocked by
lack of financial support, day care, and other necessary services when
they tried to continue their studies. They compared the actions of the
government to the behavior of their abusers: "They give you something
then they take it away—just like the man." (Interview, Literacy Learners,
Charlottetown, PEI, March 1997).

Questioning Normal

Therapeutic literature suggests that this sensitivity is abnormal in com-
parison with some assumed normal level of arousal. Events that provoke
a reaction are described as "minor stimuli" (van der Kolk et al., 1996, p.
3), but this assumption belongs to the perspective of someone who has
not experienced trauma. The person who is reacting would not describe
the stimuli as minor. It is crucial to recognize therapeutic descriptions of
the impact of trauma to understand major reactions to levels of violence
(that some might see as minor). It is also important to question the implication that healing from trauma is a process of no longer reacting unrea-
sonably—a process of moving from abnormal to normal.

In a recent thesis, Sharon Rosenberg (1997) articulated a clear critique of this medical frame. Referring to Judith Herman's analysis, Rosenberg pointed out:

> She continues to adhere to presumptions that make a distinction between those who are "ordinary and healthy" and those who have experienced "psychological harm," who, as she clearly articulates, "are no longer ordinary or healthy." It is not the enormity of impact that I question; it is the categorization that posits normal and healthy against traumatized. (p. 60)

This limitation of the concept of trauma is revealed even in the definitions. The suggestion that trauma is outside the range of normal for women is problematic. As Tal (1996) stated:

> When the APA [American Psychological Association] states that the trauma which causes PTSD is "generally outside the range of usual human experience," it is clear that "usual human experience" means usual white male experience. (p. 136)

The medicalizing of violent experiences is part of a process of naming violence as outside normal human experience. If violence is outside normal human experience, it is something that affects the *other* and is perpetrated by the aberrant. It is not embedded within our social structures and the *normal* lives of ordinary women and men. A succinct explanation of the societal tendency to see those who experience trauma as not normal was offered by Deborah Levenstein on a listserv on violence.[2] She said:

> "Victims" have traditionally tended to be seen as "the other." It is safer, I think, to categorize victims as people different from ourselves, because then that means that we are not ourselves victimized or victimizable (a new word, perhaps, but you understand I'm sure). (FIVERS, April 1997)

The medical nature of the concept of trauma offers insights and also creates limitations. If the experience of trauma is an individual health problem, then it is a private matter between a woman and her doctor or psychotherapist, not a social and political issue that requires urgent social

---

[2]The listserv is called FIVERS: Feminists Against, Intimate, Violence, Engaged, Energized, Empowered, Exchange, Research, Resources, Resistance, Revolution AND Support. Participants work in the antiviolence movement, including, for example, shelters, crisis lines, and law clinics, and many have experienced violence themselves. The coordinators are based in North America and participants are from all over the world.

change. This framing, I believe, explains why so little notice is taken of issues of trauma in relation to education. If trauma is a health problem, it is
easy to suggest that a woman "suffering" from traumatic "symptoms"
should "recover" before she participates in an educational classroom.

Healing

Although *healing* is an important concept for the individual, using this
discourse exclusively as a response to trauma excludes and silences the
major social problem that such violence represents.

> A trauma victim is a person who, in the process of recovering and working
> through the traumatic experiences struggles to make sense out of the
> memories of the traumatic event. Recovery is to eventually accept them
> and be able to face the possibility that something else like it may happen
> again. A trauma survivor is one who has successfully worked through and
> made peace with his or her traumatic memories. (Figley, 1988, p. 86)

Recovery is framed as learning to "face the possibility that something
else like it may happen again." However, as Tal (1996) clarified: "making
peace is learning to accept the world as it is" (p. 145). Perhaps it is society that needs to recover so that violence is *not* something that women
must learn to accept as a daily risk of life. In the medical model, only
the individual must be healed, not society. Like Tal, I am left with the
question of whether we need healing or a nonviolent, but far-reaching,
revolution.

The medical model suggests that the person must heal and leave the
traumatic experience behind. For some women, the concept of healing
does speak to their experience. When I tried to articulate my difficulties
with the concept in an online seminar, I received an interesting response:

> Personally, I like the term "healing" because it describes in a positive way
> the emotional and spiritual journey I have been on. What I am interpret-
> ing, though, from your statement, is that people who have experienced vi-
> olence and trauma don't need to be "fixed"—they are human beings wor-
> thy of respect, encouragement, and success with talents and gifts to offer to
> themselves and the world. I really like that, because what happens so of-
> ten, is that we are "dogooders," operating from a white, middleclass per-
> spective, that we can "make it all better."
>
>   I didn't need to be made all better. I needed to know I could make
> meaningful goals, good decisions, and that, what turned out to be most im-
> portant for me, I had choices.

Abuse does not make you abnormal. It creates barriers. (personal correspondence)

This writer illustrates the value of the concept of an individual healing journey while also recognizing the limitations of the concept of *normal*.

Recent theorizing of the trauma experience reveals the dangers of the implication that the solution to problems of the impact of violence is for the individual to heal—leaving her pain behind and returning to normal (Lewis, 1998). The conceptualization of a journey from sickness to health puts impossible demands on survivors of trauma—they are expected to be able to put their experiences behind them and *get over it*. Lewis (1998) stated firmly: "This medicalization of traumatic experience maintains social relations of power and privilege through individualizing and privatizing the site of the problem and its solution" (p. 12). Lewis offered an alternative conceptualization to contrast with the medical model of sickness and healing—the image of "living beside the violation." She asserted that the experiences of trauma "live on" and suggested a new frame of "familiarity with violence"[3]:

Living beside the violation becomes much more possible if I understand myself as someone who is familiar with violence rather than someone whose life experience is pathologized. My familiarity with violence contributes to my knowledge, my sense of strength and my capacity for empathy rather than as something tainted with pathology that must be overcome. (unpublished presentation, 1998)

Although medical diagnoses can be reassuring to a person who has experienced trauma, they can be a trap identifying her sickness to be cured, leading her to blame herself or be blamed by others when she is not cured fast enough, cannot leave the pain behind, cannot get on with *normal* life again, and cannot learn successfully.

When Does Posttrauma Begin?

In one interview, Helen Dempster, a worker in the shelter movement, gave me a vivid account of how the diagnosis of PTSD can be both useful and problematic for a woman's own sense of herself:

---

[3]These concepts were articulated by Tanya Lewis as part of her thesis defense. I thank her for the tremendous insight of such metaphors for enabling a vision of something outside the all-pervasive imagery of a journey toward health.

I think the trauma theory has been useful because it has really validated and acknowledged the experience of a lot of women that was before kind of minimized and trivialized and so it has taken away some of the victim blaming stuff and it now puts women in with refugees and political prisoners and Vietnam vets and . . . we can have more empathy or sympathy or something. "Oh yeah other people have this as well" and it has helped women in some court cases to be more credible because you actually now have a syndrome or a disorder or something or other. . . .

. . . they take away some of that victim blaming because you've got this cluster of symptoms . . . that allows us to look at this woman and say OK we can understand then why she is not totally on top of things because she is dealing with all this stuff. So that's useful . . . but some women find it disempowering I guess to be labelled as having some kind of disorder—you know it is post-traumatic stress *dis-order*, and that is not how they feel, they feel very orderly in their lives, . . . and they *are* very orderly . . . (interview, Vancouver, British Columbia, November 1996)

The same worker recognizes the limitations of PTSD because it implies that it is possible to leave the violence behind. In a society where women are always in danger, this is not the case:

. . . the "post" part becomes ridiculous because she is always dealing with . . . as women, just leaving class and going to your car in the parking lot in the dark. . . . There is no "post," you are always having to be alert, so it isn't like you've experienced trauma and there is no danger that you will be traumatized—you've come home from Vietnam and that is not going to happen anymore. . . . (interview, Vancouver, British Columbia, November 1996)

As Tal (1996) described, women remain vulnerable to the violence of their abusers:

. . . the American woman lives in fear of an enemy who stalks her today. Her enemy is free to assault her on the street, in her place of work, or in her own home. He may attack her once or repeatedly. If she hides from him, he may find her. If she asks for the protection of the authorities, he may have the right to demand she be returned to his control. If she tries to press charges, he will be protected by a legal, political and social system that is biased against her. (p. 20)

Even if women can escape from the individual who attacked them, they cannot escape the echoes of violence in everyday life. For example, Justice MacFarland (1998) revealed in her judgment that "Ms P.," who,

"In the early morning hours of December 31, 1985 . . . was raped and otherwise sexually assaulted at knife point in her own bed by a stranger," was called later that same day by a police officer:

> Shockingly on the very day she had been assaulted a police officer telephoned her while she was in the shower. She was asked why it had taken so long for her to answer the phone and when she explained that she had been in the shower—remarked that he should have been there. She was asked invasive personal questions about the number of men she was seeing at the time. Police seemed preoccupied with Ms. P.'s personal sexual habits. (pp. 16–17)

Such comments and questioning is so commonplace to be normal, only in such striking juxtaposition is it revealed as shocking.

Recognizing Trauma?

Despite the inadequacy of psychological labels and the danger that medicalization mitigates against social responses to trauma, the ongoing process of recategorization may at least support some recognition of the profound impact of trauma. More recent categorization marks a shift from previous psychological labeling that casts the blame on the victim and implied a woman's responsibility for her own victimization through labels such as *self-defeating personality disorder* or *masochistic personality disorder*. Although Herman (1992) described these earlier categories as "diagnostic mislabeling," I am more inclined to see these labels as revealing the contested and socially constructed nature of *all* labels—showing that there is no correct labeling.

The contrast between the way mental health disciplines conceptualize the survivor of public events causing trauma—such as war, flood, or tornado—and private events—such as rape, incest, or domestic violence, is described clearly by Laura Brown (1995). She suggested that:

> . . . the "self-defeating" woman who's been in a battering relationship is treated quite differently (and less well) than is the survivor of a train wreck, even when the presenting symptoms are similar. The former is assumed to have contributed to her problem, in particular because of the interpersonal locus of her distress (Brown, 1986); the latter is almost always seen as the innocent victim of a random event. (p. 102)

Although the categories have shifted and *self-defeating personality disorder* is now contested, the implication that women are responsible for their own experience still has impact. An example of how that judgment can be played out in practice is offered by the inquest into the death of Arlene May, a woman who spent many years trying to escape a violent husband who eventually killed her. Michele Landsberg (1998) wrote from her journal entries illustrating the sad truth of Tal's assertion that women may find it impossible to reach safety:

> Journal entry: May '98: the women's coalition at the inquest faces a tough challenge. Some of the witnesses representing the police, government and crown attorneys are spreading the idea that May's death was her own fault.("Why didn't she go to a shelter . . . ") Somehow, the women's legal team has to expose the distortions and prejudices that underlie the victim-blaming. Journal entry: They call Dr. Rosemary Gartner, University of Toronto criminologist and sociologist. A new picture emerges of incredible female strength in the face of horrible odds. Arlene May, welfare mother of five, battered and terrified, learns by bitter experience that the judges, crowns and police cannot and will not protect her from Iles even if she goes to a shelter. (She has been stalked by him before while at a shelter). May scrapes together a down payment on an apartment in a new, secret location; she installs new locks and motion detector lights at her home, alerts the neighbours, puts the police and shelter on her speed dial, writes her will. (p. A2)

Where those who experience trauma at the hands of another are seen as having medical problems and judged as lacking in some way, shame will contribute to silence about the extent of violence in society and little social change can occur.

Links between the experience of childhood violence and adult psychiatric problems are widely made. "Many or even most psychiatric patients are survivors of childhood abuse," Herman (1992) asserted, offering a variety of statistics to support her argument. Although she was clear that ". . . abuse in childhood appears to be one of the main factors that lead a person to seek psychiatric treatment as an adult" (p. 122), she still sought to draw a distinction between "ordinary personality disorders" and the disorders resulting from extreme situations of trauma. She discussed at length the links between so-called *borderline personality disorder* and experience of trauma, which were previously unrecognized. This clearly revealed the profound danger in such medical categorization. Medical labels such as this one can create a screen that completely draws attention away from violence as the source of the problem, focusing instead on diagnosing the dimensions of the sickness or disorder.

The ongoing attempt to find more adequate terminology to categorize the profound impact of "prolonged, repeated trauma" offers women a new label—*complex post traumatic stress disorder*—to capture the "multitude and severity of clinical manifestations" (Herman), but it does not make women safe and, arguably, contributes to keeping women at risk of violence. While attention is paid to changing the individual to help them return to normal, the violence of normal society remains unchanged.

Psychological labels cannot even fully reveal the complexity of a particular woman's ongoing struggle as she continues to live beside violation: "A single diagnosis of complex post traumatic stress disorder does not capture the nuanced complexity of how trauma lives on in a survivor's everyday life" (Lewis, 1998, p. 33). One danger in such labels is that they can appear to offer definitive information, which can then be used to judge anyone who does not correctly fit the picture of the illness harshly and make assumptions about characteristics and needs of anyone who has experienced trauma.

In education, participating in the labeling of diagnoses is an ever-present pitfall. Instead of participating in diagnoses, instructors should support learners to explore the complexity of their own experience—to understand that violence is not only an individual matter, but also a social issue, and that the aftermath of violence has an impact on learning. It is particularly important that literacy workers do not unintentionally reinforce social silences about the impacts of violence through unquestioningly using the terminology and conceptions from within the therapeutic field as if they were simply facts, rather than socially constructed frameworks that reveal, conceal, and profoundly shape taken-for-granted responses to violence.

CANARIES IN THE MINE

Survivors of violence who work in the university, I want to suggest, may be like the canary in the mineshaft. What is intolerable to us may seem like a minor annoyance to others, at least at first. There is much pressure to fade quietly away, taking our experiences up as personal inadequacies, learning to cope better with the world as it is. For feminists, the university is just one of many sites where "the world as it is" is simply not good enough. Some can "cope" better than others, but "coping" means accepting a set of conditions which make our lives and our work simultaneously difficult and invisible. (Heald, 1997, p. 46)

The shift from perceiving experiences of violence as leading to "personal inadequacies" to arguing that the "'the world as it is' is simply not good enough" has implications broadly in society and in education in particular. Conceiving those who have experienced violence as "canaries in the mine"[4] helps shift the unproblematic sense of what is ordinary and healthy and move away from judgments of overreaction assessed by those who have not experienced violence.

Miners used to carry canaries (or sometimes other birds) into mines to provide an early warning system for lethal gas. The birds were more sensitive than humans to the gas—low levels were toxic to them. When the birds keeled over, they were not seen as overreacting: Their reaction to the gas was viewed as a valuable warning that, although the miners could not sense the gas, it was present and they should get out of the mine before the levels became lethally toxic to them as well. In a parallel sense, as a society, we might view traumatized women's reaction to violence as a warning that violence is toxic to us all. We might see those reactions as useful warnings that societal violence needs to be brought under control, rather than seeing the traumatized as needing to reduce their reactions, heal, and increase their tolerance of violence. If the whole society is a toxic mine, there is nowhere for survivors to go that is free of the toxic irritant.

Sensitivities

Several survivors described the greater sensitivity they had gained from experiencing trauma as a valuable asset. Some speculated about how different life would be if their sensitivity were valued so that they did not need to try to hide it by acting *normal*. Seeing the reactions of trauma survivors not as overreactions, but as sensitivity, perhaps allows such reactions to be seen as neither good nor bad. In some situations, the sensitivity might be inconvenient; in others, an asset. As Lewis (1998) stated in her open letter to Judith Herman:

> When children growing up in captivity are seen through the lens of normativity, then their development and the survival skills that they learned are seen as being abnormal. If this mold is broken Judith, then what potential strengths can be identified and developed in these skills? Survivors develop powerful skills of observation, listening and attunement (Miller, 1981). These can take them out of their bodies and away from fo-

---

[4]Thanks to Susan Heald not only for this concept of canaries in the mine, but also for many lengthy discussions and repeated prompting to help me see how easily I can slide into accepting unproblematically what is normal and abnormal and seeing health as no longer "overreacting." Susan's immensely careful review of the draft manuscript spotted those places where I tended to slide back into accepting the frame of normal in a way I did not want to do.

cussing on their own desires, feelings, sensations. Often these skills are presented as a "problem" to be overcome. But, they are also highly developed abilities. My question is how to learn to use these abilities without being taken away from myself. (p. 51)

A question for educators is how to support students to learn, helping them to benefit from these sensitivities, rather than being taken off course by intense reactions. Educators may have to struggle to avoid judging learners who react strongly as overreacting and diagnosing their problem; instead, they should strive to address the learning situation that is problematic.

Is Violence "Useful"?

I wonder how much the current societal forms of work and family life make use of survivors' sensitivities and other consequences of violence. Does society devalue these consequences, judge them as inappropriate when they are inconvenient or too extreme, and yet at the same time depend on them? Lewis' (1998) suggestion that the separation of trauma from ordinary life has a political impact is helpful to understand how the process might work:

> By separating experiences of prolonged trauma from those of "ordinary" life, important linkages between normative social relations and experiences of violence also become obscured. Butler (1994) discusses the arbitrary boundary drawn around trauma, separating it from normal life. It is worthwhile to ask: how numb does someone have to be to tolerate working in a fish processing plant or on an assembly line? How dissociated does a person need to be to withstand the privileging of certain sexes or classes? How much distrust is essential in the daily betrayals of white people towards people of colour? What possibilities exist to disrupt normative social relations if connections are drawn across the prolonged traumas of "everyday" life? You end "Trauma and Recovery," Judith, with a discussion of the survivor's participation in the "common" and the "ordinary" as signs of recovery. Given the insidious trauma that underlies many people's ordinary life, I wonder what it is you wish to celebrate in reinforcing normativity? (p. 33)

Laura Brown (1995), like Lewis, argued that we must question the everyday nature of trauma for many:

> Feminist analysis also asks us to understand how the constant presence and threat of trauma in the lives of girls and women of all colors, men of color in the United States, lesbian and gay people, people in poverty, and

people with disabilities has shaped our society, a continuing background noise rather than an unusual event. What does it mean if we admit that our culture is a factory for the production of so many walking wounded? (pp. 102–103)

If trauma is part of ordinary life, Danica (1996) speculated why violence against women and children remains part of *normal* life. She suggested that it preserves power imbalances:

> I believe child sexual abuse and violence against women are an integral structural part of patriarchal society and culture. They are how we—especially, but not only, women—are socialized to accept powerlessness. If this were any other issue with such a devastating effect, we'd have a massive mobilization of resources, we'd have comprehensive programmes, we'd have a blank cheque to enable us to do the work that needs to be done. If any other sort of plague or virus than the one called child abuse ravaged the children and left them crippled or destroyed, we'd find the resources to stop it. (p. 150)

Others have suggested that incest conforms to the other messages a growing *girl child* is given about her lack of power (e.g., Wisechild, 1988); it serves an important purpose to reinforce that powerlessness. If normal life is violent and this violence serves a purpose in society, then it is a crucial task for educators to reveal the facade, maintaining the illusion that trauma is abnormal.

This contradictory dynamic about what it is to be normal means that the demand to act normal creates a pressure on those who have experienced trauma *and* preserves the very concept of *normal*. Rosenberg (1997) stated this issue clearly, also through referring to Judith Herman's writings:

> My concern lies predominantly with her unproblematized reliance on the categories "normal" and "abnormal," which she evokes as regulating expressions—assuming an assignment of non-traumatized people to the former, traumatized people to the latter. So long as these categories form a dominant frame through which issues of the impact of trauma are understood, those of us who are grappling directly with these impacts are continuously burdened with the requirement to make ourselves (appear) normal—enough. This not only bears a significant weight on individuals, but also ensures that these normative categories are continuously being renewed and kept in place. (pp. 58–59)

Educators have a responsibility to reduce the burden for trauma survivors to act normal and to avoid, even unwittingly, supporting the continuation of normative categories.

What Is Returning to "Normal"?

In light of the statistics on the numbers of women and men who experience violence in this society, what is *normal* is at least questionable. Is it experiencing trauma or living a life free of such experience? When Lenore Terr (1990) was studying children who had experienced trauma, she chose a control group of 26 children who she did not think had experienced trauma. During the study, she identified that 10 out of those 26 showed signs of trauma (p. 24). A graduate student at McGill told me that she had some problems with a preliminary study because she could not find anyone who had not experienced violence to be in a control group. She explained it as a problem of her research design, but I wondered:

> My minipilot project examined previous experiences of interpersonal violence (i.e., sexual, physical, emotional, and verbal abuse) with measures of learning styles (using Kolb Learning Style Inventory), attributional style (using the Seligman et al AS Questionnaire), post traumatic stress disorder, and an interview on learning experiences in university.
>
> The results are pretty preliminary, since our quasi-experimental design was messed up by the fact that we defined the area of "interpersonal violence" so broadly, we couldn't find anyone for the control group! Interesting implication for research. The effects, though are most pronounced for women who have had experiences of physical and sexual abuse (no surprise there!). What was most interesting was that even though women had, for the most part, experienced these events more than 10 years ago, and, had had therapy, they still fit the profile of chronic PTSD. (Reilly, personal correspondence)

This finding supports the suggestion that trauma survivors cannot be expected to *heal* and return to *normal*. Instead, educators must learn to teach survivors for whom the legacy of violence remains an ever-present reality.

Laura Brown (1995) asserted that traumatic experiences such as incest, battering, rape, and date rape are not unusual:

> . . . statistically they are well within the "range of human experience." They are the experiences that could happen in the life of any girl or woman in North America today. They are experiences to which women

accommodate; potentials for which women make room in their lives and their psyches. (p. 101)

Brown drew attention to the effect of such a division between *normal* and *abnormal*, asking:

> What purposes are served when we formally define a traumatic stressor as an event outside of normal human experience and, by inference, exclude those events that occur at a high enough base rate in the lives of certain groups that such events are in fact, normative, "normal" in a statistical sense? I would argue that such parameters function so as to create a social discourse on "normal" life that then imputes psychopathology to the everyday lives of those who cannot protect themselves from these high base-rate events and who respond to these events with evidence of psychic pain. Such a discourse defines a human being as one who is not subject to such high base-rate events and conveniently consigns the rest of us to the catgory of less than human, less than deserving of fair treatment. (p. 103)

Such prevalence of violence leads me to question whether violence is a symptom of a larger societal illness and to seek educational approaches that will begin to reveal the complexity of violence.

In a study of refugees who have experienced trauma, and who came from diverse regions to settle in Denmark, Inger Agger (1994) made links among the violations in public space, private space, and political space, which are usually considered in isolation. She identified that "violations in the public space almost have the character of being normal and unconscious; they are simply among the conditions for moving around in this space" (p. 142). This normalcy of violation creates a continuum, even with violations of imprisonment and torture, which might easily be seen as exceptional and outside the realm of normal experience. Agger spoke (in the third person) of what she learned during her study:

> On the way, she received new knowledge about how the power of shame can be used to control and punish; about childhood's gradual internalization, in the feeling of shame, of the power outside, and about how this feeling connected to how we understand what is pure and impure. She saw how the impure person can be made by the others to feel an accomplice to her own contamination: she could have been more careful; she could have taken care. And she also saw how the impure one can make herself responsible. When the others hurt her, it must be because she is herself evil. The evil must correspond to something inside herself, if nothing else, then to not being careful. She saw how it was part of life in the social structure always to be careful that forbidden boundaries are not violated; and how

the development of an inner power of shame contributes to creating obedient, silent and invisible women. Those who refuse to be obedient, but go out into the political sphere, are again struck by the power of shame. The political prison and its torture use the stamp of whore as the special humiliating strategy against the woman's body, and the researcher saw that strategy as an exteme variant of the control-and-punish-methods that women already know from childhood's internalization of the power of shame. (p. 126)

Agger's insights about the importance of shame as the common thread that links a wide variety of experiences of violence is crucial in allowing us to see the commonality between even the extremes of torture and the everyday sense of threat that women experience. The element of shame is central to silencing protest about all forms of violence. Shame is also key to the pressure to hide the impacts of violence and act normal.

Are Trauma Survivors Expendable?

Unfortunately, another aspect of the canary analogy also applies. The canaries were expendable. It was acceptable for the canaries to die so that the miners would know when *they* were becoming unsafe. Social acceptance of such high levels of violence against women and children suggests that those who are traumatized are also expendable. Only minimal resources for shelters and short-term counseling are provided for those who have been traumatized. Elly Danica (1996), speaking only of childhood sexual abuse, described denial that can be seen to apply to other forms of violence against women:

The escalating body count will continue as long as society as a whole maintains the following denial-based illusions: that child abuse is the individual problem and responsibility of the victim rather than a social problem requiring political will and extensive public resources to resolve it; that the nuclear family as currently constructed is a safe place rather than a threatened primary social unit that could be improved by a rethinking, and perhaps a restructuring, to ensure that it functions as a nurturing environment for children; that children are the sole responsibility of one or possibly two adults rather than the responsibility of all members of a healthy community; that there is no effective treatment for abusers and no possible deterrent, when what is really at issue is the lack of resources to fund programs and seek solutions' and, finally that everything will be fine as long as we can find a way to process a few of the most adversely affected victims by applying what I can see only as Band-Aids, such as inadequate short-term therapies, followed by injunctions to the victims that they simply get over it. This is denial at its most pervasive and dangerous. (p. 146)

In literacy work, it is important not to merely provide the equivalent of inadequate short-term therapies through inadequate, short-term learning opportunities that do not enable women to learn successfully in the face of trauma. We must recognize that for literacy learners having experienced trauma is not abnormal and learn to address the implications for literacy programming. We must support learners to see their own strengths and recognize the value of the sensitivities they learned through trauma. As Cate Sills, a literacy worker in northern Canada, said:

> . . . it is essential for literacy practitioners and ABE instructors to develop an awareness and sensitivity to the impacts of violence on learning. . . . Often, the classroom is the only safe place for women participating in literacy programming in small northern communities, where counselling support, shelters are just not available. Literacy workers need to understand the complexities of violence on the lives of the people they work with in order to provide an empathetic and helpful response to their learning needs. (Sills, personal correspondence)

QUESTION COMMON FRAMINGS

Literacy workers have a responsibility to question the complexities of understandings of violence and trauma in society to avoid simply reinforcing the pressure to return to normal and preserving the myth that it is not normal to experience trauma. Only through questioning common framings of violence and avoiding participating in simplistic medicalizing discourses can literacy workers and other educators avoid colluding in the conceptualizations that minimize and individualize violence and blame survivors for failing to cope with normal life.

We must take social responsibility for the toxic levels of violence in society. Taking responsibility in literacy programs means recognizing the effects of trauma in literacy practice and responding to them in ways that question the status quo and make visible the social nature of the problem. Educators must not collude in the sleight of hand that declares violence a problem, but obscures the extent of violence, along with who and what is served by the continuation of violence and limits opportunities for any substantial social change. Educators have a responsibility to develop new understandings of the complexity of the place of violence in society and draw on these to support survivors to learn successfully.

3

Breaking the Silence
in Literacy

The extent of violence makes it clear that violence can never be ignored in an educational program. As I talked to people and read for this project, I heard endless examples of different forms of violence that impinged on literacy learning, many of which I had not previously thought about. Literacy workers described a range of violence that they had seen or heard about in their classrooms, and spoke of feeling "inept" as they wondered what responses would support learners and their learning. Literacy learners told me about the violence in their lives and their struggles to learn. Therapists and counselors provided detailed descriptions from their observations and, shaped by their analytical framework, of the characteristics of women who have survived trauma. The brief overview here, drawn from all these sources, serves as a backdrop to a more detailed discussion of the impacts of violence on learning.

THE SLAP OF SILENCE

During interviews, several literacy workers suggested that "maybe survivors are what is normal in literacy" and you'd be "hard pressed to find anybody who hasn't been physically, sexually or emotionally abused." In contrast, another worker was very interested in the topic, but said that she had seen nothing in her classes. Other instructors and counselors were aware of incredible levels of violence in the past and present lives of the same students, but the silences around issues of violence meant that the differing perceptions were not usually shared.

Although in literacy work, as in the rest of society, many people do know the horror stories that we have experienced, and that a myriad of learners tell, these stories also remain largely invisible and have not led to change. There is little talk in the literacy field about what experiences of violence mean for literacy learning. This silence makes it possible for some workers to miss it. During my research, one worker commented that middle-class tutors would not know about violence. Perhaps middle-class women may be less likely to have experienced the violence of poverty and school failure, but they may well have experienced childhood abuse and violence in adult relationships. Silences makes it possible for programs to maintain the illusion that "it's not happening to any of our people" (Alphaplus Literacy and Violence Online Seminar, February–April 1998). When response to the issues stays with the individual, sensitive, and empathetic instructor, the program or college can preserve a silence that maintains the illusion that violence is outside the realm of most people's experience.

The lack of response in literacy preserves the sense that stories of violence are unspeakable and has impact on those with stories to tell. One literacy worker from Arizona, Ann Unterreiner, spoke of her own experience as a child:

> When I first told about being sexually abused to my grandfather, he slapped my face and told me I was a nasty little girl. It was the slap of silence I have been battling in my soul, life, and healing, since. (Alphaplus Literacy & Violence Online Seminar, February–April 1998)

That experience would make it hard to break the silence again, yet learners have spoken about needing to get their story out. Gowen and Bartlett (1997) talked about three learners in a workplace literacy program who wrote about stories of abuse in their journals. Later, when one of them had written and published her story, she explained to the instructor that she had no "space for goals" until she had told her story.

Learners telling their stories through the language experience approach (where the learners speak and the tutor writes down what they say) and publication of learners' stories are the mainstays of much literacy work. Given that, I have previously argued, we must look at the messages sent by subtle exclusions and make space for learners to speak about the violence in their lives:

> But what stories remain untold? If literacy learning includes ideas of empowerment and finding a voice, then learners speaking about their lives must be part of literacy work. Literacy workers must be prepared to respond to the truths which learners want or need to write and speak about and to offer relevant reading material. How can workers in literacy pro-

grams exclude certain realities of a learner's life as inappropriate to the literacy program without silencing learners and confirming for survivors of abuse that their experiences are "unspeakable"? (Horsman, 1995, p. 211)

Counselors have taught me the importance of setting clear limits in the literacy class: Instructors should not feel that they must always hear all disclosures, must take care to give warning before raising subjects that might lead to disclosures, and should not simply encourage disclosures. These complex issues are discussed further in chap. 3, but do not eradicate the danger of silencing stories of violence in literacy programs and of preserving the sense that violence is unspeakable.

As I traveled, I was struck by how eager many literacy workers and learners were to talk about what we can do in literacy programs to make the violence visible in ways that can help women to learn and teach successfully. Yet many workers said that they had not been talking about it in their own programs or organizations. At the start of an online seminar on the issues, I was amazed by comments of relief that there was finally a place to talk. The value of hearing about others' experiences was clear. One worker said:

I just got on line and want to leap into the discussion. . . . My desire to jump in is that I have been grappling with how to deal with issues of domestic violence in adult ed. programs for several years and have so often felt so isolated and without the opportunity to discuss with others how we understand and proactively address the issue.

Another responded to a comment: "You stated it so clearly. It is such a relief to hear someone else's frustrations and realize that it's not me!" I wonder whether there is so little talk about why learners have difficulty learning, or why they did not learn as children, because to recognize the impact of violence might fill us with despair and helplessness. Trying to make sense of what I was learning and stay with a sense of how literacy work could change as a consequence, I was relieved to read:

Witnesses as well as victims are subject to the dialectic of trauma. It is difficult for an observer to remain clearheaded and calm, to see more than a few fragments of the picture at one time, to retain all the pieces, and to fit them together. It is even more difficult to find a language that conveys fully and persuasively what one has seen. Those who attempt to describe the atrocities that they have witnessed also risk their own credibility. To speak publicly about one's knowledge of atrocities is to invite the stigma that attaches to victims. (Herman, 1992, p. 2)

The nature of the material contributes to the complexity of silence and confusion. Tal (1996) offered a reminder of the possible benefits of breaking silence:

> Bearing witness is an aggressive act. It is born out of a refusal to bow to outside pressure to revise or to repress experience, a decision to embrace conflict rather than conformity, to endure a lifetime of anger and pain rather than to submit to the seductive pull of revision and repression. Its goal is change. The battle over the meaning of a traumatic experience is fought in the arena of political discourse, popular culture, and scholarly debate. The outcome of the battle shapes the rhetoric of the dominant culture and influences future political action. (p. 7)

The literacy program is one place where battles around the meaning of trauma must be fought and violence made visible. Engaging in this discourse about violence is essential if women who have experienced trauma are to be freed from silently trying to act normal while they attempt to learn to read. They need a language about violence that supports understanding the impact of experiences of violence on the struggle to learn and reduces the burden of shame.

LEGACIES OF CHILDHOOD VIOLENCE

Violence in Schools

Violence in childhood is perhaps the aspect of violence that it is easiest to assume will not be present in the adult literacy classroom. However, although the experience of violence in childhood may be long past, overwhelmingly, workers and learners talked about the profound impact of childhood trauma on adult education. Workers and learners talked about the prevalence of learners' experiences of violence in school as children. One worker spoke of a learner with an intellectual disability, for whom school as a child was such a violent experience that she cannot bear to go to the literacy program even to help others. A learner I interviewed spoke of one experience of violence she had in school:

> . . . being terrified of my parents, being terrified of my teacher . . . grade 6 teacher who was a pervert. . . . he didn't like me from day 1 . . . I think I also challenged him in a silent way he knew he couldn't get near me and look down my shirt, or feel or touch or stuff like that, I think he also was repelled by that. I remember one time he was humiliating me in the classroom and I . . . I answered his question and he came up to me in the class-

room and he grabbed me behind the neck, by the hair and by the neck, he shook me and he dragged me outside and he threw me against the wall and he told me to stand there and he said don't you ever talk to me like that again. He said I'll come back and deal with you later.

So I had to stand out in the hall waiting, and then he grabbed me again and he was yelling in my face and he dragged me over to the stairs, and he pushed me and I tripped and I grabbed on to the railing and he said you get down to the office. And he said I'm going to phone your parents and tell them exactly what you did to me today and I went yeah and when you're talking to my mother give me the phone because I am going to tell her in fine detail what you just did to me.

He never called my parents, but I was also terrified walking home because my mother would never believe me. . . . You could come up to my mum any day of the week and say your daughter just cut my dog into little pieces and barbecued it she would say, "what the hell did you do to their dog." You could tell her any fabrication, your kid just beat up my kid, OK what did you do. . . . If I had a detention I would say that I forgot my books and got half way home and had to go back. I'd get a detention for breathing and live in fear that they would be told that. That would be an excuse to break out the leather strap, go to your room and I'm going to whack you wherever I like. I remember waiting on the bed. . . .

Home was not a supportive place, which compounded the violence the woman experienced in school. This student talked about the mixed messages she received at home, where she was told that she should learn something but also put down if she learned it. She explained that she found these mixed messages crazy-making:

Having somewhat uneducated parents, the mixed messages, I could never figure them out . . . they wanted me to excel, they wanted this amount from me, but when I brought it to them and showed them they would ridicule it. Giving me piano lessons, but making it impossible to practice, but making me feel guilty because they were paying for my piano lessons. I don't want to hear what you have to play, because what are you trying to do—be big or something?

One therapist suggested that if school is a safe place for a child who is being abused at home, school can become a place to be *in the mind* and to excel. However, if school is also a place of shaming and violence, then children day dream or disrupt the class. Adults who experienced violence as children and who cannot remember their school years likely survived by day dreaming or dissociating. One group of learners debated the question of where teachers learn to humiliate because most of the group felt that humiliation was their most consistent experience of school.

I heard over and over again that the residential school system, where Aboriginal children were obliged to pass their childhood in harsh boarding schools separated from their language, culture, and family, is an all-pervasive legacy for First Nation adult students:

> Many of the learners in the FNAEP [First Nations Adult Education Program] are courageous survivors of the residential school system. Even if they did not go to residential school they have been forced to deal with that legacy in many different ways. One woman who I look up to and respect just told me about a teacher who repeatedly broke yardsticks over the heads of the children who would give wrong answers. (Cooper, Alphaplus Literacy & Violence Online Seminar, February–April 1998)

Accounts of the violence committed in the residential school system include physical, sexual, and psychological abuse—extreme humiliation, frequent cruel punishments for *crimes* such as bed-wetting or students speaking their own language, or being unable to eat the food:

> I was only six years old. At first, when I got there, I was afraid, sort of frightened to come into such a huge home. . . . And it was kind of a frightened feeling you had. I didn't know anyone there. They talked a different language which didn't make one bloody sense. . . . We tried to get hold of the language and that was our greatest problem. So we had a heck of a time learning English . . . away from Micmac. . . .
>
> Some punishments were very severe. If you were caught doing something, such as going over the boundary line . . . you see pretty flowers and you want to get them. It wasn't much, but you sure got punished for it. You either went without your meat or you got locked up in a closet all by yourself. It's a little cloakroom. I'll never forget it. (Millward, 1992, p. 12)

Children were sometimes taken from their parents and not permitted to return for holidays from as young as 5 years until 16 or even older. Control was taken from parents and children alike:

> We are sent to the Brantford Mohawk Institute. It seems that the house allotted to us on the reserve is too small, so the Indian Agent, in his wisdom, decides to send those in our family who are of school age to residential school. I am only five years old. That doesn't matter. The Indian Agent represents Indian Affairs and they make our decisions for us. (Hewitt, 1988, p. 12)

One worker suggested that we have made more space in literacy programs to talk about school experiences than for the horrors of violent and abusive home lives. She argued that bad school experiences are often seen as the reason that children fall through the cracks and fail to learn, but thought that, although the home may have been worse, there is an enforced silence about the violence in the home. Although I agree that there is silence about the home experience, in spite of some talk in literacy programs about bad school experiences, there is little focus on how those memories may impede learning as an adult.

Childhood Sexual Abuse

There is even less mention of abuse in the family, particularly sexual abuse. We do not talk about the ways in which focusing on learning to read can remind a woman of when she was a child trying to learn and that the connection to childhood may be terrifying. We do not speak about the ways in which participating in schooling may remind of childhood and trigger flashbacks and memories that have been repressed. One literacy worker explained the impact of such flashbacks on both the learner and herself as a teacher:

> A woman was having flashbacks in the class one morning. She had a lot of nervous energy anyway but she had woken up in the night and she thought someone was shaking her bed and then she realized it was her own body and that she was having a flashback. What she wanted me to tell her was how long was she going to be in that state of inability to pay attention to anything. Because she said the last time it had happened it had lasted for a month and she wanted to get on with her work—she was meaning her writing and math with me. I said, I don't know. All I could do was say I think it's really important to pay attention to what you're feeling and I strongly encouraged her to get a counselor. . . . That sort of experience leaves me feeling quite inept. (interview, British Columbia, November 1996)

Although this flashback may not have been triggered by something in class, therapists said that participating in a group sometimes leads to flashbacks:

> If you think that the literacy course itself is causing the flashbacks I think that . . . one of the things that you have to have is some kind of perspective, in the sense that people may be so longing to have the contact with you because you are caring, that they will place themselves in situations

which are unsafe, a group situation that has too much stimulus for them.
(White, interview, November 1996)

I heard repeatedly about learners' (and sometimes also workers') experiences of neglect and physical, emotional, and sexual abuse as children:

> The accumulated research suggests that the sexual abuse of girls is far more common than was previously thought. In one study (Russel 1988) for example, 38% of a random sample of women reported that they had been sexually abused before the age of 18; 28% had experienced sexual abuse before the age of 12. (Walker, 1994, p. 91)

Increasingly there is awareness that, although most abuse is carried out by men, there is also a need to acknowledge the greater silence about abuse perpetrated by women. In her recent thesis exploring this area, Kelleher (1997) stated:

> The female survivor of female perpetrated sexual abuse has long been silenced by a culture that will not acknowledge that her experience exists. She lives in a world of secrecy, distress, anger, controversy, and fear of being ostracized and disbelieved. (p. 4)

There is a growing awareness of the serious aftermath of all childhood violence. Such abuse impacts on every aspect of the person. It may have disrupted childhood literacy learning. Northern school counselors, Pitsula Akavak and Sheila Levy, spoke of students who "lose their interest in learning anything when there's too much violence." They said students "really shut down." Experiences of abuse will continue to have an impact in a myriad of ways for an adult seeking to return to learning. As well as the direct impact on attempts to learn, workers and counselors talked about the importance of recognizing self-abuse, threats of suicide, and suicide attempts as legacies of childhood violence that may be firmly intertwined with the terror of attempting to learn and change as an adult.

A literacy worker in the north spoke of tensions within the Inuit community that led some women to feel uncomfortable with naming the abuse that had happened to them as children because elders knew and did not help. The desire to honor elders sometimes felt at odds with the idea that abuse experienced in childhood was wrong. There was fear that to expose abuse was to question the culture in ways that were not acceptable. I was told that abuse would have been much rarer in earlier times and dealt with within communities. However, some workers felt that there was tension about whether there was abuse prior to white contact or whether it was only a product of the dislocation and devaluing brought about through white contact and racism.

Several students talked about the cumulative effect of feeling that no place was safe. They experienced violence at home, at school, and on the street:

> Abuse didn't stop at home . . . it continued going to school, there were children who would wait for me and then beat me up for no reason, I had no reason for it . . . then in school some of the teachers, they were older teachers, they would pick me to be in front, I was a good student I tried hard, my parents were poor or . . . I would give the impression I was just the right victim, so I would be victimized. The teacher would still have the little stick and he would sit right in front of me and he would hit on the desk and spit when he was talking. . . . I don't know why he picked me, and then my name he would make fun of my name. . . .

The words of this student were echoed for me in Elly Danica's (1996) account of violence in every aspect of life, which she described in stark and eloquent clarity:

> In every context I was threatened. If this or that wasn't done, if I didn't give my father what he wanted, I suffered the miserable and painful consequences. At school, if I didn't do what I was told, I was hauled up before my classmates and strapped across the hands with a thick leather strap. Even among my peers, some would threaten on the playground with the bullying that they had learned from their fathers at home. There was no place I could go where violence against me was not a consideration and a possibility. And if the violence I lived with every day was not enough in church I was promised that there would be further violence awaiting me the moment life was over. (p. 123)

As adults, many learners continue to experience a wide array of violence. One literacy worker said that learners are often abused and controlled from all sides—by kids, landlords, and even program deliverers.

WHO IS IN CONTROL?

> The batterer often shows no respect for (or, in some cases, no recognition of) the autonomy of the battered woman or, if the abuse occurs in the context of a family setting, other members of the family. He treats the woman and the family members as if they were his personal property. (Walker, 1994, p. 59)

Bruising from psychological abuse may be particularly telling in a literacy program. Women often spoke of the way that being controlled and put down wore them down. One learner wanted to make sure I understood that mental abuse is "as bad or worse" than physical abuse. Another talked about the way that the put-downs felt:

> He tried to keep me under his thumb and under his control and it didn't matter what I did I was always wrong. I was always stupid.
>
> It began before then, growing up in the family situation that I grew up in, women didn't have to know much, I came from the Prairies, and if you got some education great, but its no big deal, you're going to get married you're going to have kids, you're going to bake bread and do all that stuff. So it started before then, my parents never actually told me I was stupid, but I always felt like I was, and I was never expected to do much and I never tried very hard, but after. . . . Well what I understand now is that he was just trying to throw his pain on me and I was taking it. . . .
>
> You are stupid, I can't believe it, you have no idea, on and on. . . . The body language I can't believe. . . . At first I'd fight back . . . but after a while, you can only take it for so long, I'd feel like I was shrinking. *I started to believe it. It made me scared to ask for help or try to learn, I thought I couldn't learn. So I didn't even try.* (Horizons interview, November 1996)

I recently read with horror the diverse dimensions of psychological abuse on a listserv focusing on issues of violence. The types of control and invasiveness described have included:

> Isolation from friends and family, criticism of friends and family, surveillance (you can't even talk on the phone because he listens in, if you have someone over to talk, he follows you from room to room so he doesn't miss any of the conversation etc.). I don't know how to name this one: he would argue over ridiculous things and convince me he was right. For example, I might say "Look at the beautiful sky. . . . It's such a pretty shade of blue" and he would spend hours arguing that no, it wasn't blue at all, but purple. (Kat, FIVERS, April 1997)

There were endless detailed descriptions of version after version of surveillance, control, and undermining of any possibility of knowing anything or valuing oneself in any way. It is hard to imagine how anyone could learn in the face of such oppression.

These vivid descriptions of harassment also show how easily the behavior of the instructor and the situation of a classroom could echo and remind a woman of controlling abusive behavior:

The batterer may attempt to control virtually every aspect of the woman's life. He may bombard her with questions, tell her exactly how she is to spend her time, and subject her to constant surveillance. It is not unusual for battered women to report being kept awake at night by long harangues designed to tell them what to do or being suddenly awakened to receive trivial, aversive, or frightening demands. Such harassment has obvious debilitating psychological effects, but it can also be physically debilitating (e.g., sleep deprivation). Some forms of harassment such as surveillance (which deprives the woman of privacy), sleep deprivation, and repeated periods of intense prolonged questioning are similar to those used by torturers and can constitute forms of torture. (Walker, 1994, p. 59)

A literacy worker having sensitivity about how to ask questions, reading over a woman's shoulder, and having respect for the confidentiality of a woman's writing might be crucial for a learner living in such a situation.

Deaf[1] students may be particularly vulnerable to abuse and control by family members and spouses. Deaf women lacking literacy skills have less access to television, radio, or books to learn information about resources that might help them value themselves. Workers suggested that a common issue for many Deaf women was control—of their children, their cheques, their own movements, the resources that might increase their independence:[2]

The men (including fathers, brothers, husbands, boyfriends, etc.) controlled the women and their behaviours. They were not allowed to come at night to class because the men thought it would be too dangerous for them . . . the men would not look after the kids so they could come to class . . . the men did not want them going because the other women or staff would influence the women and make them realize how controlled they were. Mostly, the men made the women question their need for learning . . . why go to school, you only need to look after kids? . . . (Wilson-Lum, Alphaplus online comments, February 1997)

Workers in the Deaf community talked about their frustration of not knowing how to support women who were controlled and dependent and who had little say over their own lives. In particular, women who have not had the opportunity to learn American Sign Language can remain

---

[1]Although I understand that there are debates in the Deaf community about whether the capital D should be used in all instances, I use the capital D for Deaf throughout this book to emphasize the culture of deafness.

[2]Resources such as TTY, flashing lights to signal the doorbell, baby crying, and so on can all increase a Deaf person's freedom to live independently.

dependent on family members or spouses to interpret for them, making it harder for them to resist the ways they are controlled and harder to leave. One worker spoke of a woman who had been abused for 25 years by her father. When she started the program, she only knew signs for such concepts as *stupid* and *wrong*. Apparently she made slow progress and so was dropped from funding as a "waste of money." I was also told about a Deaf woman who had been raped and became pregnant. Although she had an abortion, she did not have any opportunity to go to a counselor. For the time being, she continues in the literacy program trying to learn despite this trauma. If she is unable to learn fast enough, attend regularly enough, or simply needs to take a break for a while, she is likely to be judged as unmotivated and dropped from the program. Deaf literacy students are particularly vulnerable to being dropped from support. In Ontario, for example, Deaf students are funded by Ontario Disability Support Program.[3] If they are judged to be not making sufficient progress, because of their pace of learning or because of absences, they are dropped from funding and from the program.[4]

Sometimes women did not object to the control exerted by the men in their lives, but the literacy workers were disturbed. One worker said that when her program, which serves people who are on the street, made the decision to exclude a woman's partner from the program because he was abusive, the woman was angry with the program and quit. Workers talked about how frustrating they find it when they cannot help a woman achieve safety:

> It's even more difficult for me when I know that a woman is in a really dangerous situation and her partner is also a learner. . . . If she is sharing that information and she's interested in getting support then we can establish some boundaries. If she is not interested in that, or doesn't feel safe to do that, then I can't establish boundaries with him. It's not a safety issues if she hasn't shared with me—where I suspect. So I can't take an action to make her safe if she doesn't want it. That part can be really frustrating. . . . It's like, do I have to be pleasant to this person when I know the bruises came from you? If she's not ready to share that then I can't make it a safe

---

[3]The Ontario Disability Support Program replaced the Vocational Rehabilitation Services and the requirements have become increasingly strict. With an increased focus on getting students into the workforce, those with limited American Sign Language (ASL) skills are unlikely to be allowed to stay long enough to develop good communication skills.

[4]My thanks to Deanne Bradley, who facilitated my access to Deaf literacy workers in Ontario and provided extensive information in an interview as well as e-mail correspondence.

place for her. (interview, Community and Street Program Literacy Workers, Toronto, February 1997)

Another woman student asked that the program provide her partner with progress reports on her. The program considered his behavior controlling, but the woman experienced his attention as valuing her. A program worker said she saw this woman as having had so little attention and being so devalued throughout her life that any male attention was extremely important to her.

Workers who worked with homeless women spoke of the ways in which men pull women in and out of homelessness. The line between being homeless and not may vary based on whether the man they are in a relationship with has accommodation. A woman on social assistance in Toronto, for example, who has a male partner does not receive a cheque; instead, it must go to the male unless she can prove he is not paying the rent regularly. Even when women are simply sharing space with a man, the man is assumed to be a spouse and the cheque goes to him. Women's lack of control over their money makes them dependent and might make them more vulnerable to abuse. Workers talked about the prevalence of violence on the street and within shelters and drop-ins and the tension between the men as defenders of "their" women from other men on the streets *and* also their abusers.

One worker who works with students with intellectual disabilities remembered how difficult she had found it to decide what to do when she thought a woman with intellectual disabilities was being abused by her caregiver. She realized how little choice the woman had of safe places to live; she questioned whether the situation would simply be worse if she tried to initiate a process to reveal the situation. Intellectual or physical disabilities can increase women's vulnerability. Women with intellectual and physical disabilities are more likely to be targeted on the street and may be dependent on caregivers in the home or in group homes. Caregivers may be demeaning and abusive; even the assumption that a woman cannot do something may limit her potential to learn and decrease her self-esteem. The dependence women have on their caregivers may make it difficult for them to complain about any level of abuse, put-down, or exclusion. When women do complain, they are less likely to be believed and to be removed from the dangerous situation. The consistency of ill treatment may mean a woman has known little else, destroying all self-esteem and making violence normal.

Adult learners who were labeled as children and sterilized without their consent, or placed in institutions where they were mistreated in many ways, are not uncommon in literacy programs. Ticoll and Panitch (1993) drew attention to compilations of statistics that suggest the prevalence of abuse in the lives of women with disabilities:

> . . . a compilation of national prevalence studies suggests that from 39 to 68% of women with an intellectual disability will be sexually abused before they reach the age of 18 (The Roeher Institute, 1986). A number of studies on the abuse of women with disabilities generally would support the suggestion that this population, which includes women with physical as well as mental disabilities, is highly vulnerable to sexual abuse (Stimpson and Best, 1991; Sobsey, 1988). Furthermore, anecdotal evidence strongly suggests that not only have many women with an intellectual disability been abused, but there has been little, if any, opportunity for them to talk about what has happened to them or to get the support they require to deal with their experiences. (p. 85)

Ticoll and Panitch made clear the range of factors that make women with intellectual disabilities particularly vulnerable to abuse. They included in their list: segregation/isolation, lack of decision-making power, lack of self-esteem, lack of access to community-based services, and poverty. They reminded the reader that it is not having a disability per se that makes a person vulnerable to abuse, but the presence of these factors:

> When individuals are not impoverished, when they have employment and education options, when they have a network of friends, when they live in safe housing conditions, and when they can develop a positive sense of self and self-image, they are much less likely to be abused. (Ticoll & Panitch, 1993, p. 85)

ESCAPING VIOLENT SITUATIONS

Many of the situations I heard about during interviews involved women trying to escape violent situations. Some were leaving situations of public violence only to become more trapped in private domestic violence; others left an abuser only to be further trapped in poverty and increased vulnerability to the batterer.

Women working with immigrant women, especially refugees, spoke about women who have left war-torn countries and have experienced the violence and horror of attacks on themselves and their families. Some have endured arrest, imprisonment, and torture. One counselor spoke of women dealing with flashbacks, nightmares, disrupted sleep, and depression as a result of their experiences and coping with so many problems that they are exhausted. Taking on education while the aftermath of trauma is so vividly present in daily life is an enormous challenge. Yet for many in literacy and ESL training, this is the unspoken reality. The nature of the educational setting, interactions, and curriculum are all crucial in making learning possible or impossible. Yet funders often judge the attempt to recognize these needs as trying "to be all things to all people" rather than simply the bare minimum to make learning possible.

Immigrant women also have added deterrents against leaving violent partners. They may fear being alone in a foreign land, fear the disapproval of their community, or have difficulty with language. Language barriers, unfamiliarity with the system, fear of the police, and racism may all make it harder or impossible for some immigrant women to access shelters[5] or the "protection" offered by the legal system. If women have been sponsored by their spouse, they may fear being sent back to their country of origin and may not be eligible for assistance in Canada. A study of spousal abuse in the South Asian community in British Columbia illustrated the role of sponsorship in trapping women in abusive situations:

> . . . the husbands abandoned their responsibilities of sponsorship support to help settle their wives in Canada. Instead, they transformed the sponsorship into a form of new power over their wives. The result created nearly insurmountable inequity in their relationship and made the women socially, psychologically and financially dependent on their husbands. (Dosanjh et al., 1994, p. 1)

They may be far from family and friends who might be able to support them. The following account from a literacy worker made me think of how few women might be able to rely on such help from their parents and to question how else they would be able to get free:

> . . . a former student of mine who came to Canada from India to meet and marry her husband, thousands of miles from any close blood relative. She soon found that her new home was not a paradise. She was being abused both by her new husband, who had a drinking problem, and soon by her mother-in-law. Her mother-in-law beat her for complaining about her situation. . . . When my student told her husband's family that she had been to see . . . [an Indo-Canadian immigration counsellor in that community who

---

[5]A recent e-mail from British Columbia mentioned the difficulties some immigrant women have in getting support from a shelter: "Lacking the resources to effectively deal with second language learners, and lacking space in general, some shelters do not admit some new immigrants/refugees and especially not people without the proper immigration paperwork."

has done many heroic things for women in that situation] the family was instantly afraid, and stopped abusing her. Very shortly, however, they moved away. . . . I heard that, about one year later, my student simply left her husband's family and went back to India. She left all of her things, got in a taxi with her baby daughter, and went to the airport. She had convinced her family in India to arrange for the ticket. (Alphaplus Literacy & Violence Online Seminar, February–April 1998)

English programs for new immigrants do not routinely explain the possible sources of protection, such as shelters, when they introduce many other aspects of life in Canada. Yet the study carried out by the India Mahila Association suggested that women's "limited knowledge of resources available" was a factor in women staying longer in abusive relationships. They stated: "The women cited that they did not know who to go to for help since they had limited opportunity to become informed and to develop relationships outside the extended family" (Dosanjh et al., 1994, p. 2).

In British Columbia, a family violence curriculum has been written for newcomer English programs. Like other curriculum I have seen (Hawkins, 1984, Lovell, 1993), my major concern is that it offers somewhat simplistic assurances about the protection offered by the police and legal services and suggests that leaving a violent man will make a woman safe. Despite its limitations, it is an innovative attempt to open up the topic of violence within ESL programs. Unfortunately, I was told that it is rarely used in the classroom.

Violence of Historical Racism

First Nation instructors talked about the experience of the residential school system, reminding me that the closure of the schools has not meant an escape from the legacy of the violence perpetrated through that system. Adults who endured the myriad layers of cruelty and destruction have to find ways to live with the ongoing legacy of pain. Addictions of various sorts provide one way of burying the pain and expose both adults and children to further violence:

I have seen and experienced a lot of abuse as a child that was the result of alcohol. I remember my Mother being battered many times, and the fear I felt. Too afraid to move, yet afraid that she would die from the injuries she received. My sexual abuse started then. There were many who took advantage of me while my parents drank. They had no idea what was happening to me. I was too afraid to tell, scared that when I was alone that I would be beaten. I was told that if I said anything to anyone I would pay for it, that there wasn't anyone to protect me, so I wasn't safe. (Audrey G. cited in Steel, n.d., p. 7)

Adults who were incarcerated in residential schools as children often had little opportunity to experience nurturing parenting. That legacy of violence may continue as that generation of adults becomes parents and must discover anew nonoppressive ways to bring up their own children. This ongoing legacy has been named the *residential school syndrome*—marking the impact, but naming the ongoing consequences in medical terms.

The residential school system was intended to assimilate First Nations—"kill the Indian and save the man" (Pratt, 1888; cited in Ahern, 1978)—and participation was enforced. The ethnocentric and racist assumptions of the superiority of individualistic, capitalist values over aboriginal community and cultural values was the underpinning of the school system. Children were prevented from developing pride in their culture and identity, separated as they were from family, community, and culture at an early age and *educated* to believe that their own culture, religion, and way of life was inferior to white *civilization*. This destruction of culture and identity continues. One instructor spoke of her own childhood experience:

In the seventies there was a lot of racism towards Native people. . . . People always harping on what kind of a name is that. . . . One teacher actually saying I thought we killed all of you people off—because it was a native name. I said it's native and . . . he's like what do you mean native? I said "Canadian Indian." He said "Oh I thought we killed all of you off." and I just kinda looked at him and that's in grade five and I remember thinking "Well you know—you did a pretty good job"—because I was visualizing my uncles. . . . (interview, First Nation Instructors, Toronto, January 1997)

Instructors told me that in First Nations programs they take it as a given that everyone has experienced violence. If learners did not experience the residential school system itself, they are sure to have experienced the violence of its aftermath and the ongoing racism and insults that have inevitably assaulted their self-esteem and pride.

White workers in the north spoke about the added stresses of isolation and cultural oppression, suggesting that the move to settlements has meant that men's traditional skills are no longer valued, putting added pressure on relationships. It is often hard for women to escape violent relationships in a small, remote community, where the abuser may remain in the same community or return after time in prison.[6] When the woman seeks to escape violence by moving away from her community, she may leave that particular man behind. However, the daily violence of racism may be more vividly present and harder to endure in an urban center, where she is also isolated from her own family and community.

Living in a Shelter

Women working in the shelter movement spoke of the impossible demands on women who have recently left a violent partner and must pull together the necessities of life. They may be in temporary housing trying to arrange transportation, schooling, and work. They may have new accommodations, but have to deal with the terror of managing alone when they have been continually insulted and convinced they cannot cope. They may be trying to manage in a new situation where money is tight, when they previously had little access to money or money was entirely controlled by their spouse.

A woman with children has to find day care that she trusts will keep the children safe from the abuser and support those who may be traumatized by the violence they have witnessed or experienced and who may be furious at the disruption in their lives and the loss of their belongings. Several program workers spoke of the need for day care in or near literacy programs for that reason. One literacy program designed particularly with the idea of reducing barriers to learning has a day care onsite. Policies prevent giving out information about children there and staff have changed the access to the center based on an awareness of the need to keep children safe from spouses who might snatch them. A worker from a program working with women in second-stage housing, which does not have on-site day care, saw this lack as a major barrier to women's learning. She talked about how hard it is for women to concentrate when they are worrying about the safety of children and cannot look in on them for reassurance.

A series of practical problems for women living with violent men or who have recently left violent partners were raised by one woman work-

---

[6]Challenged by this complex picture, some Inuit elders have proposed a new system in contrast with the shelters where women alone seek refuge. Suggestions I have heard include a residence where men must address their problems in traditional ways and locations where a couple can live closely observed and supported so that community involvement and knowledge of the situation will change the man's behavior and keep the woman safe.

ing in the shelter movement. She spoke about the challenge for women to concentrate when they cannot be sure that their children are safe from the batterer. She talked about the effort to get to class, as well as the lies, fear, and practical barriers for women who are still living with a violent man or who have left and are being stalked. She talked about the challenges of temporary housing and the difficulties of transportation. She talked about how women who have to cope with being in danger in their daily life, or with the chaos of transition, will need not only a supportive environment, but also warm-up activities designed to help them concentrate and leave their stressful situations behind. They also need exercises that include the emotional component to learning and help them feel positive about their ability to learn.

Few literacy programs talked about the availability of resources that make it possible for women to leave a violent partner or maintain safety once they have left. The staff in one program told me that they had information on all the resources available in the region that might help a woman to stay safe in the lobby of the program on display with all the other program information. They thought this visible availability was important because it meant that a woman did not have to speak to anyone to access information. This easy availability might be important, thus it seems surprising that I did not see many antiviolence posters, posters from help lines, or flyers listing resources prominently on display. It might also be useful if programs had a sign up saying that, if you do want to talk to someone in the program, here is who you can talk to and when. Otherwise the implicit message might be that a literacy program is not somewhere you can speak about what is going on in your life even if it is getting in the way of literacy learning.

Women may be terrified of increased risk of violence because they have left a batterer and may be struggling with the legal system to keep themselves and their children safe. Northern shelter workers talked about the added difficulties for women's safety in small, remote communities where violent men may return to their community even if they have been imprisoned and where women may have to completely leave their community to escape. Reading the interactions among shelter workers and other advocates of abused women on a listserv has alerted me to how complex the process of seeking safety can be. They have written about the difficulty in getting restraining orders, the lack of enforcement of court orders, women being seen as *malicious* if they accuse their abuser of abusing the children, women charged with assault when they fight back while being abused, women losing children to "protective" custody (judged to have failed to protect them from the violence of their spouse), or women losing custody to the father accused of making *malicious* accusations.

There is tension between the needs of mother and children. One literacy worker worries that, when she tells a woman about the law requiring one to report any suspicion of child abuse to social services, she discourages the woman from talking to a counselor. Although this law may be crucial to protect children, it may also increase the isolation of a woman who is in a violent situation because she may fear that talking to anyone about her situation as she seeks support will mean that her children are taken from her:

> It is the law in B.C. that if anyone knows of violence in a home where there are children, they are to report it to Social Services if there is any chance of the children being abused. . . . In this phone call with a woman I barely know, I had to tell her that she might find if she talked to counselors, which she was considering, they may come to a place where they felt they had to report.
>
> Every time I tell someone about this, I feel like I'm isolating them and cutting them off from help. And at the same time, I worry about the kids. The law here really complicates things—which are complicated enough by trying to help the woman balance her needs and her kids needs—and by my own sense of concern for the kids. (Alphaplus Online Seminar, February–April 1998)

A shelter worker in Prince Edward Island talked about the need to report any suspicion that a woman is being abusive to her child and the tension that creates as women who have fled violence and control find themselves controlled again. These tensions can leave educators with another layer of responsibility and tension about the need to act *correctly*, which may lead some to prefer not to know too much about their students' lives.

Occasionally women working in women's services talked about the inadequacy of services for those with addictions, arguing that they frequently address the symptom rather than the cause. They suggested that the addiction is a coping mechanism for those who have experienced abuse and so the issues of abuse cannot be ignored if the attempt to support women to free themselves from addictions is to be successful. The lack of recognition of abuse in addiction programming means that women who take drugs or alcohol to numb the pain will simply feel worse if they try to change their pattern without addressing the source of the pain. Literacy workers also talked about learners who were on a whole range of medications as a result of violence, which also interfered with learning. One shelter worker, Helen Dempster, said:

Women get over-prescribed drugs from their doctors. It is still one of the number one solutions that is offered by the family doctors, an anti-anxiety or an anti-depressant, there are so many side effects to a lot of them and sometimes they are offered both. We're now struggling with this stuff in BC—where is the link between substance misuse and violence against women in relationships? We are trying to come to terms and find out information about that. And when we say substance misuse we are also including prescription drugs, that are prescribed for the women. . . . When a woman comes into a transition house we ask them to turn in their meds, just so that we can keep them locked up in the office and away from kids hands. And then they are free to come and get them and take them. She often gives us this small shopping bag of about four or five or six different things that she is on to help her sleep, to help her get over anxiety, depression—she's got some nausea not keeping food down. (interview, Vancouver, November 1996)

Literacy workers questioned the effect of such medications on learning and women's behavior in class and wished they knew more about how to work with learners who were affected by drugs.

The overwhelming array of violence that many women are coping with, including the violence of poverty that is so frequent it is commonplace, can leave instructors with continual tension over whether to focus on these issues, the literacy learning, or a complex question about how to find a balance between the two:

Sometimes we never got around to reading and writing because the stories I heard just blew me away. I know we all have experiences where we sit there and listen to people tell us about what happened in the last twenty-four hours. Poverty—linking violence and poverty is something I want to do here today—I just want to put those two together. Living in shitty places where the toilet floods where the landlord turned up in the middle of the night, where they fight on the street, the break-ins that happen, the purses get stolen. Sometimes 9:00 o'clock in the morning everyone walks in and I start to hear the trauma that people are living with daily in Vancouver I guess—or (from others "it's everywhere") and then one person tells me and then another person starts to talk about what happened to them and then another person. . . . I hear all this stuff. . . . So there's a reality change between my life and the students and it's about money—I have a safe place to live. (interview, Salt Spring Island, British Columbia, November/December 1996)

This instructor spoke of the students leaving "standing up straighter" when they have been able to spend time talking about the daily realities of their lives. However, other instructors talked about the value of leaving that pain behind by focusing on what they came to do—the reading and writing—and gaining the satisfaction of successful literacy learning. Several instructors agreed that they were always aware of the tension between achievement through work or addressing the realities of the issues. Some tried to find a balance that included both.

DANGER IN EDUCATION

For some women, even the classroom is not a safe place. I heard repeatedly about violence *in* the adult literacy classroom. I was told about situations where women students were harassed by male students inside and outside the classroom. One worker spoke about subtle harassment that led a woman to drop out of the program. Several workers spoke about how violent interactions are taken for granted and suggested that there is an aspect of denial in the inability of programs to address this. Often programs and colleges did not address the problem in a way that made the woman feel comfortable enough to stay. In contrast, programs that served people on the street described a level of violence that was staggering—coffee cups and chairs flying at times—but spoke of clear program policies about all levels of violence in the program.

I heard of teachers whose derogatory, racist, and sexist put-downs of students were a form of violence that made it hard to learn. One group of instructors said that they hear from learners that some instructors frequently get angry and reveal racial hatred or call learners *stupid*. Insults, criticism, or racist, sexist, or ableist comments can also be offered by other students, and many instructors do not take these on, perhaps taking them for granted as ordinary. I was also told of innuendo and humorous comments, which are not experienced as funny by the recipient, being aimed at instructors who felt unable to adequately address the situation. On several occasions, discussion was opened up around the violence of swearing and foul language. Programs that had specific, laid-out policies that excluded such language and the speaker if they continued were again programs that served people on the street, where high levels of violence are always visible.

When partners are in the same class, it may be particularly difficult for the instructor to find a suitable way to respond to one partner putting down the other. Even the way the instructor speaks to a partner can have the danger of contributing to the man's violent control, as Karen Ritchie, a literacy worker from New South Wales, Australia, described:

Another episode that causes me great pain, was a woman's look of terror when I praised her work. Her husband is in the same class. I realized the situation when he immediately put his work in front of me. I also praised him. When my student came in to class next day with a black eye, I wondered if I had praised him enough! I will need to be extremely careful in future when I have "family" groups or groups with connections to one another. (Alphaplus Literacy & Violence Online Seminar, February–April 1998)

Having abusers and the abused in the same class was described as a common situation in mixed literacy classes, which led to great tension for instructors who tried to create safety for those being abused. Many instructors face the difficulty of trying to support women to enable learning while not making any comments that escalate the partner's violence. Instructors may be left feeling that they are walking on eggshells.

I heard about women for whom the classroom felt like a precious safe place or at least safer than anywhere else in their lives. For these women, even those in crisis, it was one place where they did not feel terrified of the abuser in their lives. There are a variety of statistics about violence in adult relationships. Statistics Canada figures for 1993 state that:

One half (51%) of Canadian women have experienced at least one incident of physical or sexual violence (as defined by the Criminal Code of Canada) since the age of 16. Twenty-five percent of all women have experienced physical or sexual violence at the hands of a marital [includes common-law] partner. (p. 2)

Such statistics suggest that there will be many women in classrooms who have experienced or are currently experiencing violence as adults.

For some women, the violence in their lives follows them to school. Instructors, learners, and counselors spoke of situations where women's male partners chose to escalate the violence when women returned to school. One worker said that when women get "uppity," men become more violent. A woman thinking that she deserves an education, gaining confidence as she sees herself able to learn, or getting the satisfaction of beginning to achieve success is clearly *uppity*, and perhaps even beginning to imagine the possibility of moving away from his control.

One instructor spoke of the crisis in the classroom when a woman decided she was ready to leave her violent husband. She wrote her husband a letter and gave it to many in her class to read before she gave it to him. The instructor feared that this action would mean the student could be exposed to more violence before she left the marriage. Because family members were also in the class, it seemed unlikely that this student would feel safe to continue in the program. One counselor I talked to spoke about the importance of "controlling the speed of the split" because otherwise it "backfires." I am not sure whether a literacy worker is in a position to control the speed, but that comment resonated with the story and reminded me of the complexity of demands placed on instructors.

Women may have decided to return to school to prepare to escape the violence, but the immediate result is often that the man becomes more violent. As the woman empowers herself, the man tries to assert his control—to dominate and escalate the violence. This complex dynamic of threat and desire connected to education for women has been explored by Kathleen Rockhill (1987). She argued that this is a central dynamic for women:

> In order to look at how women's participation in education is embedded in the power dynamics between men and women, we need to look at how power operates in the concrete practices of everyday life: the direct opposition of men to women's participation in various forms of schooling; the general forms of male resistance to woman's participation in activities that may challenge her performance of traditional duties, as well as her gendered sexuality; the effect of male violence upon a woman who lives in the daily face of its threat, even if the violence is not explicitly directed against her participation in education programs. At its most fundamental, we need to ask how man's ownership of woman's labour and sexuality, her body and mind, affects her participation in education, and how education poses a threat to that ownership. (p. 316)

One instructor said that she particularly hears from older women, whose husbands seem threatened that their wives are going back to school. She heard a range of ways that men sabotaged the women's schooling and sought to control their behavior. She spoke of how threatening it was for women to feel divided between their family and community obligations and their own education; she felt it was crucial for instructors to "honor" what a woman needs to do to reduce the tension and make it possible to learn.

Interviewees also spoke of the need to honor the work that instructors do as they seek to respond adequately to the disclosures of current or past violence from women in their class. They also spoke of the lack of recognition of the danger they sometimes feel from violent men. I heard of situations where women instructors felt threatened by a male student in the classroom or feared being followed home. One college instructor said that, although she had reported her concern that one of the men in her class was dangerous to the college authorities, she did not feel she was taken seriously. I heard an account of a worker, from a program serving people on the street, who was stalked and attacked—hit over the head with a two by four and knocked unconscious. At that program, the staff said death threats were a daily occurrence. That staff clearly watched out for each others' safety. Although they seemed to have grown accustomed to the daily sense of danger as part of their everyday work life, they were clear that it contributed to a high level of exhaustion and burn out. For the most part, there appeared to be little institutional action to ensure learners' or instructors' safety and sense of comfort in the educational setting. A *Toronto Star* article quoted figures from a Canadian Union of Public Employees survey, reporting that:

> 61.2% of female respondents had experienced at least one incident of actual or threatened violence on the job. 52% reported three or more incidents and 20% reported receiving death threats. (*Toronto Star*, 1993, p. A14)

Although I did not hear about learners' experiences of violence at work, I can only assume that for some of those in paid employment this aspect of violence also would have been present.

I frequently heard of women who were being stalked, who were trying to learn while their husband (or ex-husband) was outside the school waiting for them, and who were struggling to attend school and learn in the face of escalating violence. This violence is a very real threat: "Of all women murdered in Canada, 62% are killed by their partners, most often after they have left the abusive relationship." (War Against Women Report, 1991, p. 7). Several workers talked about what this level of terror means to the individual threatened, as well as to others in the class. Women in a program that served women in second-stage housing spoke in particular about the impact on the entire class when any woman experienced violence.

Many literacy workers spoke of women's erratic attendance, which was due to pressure from controlling men who prevented their regular attendance (or their study at home), shame over attending school with the bruises that would reveal they were being battered, or severe injuries. As one college instructor said: "Another student just isn't coming because she's been beaten up so badly she can't walk!! I have seven women in this class—I know four are dealing with this stuff." (personal correspondence, 1997).

For programs where regular attendance is required to maintain a place or where students are funded, students who are experiencing violence can be dropped off support or out of the program—controlled again, but this time by those in a position to judge them as not serious, not motivated, or not making sufficient progress. The same instructor said:

> Last night as I was leaving I talked to a missing student on the phone and she allowed as how she hadn't been coming because she had a black eye. "I guess my boyfriend just got a little too drunk." (Alphaplus Literacy & Violence Online Seminar, February–April 1998)

RECOGNIZE THE PRESENCE OF TRAUMA

Experience of trauma and its aftermath—whether it took place during childhood or as adults—is likely the present reality for many, if not most, literacy learners. In literacy programming, we cannot take refuge in the silence about such trauma—it is vividly present in the classroom in many dimensions. The experience of trauma cannot be framed as abnormal and individualized. In literacy programming, we cannot fall into the trap of suggesting that learners can go away and *heal* from the trauma and come back to class when they are ready to learn. We must recognize the effects of trauma and create literacy opportunities that are viable for learners who are "familiar with trauma" and will enable them to learn while they continue to "live beside the violation." We cannot diminish learners by maintaining a silence about the extent of violence in society or by understanding their experience in terms of pathology and ill health. We need to recognize the value of those who warn society about the dangers of normalized violence, honor the increased sensitivities that living with trauma brings, and design literacy programming that supports learners, despite the violence they have experienced, to value themselves and develop their literacy skills.

II

LEARNING IN THE CONTEXT OF TRAUMA

It is impossible to remove the impact of trauma from literacy programs or perhaps remove it from any educational setting. Although many argue that learners who have experienced trauma and who need to "heal" should be referred elsewhere for counseling, there are major problems with the attitude that learners can go away and heal and then come back and learn. There is no place free from violence—no place to retreat for healing. Even when learners have already worked or are concurrently working therapeutically on their trauma issues, they still bring their trauma issues along when they come to class.

Several literacy workers spoke strongly about the need to recognize that issues that surface in literacy need to be addressed in literacy perhaps as well as elsewhere. Evelyn Battell, an adult basic education instructor in a community college, illustrates this issue with a comment about a student who had already been in extensive therapy, but began to have trouble when she started working on math:

> She thought she pretty much had sorted out her childhood but math has brought it back BIG TIME. She is going to keep a journal—she's very articulate and observing. We are talking a lot as she struggles but the struggle is really extreme and I'm worried. . . . (personal correspondence, 1997)

If, in literacy programming, we do not recognize that trauma issues are present in the literacy classroom and that instructors' actions can help or hinder learners' processes, we leave learners and workers isolated and unsupported. As Evelyn Battell described the impact on the learner she is working with, her sensitivity and support is clearly crucial:

When she arrived she couldn't feel her lower extremities at all. A couple of times through the test she was having trouble breathing. I did everything I could—let her talk about it—gave her help with the questions to make it more like a class and not a test, etc., etc., but she was determined to go on with it. Finally she quit and left—she was okay I think—I urged her to figure out how to care for herself in the afternoon. (personal correspondence, 1997)

This brief note speaks volumes about the layers of difficulty experienced by a single student and, in turn, one instructor seeking to support the student to find her own path to learning in the face of traumatic experience and its impact on her learning. Perhaps this is a particularly extreme account. Perhaps literacy workers may hope not to frequently deal with such severe difficulties, but these are impacts of trauma that may often be present, but invisible, in the literacy classroom. For example, this particular student might have felt stupid and ashamed at missing the test and feeling unable to sit through it. An instructor who had no other possible explanation might, without opening up, talk about what is going on for the learner, simply assume the student is not serious and not motivated. Another student might be less articulate and observing, less emotionally ready, less comfortable trusting the instructor, and unable to offer the instructor clues about why she misses class or tests. Another instructor might be too overwhelmed with the demands of all the students (and the demands of the program, the curriculum, the record keeping, or issues in her own life) to be sensitive to what is going on for each particular student. This case illustrates the value of recognizing the presence of trauma impacts in the classroom.

Therapeutic discourse suggests that a series of impacts follow the experience of trauma and that, even for a student who never discloses her experience, impacts of violence can operate in the classroom. What these impacts look like are discussed in detail in the next chapter. Therapeutic discourse offers literacy work the possibility of knowing what these impacts look like. It can offer instructors who are struggling to do their best to help students learn a place to develop awareness as well as approaches and supports for addressing these issues. Workers who are acutely aware of the nuances of violence reported how much easier it would be simply not to see than it is to see and work without knowledge and direction: "It is in fact easier if you pay no attention to this and don't talk about it!" (Battell, personal correspondence). This work begins an exploration of what might be seen differently and what might lead to new approaches in literacy. It seeks to provide a forum for workers to explore creative alternatives for teaching and program models that support those who have experienced trauma to learn.

Therapeutic discourse suggests that control, connection, and meaning are significant issues for anyone who has undergone trauma. These issues should be explored in the context of literacy learning. Rather than addressing these issues as aspects of individual healing, our focus should be on control, connection, and meaning as integral to learning, including literacy learning. For learners to set goals and make changes in their lives, addressing these factors is crucial.

Recognition of the whole person offers potential for literacy learning. My knowledge about recognition of four aspects of the body comes primarily from various First Nation educators, who explained the concept of the medicine wheel and balance among the four aspects of the person. Aline LaFlamme, a pipe carrier I met in Yellowknife in the North West Territories, made the concept most powerfully clear when she drew the medicine wheel. Instead of a balance among the four quadrants, she drew most of the circle as the mind, with two tiny quadrants for the body and emotions and an even smaller section for the spirit. She said her drawing illustrated the lack of balance in North American society, where the mind is given far too much weight. She helped me see that, given this emphasis, it is not surprising that literacy learners, who are not judged as excelling in the mind, often feel they are not valued. When I described this off-balance wheel to Susan Heald, survivor, women's studies professor, and advisor to the project, she used it to illustrate that healing for individuals can be problematic if healing is learning to function better in a sick, off-balance world.

Much therapeutic literature suggests that a central task for the trauma survivor is to connect body and feeling, to reintegrate the self, and to integrate her history of trauma with other aspects of herself—to *heal*. Lewis (1998) captured a central contradiction in this concept of a return to normality:

> While therapy teaches the survivor to connect body and feeling and to listen to the messages from that reconnection, the general social context will not support the survivor in this work. Brown (1995) states that denial and minimalization are necessary to cope with "insidious trauma." Most women live out degrees of constriction in fulfilling their care taking roles. Given how capitalism severs the public from the private, the mind from the body and feeling, the individual from the community, those who consciously at-

tempt to connect body/mind/feeling/spirit are extraordinary, not ordinary. Through the struggle to connect the survivor engages in politically transformative work that remains unseen and unacknowledged in a diagnostic model that asserts normal life as its goal. (p. 35)

Within literacy learning, there is the potential to move away from the diagnostic model and support literacy learners in learning and claiming their power while questioning the narrow concept of *normal life*.

4

Beyond "Normal" Appearances: "Hidden" Impacts of Trauma

Hearing about impacts of trauma from therapists, counselors, and literacy workers led me to explore the range of learning these impacts require and to recognize that this hidden learning takes energy away from the literacy learning process for many students. This chapter introduces these concepts and examines new possibilities for literacy practice; it takes into account the full scope of learning necessary for learners to successfully improve their literacy skills. These issues create areas of learning that women must struggle with if they are to be successfully present—with full attention—in the classroom and learn to read. When these issues are not recognized, they can become barriers to successful learning.

The added layers of learning that these impacts necessitate seem to explain why it takes some time for many learners to build better literacy skills. Yet when I suggested to counselors and literacy workers that impacts of trauma might explain why it takes *so long* for learners to significantly improve their literacy skills, several women were indignant with me, insisting that it does not take a long time. They argued that unrealistic expectations of how fast learning should take place is the problem, not the speed at which learning occurs. Given what many illiterate women have to cope with as they begin to learn as adults, the expectations are unrealistic.

Recently, more talk in literacy focuses on *outcomes*, as various government initiatives seek to make literacy programs accountable and to fund only visible progress. This government-generated discourse needs to shift to include the complexity of issues many learners are dealing with when they take on literacy learning. Much of the learning that has to take place—learning that takes the energy of the learner—is not visible to learners or workers, let alone planners and funders. Learners and workers are likely to be frustrated, wondering why there is not more visible progress, rather than noticing the layers of learning that are taking place alongside the more direct literacy learning. It is crucial to make these areas of learning visible for learners, instructors, funders, and policymakers so that situations that allow women to learn successfully can be created.

Listening to therapists and counselors and reading literature on the effects of trauma experiences, I was aware of tension between the wealth of understanding that the information I was learning seemed to offer about behaviors I have seen in many people—literacy learners, other workers, and myself—and the profoundly problematic creation of a divide between those who have experienced trauma and other literacy learners. Therapeutic discourses necessarily pathologize behaviors. Yet more and more, I see that trauma impact behaviors are demanded by a society that requires people to become numb and fragmented to survive intolerable situations. As I was drawn into these discourses, I began to reframe some earlier experiences in literacy and rethink approaches to many problems in literacy work. I was also frustrated by the slippery slide into pathologizing such behaviors—into perceiving anyone who behaved in a particular way as *other*. I began to see how easily I share in and reaffirm a concept of *normal*.

Working within the categories created in therapeutic discourse offers new insights that I think will benefit literacy work. Yet working within these categories, I also become complicit with the framing of these categories as *other*. My position is inherently contradictory, as Spivak (1987) pointed out: "It is impossible, of course, to mark off a group as an entity without sharing complicity with its ideological definition" (p. 118).

Throughout the chapter, this tension remains present as I describe behaviors that are significant in adult literacy learning and also recognize such behaviors as commonplace in society broadly. To counter the slippery slide into pathologizing, I return to my earlier assertion that our strategy must not be to separate out trauma survivors for treatment different from other learners. Instead, we must focus on all learners as whole people, stress the importance of drawing on their strengths in all approaches to literacy learning, and avoid focusing on survivor behaviors as individual problems.

ALL OR NOTHING

All or nothing is a theme that can frame a learner's reactions to issues of trust, boundaries, and openness. Heather Bain, an Edmonton-based psychologist, talked about trauma survivors as frequently showing opposing patterns at the same time—moving between complete control and abdicating control, between complete trust and no trust at all, between a defended self and no boundaries or self-protection. She spoke of women switching between extremes and having enormous difficulty with ambiguity:

> All or nothing—100% or 0%. . . . I think it would be a really evident pattern, you may see students who do really really well for a while and then maybe do less well, but certainly they're still viable within the program, but they won't consider that they're still viable and they'll leave, because there's no middle ground, there's not a continuum, there's just that switch from I'm here and I'm doing well—to I can't cope with this, I'm failing I'm doing really really badly. . . . (interview, Edmonton, December 1996)

This insight offers me a way to see behavior of the learner I tutor, which I had found confusing and contradictory. It gave us new ways to talk about what goes on for her when she abdicates all control one minute and fights for complete control the next. Heather Bain suggested that it would be valuable for women to learn to find middle ground. She stressed that if one pattern is present, you could expect to see the opposite also:

> . . . there often is no middle ground and healing is partly about creating that middle ground, so I think if you see one pattern you also need to assume that the opposite is there somewhere, and it may not be played out in the moment, it may be played out next week, or it may be played out somewhere else. But the opposite is always there. . . . (interview, Edmonton, December 1996)

Another aspect of *all or nothing* that therapist Clarissa Chandler spoke about was a tendency for survivors to make enormous, heroic efforts, but to be less likely to carry out daily, on-going work. The idea of daily effort gradually leading to change was described as often foreign to survivors. Those who grew up in violent and chaotic homes have little experience of seeing regular effort lead to results; they are unlikely to have been given the support or space to work at learning something regularly—to do homework regularly and see the results of their own learning. Clarissa Chandler said survivors are often amazed that what they need to do is consistent daily activity, aghast that something so boring is required:

> . . . what happens to the experience of neglect, and the impact of neglect, is that you don't have . . . the day-to-day tools to live your life in such a

way that you are supported to have what you want, because the nature of trauma is that you have to take your day-to-day needs, set them aside to survive some traumatic event at the moment. This means that part of your organization is that day-to-day self-care is negotiable and that's what really makes me able to survive and succeed. . . . So neglect, is what people have no comprehension. . . . Neglect is the structure of everyday life. Or another way to look at it is self-love, self-care, self-responsibility is the concreteness of everyday life—being able to get out of your bed, brush your teeth, go for a walk, exercise, figure out your food, figure out your sleep, figure out what you might need out of life—that would be considered hum drum, boring, what does that have to do with me? (interview, Toronto, November 1996)

I asked a group of literacy workers in British Columbia, most of whom work in full-time community college programs, whether this resonated. They replied that it strongly reminded them of the students who come in at the beginning of the year ready to make an enormous effort, convinced that this time they will *just do it*. They spoke of students who seem to wind themselves up to a point of hysteria to get to class and take on the impossible—trying to be superhuman. Workers suggested that perhaps trying to be superhuman came from not knowing what is real or possible. All the workers said that they have a sinking feeling when they meet students with this outlook because experience tells them the students will drop out soon after, feeling they are not doing brilliantly. Several learners also described their own experience in similar ways. Frustrated instructors wonder how to help students stay in for the long haul. Students are also frustrated, having thought it would be different, that this time they were going to work really hard. These students can easily be labeled *not serious*. The insight that they may not have had practice with the concept of daily work leading to change suggests new ways to think about approaches to help them learn successfully.

Totalizing, another dimension of the *all or nothing* concept, is the tendency to move instantly from one example to *it is always this way*. One mistake means I always make mistakes—I am stupid and nothing will change. Further, you let me down once, so I can never rely on you, you will always let me down, I will never trust you again over anything. Heather Bain suggested that this *all or nothing* pattern means that the "facilitators will often be idealized or hated." Obviously this, too, can create a challenge for the facilitator. Clearly these tendencies could be problematic for literacy learning and could undermine the possibility of seeing mistakes as simply part of learning and then continuing to regularly practice writing or reading.

Living With Extremes: Identifying Middle Ground

Students who have lived with violent men—fathers or husbands—spoke about how their experiences of abuse created a life of extremes. When one woman in Prince Edward Island tried to make the point clear from her own experience, other learners in the group knew exactly what she was talking about:

> ... living with abuse is a life of extremes. Things are either—you're getting bouquets of flowers delivered in the snow outside your door, or you're being woken up 2 o'clock in the morning with a knife at your throat. It's extremes. Finding balance, I think it's beyond confidence in yourself. You don't even know who you are, you know. If you've been told since the day you were born you're a piece of shit and you don't have a brain, much less ever use it, you carry that on through the whole life, you don't know who you are. (interview, Charlottetown, PEI, March 1997)

After coping with such extremes, finding balance is an enormous challenge. In violent households, you are either right or wrong. There is no possibility of negotiation, no middle ground, and no questioning those with physical power or authority. Being wrong can lead to violence, but arguing that you are not wrong can be even more dangerous.

Although I am concerned not to use the depiction of *all of nothing* to create a sense that survivors have a unique problem, the insights offered by this concept might be of value to all literacy learners. The group of literacy workers who met in Edmonton were prompted by the discussion about all or nothing to notice that literacy and illiteracy are also constructed in our society as all or nothing—either you can read or you can't. Although many learners' experience is that they can read to some extent, both learners and others will say they cannot read. This dichotomy masks the actual middle ground—reading with difficulty. A tendency to see things in all or nothing terms is not unique to survivors of trauma, but a common process of categorization that tends to create rigid dichotomies. These dichotomies frequently specify the divide between the norm and the other—like the literate and illiterate, or the able-bodied and disabled—providing sharp separation.

I found that when working closely with a student, looking at her actual experience of reading and writing has helped break down the divide between illiterate and literate and helped her see the gradual improvement in her reading. She has begun to recognize middle ground and to observe the gradual change in some of the less tangible things she is learning. Now that I am aware of the pattern of all or nothing, I am more able to observe it and less likely to get offended. For example, learners at the end of one learner leadership project described it as "wonderful," yet later told me it was "completely useless." When I see the comments as part of the pattern of all or nothing and notice, that in my own reports, I wanted to decide whether it was good or bad, new options open up that leave more space for an assessment that includes both strengths and weaknesses. Working on making the middle ground visible, exploring what makes an activity a little better or a little worse, might avoid the pattern of all or nothing and create the possibility of more choices. Curriculum that helps make middle ground or small improvements visible and includes more exploration of what leads to successful learning might be useful to all learners.

The *all or nothing* notion suggests that a variety of modes that help learners see gradual progress might be useful. Portfolios of work could be used to help learners see incremental changes in their work. Writing a journal entry each day about what they have worked on or learned might provide a useful record over time. Mentors and role models might also be a support for learners as they struggle to continue in the face of frustration that no single thing provides total success. One learner spoke about the importance of the role of a sponsor in Alcoholics Anonymous groups—someone who, as she put it, "believes in you until you begin to believe in yourself." A similar support might also help learners stay involved in literacy long enough to recognize the possibilities of daily work and appreciate the achievements made in middle ground.

PRESENCE

Therapists and counselors I interviewed often spoke of experiences of trauma leading to *dissociation*. Therapists use this term to refer to a process whereby a person who is experiencing unbearable trauma distances herself from her body to separate herself from the trauma. This response, sparked to survive the initial trauma, can become an on-going state into which a survivor may unconsciously slip. Heather Bain began our interview by speaking about dissociation:

> I begin with dissociation because it's the big one. I work mainly with adult women and I see that adult women who've experienced trauma in their life will either use school as a way to cope, or escape. So they do really really well or else they can't cope with school at all and they drop out early, or there's big gaps and you know there's dissociation, that ability to separate and to move out of the traumatic experience and to shut that off. But what happens is that anything that reminds a kid or an adult of that expe-

rience can lead to a separation. The cues can be unnoticeable to us, or they can be really minimal. . . . (interview, Edmonton, December 1996)

A recent study suggested that dissociation is particularly connected to childhood trauma because even assault victims dissociated more if they had "histories of childhood physical and sexual abuse" (Dancu et al., 1996). Absence without physically leaving is key to the concept of dissociating.

The authors of *The Courage to Heal*, a self-help book for "women survivors of childhood sexual abuse," provide a straightforward account of this process, although they do not use the term *dissociation*:

> One of the common ways children deal with the unbearable experience of being sexually abused is to flee from the experience, to split. [they explain that although the term splitting has a different "clinical definition" they use it to describe the feeling the survivor has when she separates her consciousness from her body, or "leaves" her body] Most survivors have experienced this at least to some degree. In its milder form, you live exclusively on the mental level, in your thoughts, and aren't fully present. At its most extreme, you literally leave your body. This feat, which some yogis work for decades to achieve, comes naturally to children during severe trauma. They cannot physically run away, so they leave their bodies. Many adult survivors still do this whenever they feel scared. . . .
>
> You may consciously choose to split, but sometimes splitting happens spontaneously when you don't want it to—when you're in the middle of a serious conversation for example or making love. (Bass & Davis, 1988, pp. 209–210)

Literacy workers are familiar with the idea that many learners have difficulty paying attention for any stretch of time and often appear to be daydreaming or bored. Some literacy workers identify those who are not paying attention as not serious students or unmotivated. Others might wonder about learning disabilities, intellectual disabilities, fetal alcohol syndrome, or attention deficit disorder. Alternatively, literacy workers might judge that their own teaching is not interesting enough and be continually looking for ways to make the class more interesting—to hold the learners' attention better. Whatever the judgment as to the cause, the result of learners not appearing to pay attention is likely to be frustration for workers and learners alike. One instructor at the Friendship Centre in Brandon, Manitoba, told me that she worked with many students who, although they were in the class regularly, were frequently so spaced out that they did not even recognize their own work. In consequence, and similar to their childhood experiences of missing a lot of school and not getting a good grasp of the material, they missed a lot although they were physically in the classroom. Again, they were not able to understand the whole. Students often said to this instructor that they must be stupid if they were in class and still had not "got it." They had no other explanation. This is where understanding dissociation and the concept of presence can be vital.

In literacy, it is crucial to explore alternative explanations to allow us to move out of the frustration and inescapable judgment of stupidity. Lorna Gallant, a therapist in Prince Edward Island, suggested that, for children who experience trauma, dissociating or spacing out is one strategy to leave their memory of the trauma behind and continue to function. Some children may leave into their minds, focusing on thinking, and are likely to be extremely successful in school, whereas others act out. I have heard literacy learners say that they used both *spacing out* and *acting out* to survive their schooling, but spent little time focused on the lessons and fully present in the classroom. Both these strategies may be ways to *leave* the classroom because acting out often would have resulted in being sent out of the classroom.

Counselors speculated that factors causing children to rely on one option and not another could include the age of the child and whether school was a place of violence. If a child was already successful in school, focusing on schoolwork could become a viable strategy to escape the violence. If abuse began at an early age, it would be harder to stay present long enough and discover the possibilities of escape into the mind. School that was also violent and oppressive might offer no safe haven of intellectual achievement. If racism, classism, or ableism adds layers of insult, exclusion, and limited expectation, school would be unlikely to offer a safe haven to explore knowledge. Anne-Louise Brookes (1992) described her own childhood experience after she had been *changed* by her experience of abuse:

> I remember crying in the night. I found it difficult to hear Mrs. Patterson when she spoke in the classroom. I felt as if she were speaking from beneath tumbling water, or from the end of a long tunnel. She assumed I was daydreaming. I stopped imagining that I might one day be a teacher. Teachers were required to stand up in front of their students. I knew I wouldn't be able to stand up in front of people and talk. Not me. Everyone would know, I thought. No longer did my imagination dance me through the leaves. The sound of ringing church bells irritated me. Mostly I felt ashamed, different. I am an incest survivor. I was changed. . . . (pp. 21–22)

Her family moved to New Zealand and she described the changes that made:

> In a way, school was easier. Reading was a pleasure which enabled me to escape, when I needed to from myself and from others. Teachers reported me a good student. Being a good student was easy. It was easy, that is, until I was expected to stand up or speak in front of my classmates. This was painful. Afraid, I would vacate my body so as not to remember. (pp. 21–22)

Anne-Louse Brookes reported that this is still a strategy: "I still vacate my body when I am afraid" (pp. 21–22).

Betsy Warland (1993) wrote, "I forgot how to read in grade 3." She first gave the explanation offered at the time about the new school she moved to, then added:

> there's another reason I forgot how to read in grade 3.
>
> A reason that shook my faith in the written word far more profoundly. I was being sexually abused. As is nearly always the case, my abuse was unacknowledged. Invisible. And, as is often the case, my abusers' words placed the blame on me.
>
> Read. Ar-; To fit together. Old English raeden, to advise: READ; REDE, raeden, condition: HATRED, KINDRED.
>
> Although we weren't Bible thumpers my family was a religious one. My parents were the "pillars of the church." We were raised to believe that when we rebelled or simply disagreed with their opinions we were disobeying "God Himself."
>
> The written word was The Bible—The Law: one in the same. The Word was The Truth. No questions asked.
>
> in grade 3 I lost faith in words.
>
> At 43 I understood why. (pp. 34–35)

I wonder how many literacy learners forgot how to read, separated themselves from their childhood abuse, forgot that whole time in their lives, and mistrusted words to protect themselves from the words used to blame them and misrepresent their experience and from unbearable memory. Some literacy learners have written about why they could not learn in school. Ann Green (1990) wrote:

> I loved going to school just to get away from the drinking and the fighting. But I could not learn because of what was going on at home. I was too worried about my brother as there was hardly any food to eat, or wood to keep us warm. (p. 3)

Josie Byrnes (1977) described her response to living in poverty and being neglected and mistreated:

> I took to living in a dream world where I could become top, and people were friendly with me. Oh, yes, I were clever, so clever the teacher was asking me the questions. I try not to day-dream but I still say it's the most friendly place in the world. It was the only place I could turn to as a child. (pp. 22–24)

In medical literature, *dissociation* is described as a "way of organizing information" (van der Kolk, van der Hart, & Marmar, 1996). *Primary dissociation* describes the memory of a traumatic event, which, rather than being integrated into consciousness, is split into its different aspects—sound, smell, sight, and touch. These memories may then intrude in flashbacks and nightmares. *Secondary dissociation* is the spacing out described by Bass and Davis. My concern is that the concept of dissociation, and particularly the more medical interpretations of it as a disorder or ailment, suggest that it is normal to be present and abnormal to be dissociated. This *all or nothing* approach can easily make the complexity of degrees of presence, and the wide range of factors that might lead to greater or less presence in a particular situation, disappear.

It is important in literacy to avoid sliding into pathologizing learners as ill because they dissociate or focus on diagnosing whether a learner is dissociating or merely daydreaming or distracted. Consequently, I choose to use the word *presence* to focus on the nuances of presence, rather than on dissociating or absence as a problem, and to move away from a divide that posits daydreaming as a healthy, natural phenomena and dissociation as a symptom of trauma and ill health. A focus on what constitutes presence avoids the suggestion that absence must always be problematic or has only one cause. There is no benefit in simply replacing one framework of judgment (motivation) with another framework (dissociation). Instead, new and nuanced discourses are needed that allow us to recognize impacts of abuse and conceptualize new ways of working that neither medicalize the issues nor preserve invisibility.

The frustration caused by the failure to learn and the accompanying label of stupidity make it crucial to discover new explanations that might lead to new possibilities for learning. The recognition that many learners have difficulty staying present for a variety of reasons could become part of the everyday discourse in literacy programs. The issue could be mentioned when a student enters a program and could become part of the talk about what will happen in the class or group, part of staff and volunteer training. Normalizing the concept of presence would make it possible to create space for learners to begin to notice when they are more or less present and what factors—in their own lives, in the classroom, and in the program more broadly—contribute to the ability to stay present in a particular situation.

One therapist spoke about the importance of honoring dissociation as a brilliant survival strategy for enduring the unbearable. Recognizing the process as one that survivors have *learned* and one that spiritual leaders may spend a lifetime seeking to achieve may be particularly important for literacy learners, who often feel they are unable to learn anything. Several survivors have also pushed me to recognize the value of spacing out. During an online seminar, Ann Unterreiner said:

> I must maintain a practice of honoring the needed protections that dissociation offers a survivor. If they did not need to dissociate they would have let it go. (Alphaplus Literacy & Violence Online Seminar, February–April 1998)

In contrast, the therapeutic literature—both the clinical literature and the self-help—takes the approach that it is important for survivors to learn to stay present.

> It has been repeatedly observed that once people have learned to dissociate in response to trauma, they tend to continue to do so in the face of subsequent stress. Continued dissociation may not only interfere with the conscious processing of current information; it also prevents the exploration of alternative ways of coping, and thus interferes with general adaptation. Even if tuning out potentially frightening stimuli helps to keep a person from feeling overwhelmed, in the long run trauma victims are in danger of having difficulties with active problem-solving strategies; that is, they may consolidate a helpless and passive social stance. (van der Kolk et al., 1996, p. 316)

Bass and Davis (1988) suggested that dissociating or splitting is something a woman may want to learn to control. They suggested a series of strategies to learn to stay in the present moment:

> Remember to breathe . . .
> Pay attention to when you split . . .
> Be willing to feel . . .
> Make the commitment not to split unconsciously
> Reach out . . . (p. 210)

One survivor wrote about dissociating as a survival skill and about her own challenge learning to stay present:

> It is a strange paradox that the ability to dissociate and split is one of the most important survival techniques I developed as a child, and that it then proved to be one of the most difficult things to let go of and overcome as an adult, when I began the work of healing. Of course it was hard to let this go—for was it not what had kept me alive? How could I survive without this split, which so conveniently kept the pain at a distance, at least sometimes? But I learned slowly, so very slowly, to feel safe, and then I found I no longer needed to dissociate, leave my body, fragment, hide. (Danica, 1996, p. 18)

She drew attention to the importance of a sense of safety as crucial to beginning the process of unlearning dissociation as an automatic response.

A central question about literacy learning is how much presence is needed to learn. When I discussed this issue with several colleagues, they reminded me that few of us give our full attention to everything that we do or perhaps even know what *fully attentive* would look like. Much work can only be endured in a semipresent state. Perhaps society benefits from a certain degree of dissociation while pathologizing it as a problem. As noted earlier, Tanya Lewis (1998) asked, "How numb does someone have to be to tolerate working in a fish processing plant or on an assembly line? How dissociated does a person need to be to withstand the privileging of certain sexes or classes?" (p. 33). Total attention is extremely exhausting and may not be necessary to learn. Yet a student who *leaves* frequently will have difficulty learning especially if she does not even know that she has left and is unaware that she has missed a portion of the lesson. The goal for literacy learning may not be for every learner to be completely present, but rather to find middle ground where sufficient presence allows continued learning over time and remembering the work later. Being aware of the degree of presence and whether it is sufficient for the task is an important aspect of middle ground.

Presence and Possibilities for Learning

If *spacing out* is named as something many learners struggle with as they seek to learn literacy, and if the classroom is a place that is accepting and supportive of the variety of challenges learners will be facing, then, rather than having to be ashamed of spacing out and hiding it—their likely school experience—learners can try to become more aware and conscious of what is happening for them. The instructor and group can learn to work together to enhance the possibilities for the presence of all learners as well as the instructor.

A first challenge for learners may be beginning to learn to recognize when they are more or less present and beginning to become aware of why and of what sort of situations contribute to their ability to be present and what situations lead to greater distance. Then a learner might want to assess what amount of presence or distance works for her and what amount stops her literacy learning. Would she be able to learn better if she were more present? Does she want to learn to stay more present? Students might be encouraged to think about their own lives—reflect on what is going on generally for them. Do they have crises happening in their lives? Are they having nightmares and trouble sleeping? Are they well rested and full of energy for the class? Do they want to or can they make any changes in their lives that would help them be present? Do they want to explore their experience of absence? As an individual, a learner might want to strategize whether there are any changes to be made in her own life and what she needs to permit her to be present enough to engage in learning.

As a group, the whole class, including the instructor, could look at how the learning situation or program functions to assess whether there are changes that might help many learners to be more present or lose less ground in their learning during the times that they are less present. They might reflect on the class. How comfortable are they feeling in the class, physically and emotionally? Does the topic of the class interest them? Are they relaxed? Anxious? Panicked? Has something in the classroom made it hard to stay present or connected them to early trauma? As psychologist Heather Bain pointed out: "It could be really minor, it could be the tone of a voice, it could be a school bell, it could be the quality of light, on a particular day" (interview, Edmonton, December 1996).

Are there factors that might help make the place seem safe and the people trustworthy? It is crucial that the program take responsibility for the situation in the classroom. Is the situation as safe as possible? What sort of triggers—actions or events that trigger past coping strategies—are present? Triggers might include loud arguments—men who tease, are abusive, or make sexualized comments. The tone in the classroom might be too much like school or generally disrespectful. Some women might find it helpful if the room is less like a traditional classroom.

Yet as Heather Bain suggested, women do not space out only because of feelings of fear or panic. Many mundane and ordinary situations might remind a woman of when she was abused and trigger her spacing out. This awareness is important so that an instructor is not left feeling responsible—thinking that she must have done something wrong—when a woman spaces out. Instead, an instructor can more easily become a co-investigator with each woman and support her in her own investigation without becoming defensive. A woman's presence should not be her problem alone. It should be a collective challenge for the class and instructor to make the program as supportive of learning as possible for all the learners present, as well as to support any individual learner in addressing her own challenges.

One possible approach is to work in ways that might help each student explore her own presence and learn to stay more present. Heather Bain offered several helpful suggestions:

> I think that small chunks are really important because generally people don't learn to stay present all the time, they hop in and out. I also think that it is really important that permission to leave is always given because often kids have been trapped and they need a way to leave. So we don't want to take away the only way of leaving. We want to really say it is okay to leave and there are other ways to leave. So access to the door, and making sure that it is really easy to get to the door, or maybe someone needs to sit near to the door. It's important not to have backs to the door. . . . Maybe even build a focused time and doodling time. I know often with clients I'll have to do that in different ways, build in times when they are present and build in times when they are able to be gone. (interview, Edmonton, December 1996)

In a supportive environment, learners could develop many more ideas to support their learning. If women can begin to explore their options in a safe environment, gradually they might be able to walk out of the room when they feel uncomfortable, rather than automatically spacing out, perhaps with no awareness that they have done so. In this way, they can break out of the automatic response and take more control over their choice of strategies, finding new alternatives to spacing out. Each student might be able to gradually learn what helps her to stay present or to return when she spaces out.

One learner told me that if she sits where she can see out the window, she leaves more easily, but sitting beside someone she feels safe with helps her stay. Sometimes she will choose to sit where she can look out the window because she knows she needs to give herself that option; other times she will choose to sit elsewhere and struggle to stay present. Factors such as how comfortable she is feeling in the group, the work they are doing, the group energy, her own level of energy, what else is going on in her life, and her level of health that day all affect her choice of seating on a particular day. This learner has identified middle ground for herself, where she does not expect to be totally present at all times. Instead, she recognizes what is possible on a particular day. Becoming more conscious of her own degree of presence and factors that enhance or inhibit it has allowed her to learn to strategize how to create the best learning situation for herself. This might not be possible if she felt that she was failing, or was criticized by others, whenever she was unable to stay present. She might then focus her energy on hiding her level of presence. If the whole issue remains unspoken, she receives no support to help her learn about her own patterns and needs or develop her own strategies.

During an interview session in Iqaluit in the North West Territories, Darlene Nuqingaq, an elementary school principal, observed that a retreat room available for students functioned to allow students to leave fully when necessary. Perhaps it reduced the need they might otherwise feel to space out or act out. Monitoring the room, this principal had noticed that students seemed to go there when they needed to be alone and returned to their classes as soon as they were ready. She believed that, rather than the room becoming an easy option for those who did not want to work, as some had suggested it might be, it reduced the likelihood of patterns that might block learning. With this alternative in place, acting out and spacing out are not the only way for a student to escape from the classroom, and "students learn to take responsibility for identifying what they need at the time."

Similarly, a creative room (or corner of a room) for adult learners to retreat to might be a wonderful option in literacy programs. One program I visited had two areas in their classroom: one with chairs around a table, the other with comfy chairs and sofas and cozy quilts to retreat under. Learners and staff said they sometimes used the space for their work; at other times, individual women could use it as a way to leave the group and take care of themselves while still being able to hear what was going on. This is another example of middle ground, where the learner does not have to choose between leaving the class entirely or staying and participating.

Heather Bain also pointed out that the ability to leave the body and space out means that a woman may not be good at being *in her body*. She may not listen to the messages of her body well and may not take notice when she is feeling unwell or simply uncomfortable and unsafe.[1] One instructor wrote a vivid account of what she notices when a student does not seem to be in her body:

---

[1]The connection to the body and how that might be taken up in a literacy program is examined in more depth in chap. 6.

A lack of presence can show up as a kind of clumsiness. Not only will a student not be able to think and answer, they will not be able to sit at a desk without knocking over a coffee or their own books. They may kick packsacks that are lying on the floor near other people's chairs. They may reach for chalk and two metre sticks and three chalk brushes will fall off the ledge. The body shows when you're not in it. (Patterson, personal correspondence, September 1999)

As a learner explores whether she is present and what makes it possible for her to stay or leave, she may need to learn to listen to her body and leave when she is not well or not comfortable in the situation. This therapist suggested that activities that help women to ground themselves in their body—such as physical movement—while learning might help them stay present. However, she also warned that the reason women have difficulty connecting with their body is because it can be a source of painful memory. Consequently, helping a woman connect to her body might also open up access to pain she has shut off. Even when a program and instructor go to great lengths to make it possible for women to explore their presence, it may still be a slow and difficult process as women struggle with recognizing their own reactions, pain, memories, and established patterns and experience the possibility of being in control of learning in this way.

Exploring Spacing Out

Care needs to be taken to ensure that survivors learning *not* to dissociate rather than exploring dissociation does not become the focus; this could easily pathologize daydreaming and lead to judging everyone not paying attention as dissociating or criticizing those who continue to space out. Tanya Lewis' (1999) discovery of language to speak of the pleasures of spacing out, captures the need to move away from viewing it only negatively:

> Until now, I have had neither the language nor the knowledge to express my grief at the need to return to a pedestrian body after being able to fly. I greet this with as much enthusiasm as Peter Pan being asked to grow up. I am homesick for an experience I cannot even name. I live with a sense of having voyaged, a sense of living with knowledge and connection that cannot be expressed in language, and which, to my puzzlement, others do not seem to share. (p. 33)

Lorna Gallant (1997) suggested that she would encourage a learner to explore what she learns when she spaces rather than encouraging her to try to control her spacing out. Can learners write about how it feels, what they see and think, where they go, and what they are aware of when they leave—the moment of departure? In response to my mention of the learner who avoided sitting where she could see out of the window when she wanted to try not to space out, Lorna Gallant suggested the learner might want to sit by the window and write about what she sees as she looks at the window when she is present and when she leaves. One instructor was wary of trying this option and unclear about what she might be opening up, which points to the importance of ongoing connections with counselors who can offer support to both learners and instructors.[2]

Susan Goodfellow, a counselor who leads small groups of women who have left abusive partners, said she often discusses with the women what touch is acceptable to them; when they *leave*, she comments so that they can speak about what happened if they choose. She stressed that it was particularly important not to touch unless that had been agreed to. She does not ask questions in a threatening way, but gently checks in if a woman leaves. One learner in Toronto reported to me that if there is someone in the group whom she feels comfortable with, she feels okay having him or her put a hand on her shoulder, when she appears to be spacing, and asking her a question about what is going on for her.

This shift of focus—from avoiding spacing out to exploring it—might also help literacy workers develop curriculum that explores presence and the factors that strengthen and diminish presence for all students. For example, a check-in process or talking circle at the beginning of the class could help learners recognize factors that hinder their presence and might help some learners leave some of the pressures that diminish the possibilities of fuller presence behind and turn more attention to learning. In a class I teach, I have begun to ask students what helps or hinders their presence in class. Although these are not literacy learners, the lesson I have learned from this process is that sharing the types of issues and problems that distract and exhaust learners seemed to help them set those things aside and focus. Through this process, a student might recognize the degree of presence she is able to have that day and negotiate the sort of work she can accomplish. Maybe it is not a day to learn new things, but she can do other work. Instructors working with refugees who have experienced trauma talk about the importance of choice:

. . . if my student is having a really bad day, if my student is not comfortable working with the opposite sex, or a student who is normally coping

---

[2]Possible connection with counseling is discussed at length in chap. 7.

pretty well with the language is trying a new anti-depressant drug with their psychiatrist, and they're drowsy, or their attention-span is shortened, how do I provide that person with choice in every activity? (Hrubes, 1997, p. 4)

Some days a learner may also decide that she cannot be present and would be better off attending to the problems distracting her. Other days she may choose to stay in class if it is a safe retreat for her. With the recognition that she is unable to attend well, she might be less hard on herself if unable to learn or remember previous learning. Overall, any process that helps all students—whatever their distractions—recognize what blocks and enhances their attention to learning and to make appropriate choices for themselves can help with learning.

Reflecting on a learner leadership activity I led, I became aware of the varying degrees of presence of different participants on different days. I was fascinated and frustrated by the ways in which those who seemed most absent drew my attention. I felt less and less able to reach those who were present as I watched those who stared out of the window, who seemed disengaged from the process, who regularly arrived late and frequently missed sessions, or who often stood near the door or distant from the group. At the time, that observation remained a private struggle of mine to pay better attention and not be distracted by participants' various distancing activities. Reviewing that activity from the perspective of impacts of trauma, I can see the value of taking time to talk about it.

During an online seminar, Christina Patterson, an instructor from British Columbia, mused about her own presence:

I try to listen when students are telling me about their lives but I can't listen as well when I am thinking about my own agenda. I'm aware when I'm waiting for an opportunity to stop this flow of talk and head us back to where I was trying to take us. Sometimes we agree to talk about things later, but that's not always the point either. I can see that some of it is about students needing to tell me now why they are unable to focus. I hate to think of the student spending so much energy to explain to me why they are unable to focus when really my attention is looking for a break in the ideas. Talk about not being heard! (Alphaplus Literacy & Violence Online Seminar, February 1998)

Instructors in programs that are tightly structured may be particularly vulnerable to the pressure to *get back on track*, but in any situation, instructors are likely to struggle with their own internal pressures about what is appropriate or useful. The opportunity for reflection by practitioners can lead to changes that enhance everyone's presence and ability to learn and teach.

Spacing Out Strategies

As I imagine these possibilities and wonder how they might alter literacy programming, I can see tensions that might emerge. Balancing the responsibility of the individual learner, the group, the instructor, and the program in this area is one possible place of tension. The emphasis could be placed solely on the individual to be aware of her own presence and learn to stay present. It also could be placed on the instructor to create the perfect classroom setting and process to enhance every learner's presence. Recognition of shared responsibility, combined with an attempt to maintain a balance between what it is possible for a program and an instructor to take on and what it is possible for an individual to do, is important.

A second risk of this shift is excessive focus on presence and on creating an appropriate learning situation for each learner, to the point where it becomes an obstacle to learning to read. Liz White, a Toronto-based therapist in private practice, alerted me to the importance of staying on track with the task to be accomplished, avoiding getting side-tracked, and taking attention away from the scary task of focusing on reading and achieving success. Tanya Lewis explained that part of what happens may be that taking on a difficult task brings back the endurance and shame of the experience of abuse. Developing tolerance for difficulty and skills for hanging in may be part of the challenge of learning something difficult. Reorganizing the classroom and focusing on presence could become an easy escape from the challenge of literacy learning. It is crucial to recognize this danger and maintain a balance so that attention to presence enhances learning to read, rather than derailing it.

In any group or class, there are challenging questions about how much time and attention to devote to issues of presence. Learners who want to focus firmly on literacy development might find a focus on reflection and issues of presence frustrating and irrelevant. However, if such work is always embedded in reading and writing tasks—both private journal writing and more public, group activities—the relevance to developing literacy might be more apparent. Such reflection could also take place in a separate program before or alongside the literacy or academic activities.

As literacy workers become more aware of the range of absence and presence for themselves and for learners with whom they are working, a far more in-depth understanding and exploration can take place of how presence intersects with literacy learning. These possibilities raise many questions. In literacy, can we help people learn to stay present? Can we help people value and learn by their absences? Is that viable? When should it be talked about? Who would do it? What limits and what enhances an instructor's ability to stay fully present? The space and time needed to take on these issues are daunting. The training needed for paid workers and volunteers must also be considered. Developing an awareness of the complex nature of presence leads to new questions about enhancing presence and improving learning.

LIVING WITH CRISES

Therapist Clarissa Chandler explained that a child born into a family where there was never safety has always lived in a state of *emergency*. For this child, the experience of living without crisis is not only unfamiliar, but creates as much panic as the response to pain because the child, and later the adult, has no information about what sensations outside crisis should feel like (Chandler, n.d. *Weaving the Story*).

Instructors reported many crises in learners' lives, commenting on the energy these crises consume and that they may make it impossible for a learner to be sufficiently present to focus on learning to read. Workers often struggled with feeling that, given the sheer volume of crises, the student must in some way be responsible. However, they were also well aware that lack of resources did lead to multiple crises and offers few possible solutions. Apprehension of a child by authorities and placement in foster care, health or other problems with children, loss of housing or other housing crises, and loss of a job or the endless hunt for a job are all common features in learners' lives. Instructors felt tension between recognizing the difficulties of addressing crises with few resources and feeling patronizing when they expected less of their students because of their lack of resources. The therapeutic discourse seems to offer useful insights here.

Therapists and the therapeutic literature talk about how scary it can be for someone used to living in a state of crisis to live without crises. Waiting for the next crisis creates continual tension and expectation. For some women, it may be easier to provoke or look for the next crisis, rather than continue waiting for it. A group of workers described crises as a way of "putting off success and change." Yet one woman said that, after living with crisis all her life, she had no sense of who she would be if she were not in crisis. Over many years now, I have watched the student I tutor go from crisis to crisis. If there is no major crisis in her own life, she will take notice of the horrors on the news, in her apartment building, that her friends are experiencing, or perceive something as a crisis that at another time she might experience as minor. Whatever the issue, the impact on her is often huge and always takes her attention away from her learning. Now we talk about her discomfort with and distrust of calm and her familiarity with crisis. We strategize together about what will help her address the crisis or separate herself from it so that she can return to learning as quickly as possible.

Mary Beth Levan, a counselor in Yellowknife, North West Territories, wanted to make sure I understood that the experience of trauma "rewires the nervous system" for fear and escape. She said trauma survivors are "running on adrenaline" and spoke of the need for "rewiring" again so that the system was ready for "sanity, peace, calm." The therapeutic literature describes this *hyperarousal* of trauma survivors in this way:

> They have an elevated baseline of arousal: their bodies are always on the alert for danger. They also have an extreme startle response to unexpected stimuli, as well as an intense reaction to specific stimuli associated with the traumatic event. (Herman, 1992, p. 36)

Although I find this description problematic, as discussed earlier, it does draw attention to a level of tension experienced by many survivors. Working with a survivor, I have found myself helping her to become aware of her own style by using the analogy of a thermostat set very high so that she experiences each crisis as large and threatening. Increased awareness has helped her recognize what is happening and begin to *rewire her system* so that she is coming to know and value a state that is less crisis-ridden.

Both constant crises and high ongoing levels of tension are significant barriers against trying to focus on literacy learning. Calm and relaxed attention is more likely to facilitate learning than a high level of tension, which easily slides into panic. In a state of panic, trying out new possibilities and remembering existing knowledge may be equally impossible. These insights can be valuable in adult literacy work. Instructors may be freed from some frustration in the face of ongoing crises in students' lives and from subsequent self-criticism for judging harshly. Instead, workers may be able to notice patterns that impede learning and support learners recognizing these barriers to learning. Eventually, a sensitive worker might be able to support a learner to recognize her own patterns around crisis and tension, find strategies to address the crises she faces, and seek out and find pleasure in a calmer place, rather than remaining in a constant state of crisis.

TRUST AND BOUNDARIES

> . . . abuse is an assault on three of the most fundamental prerequisites for what we could call "basic trust": the world is benevolent; life has meaning; I have worth. (Agger, 1994, p. 13)

Trust, and the attention to whether it is safe to trust, is another issue that workers and counselors spoke about as taking up energy and impeding learners' presence in the program. One of the staff in the Horizons Program, a transition program for women in British Columbia, spoke about the time learners need to assess how far to trust the teacher:

> I look around the room and I see faces still going when are you going to let me down. It takes so long, it adds so much pressure to the adult learner to go through all the trust process with each teacher, it adds extra time on to the learning. Which I think is really important because if you don't do the checking the person out you're not going to learn anyway. But it's placing extra pressure on the relationship. We try to say trust your gut, set your boundaries and at the same time we know that's adding extra pressure to the learner. An eight-year-old doesn't go through that, either they do it or they don't. We ask a lot of adults. (interview, Horizons Program, Duncan, British Columbia, November 1996)

This worker was conscious of the time learners needed to build trust with each new instructor, and so was cautious about bringing in temporary teachers or workshop leaders. She recognized that it was hard for women to feel comfortable with each new person, and that the energy expended to check out whether a person was trustworthy added time to the learning process.

Elly Danica (1996), a survivor who spoke clearly about her own difficulties with trust, added a further dimension to the problem of trusting: "The first thing I learned, in a long list of strategies to survive my childhood, was not to trust anybody. The second thing I learned was not to trust myself" (p. 17). If you cannot trust yourself, you cannot decide whether to trust others. Your gut, or instinct, is not to be relied on. You cannot know who to trust and who not to trust. You may not know whether to trust your own sense of danger:

> Accurately assessing whether an activity or situation is merely fear producing or truly dangerous and what can be done to be safe is another problematic area for survivors . . . Because survivors were taught, either explicitly or implicitly, to mistrust their feelings and perceptions, their ability to discern realistic levels of pain, fear, and danger have been impaired. In some

situations, a woman's fears may be so high that she confuses fear with real danger, or she may be so used to discounting or disassociating with her fear that she does things which are indeed dangerous. (Warren, 1996, p. 134)

Therapist Liz White pointed out that there is no point assuring a survivor that you are trustworthy; it cannot diminish the time taken to build trust. Instead, recognize that you will be tested and avoid getting defensive and impatient while the slow process of building trust takes place; taking care in this way is more likely to move toward a level of trust that enhances learning.

Therapists use the term *hypervigilance* to refer to the level of alertness at which survivors may observe the tensions in a room. Many survivors I talked to spoke of this alertness as valuable and argued that if such sensitivity could be learned without the pain it would be wonderful. Like learning to leave the body, some mystics spend years trying to acquire this attunement. Herman (1992) stated that, "chronically traumatized patients have an exquisite attunement to unconscious and nonverbal communications. . . ." They pick up the vulnerability of the "therapist" and notice "fluctuations in attention" (p. 139). Herman went on to talk about a dynamic that instructors might recognize:

The patient scrutinizes the therapist's every word and gesture in an attempt to protect herself from the hostile reactions she expects. Because she has no confidence in the therapists's benign intentions, she persistently misinterprets the therapist's motives and reactions. The therapist may eventually react to these hostile attributions in unaccustomed ways. Drawn into the dynamics of dominance and submission, the therapist may inadvertently reenact aspects of the abusive relationship. (p. 139)

Although Herman seems to assume that the therapist always has benign intentions and the survivor is always wrong in her judgments, these words also alert literacy workers to continually question whether we are being trustworthy and whether our behavior in any way replicates an abuse of authority—the authority we hold in our power as teachers.

The Trustworthy Teacher

Potter (1995) drew attention to the moral requirement of the one being trusted when she said: "Take care not to exploit the power that one has to harm the trusting person" (p. 71). To raise the issue of trust is to open up the question of what it means to be trustworthy. One suggestion of what it might mean to be a trustworthy teacher is offered in the following quote:

> The power granted by her [the teacher's] institutional role then confers upon a teacher increased responsibility to be nonexploitative and nondominating with regard to her students' (potential) trust. This responsibility is especially crucial when, for instance, the student is a woman of color and the teacher is European American, or the student is lesbian and the teacher heterosexual, or the student's class background stands in contrast to the teacher's mastery of academic discourse. (Potter, 1995, p. 72)

Potter is talking about the teacher in an academic context, but these issues of power also apply in the literacy context. Literacy teachers may have less power to grade, but their response to a student may still hold enormous weight. Differences of class, race, and educational level may add to the danger, particularly if workers look down on learners in any way. Clarissa Chandler described the problem:

> So if you have somebody who was also sexually abused, and dealing with that kind of class discrimination and you start to try to teach them to read, it is like you are trying to touch the most vulnerable spot in them. So you cannot put your hand on that vulnerable spot and also demonstrate any of that class disdain. . . . So you have to be able to communicate the lack of judgement, and even if you can not communicate the lack of judgement, you must communicate that it is your lack in lack of judgement. That it is your limitation, not their limitation, your inability, your lack of capability to teach, not their inability to learn . . . Because you restimulate those feelings of humiliation and shame. That is not the state of mind . . . I can't learn. The key resource is to create this emotional, restful state so they can attend to the self here and have control. (interview, Toronto, November 1996)

A critical question is whether instructors teach and give feedback in ways that shame learners and add to the abusive message that the student is not okay:

> Every time a teacher gives out overly harsh feedback, a survivor will have to try and "survive" not only the abuse but the new messages of being less than okay too. (Potter, 1995, p. 81)

A student who is a trauma survivor speaks from her sense of power in the relationship:

The teacher holds an almost excruciating amount of power over me. They have the power to reinforce all the old messages if they choose to. I realize that I have the control not to hear some, but if I choose not to hear some messages, how can I trust that the ones I do take in—are valid? For me, I need to trust fully for the new messages to be valid. (Potter, 1995, p. 82).

One group of learners spoke about their difficulty trusting any comments about their work or their ability. One learner in the Horizons Program said that she had worked so hard to exclude all the judgment that she was stupid that she could not let in a judgment that she was smart:

I was always on the honour roll, but I wasn't allowed to know that because it wasn't being humble enough, putting myself on a pedestal, trying to act smarter than I really was, because after all you're so stupid you're never going to go anywhere, you're not going to do anything all you're going to do is work in my store. Turmoil of where the hell do you stand in any given day. The tension of never knowing when they were going to flip and then hearing the messages, I'm number six in the line of kids, I've got four older brothers and an older sister, they've lived through that crap so they're also pouring that crap down your throat, so they're also doing it as well as your parents. The hardest thing in this class was reading notes saying I was intelligent. (interview, Horizons Program, Duncan, British Columbia, November 1996)

This represents a major challenge in literacy. Many learners have continually been told they are stupid—in school, at home as children, and then by controlling and violent spouses as adults. Leaving those messages behind and trusting new messages from their own experience in the classroom and from instructors may be a crucial transition toward believing it is possible to learn.

I wonder about the limits of trust in literacy. How reliable are workers? Do we always give feedback in a way that is not damaging? In literacy, it may be crucial to be careful in any interaction about honesty and to recognize that a learner's responses may be shaped by past history and more than a *reading* of the actual words. For example, when workers assure learners that they are happy to teach something several times or tell a learner that she is "doing well," does the learner scrutinize every word and underneath the words hear a different message—perhaps one of frustration, impatience, or failure? When workers assure a learner that it is great to have her on the board of a community program, but struggle with the tension of slowing the board process down to work for the learner, does the learner read that she is a burden and not trust the worker's assurances? One learner described learners in a leadership project as "a bunch of watchers" with incredible skills at watching people and sensing danger. Exploring what is observed in that watching process might reveal information useful to all participants in an interaction.

Understanding the impact of violence issues on learning is a bare minimum for all teachers if they are to be trustworthy teachers of trauma survivors:

> A trustworthy teacher with regard to survivors is one who has acquired sufficient information to be able to open up the subject in the classroom when appropriate; who continues to gain understanding through a search for knowledge that is both cognitive and self-reflective about her own fears, prejudices, and experiences; who develops a comfortable, confident, and grounded understanding of the interplay of the psychological and political structures that perpetuate abuse; who explores the intersection of the legacy of incest with students' diversity' and who is committed to doing her part to undo the effects of abuse on adult learners. (Potter, 1995, p. 80)

Trustworthiness also implies that an instructor who knows that a learner has survived trauma will not judge the learner as "being marked, deformed, or wounded creatures who need to be nurtured back into 'normal' society," but will still value the learner, respect her ability to learn, and recognize the phenomenal strength that enabled her to survive trauma.

Trust and Betrayal

Several therapists talked at length about issues of trust and explained that, once trust has been betrayed, especially in childhood, a person expects to be betrayed again. This intense distrust leads to a woman continually looking for the meanings behind superficial words. Therapists suggested that it is crucial to avoid making promises you cannot keep and stressed the importance of always being reliable. Trust can often be all or nothing, so any breach of trust is major. Helen Dempster, a worker with the Society of Transition Houses in British Columbia and the Yukon, also stressed the importance of literacy workers being reliable. They need to avoid being perceived as part of the *system* that lets down women leaving violent men by failing to provide safey.

Several therapists said that the issue of betrayal was so major that they had learned to avoid springing any changes on their clients. For example, they let their clients know well in advance if they are going to be away so that they can work with their clients to look at how they will look after themselves and acknowledge their feelings. Liz White said:

> ... there is something about being able to trust that I'm not going to come next week and get a bomb dropped—because there's a sense of betrayal. (interview, Toronto, November 1996)

Heather Bain talked similarly about trying to be as trustworthy as possible. She also suggested that, although ambiguities are hard (as they represent middle ground), it is important to help a survivor recognize that not everything will be absolute and knowable ahead of time and to teach strategies for dealing with change.

This simple information about betrayal gave me a new way of looking at a situation I experienced in the past. For some time, I ran a women's literacy group. The group knew well ahead that I would be away for the summer and would return to continue running the group in the fall. During the summer, however, the program learned it could begin a project to redesign the tutor training, and I eagerly applied to take this project on. The consequence of this new development was that the women's group was allocated to a new staff person. Several members of the women's group were furious, insisting that I should continue to lead the group. Although it created much anger, the staff felt that they needed to be able to make decisions about the program and stuck to the new staffing plan. In the light of the information about trust and betrayal, I see the incident differently. The learners' issue may have been betrayal of trust rather than wanting to control staffing decisions. I had left, promising to return, and then did not. Based on this new understanding, I would have tried to return to the group, even for only 1 or 2 weeks, to carry out a process of closure and avoid the sense of betrayal and dishonesty that caused a crisis of fury and tension in the program.

Therapist Clarissa Chandler suggested that abuse causes a woman or child to focus on the abuser's reality, trying to understand his (or her) thinking to maintain safety. This distances the survivor from her own knowledge and leads to lack of trust in what she knows, which has a profound impact on learning:

> Trusting in at least some things is logically necessary in order to make judgments at all (Wittgenstein 1969). Being a member of a community of knowers, Code argues, allows us to draw on a body of unarticulated assumptions about the reliability of others' words. As she emphasizes, trust "is a condition of viable membership in an epistemic community. In fact,

the very possibility of epistemic life is dependent on intricate networks of shared trust" (Code, 1987, p. 173). (Potter, 1995, p. 71)

This difficulty with being a knower is fundamental. Sylvia Fraser (1987) talked about her intellectual pride and the devastating effects of beginning to recover memories of childhood abuse: "My pride of intellect has been shattered. If I didn't know about half my own life, what other knowledge can I trust?" (p. 253).

In literacy, we need to develop ways to help learners build trust in their own knowledge and trust in their ability to judge the safety of a situation and the trustworthiness of others. Processes such as journal writing, timed writing, and reading out loud can provide the safety of practice in a challenging situation, yet one where the learner always has the option of opting out instead of taking a turn and is only briefly in the limelight. Literacy instructors I interviewed used a variety of approaches to support learners to become comfortable with their own knowledge. Several workers invited groups of students to use the board, where they worked out math problems in full view; others encouraged learners to do some work loudly and boldly. One instructor described "spell and yell"—an approach to teaching spelling where she encouraged students to yell answers as a way to gain confidence.

Workers need to be sensitive to learners' levels of comfort and avoid pressuring women to take on something that may be terrifying. Therapist Kathleen O'Connell, a counselor and educator based in a community health center, advised literacy workers to be careful about what they ask women to take on in class:

> Another example that I am thinking about in terms of learning would be women, as adult learners, being asked in a class to say something personal about their lives, or to bring something personal in, to tell a story. For some women, especially when there are various forms of violence including assault, this can be enormously threatening. If she is in a bad space, is depressed . . . then the idea of her sitting or standing in front of a group and sharing a personal story can be really frightening . . . she can feel there is no way that she can sit and have everybody's eyes on her and be centred out. . . . So for teachers and tutors being able to be really flexible about that and finding ways to avoid pressuring women and centring them out is really important. . . . (interview, Toronto, November 1996)

This caution is a useful reminder for workers to be sensitive to all learners, supporting them to take on challenges without pushing them to expose themselves to a situation that feels terrifying.

Strategies to help build learners' trust in their own knowledge, trust in their ability to judge the safety of a situation, and the trustworthiness of others could be developed and used more consciously in literacy programming. Trust-building exercises would also be important to strengthen the trust between all members of a group and to support learners in learning to take controlled risks in a literacy setting.

Rescuing Versus Respecting Boundaries

The therapeutic discourse about boundaries has increasingly moved into popular language. I use *boundaries* here to denote the separation among people that preserves each person's integrity as an equal adult. Although what constitutes acceptable boundaries is a contentious concept—not all would agree on what is reasonable—the concept draws attention to a problematic area in literacy education. The separation among learners and between learner and instructor can slip to such an extent that the potential for successful learning and teaching is compromised. I heard repeatedly from therapists and counselors that, to be trustworthy, workers had to learn to respect their own boundaries and the boundaries of others and support those who do not have good boundaries to create them.

Counselors spoke about the importance of workers recognizing when their own boundaries have been crossed, using their own anger as a guide, and learning to create the limits necessary to avoid feeling burned out, used, and angry at those who make demands. This work is crucial to workers' energy and emotional state. The ability to re-instate boundaries when they have slipped is also an important skill to model for women who may not have learned even the simple right to keep boundaries. Many workers also may not have a sense of the right to keep boundaries. Instead, they gain their sense of identity from being caring and supportive—always available to help. Rather than being able to model good practice for learners, workers may also be caught in a boundary-less trap.

Many literacy workers spoke about their difficulties creating limits and boundaries for themselves. A typical example of workers' ambivalence was one worker's account of closing her door after class and trying to ignore students who knocked. When we talked about it, she recognized that she had never given herself permission to tell students when she was and was not available to them and to ask them to respect her boundary. Instead, she said she felt angry that they hammered on her door when she needed to get office work done. Other workers often talked about not even setting such basic limits, feeling unable to set any boundaries because they felt they had to stretch to meet their students' needs, which were too critical to be denied. In the face of this need, workers often felt obliged to disregard their own needs or desires. Obviously there is much work to be done for these workers to find a balance between their own needs and the needs of their students.

For workers, respecting learners' boundaries may be especially hard with learners who do not maintain good boundaries. Toronto literacy workers working with people on the street talked about many learners in their programs lacking boundaries; the workers worried about how vulnerable this made the learners. Two workers expressed concern when learners revealed this lack of boundaries, not just to a staff person, but in a mixed group:

> A. . . . people with no boundaries who meet you and immediately are telling you the most intimate, traumatic things, right? I think that is a big issue.

> B. When they come in to share it with a bunch of men in the front room I have a harder time with it. . . . It's happened a few times where a woman has come in and suddenly said "Sorry I was late 'cause I got raped last night." And suddenly the whole room goes dead. And it's usually a roomful of men and maybe one other woman. And you can't say "Shush, you're not supposed to say that," this is serious and she deserves to own it, but all of a sudden the whole room has gone quiet and she's become so vulnerable, and she doesn't—may not be aware for lots of reasons—understand where she's put herself. And then another woman will say "You know, I understand what you feel like, because it happened to me last month." And it's there, and there's no privacy for them and no respect. Sometimes if you're really lucky the other men will leave the room. Some are there to be supportive, there have been some times when I think it was genuine, but there are times when—they may—they're such a vulnerable group of men, some of them are—at this point, they're just as traumatized as the woman was, because they're dealing with their own issues. (interview, Community and Street Program Literacy Workers, Toronto, February 1997)

Much therapeutic literature describes sexual abuse as a form of trauma that violates boundaries. For example:

> This impaired ability to trust one's perceptions and act on them also extends to setting appropriate boundaries. The essence of sexual abuse is having one's most intimate boundary—the skin on one's body—violated. (Mitten & Dutton, 1996, p. 134)

> A sexual relationship between family members is an extreme threat to the boundaries of the system. . . . Such a relationship is therefore connected

with a severe risk of pollution and contamination and thereby also with secrecy and shame. (Agger, 1994, p. 44)

I question whether it is the sexual relationship that is a threat to the boundaries of the system or whether the threat lies in breaking the silence and revealing that the taboo against incest has been broken. Trauma caused by the actions of other human beings are boundary violations that "confront human beings with the extremities of helplessness and terror" (Herman, 1992, p. 33) because their power is unable to prevent the actions. Literacy workers who met with me in Edmonton spoke of trauma leading to either building a wall or being completely exposed. They saw problems created from being overdefended or underdefended. They also talked about the difficulty of living behind a wall. From behind a wall, you cannot easily test out the safety of a situation; instead, you have to leap the wall right into the middle of a situation. This awareness about the complexity of boundaries is important for workers seeking to preserve a balanced boundary while respecting the boundaries of others. Many workers may find it particularly challenging to avoid falling into the rescue trap and taking care of the person who seems underdefended and vulnerable.

Learners' crises can easily lead staff or tutors to rescue, ignoring all boundaries, rather than respecting the learners' strengths. Rescuing may make a learner feel less competent—as if only others can solve her problems. Although some learners even ask to be rescued, when workers take over, further problems are created. Although Herman's description of this complicated connection around rescue is rather prescriptive, it does offer insights into some of the crises and tensions that can easily occur within a literacy program:

The survivor oscillates between intense attachment and terrified withdrawal. She may cling desperately to a person whom she perceives as a rescuer, flee suddenly from a person she suspects to be a perpetrator or an accomplice, show great loyalty and devotion to a person she perceives as an ally, and heap wrath and scorn on a person who appears a complacent by-stander. The roles she assigns to others may change suddenly, as the result of small lapses or disappointments. . . . (Herman, 1992, p. 93)

Although Herman's quote captures some truths of the experience of survivors, the situation is described from the place of normalcy. Lewis (1998) used this quote from Herman to argue for a more nuanced understanding, beyond normalcy, that recognizes a range of power issues:

. . . a more complex understanding of the survivor's experience in relationship by analyzing how domination is embedded within normative relational standards. Incest is only one relational site among many in which hierarchies of power and privilege are established, taught and maintained.
(p. 146)

This reminder that the experience of trauma intersects with other
hierarchies of power is crucial because worker–learner is a hierarchical
relationship. It is particularly important that the instructor support learners to honor their own boundaries and avoid pushing them to override
boundaries. As I have become more aware of the complexities of the issues of boundaries, I realize how easily encouragement for learners or colleagues to give something a try or take on a challenge can move into dangerous terrain of disrespect for a colleague or learner's own judgment of
boundaries.

Therapists suggest that, for therapeutic work to be carried out safely,
clear boundaries need to be agreed on between a therapist and client.
This clarity would also be beneficial in literacy:

> Secure boundaries create a safe arena where the work of recovery can pro-
> ceed. The therapist agrees to be available to the patient within limits that
> are clear, reasonable, and tolerable for both. The boundaries of therapy ex-
> ist for the benefit and protection of both parties and are based upon a rec-
> ognition of both the therapist's and the patient's legitimate needs.
> (Herman, 1992, p. 149)

Agger's (1994) description of the importance of boundaries to protect the
researcher or therapist offers an elaboration that seems to apply to literacy work:

> The confrontation with violence demands a defence of some kind, but the
> researcher (and therapist) must try to be conscious of how she or he pro-
> tects herself, must try to maintain boundaries so that she or he is experi-
> enced as safe and secure; but these boundaries must not be so rigid that
> the researcher is experienced as cold and distant. (p. 19)

Obviously there are cultural differences around what would be experienced as safe or cold and distant that make it harder to judge the line in
each instance. However, an awareness that it is important to find that
balance could be beneficial for workers and learners in adult literacy.

In literacy, then, the task for instructors is to respect the boundaries of
learners and support learners to recognize both their right to create or

maintain their own boundaries and their responsibility to respect the boundaries of others so that a respectful and safe learning environment can be maintained. In a safe learning environment, each learner can pay attention to learning undisturbed by fear and anxiety about the danger of further boundary violations, whether subtle or direct. The instructor, or literacy worker, as the one with power in the situation, has a responsibility to take on the complex tasks of recognizing boundaries and creating a safe learning environment. As Potter (1995) suggested:

> I do not mean to suggest that student survivors have no responsibility to set or observe boundaries; nor do I mean to suggest that survivors are not autonomous and therefore need to be paternalistically cared for by teachers and others. . . . My reason for emphasizing teacher responsibilities . . . is that, given the intersection of trust with power relations and the vulnerability involved in trusting another, the person who stands in a position of power bears more of the burden for establishing trustworthiness and cultivating trusting relations. (p. 85).

Counselor Kathleen O'Connell stated that one obvious aspect of boundaries must be clarity about touching. A hand on the shoulder, a pat on the back, or a hug may seem a supportive gesture for some, but could be invasive and traumatic for others. Basic respect for the boundary between one person's body and another's is important if the classroom is to be a place where a survivor can relax and feel safe. Alternative ways—through words and looks of encouragement—would need to be found to show support, and encouragement, or sympathy. The classroom offers quite a challenge for women who are not comfortable being close to others, or close to men in particular. Working together at a computer or in a group at a table might be extremely threatening for some students. The proximity of an instructor, an instructor coming up behind a student to help, or an instructor towering over a student who is sitting could be problematic. A male instructor might need to be especially sensitive to what might disturb students and negotiate issues such as touch, closeness, and relative height.

Between Literacy and Therapy: Program Structures as Boundaries

This study raises complex issues about boundaries because it questions the divide between literacy and therapy. Some literacy workers firmly assert they are not therapists and create a strong boundary between literacy work and therapeutic issues. Others insist that it is impossible to set a boundary to listening and believe that if a learner needs to be heard that need is sacrosanct. Although one therapist, Liz White, was particularly clear about the importance of focusing on the task that you are there to do—working on reading and writing—this study has revealed that the issues of violence cannot be entirely excluded. If these issues are relegated only to the private realm of therapy, then literacy programming perpetuates the myth that it is possible to exclude the impacts of violence from the classroom. In this way, educators participate in creating the illusion that the consequences of violence are individual matters to be addressed in the privacy of therapy and participate in preserving discourses of normativity. Striking a balance that neither blurs literacy and therapy together nor excludes and silences the issues that emerge in literacy work is particularly challenging. Encouraging workers to feel that they must listen to all disclosures, and suggesting that disclosures should not be allowed, are both inappropriate strategies for literacy programs.

Programs may be more or less *boundaried*. In college programs, where the roles of instructor and students are clearly defined and the expectations of instructors are spelled out, structures make the boundaries clear. Instructors are in the class for defined hours, during which time they teach. Although many instructors may be warm and empathetic and listen to disclosures, the structure of the program helps to create boundaries. The instructor is not a friend, available at any time, but a person with a clear role to teach literacy. In colleges, there are also usually counselors available, so there is a greater chance of keeping the instructor role separate from the role of counselor. These structural boundaries may make what they can expect in interactions within the program clearer for learner and worker alike.

In contrast, in many community-based programs, there has traditionally been little structure and few boundaries in place. Several workers said that cutbacks have led to staff having to impose more clear-cut limits. Although this may be problematic in many ways, particularly for learners, who feel let down by the shift in availability and service from the program staff, this shift has at least had the advantage of creating greater clarity about roles and boundaries. In community-based programs, there is usually no staff room for the worker to go to separate herself from the learners' needs and demands. Staff can always be interrupted. There are no set hours when they are available. Often warm friendships develop between worker and learner and the boundaries between roles can easily be blurred.

Community programs often value shifts from institutionalized relationships. Where learners are also volunteering on committees, or where volunteers are teaching, roles become strongly overlapped. Often staff, volunteers, or learners have access to home phone numbers, lend money, or help each other out in a variety of ways. This building of community, and freedom from the rigidity of prescribed roles, is a major strength of community programs and does have many advantages, modeling the value of a different form of community. However, it can also lead to boundaries not being maintained, to rescuing, and even to possibilities of reabusing, as power imbalances are masked and unacknowledged. Such programs can resemble a family, which may be terrifying for some and may replicate problems such as creating favorites, insiders and outsiders, and making power issues invisible. Sometimes learners are angered by the suggestion of friendship, rather than a teacher/student relationship, seeing dishonesty in the lack of clarity about the boundaries.

Staff from programs that serve people on the street spoke about maintaining greater clarity about boundaries in contrast with other community-based programs. They felt that they had many more rules and had gradually increased structure as they sought to make their programs more effective places for literacy learning and to decrease the violence in the centers. They had learned to become more proactive and less crisis-driven as organizations. Some of these workers worried about their role as enforcers of rules, but they also commented that the rules avoided situations of crisis familiar in other programs. In street programs, learners who break the rules have to leave, but they can come back the next day. In other programs, tensions can simmer with no mechanism to defuse them.

During this study, I began to see that, in an institutional setting, workers have to work hard to disregard boundaries, whereas in community-based programs, they have to work hard to create them. The dynamic between tutor and student is particularly challenging because the relationship may develop into an unstructured friendship. Problems can occur when tutors, staff persons, or learners take on more than desired and fail to maintain their own boundaries. They are then angry, often with another person who can be seen as responsible for invading boundaries. Counselor Kathleen O'Connell spoke about the importance of helping learners assess ahead of time what will and will not be comfortable places to disclose. Instructors in some programs spoke of the challenge of working with learners who disclose to volunteers, revealing too much, either for their own sense of safety or for the tutor's.

This raises many questions. In community programs, do we preserve an openness that invites rescue and risks re-abusing? How can tutors, staff, and learners create clear boundaries and respect the boundaries of others? What should be included about boundaries in tutor-training or follow-up workshops? Some programs do include some aspects of boundaries in tutor training based on the recognition that some learners or tutors may be isolated and want more from the tutoring relationship than the other can give. Currently few programs raise the complexity of these issues, perhaps fearing they might deter new volunteers from continuing.

TELLING

> There are never enough words or the right words, there is never enough time or the right time, and never enough listening or the right listening to articulate a story that cannot fully be captured in thought, memory and speech. (Laub, 1995, p. 63)

Dori Laub, psychoanalyst and cofounder of the Video Archive for Holocaust Testimonies at Yale University, has described the profound difficulty of speaking about the experience of trauma. Tanya Lewis (1998) described this further from her own experience:

> While bringing language to the experience of trauma is part of integrating memory, the nature of language means that some of the experience is inevitably left behind . . . . Distance is created between the embodied experience and its expression in language. . . . Experience may be excluded from expression in language or it may be framed in particular ways. For me, there was always this struggle about what I would leave behind by speaking and how what I would say could be most accurately framed in language. My reluctance to speak about what I was experiencing was both my terror of breaking silence and the difficulty of bringing language accurately to the child's experience. (p. 128)

I have read about "telling the secret" as "empowering" (Dinsmore, 1991, p. 37), and many therapists talk about the power of bearing witness to stories a woman may have always believed unspeakable.

When children are abused, they frequently receive dire threats about what will occur if they give away the secrets. Abused children are often told that they will not be believed, that they will be punished, or that they will cause others to be harmed. An understanding of impacts of violence must lead to an increased awareness for all teachers of how to teach in ways that honor learners' silences as well as their words. Instructors must be cautious about judging students based on their participation. As one instructor, drawing from the experience of her student, explained:

Experience of violence might make students "lose" their voice and if that quietness is honored and the student is supported and validated we, as instructors, might in some small way be instrumental in their journey to "find" their voice again. (personal correspondence)

Adults living with a violent partner may experience a silencing that denies them a voice. The more they are told they are stupid and know nothing, the more they will be unable to trust what they know. One literacy worker described her experience in a collection called "Through the Eyes of Teachers." She gave an example to illustrate the ways in which she was silenced:

Coming out of a movie once that left me very thoughtful, I began to speak my mind in the car on the way home. "I think," I said, "that human beings are basically good." I wasn't aware I was attempting a philosophical dialogue on human nature and the good of humankind. Hank responded with anger and violence, "Just shut the f– up you don't know what the hell you are talking about." That was one of two typical responses he had to my attempts at independent thought. The other was to ignore what I had said as though the words had never been spoken. He'd introduce a new topic as though I had not spoken.

Me: "I think human beings are basically good."
Husband: "What are we having for supper tonight?"

Ironic, the parallel between his control of conversation and the same method used by some instructors in classrooms to redirect conversation . . . or maybe not so ironic?

By the time I left him I stuttered, not from any physical ailment, but from humiliation. I'd be in a group of people and it would become my turn to speak and as I looked around the group and found their eyes on my face and that I actually did have their attention and they seemed to want to hear what I had to say, I would blush and stammer. (Emerson, n.d., pp. 40–41)

Learners who have been denied a voice and developed a fear of speaking have to struggle with telling their own stories, what they will allow themselves to reveal, and what they believe will be allowed in the school setting.

Several therapists and counselors stressed that it is not the *telling* that is important but the *listening*—being heard by a caring listener. Clarissa Chandler said that the "restoration of value and dignity" is to have somebody listen to the story, to validate it, and to restore positive treatment. She says there is "no hope if this is me" if the trauma is all she is, then a woman can only assume she deserves to be treated badly (Chandler, n.d.,

Weaving the Story). In a presentation on flashbacks, Clarissa Chandler went further to stress:

> . . . to vomit up the old memory is to leave her only wounded, she must externalize the memory and internalize a new image of herself—if she does not internalize, no healing occurs so both pieces are essential. (Chandler, n.d., *Flashback Management*)

Much of the best current literacy practice includes learners writing about their own lives. In this way, curriculum that is relevant and meaningful to learners' lives can be created. This approach can be critiqued as a liberal approach because it can imply that the true or authentic self can be expressed. If it is not used critically, it can become a device that simply encourages learners to write themselves into dominant discourses—the very discourses within which they are devalued—rather than creating the potential for learners to challenge these discourses, creating new discourses that offer alternative accounts of their experience. Despite these limitations, this practice is widely used to provide reading material relevant to learners lives and to give learners experience as creators, not only as consumers, of the written word.

Learners at Chapters Literacy Program in Alberta talked about what it meant to write about their experiences. One woman said that she was still writing down all the bad things that happened to her and then tearing them up to leave them behind. Learners can discover the commonality of their situation with others through reading other similar stories (Gaber-Katz & Horsman, 1988; Horsman, 1995). Often learners are asked to write journals; sometimes these are *response* or *dialogue* journals, where the instructor or facilitator writes a reply or reaction after each journal entry. Beginning literacy students are asked to tell a *language experience* story, where an incident from their own lives becomes the basis for their own reading. If learners feel they must be careful about what they reveal during these activities, energy again is being expended to take care about what to reveal and what not to reveal. Emerson's earlier mention of the approaches used by instructors is a reminder that the ways the instructor seeks to control discussion might remind a learner of earlier silencing and give her the message that it is still not safe to speak without expecting to be shamed.

I am not suggesting that the more open learners are in the literacy classroom the better. I want to draw attention to the energy learners put into deciding what they will say or write and to worrying about whether they will be shamed. This tension and fear is another distraction from the task of developing the ability to read and write with ease. Shelter worker, Helen Dempster, suggested that learners may be continually asking themselves, "Can you hear, or will I have to take care of you?" and "Can you hear, or will you shame me?" Clearly these doubts take us back to the question of trust.

When learners have built some trust that the classroom is a safe place to take risks in learning, they may be tempted to be more open with the stories of their lives. This creates a tension—in the form of the demand that the instructor and learners be able to hear.

> When the traumatic events are of human design, those who bear witness are caught in the conflict between victim and perpetrator. It is morally impossible to remain neutral in this conflict. The bystander is forced to take sides.
>
> It is very tempting to take the side of the perpetrator. All the perpetrator asks is that the bystander do nothing. He appeals to the universal desire to see, hear, and speak no evil. The victim, on the contrary, asks the bystander to share the burden of pain. The victim demands action, engagement and remembering. (Herman, 1992, pp. 7–8)

Some learners need their stories to be heard, whereas other learners may want the classroom to be free of the danger of having to hear disturbing stories. The instructor or other learners may not be in a position to "share the burden of pain" because their own pain may be too raw.

Learners may need support to recognize the limits of what they can hear and set appropriate boundaries for themselves. As one online seminar participant, American university-based researcher Daphne Greenberg, reminded us, it is crucial that learners not say too much and then go home and react to what they have done and that listeners do not take on too much:

> It is also critical that others who hear these stories, do not go home and experience similar psychological reactions. Just like we encourage people to say that they don't want to share something, it is critical that we also create an environment where listeners (our learners) can say that they don't want to hear something. Often hearing these stories can trigger flashbacks for individuals abused as children. (Alphaplus Literacy & Violence Online Seminar, February 1998)[3]

---

[3]Although this writer focused on the needs of learners, the needs of instructors are also important. Those are discussed in chap. 8.

Yet too much caution on the part of instructors can lead to so much anxiety about learners' sensitivities that everyone might be silenced. Later in the seminar, another participant in California, Beth Sauerhaft, brought us back to the importance of finding a balance:

> To me it is a given that to see our students only through the lenses of trauma is clearly a mistake. Even as we learn more about building sensitivity and approaches to responding to trauma in literacy programs, there is always a thin line in terms of recreating the oppressive dynamics of paternalism (even and sometimes especially by women) when we get overly concerned about the impact of a particular book or story on our students for this often becomes a rescuing dynamic that can undermine a group's sense of power and agency. (Alphaplus Literacy & Violence Online Seminar, March 1998)

Beth Sauerhaft reminded us that it is important for instructors to check in with our own feelings to know when our own fears are holding us back from introducing issues that might open up writing about harrowing experiences. She also stressed that learners must always be able to choose when they want to participate.

Literacy workers suggested that, within the literacy field, we are more focused on helping and may feel that we must do something in response to hearing learners' stories. It is crucial that workers not think they must *fix* things or resort to correcting grammar in the stories because they are uncomfortable with feeling helpless. Herman (1992) affirmed that there is value in bearing witness because the witness: ". . . contributes to constructing a new interpretation of the traumatic experience that affirms the dignity and value of the survivor" (p. 179). Workers also spoke about the challenge of working with students who seem to be stuck in a place where they repeat the same story over and over again. They questioned why this occurs and speculated about what they could do to help the learner feel heard and begin to tell new stories about her life.

Space for Fun and Humor

In an attempt to make space for the harsh stories from learners' lives, literacy programs may be at risk of focusing only on pain. If the focus is only on pain, there is no space for hope, for belief in the possibility of change, and for joy in learning. Several therapists and literacy workers stressed how important it is to also make space for fun and humor to shift the energy. One literacy worker drew on her own experience when she said that children in violent or alcoholic families are often not allowed to be frivolous—to laugh and play. Humor can be threatening for women who have been the butt of humor as children or adults. Teasing is extremely hurtful when it is loaded with put-downs. She felt that creating the possibility for humor, and joy, and laughter that is not at anyone's expense was very healing.

Finding a balance and assessing when to move to activities that create the possibility for joy and pleasure can be extremely difficult. One instructor from British Columbia told me of a tutor who, when a learner had spoken of the horrors of her life, asked if she could not find something "more cheerful to talk about." Clearly such negation of pain is horrifying, but a balance that allows space for joy as well as pain may be crucial. A First Nation literacy instructor based in Toronto said that she always tries to make her class fun because she knows that for some learners it may be the one escape from the pressures of the home.

The participants and staff of Chapters Literacy Program in Camrose, Alberta, run by Deborah Morgan, revealed a way to create balance between pain and joy. That program seems to use the writing process to make space for learners to write about the grim and tough in their lives as well as to provide a healing process with opportunities for lightness, humor, and play. It made me aware how unusual so much space for play and fun seemed for a literacy program. I thought perhaps play has not often been present because literacy workers want to be careful not to treat adults as children or have felt constrained by demands of curriculum or required outcomes. The descriptions the students gave of the pleasure they found in activities like playing in a playground on the swings and slides and then returning to the program to write about the experience was fascinating. They talked about how much they enjoyed such *fun* when they had not had much chance to have fun as children. One of the instructors began and several learners joined in trying to give me a feel for what they did and why it was important:

> We had a student who had never had a photograph of herself before. So we went to the park and spent a whole afternoon being models and being photographed, and we had a fantastic time, and we all were able to go home with pictures of ourselves. . . . Then we came back and wrote about it: how did it feel to have your picture taken? How did it feel taking a picture of somebody else? Always [back] to the writing. That's sort of the key, no matter what crazy escapade we get onto, we write about it. (interview, Chapters Literacy Program, Camrose, Alberta, December 1996)

They described another occasion when they earned some money and used it to go away together and have a wonderful time:

A: So we've tried to do things that we might not have had the opportunity to do otherwise. To know what to look forward to, what to aspire to. . . . Because a lot of people just thought "I'll never get a chance to do that, because I don't deserve it. . . ."

B: It sort of can all be summed up in a way as play. . . . It's about "I feel like doing this, let's go do this"—the blowing bubbles down Main Street kind of thing. . . .

C: . . . all the learning experiences that we've done here, it isn't just add and subtract and this and that. That doesn't necessarily prepare you to go out into the world. It's this that prepares you to go out into the world.

During that outing, one learner apparently said: "I never knew what good was. I never knew that things could be so wonderful" (interview, Chapters Literacy Program, Camrose, Alberta, December 1996). The value of focusing on enjoyment was confirmed by therapist Liz White, who reminded me of the importance of creating opportunities for learners to "develop the role of 'enjoyer.'" She suggested that might include using a variety of topics for writing, such as describing "moments of appreciation of music, of spring, of a friend, of a movie" (personal correspondence, 1999).

The staff and students at Chapters Program also described a writing project focusing on pleasure—a gratitude journal. I was initially quite sceptical about setting a task to write each day about three things you have to be thankful for when you live with violence or its legacy or poverty. However, when the students talked about what it meant to write such things as "I am thankful that I didn't have a drink yesterday," I began to hear what it meant to them to focus on the positive and the added strength it gave them. The learner I tutor and I have tried this out for ourselves and I can see that it has begun to help her tell different stories about her life—to move away from only focusing on the pain. I can hear a shift as she focuses on joys and reasons to live, rather than despair, anger, and pain. Learners at Chapters Program talked about these processes—experiencing, writing about the experience and being heard, focusing on opportunities to notice the positives, as well as space to tell the worst—as helping them come more alive and begin to notice the world more. Learners also spoke about a sense of acceptance. Nothing was too terrible for the rest of the group and the instructor to hear and respond with understanding. One woman said that she started to feel good about herself and to notice how things work; she began to be more aware of emotions and her growing understanding. They all agreed that the gratitude journal helped them change their thinking and feel less hopeless. Instead of "Things will always be this way, nothing will change," they could focus on what they have learned and how they can try to stop further abuse happening to them.

When I think about how to bring play into literacy learning, I fear that instructors who are not comfortable with the grimness of many learners' life histories, or who do not fully respect learners as adults, could use this suggestion as a justification to silence stories that are hard to hear or treat learners like children. The key for students at Chapters Literacy Program was clearly balance, so that in the group they could share the pain and, as they put it, "try out what good is."

CREATING THE LITERACY PROGRAM
AS A SAFER PLACE

The therapeutic literature on incest perceives these reactions in terms of being "triggered" in which past trauma intrudes on present day life bringing strong emotions of terror, rage, or grief (Herman, 1992). The therapeutic goal is to gain sufficient insight into past trauma and practice to control these moments (Bass and Davis, 1988). Because my terror and rage are "inappropriate" or pathological according to social norms for the activity, my reaction, not the social relations to which I am reacting, becomes the site requiring change. . . . Although being "triggered: is viewed as a "problem," it is also an invaluable, if costly way to see through the blinders of ordinary life to its underlying social relations of power and privilege. (Lewis, 1998, pp. 83–84).

It is crucial that literacy programs respect the *canaries* in literacy programs and seek to create a setting that is not toxic and that supports literacy learning. Violation of safety is a central aspect of trauma. This is particularly true for survivors of incest, where those who should have helped preserve a child's safety and helped the child to learn a sense of safety instead violate the child's safety. For some learners still involved in a relationship with an abusive man, the literacy program can be a rare place of safety. This may mean that some learners want to be there even when they are in crisis and unable to learn. It is already clear that in the literacy program safety is a complicated concept. Some learners want the program to be a safe place to tell their stories; others want it to be a place safe from hearing disturbing stories. Some want to be free to express their anger or rage; others want a place that is safe from experiencing any form of violence, including outbursts of anger or frustration.

Many literacy workers talked about the challenge of creating a safe space in their program. Some spoke of the limits of their power to create a space that would be experienced as safe by all learners and where they would be free of harassment or more subtle pressures. This was especially true where racism between groups created tensions and where participants had connections and relationships outside the classroom. In such circumstances, the power of the instructor to create a respectful and safe environment for all is often limited. One community college instructor from British Columbia described her experience:

> I have that problem with people coming into classes with histories with each other, so it's impossible for me to make the classroom safe for both of them. Their families have been feuding for years, or this year I have somebody who is in the class who told me the second day of class that she was laying a charge against the brother of one of the other women in class for attempted murder. . . . Then this year also I have a problem where one of the women who has been being severely battered, she's just left her husband a couple weeks ago. Her husband who she left, his sister is also in the class and so she did things this year that are very strange. Like she handed this letter all around the class that she had written to her husband . . . before she gave it to the husband. What she was doing in fact was looking for support from the other women in the class, because she's in this situation where no one will really believe that he's as bad as he is. Particularly, his family won't believe it. And so she's looking for support from other women in the class . . . which totally freaked out her sister-in-law. Her sister-in-law came to me and said "I can't come to school any more, because my brother is going to be asking me to spy on his wife. . . ." I can't make that class safe for all of those women. They can't all be there. But in fact, we don't have any other place for them, and so one of them offered to move into the next class up because her skills are kind of borderline, but basically it's impossible for them all to be there safely and it's impossible for the whole group to deal with the fact that they're not there safely because they don't want to deal with each other—in the classroom, they don't want to deal with each other, and there's lots of people in the class who don't have any interest in giving them any support around those issues—they just want to get on with the work. And so it's an undercurrent that's always there. I've had that before to a greater or lesser extent; this year it's bigger than usual, but that kind of family infighting that they bring with them is really hard to deal with, because I can't deal with it. (interview, Salt Spring Island, British Columbia, November/December 1996)

This instructor clarifies the challenge she experiences in trying to create safety in her classroom. She works hard to create as safe an environment as possible, yet her resources are limited when all the learners cannot be safe in the same classroom and there is nowhere else for them to go.

Despite these limitations, several workers spoke of their sense of responsibility for creating a safe classroom or program and were aware that, in their absence, a level of harassment took place that they did not allow. Workers working with torture victims spoke particularly of the need for a calm atmosphere that is not too distracting so that learners can feel safe and relaxed. Some program workers spoke of how stressful and active a role they have to play to try to create a safer space. For others, I wonder whether that work goes almost unnoticed, but adds to their level of emotional exhaustion and bone-weary tiredness at the end of the week, making it crucial that they are sensitive to their own needs.

The level of energy required was particularly striking in accounts from programs that work with people on the street. In those programs, the commitment to creating a place that is safe for all learners requires an active policing role on the part of workers to ensure learners do not bring weapons into the program and remove anyone who is violent or abusive from the space. Although workers spoke of the importance of the safer space they were creating, they also spoke of the exhausting task of enforcing it and the tension of being the recipients of anger unleashed when they barred students from the program. They stressed that creating a safer space is an ongoing challenge that forces them to recognize the power dynamic in which they impose limits and struggle continually to maintain them in the face of the threat of violence:

> I think it's really hard to . . . the pressure and responsibility on the staff of a program like ours to make the space safe for women, and yet how that in itself can be an all-consuming role, and how exhausting that is, and how that constantly puts you in conflict with men. (interview, Community and Street Program Literacy Workers, Toronto, February 1997)

Attempting to create safety for all in street programs means challenging the violence of some and following a set of rules. For those who are repeatedly told that their behavior is not okay, the program may feel far from comfortable. Workers from several programs serving people on the street talked about the clarity of rules and agreement among staff about acceptable and unacceptable behavior. Most described being extremely proactive, rather than reactive. Staff in the Beat the Street program spoke of having clear rules that sought to exclude violence from the program:

We've taken a whole different approach. So it's preventive. We ask people for their weapons at the door.

We hope that they'll give them to us.

We don't wait to find out if they've got one in the building. And we tell them that we'll return it within reason. So if someone has a gun, sorry, we're not returning it, we'd like you to leave. We take things like people's cane. Oh, pool cues are deadly. No pool cues, no pipes. . . . (interview, Community and Street Program Literacy Workers, Toronto, February 1997)

They keep the door locked and always have a staff person at the door to take any weapons and any symbols of hatred or racism that the students may be wearing. T-shirts with symbols of hatred have to be turned inside out if students are to be allowed inside. If a student is violent, he or she is asked to leave the program. The student is only allowed to return after he or she have discussed the behavior with a staff person.

A proactive approach to addressing questions of safety is less common in community programs, which work with a broader range of students. Perhaps it is harder to decide when to intervene when subtler violence, such as swearing or sexualized comments, makes the program seem less safe for some learners. When a man in one community program made a comment about "all the pretty girls," I wanted to tell him that such talk, which I am sure he intended to be flattering, could be offensive and scary to many women, but I hardly knew where to begin. Several learners talked about the value they found in a woman-only space even if it was a limited time meeting in a women's group. A learner from the Horizons Program said she could not cope with a male teacher:

My wound is so deep. I cannot have men as teachers. . . . I have not overcome that. . . . I cannot relate to the way they teach. (interview, Horizons Program, Duncan, British Columbia, November 1996)

In contrast, learners in Alberta who had a male staff member in their program spoke of the value of rebuilding trust through working with a gentle male who treated them respectfully. Joy So, a literacy practitioner in Winnipeg, suggested that tutors in her program modeled the possibility of different, respectful, nonviolent interactions. This alone might help a woman begin to believe they do not deserve to be mistreated and hurt:

Some of the volunteer tutors are older males, who are retired and are looking for something to do with their extra time. Although they're highly effective tutors, they're also great because they model appropriate behaviour and how men should treat women. A lot of female students have remarked, "He's just such a nice guy, I don't really meet men like that." (interview, Winnipeg, Manitoba, December 1996)

Herman (1992), describing the therapy interaction, spoke of the importance of clarity of rules and boundaries as determining safety in the interaction: "The two most important guarantees of safety are the goals, rules, and boundaries of the therapy contract and the support system of the therapist" (p. 147). However, in literacy, it is not so easy to create safety for everyone involved in the interaction. Some suggested that contracts should be set up in literacy. However, because this form is commonly used by welfare workers, this might reduce, rather than foster, feelings of safety. The Chapters Program in Alberta created a code of ethics that provided a framework to create safety and build trust in the program. It included such items as:

While I am a participant in the Chapters Program, I will:

- respect the individuality and ability of each person in the program
- not pass judgment on others and be fair and constructive in my feedback
- help create an accepting classroom environment
- be allowed to *pass* on activities that I do not want to participate in
- honor the people in the program by not using their names or unpublished work in discussion about the program outside of the classroom
- give everybody equal opportunity to speak and participate in the program
- understand that it is okay for me to express my own needs (i.e., quiet time, time out, etc.)

Such an agreement, negotiated with participants in the program, might help create a sense of safety and confidentiality for all participants. For each learner, the experience of being treated respectfully by the instructor and other learners will create a safer place to develop confidence in her abilities and her potential to learn to read.

RECOGNIZE AND RESPOND
TO IMPACTS OF TRAUMA

Seeing the complexity of awareness needed by both workers and learners around issues of all or nothing, presence, trust, boundaries, and crises adds awareness to why learning to read is a difficult and lengthy process.

Where the struggles around each of these issues are ones that a literacy learner has to carry out in privacy—because to reveal her difficulties in these areas is to be judged as *abnormal*—then the energy required is compounded. The learner needs energy not only to struggle with the difficulties, but also to hide this struggle. Therefore, it is crucial that within the literacy program the range of what is normal be broadened and the discourse opened up to reveal the struggles and learning that many learners will be engaging in as they seek to learn successfully. All instructors need to design educational processes that will enable learners who have experienced trauma to learn.

Recognizing the range of impacts considered here begins to point toward ways that literacy programs might operate differently. For example, a variety of approaches might help learners identify middle ground and persist in the day-to-day routines of learning. There are many different ways that the classroom could be organized to support learners' presence and enable them deal with the challenge and panic associated with trying to learn difficult material. Practical changes such as the organization of the room or short lessons with frequent breaks might have a powerful effect. Acknowledging that crises are an ongoing feature of many learners' lives could lead to a variety of strategies to assist learners to strategize about how to set the crises aside to focus on learning. When program workers actively question what it means to be trustworthy teachers, become clear about their own boundaries, respect the boundaries of others, and support learners to set their own boundaries and respect those of others, they create a safer setting where learners can relax and focus on their own learning. When instructors actively build trust and support learners developing trust in their own abilities and knowledge, important learning breakthroughs may occur. Creating balance that makes space for speaking and writing about pain as well as enjoyment and pleasure is part of the process of creating the literacy program as a safe place to learn.

If the challenges learners face are made an active part of the curriculum, then all learners benefit from the following: (a) exploring what it takes to be fully present in the classroom and from the knowledge gained from the times of less presence; (b) discovering a deeper understanding of ambiguity and middle ground rather than staying with the stark contrasts of all or nothing; (c) considering crises and how to live both in and out of crisis; (d) examining questions of trust in terms of the possibility of trusting their own knowledge and trusting others in the class or group not to judge and put them down; (e) learning to set boundaries and respect the boundaries of others; (f) deciding which stories to tell when; and (g) creating and experiencing a safer place to learn.

The challenge of recognizing the layers of learning necessitated by trauma impacts is not one that only applies within the classroom; it also requires that structures and lengths of programs be changed to accommodate these needs. Currently the funding constraints and bureaucratic structures that shape literacy work are limiting the recognition that a whole range of learning is integral to the literacy learning process. These challenges must be recognized so that the accessibility of literacy is not limited to those few who can learn fast and easily.

5

Learning in the Context of Trauma: The Challenge of Setting Goals

Judith Herman (1992) described trauma as caused by events that "overwhelm the ordinary systems of care that give people a sense of control, connection and meaning" (p. 33). Many writers have suggested that, for trauma victims, therapy should be directed at helping the survivor regain a sense of control, connection, and meaning in her life. This shows an inevitable overlap between literacy and trauma. Issues of control, connection, and meaning are central to literacy learning because they are integrally connected to the tasks of setting goals—increasingly a central aspect of how literacy programming is being organized. Setting goals may seem a straightforward task, where simple skills can be taught to those who find it difficult. However, for survivors of trauma, setting goals may be far from simple. The difficulty lies not simply in learning skills, but in a far more complex intertwining of issues. An exploration of the nuances of each area offers some beginning insights into why they are regularly fraught with difficulties in literacy programming and suggests new program directions and possibilities.

CONTROL

The suggestion that trauma entails being controlled and being out of control—and that, consequently, one effect of trauma is that the whole area of control becomes difficult terrain—offers interesting insights for literacy work. By *control* I mean the possibility of influencing an outcome or the belief that it is possible to influence an outcome. Therapists described women who have experienced trauma as engaged in a continuing struggle with control, feeling that they cannot have control, trying to hold on, and not wanting to be responsible. Therapist Heather Bain explained:

> . . . having control, the issue of control is a huge one. . . for a traumatized kid, or adolescent, or even adult, there is no sense of being able to control the environment. The environment is totally unpredictable and whether or not they are going to get hurt is unpredictable. There is nothing they can do to prevent it. There is nothing they can do to create safety. So everyone I know that has experienced some form of trauma needs a high level of being in charge. I'm sure that's true of a learning situation as well. . . .
>
>   I think it is the paradox of helplessness—the experience of helplessness on the one hand and the desire for control. There is a tremendous desire for control but there is an inner experience of helplessness and often a belief that we have no control and so you are going to get both [patterns]. . . .
>
>   . . . trauma is a series of paradoxes and so, you get totally opposing patterns happening at the same time. Some of that is the switch between extremes because it's about extremes, it's about all or nothing, helplessness or total control. (interview, Edmonton, December 1996)

This could be helpful to understanding some interactions that take place in a literacy program; it might also assist in revealing why many approaches in literacy often lead to explosions, conflict, and layers of tension. As discussed later, when literacy programs seek to be learner-centered—encouraging learners to control their own curriculum, set goals, and take a role in running programs by sitting on committees and boards of directors—they set up processes that can take learners into the difficult terrain of control.

The stories I heard from literacy learners and workers clearly revealed how much violence is about taking control away from the victim. Many experiences involved women being controlled by others. One learner at Malaspina College described her own experiences with a violent husband in terms of control:

> . . . he wanted me to go out and make more money. I was waitressing but that wasn't enough—I was to make more money to help him out . . . and extreme jealousy.
>
>   He wasn't happy in his life so he was also pushing me to do—whatever—that would solve all the problems and make everything hunky dory. . . . But no matter what I did. it wasn't going to make him happy inside. That's why I ended up having to leave the marriage, because nothing I did could ever solve his unhappiness and he tried to keep me under his thumb and under his control and it didn't matter what I did. I was always wrong. I

was always stupid. (interview, Malaspina College, Duncan, British Columbia, November 1996)

Women who return to school are often coping with increased levels of control and even sabotage of their educational efforts added to the strain and fears of going back to school:

> When you have a student population of older women returning to school, their husbands or partners could be threatened by this decision, taking some initiative, a step towards independence in their lives. . . . I have known students whose husbands or partners insist on reading all their notes, or insisted that they only take courses with female instructors, monitor who they talk to—if they were seen talking to a male student it would be reported to them. They make it difficult or impossible for those women to feel strong. (personal correspondence)

Abusive men often control access to friends, family, and money. Through their approval or disapproval, which may be expressed as physical violence, they often control everything a woman does and does not do. Women's writing on a listserv about psychological violence included horrifyingly detailed controlling methods. One described her husband driving her to work, keeping her wallet and ID, and then calling her regularly at work to check on her. It is not uncommon for people to think that violent abusers are simply out of control, but theorists suggest that, rather than being about lack of control, violence is about the abuser's need to be *in* total control:

> It's vital to understand that battering is not a series of isolated blowups. It is a process of deliberate intimidation intended to coerce the victim to do the will of the victimizer. The batterer is not just losing his temper, not just suffering from stress, not just manifesting "insecurity" or a spontaneous reaction "provoked" by something the victim did or (as psychologists put it) "a deficit of interpersonal skills" or an "inhibition in anger control mechanisms." These are excuses for violence, popular even among therapists who work with batterers; yet we all know aggrieved, insecure, stressed-out people with meagre interpersonal skills who lose their temper without becoming violent. We assume, then, that the grievances of the violent man must be worse, and that under extreme stress he has spun out of control. He looks it, and that's what he says: "I wasn't myself." "I was drunk." "I went bananas." "I lost it." "I went out of my mind." It's lines like these that provide a public excuse and deceive a battered woman into giving one more chance to the so-called real, nonviolent men underneath. But in fact that

violence is himself, perfectly in control and exercising control. (Jones, 1994, pp. 88–89)

People who are marginalized in society are more at risk of being controlled. Deaf workers talked about the layers of control exerted by family, exacerbated for women who use gesture only and have to communicate through their family. Deaf women also live with the threat of having their children taken away. Women with intellectual or physical disabilities are vulnerable to the control of their caregivers. First Nation people were removed from their families to attend residential schools, where those in control denied them the use of their languages. Some have suggested that this violent removal from family created a generation of adults who do not have experience being parented themselves; instead, they have experience of traumatic abuse (interview, First Nation Instructors, Toronto, January 1997). Survivors of the residential school system may find it challenging to discover how to parent their own children with gentle control when they have experienced control that was violent and violating.

Many learners spoke of welfare workers controlling them. Some did not want to take government money to avoid being under welfare's control. They described pressure to search for and get a job, to get their hair done, and to be at the training or literacy program every day even when they or their children were sick. Learners on welfare complained about home visits and about living on too little money. Women who left abusive husbands talked about dependence on government money as continuing the feeling of being abusively controlled. One counselor said: "Repressive situations can trigger memories of repression." Another suggested that lack of control is a humiliating experience, like those listed earlier, whereas control leads to pride, joy, and pleasure.

Therapists suggest that trauma leads people to have a strong desire for control and an equally strong belief in their helplessness and inability to exercise control. They also say that children who are abused cannot bear the knowledge that they have absolutely no power to stop the abuse and find it easier to believe that they have caused the abuse because they are *bad*. This permits the hope that, if they become *good*, the abuse might stop.

When it is impossible to avoid the reality of the abuse, the child must construct some system of meaning that justifies it. Inevitably the child concludes that her innate badness is the cause. The child seizes upon this explanation early and clings to it tenaciously, for it enables her to preserve a sense of meaning, hope, and power. If she is bad, then her parents are good. If she is bad, then she can try to be good. If, somehow she has brought this fate upon herself, then somehow she has the power to change it. If she has driven her parents to mistreat her, then, if only she tries hard enough, she may some day earn their forgiveness and finally win the protection and care she so desperately needs. (Herman, 1992, p. 103)

Child abusers and batterers frequently exacerbate this process of self-blame by blaming the child or spouse, suggesting that the victim caused the mistreatment[1]:

The abused child's sense of inner badness may be directly confirmed by parental scapegoating. Survivors frequently describe being blamed, not only for their parents' violence or sexual misconduct, but also for numerous other family misfortunes. Family legends may include stories of the harm the child caused by being born or the disgrace for which she appears to be destined. (Herman, 1992, pp. 103–104)

These passages illustrate how control becomes an important terrain for those who have experienced trauma. Feeling out of control, trying to regain control, not wanting to own any control, controlling in hidden manipulative ways, feeling responsible, and disowning responsibility are all complex and fraught areas. At the same time, seeking control, but feeling helpless and believing it is impossible, is a contradictory dynamic.

Heather Bain described women who have survived trauma, particularly childhood abuse, as frequently struggling with an all or nothing concept of control—trying either to have complete control or to give over control completely. A group of learners in Prince Edward Island said: "It's all about control." Being in control also entails being responsible, being blamed, and blaming oneself. Freedom is scary because no one else can be blamed. Heather Bain described some adults who were traumatized very young as getting caught in a *you fix it* place, still looking for the adult to meet their needs in a way that did not happen as a child. Several therapists talked about the support an adult needs to recognize where this attitude comes from and why it takes so much time and work to move beyond it. Other cultures may offer different ways of framing the challenge of the individual within community besides being in control. First Nation communities, for example, speak in terms of finding *balance*. Creating plans or goals for the future requires some ability to imagine taking control or seeking balance, thus a person who has been traumatized may need to learn new skills to imagine that change is possible and to take steps to move toward it.

---

[1]Women raped by strangers are also often blamed for walking in the wrong place, dressing provocatively, or for some reason judged responsible for their fate. Women may also blame themselves, perhaps also wanting to believe they have some control over their safety in the future.

Control in Literacy

As noted, many literacy programs stress learner-centered learning, where learners design their own individualized plan, control their own learning, and set goals. This foregrounds the terrain of control within literacy. Some programs also seek to involve learners in sharing control of the program through participation on committees or boards of directors. This *mine field* is often entered without preparation or even awareness of how complex and problematic raising control issues may be for some literacy learners as well as for some workers.

Therapists' accounts of difficulties with control resonated strongly with my own experience tutoring a learner who has experienced major trauma. She used to drive me crazy when she would blame me for something entirely beyond my control, or I would hear her, jokingly, but repeatedly, criticizing other literacy workers for such things as not stopping her from doing something or blaming them for something they had no control over. More and more now, we talk about issues of control and she strategizes how to take more responsibility and even to say "no" sometimes.

Literacy worker Beth Sauerhaft wrote on an online seminar about the value for a learner of learning to say "no":

"Before this class I used to be a "yes" person. Now I know the importance for my health and my life to say 'no.' I teach this to my fifteen-year-old daughter and I think she respects me more."

These words come from the journal of a former student of mine who participated in a health and literacy class dealing with breast cancer and environmental justice issues. Ana, (not her real name) a woman in her 50s from Mexico, experiences emotional and verbal abuse from her husband. In the name of building student leadership and involvement in literacy and community programs, particularly among underserved women, practitioners often make it difficult for students to say no to what soon becomes a limited and prescribed definition of leadership such as students being active in program boards, conference presentations and staffing the program. Ana thanked me for explicitly telling her and all the women in the class that they could and should say no to any invitations I extended to them to be more "involved" in things if it overextended them. She told me that she was able to practice saying "no" through her relationship with me and it then made it safer for her to try this in other contexts, like with her doctors, other staff at the literacy program, her husband and other controlling family members. She knew (because I made it very clear) that I would continue to extend invitations and encourage students to participate in all aspects of the learning process. She appreciated that I knew there were other demands for her time (she cares for her elderly mother who is ill, has a youngest daughter still at home and other stresses, not to mention dealing with her husband). Ana came to understand that I could hear "no" not as a rejection but as her evaluating what was best for her. (Alphaplus Literacy & Violence Online Seminar, February–April 1998)

This focus on the literacy program as a safe place to explore saying "no," as well as "yes," requires that workers are not caught in an all or nothing place around control, where they might be likely to take offense and snatch control back when events do not unfold as planned.

Thinking about how to support "learners to learn to navigate their own processes of being effectively in control" is a central question for learner leadership. If the area of control is like walking in a mine field while assuming you are not, just to know it is a mine field may be a key insight. In a mine field, it is wise to tread warily and, at the ready, to not retreat rapidly. There may be a need to stand still, do lots of exploration of what is happening, and then proceed with care and consciousness. Of course, it is important to recognize that it may not be a mine field only for learners. Workers, too, may struggle with issues of control. For learners, volunteers, and paid staff who are attracted to leadership activities, exploring the potential to be in control may be particularly important and difficult work.

Donna Lovell, a learner who participated in a learner leadership project I conceptualized and facilitated with Donna Jeffery, thought that control was a crucial issue in that project. She thought a lot of time and energy was spent by learners finding out "are we really in control, even if you don't like what we do." Donna Lovell often feels that learners are offered a false promise in literacy—through the implication that everyone will have control. In her view, that is only a game, and control will be taken back as soon as something goes wrong, with the judgment on learners that they just weren't capable. In our discussion, we struggled to understand each other. I felt that, rather than thinking the learners are not capable, I was liable to hang onto a certain amount of control because I am paid to take responsibility for accomplishing the agreed on task. If I snatch control back as things begin to get messy, I am likely to do so thinking *not* that *they* cannot do it, but that *I* got it wrong and I may fail. We laughed over our different analyses—the realization that we both had control issues and both were convinced that we would be judged to be at fault.[2]

---

[2]This conversation formed part of a reflection process that contributed to a chapter I wrote on learner leadership (Horsman, in press). I thank Donna for her insights and generosity with her time (and baking).

The richness of that conversation made me think it would be interesting to open up discussion about such issues early in a learner leadership activity. We agreed that not everyone would find it easy to engage in such discussion, but thought there could be ways to make the discussion straightforward. Useful discussion could be stimulated by introducing ideas such as: what would count as *success* and *failure* in a project; places in our lives where we feel we have some control; what we do when we feel out of control; and blaming others and taking responsibility.

In that conversation, this learner and I also recognized that not everyone wants control, and that most of us do at some times and not at others. Avoiding responsibility and blaming others was a pattern we both knew well. It is crucial to make as much of this visible as possible, otherwise learners may conclude that a worker has taken back some control—not because the worker became scared, but due to losing confidence in the learner—"they didn't really think I could do it"—or because they had only pretended to give over control. Without discussion, a sense of the workers' dishonesty, distrust, and layers of anger build up each time something goes wrong and may become an insurmountable barrier to good working relations between workers and learners (Horsman, in press).

Interviewing therapists, counselors, and literacy workers, as well as thinking about how literacy would look if we put these issues front and center, has led me to wonder how issues of control could be taken on with more awareness throughout literacy programming. These initial ideas need to be developed further to create curriculum and programming. During my research, several literacy workers talked about the importance of the program putting as much control into the learners' hands as possible while exploring questions of control with learners. Literacy workers mentioned exploring the idea of being in charge with students as a way to help them to begin to move toward taking charge of their own learning. An instructor in British Columbia asked students to think of a place where they were in charge. If they could not think of a place where they were in charge, she suggested driving a vehicle as a time when they might have known the experience and used that situation to help them imagine being in charge of their learning. Reflecting on being in charge in some situation can give learners an analogy to begin to get a hold on what being in charge of learning might look like practically.

Stopping and Starting

Regardless of the structure of a program, learners may need to start and stop when they choose and move onto new work, or back to old, when they are ready. Learners who start and stop, perhaps repeatedly, may be exploring taking control, rather than lacking in motivation. Several First Nation literacy workers in Toronto spoke about the advantage of designing programs that allowed women to stop and start as necessary:

> I think one of the things we learned at Native Women's Resource Centre was not to have our feelings hurt if people phoned and made an appointment with us and didn't show up, and phoned again and said sorry I didn't make it, didn't show up. There are real reasons people were at a certain place in their lives, where they knew intellectually that they wanted to do something, but there was something within them holding them back from doing that. So they weren't following through with things and it wasn't because, you know, they're lazy or whatever, it was just they couldn't at that point in time. . . . And that's why I always tell people who are applying to the project that you can come and start whenever and you can leave whenever you want and you can always come back whenever you want. There isn't a sixteen-week program you have to come to every day and that kind of thing. I think that really helps with some women, knowing that [the instructor] is going to be there every week . . . and you can come there, and know that she is going to be there.
>
> I know one student was coming along and then her marriage went through a crisis and for a while she wasn't coming and that, then when she came back she started to apologize and tell me what happened. And I said, well don't apologize, you have to handle something, you have to handle something, and the program will be here . . . whenever she can make it. . . . I didn't want her to feel that she had to apologize for going through a crisis. I wanted to just convey that I understand, and that she is not going to lose marks or fail or something, because she is not consistent. And when she's there, we try and make a good learning experience, and have fun, and just leave the world outside and do something that she really wants to do. You know—just space and time. (interview, First Nation Instructors, Toronto, January 1997)

Similarly, First Nation literacy workers in Yellowknife spoke of the value of running a flexible program where learners can say they are going to join the program but then not show up. They spoke of learners "coming back three, four times, and then five times, and then they stayed." They explained that the stresses in a woman's life may make it difficult for her to continue, explaining that it may even take 2 or 3 years before someone is able to continue. One worker said: "I don't control their time, they control it and when they are ready we're there. I allow them to choose" (interview, Yellowknife, NWT., March 1997).

An article about sexual abuse survivors learning outdoor wilderness skills eloquently described the learning involved in being able to choose to start and stop:

One half-hour into a day rock-climbing clinic, Pat told the leader she was going home. The leader, of course, had a pang of disappointment. However, she said to Pat, "I'll walk you to your car." En route, they chatted about the morning and Pat told the leader that she was in therapy for sexual abuse and felt too exposed during the clinic. The leader said she understood, asked Pat if she could call her later that week, and bid her good-bye. That week, the leader called Pat and invited her to join the group on a clinic the next weekend that would have less people. Pat accepted and participated. The following week, Pat attended an intermediate climbing clinic. Again, after a half-hour, she needed to leave. She returned a few weeks later to complete an intermediate clinic. She shared with the leader that by being able to say she felt exposed and needed to leave, then leaving without leader criticism, and being welcomed upon her return, supported her healing process. Women survivors are often afraid to say they need to leave, or to say no. They are afraid their "no" will be interpreted hostilely and they will be abandoned. When they were small children this would have threatened their survival. In this case, the value for Pat of saying, "No," leaving, and returning was substantial. The leader gave Pat a gift of knowing that she could set her own limits without being abandoned. In many other instances, it is appropriate for leaders to hear and honor a woman's choice to say "No," or that she needs to stop. (Quoted in Mitten & Dutton, 1996, pp. 137–138)

These comments suggest that the process of starting and stopping is a learning process, not a failure to get down to learning. These accounts draw attention to the restraint necessary to refrain from pushing someone to continue—from rejecting or judging them for stopping. The stance that respects a learner's choice and maintains a link to encourage return is a sensitive balance. It is possible that we lose that balance when no connection is made after a learner drops out and when we push, persuade, and cajole a learner into continuing in class, sitting on a board, or attending a conference, although she appears reluctant.

When I included this story about wilderness education in an online seminar, one worker sadly responded that it described a pretty idyllic situation. She said: "I am glad the story in your quote ended so happily." She was not feeling so optimistic about one of her own students or about the potential for her program to accommodate the student's needs:

I dealt this a.m. with a student who needs to leave our program, but she doesn't want to and our program is the place where she feels she is getting something for herself. I want to run a place where they can come around, hang out, check back in a week or a month or a year and pick up where they left off—I want her to know that what she is doing here is also valued by us not just by her.

> I want enough money and freedom and resources to be a healing place. So often when they come and tell me they are going to leave they are really saying I'm sure you'll be mad and someone is making me and probably you think I'm wasting my time anyway. I believe more and more that when they can have a successful experience with reading writing etc. they get hold of a piece of their own selves—being successful—that often they and no one else in their world ever thought they would get a hold of. (Alphaplus Literacy & Violence Online Seminar, February–April 1998).

Ongoing experiences of violence may lead women to drop out of the program or stop and start participating in a program due to changes in the level of violence or her ability to withstand it. Programs that are *healing places*—where students can start and stop as they needed, where they are not judged as making inadequate progress or not serious or excluded as a consequence of irregular attendance or slow progress—offer new possibilities for women who are experiencing violence or its aftermath.

Several other workers spoke about the frustration they feel about program restrictions that limit the amount of time a learner may stay in the program and demand documented progress. These restrictions make it difficult for workers to support learners who need to stop and start and whose learning includes invisible aspects, such as learning to stay in the classroom. In the online seminar, Beth Crowther, who taught literacy in Texas, said:

> Unfortunately, in programs where students have time limits on how long they can stay in a literacy class and quantitative, documented progress and movement to the next level is key, the seemingly (I stress seemingly) lack of "progress" and the time it can take to experiment with and gain control and meaning in learning is all to often seen as a failure not only for learners, but for teachers as well. It was frustrating. (Alphaplus Literacy & Violence Online Seminar, February–April 1998)

During the seminar, other workers were relieved to hear their frustration was shared. Despite that relief, frustration with the external limits remained central to much of the literacy workers' talk about possibilities for changes within literacy programming.

A Balance of Structure

Support for learners to control their own pace of work and choose the work they are ready for can be an important step in exploring control. Although that might suggest that a program that allows substantial leeway for learners to be in control of their learning is ideal, too much freedom can be difficult particularly for those who have not had much experience being in control. Several workers talked about the terror that learners seem to experience when everything is wide open. It may also be that a program that looks structureless and wide open for learners has hidden layers of expectations and judgments about what *proper* participation looks like. Many learners need support to recognize what work may be useful to do and to notice their own progress. Often learners veer toward workbooks and even meaningless exercises because they can provide a satisfying sense of accomplishment as each one is checked off. Supporting learners to gain a sense of control while taking on more varied and complex tasks is an important challenge. A combination of boundaries and structure alongside the freedom for a student to exercise some control may be the delicate balance that makes it possible for a learner to explore her own limits and learn about making choices and being in control.

When I talked with a group of experienced practitioners in British Columbia, we all became interested in the concept of structure and regular patterns and what that might offer learners. We discussed the value of learners becoming familiar with a routine, predictable structure and yet also knowing they can expect pleasant surprises and contrasts:

A: I think that the way the instruction is delivered has to be really structured, but the content can have the surprises, and the pleasant little breaks. One year I had a really difficult reading class, this would be an advanced reading, and there were quite a few people in there that I had a lot of apprehension about their completing the course, even though some of them had taken it already. So I structured it far more than I normally do. But our environmental unit became a unit about animals and conservation, because they liked reading animal stories. So I sort of had the themes in there that had pretty serious implications for anybody that was into the serious side but they really [had fun]—and their achievement was better in that class than I would say some of the much better, more capable, groups that I had that I was much less structured about. . . .

B: What sort of things did you structure that you hadn't structured before?

A: We had a routine for reading a story. And we did every story, every newspaper article, exactly the same way. And they seemed to like it. They knew exactly what was going to happen when they walked in there, and they would start joking with me, they would provide the fun. And I was quite amazed, because they were not a group of people that I would have expected to feel competent enough to joke with their instructor. Because a lot of ABE students aren't—they don't do that much.

B: So maybe that structure meant we know what we're going to do and then it frees up this other little part.

C: Perhaps it builds some safety and some trust. (interview, Salt Spring Island, British Columbia, November/December 1996)

This group of literacy workers had extensive discussion about the value of structure—some wondering whether they might want to introduce more structure than they had previously—while also wanting to keep a balance of risk-taking, challenge, and interesting surprises. All agreed that an important part of the routine was that learners were encouraged to feel comfortable with opting out of any activity or choosing to opt out if they chose.

During the online seminar, several literacy workers commented on the difficulty they have *selling* individualized learning to their students. Although there may be many factors involved in this reluctance, I question the value of individualized learning rather than group work. I wonder to what extent the students' difficulty with the approach arises from the extent to which they are expected to make their own choices about appropriate work for themselves. Literacy worker Diana Twiss of British Columbia described an occasion where she began by providing more structure and led students toward making choices, instead of trying to persuade students that an individualized approach is a good thing:

The group I am working with is self-paced individualized English upgrading. But they don't want that. They want a structured paced class. Something that has a beginning and a definite end. Early in the semester the students generally have such a low sense of their abilities, they look at me rather sceptically when I give the individualized-approach-to-learning chat. This semester I did things differently. I started with a structured format that had a lot of flexibility and choices. That seemed to help them get a better idea of what individualized is all about. But the time factor is what wears me down. (Alphaplus Literacy & Violence Online Seminar, February–April 1998)

Once I began to think and talk about approaches that might provide a reassuring and clear structure, while allowing for the possibility of choice and freedom within careful boundaries, various possibilities emerged. Ideas I had heard about previously came to have new meaning. One interesting idea used in a community college setting in British Columbia by two instructors, Evelyn Battell and Kate Nonesuch (which they said they drew from Sylvia Ashton-Warner) was *inhale and exhale rooms*. This is a team teaching approach. In one room, there is always an activity happening so that students can *inhale* new material. In the other room, there is no activity, but a teacher is always available as a resource person. Here students can *exhale*, working on something sparked from class or on material they need to work on for themselves (e.g., a letter they want to write, a form to be filled in, etc.). The availability of these two options means that students can always make a choice. That choice is framed by the structure and they are not pressured to choose their own material to work on. If they are in the inhale room saying that they do not want to do the work that is happening there, they can always go to the other room and do what they choose. Similarly, if they are in the exhale room saying that they do not know what to do, they can go to the other room and take the class on offer.

Another structure that supports learners to take responsibility for their own learning is a rule that one of these instructors has in her classroom: No one is allowed to be bored or to bore others. Kate Nonesuch explained:

> . . . many of them come feeling that they're stupid. They failed in school because they're stupid, they're not learning because they're stupid, and if you're in a classroom situation where people are not learning because their stuff is in their way, then it's important for them to notice that it isn't because they're stupid that they're not learning at this particular moment. It's because their stuff is in the way. It's important for me to see, so that I don't keep trying to get them to work on proofreading when they can't do it, but also they begin to have the skills to recognize their own ways of learning so that they can say to themselves "I can't do this right now because I have to deal with this other thing." They can also recognize times when they can learn, and that seems a really important skill to give them. Often people come to me and say "This is boring." We have a major rule in our class that you're not allowed to bore anybody else, and you're not allowed to be bored; if you say something is boring it gets changed immediately.
>
> When people say "I'm bored. This is boring." often what it really means is "This is too easy," or "This is too hard." Then it's time for me to figure out what kind of work I should give them that would be better for them and it's a time for them to figure out the same thing. We have a problem to solve together. I think that the more opportunities we can give them to understand their own ways of learning, the better their learning is. . . . (interview, Salt Spring Island, British Columbia, November/December 1996)

When Kate Nonesuch described this approach to other literacy workers, another long-time worker said, in her experience, learners sometimes say they are bored as a way to speak about dissociating or that they cannot handle what is being talked about. Kate continued, saying:

> I think that one thing I do get by having that rule about not being bored is that people then can say "I'm bored," whereas they can't say "I'm disassoci-

ating," or "I'm frustrated 'cause I can't figure out what the heck anybody's talking about" or "I'm afraid." They don't have to say that, they just have to say "I'm bored." That' s a clue to me that I'm supposed to step in, a way of tipping me off that there's a problem. (interview, Salt Spring Island, British Columbia, November/December 1996)

This instructor's approach—creating a rule that you cannot be bored—clearly provided some humor in her class while providing the possibility for learners to explore being in control of their own learning and the situations that block it. She also used this device to help learners take more responsibility when they create learning situations for others—because they are also responsible to not bore others:

I often get people to make presentations, and ordinary student presentations are always boring. So we start with that, you're not allowed to bore people, which means that you're not allowed to stand up here and read something that you've written on some topic that you know nothing about. If you're going to make a presentation to the class that's going to last longer than thirty seconds, then you have to find a film, or a piece of reading, or something that's interesting, and it means that you have to preview the film. You can't just bring it in, because it might be a boring film and you would be guilty of boring us all. You have to go and preview it. If you're bringing in a reading, you have to understand all the big words, because if we can't understand them we're going to ask about them, and if you don't know, then we're going to be bored. So it's kind of a catchall, it works in all kinds of ways. Again, it develops that skill of figuring out what's getting in the way of their learning right now. (interview, Salt Spring Island, British Columbia, November/December 1996)

This simple structure—no boredom allowed—can gradually develop learners' abilities to take responsibility for their own learning and to collaborate with the instructor to create situations where they can learn and help other students to learn.

Taking Safe Risks

Several interviewees explained that freedom can be extremely scary because of the danger of getting it wrong. Learners who have been abused as children may have "huge issues around making mistakes." For a child with this belief—that if she were only good enough she could make the abuse stop or the abuse is her fault—trying to always get it *right* may make it hard to take the risk of trying to learn something challenging. If she has been punished arbitrarily or severely, the implication of the failure of anyone to protect her or stop the abuse is that she must deserve it, so making mistakes may be terrifying. Heather Bain explained:

> Kids often try to be good enough because there is an illusion that if we just find the right way to do it, they'll stop hurting us, and so *making a mistake can be a matter of life or death.* It is often not a small thing—it looks small to us—and with it that desire to please and that desire to placate, because I think every little kid searches for ways of being heard. Usually they say it's because I'm bad and if only I was better, or if I was good, or good enough, something—then it would stop. . . . I think that as kids we can't handle that we have no control. As adults, we can barely handle it. So we internalize it and make ourselves responsible, because it's easier to live with than just the randomness, and the unpredictability, and the fact that we have no control. So making a mistake is not a small thing, it's big. . . . [So its valuable] just to give choice where it is possible to do that and to encourage people to make the choice—even if they seem like six of one, half a dozen of the other. (interview, Edmonton, December 1996)

If any of these circumstances have compounded the usual everyday embarrassment with making mistakes or being wrong, literacy workers may face an enormous challenge to support students in learning to make choices, to put their words out there both loudly and in print, and to see making mistakes as part of the learning process.

Kate Nonesuch talked about an approach she uses with writing that encourages risk-taking within careful bounds so the risk will boost confidence rather than diminish it:

> . . . when my students write I type up everybody's work and make copies and hand it out to everybody, and we talk about what's good in it and so on. They can choose not to have a piece copied, or they can choose not to put their name on it. It feels like a risk to them at the beginning of term, first, to give it to me and say you can copy it, and second, to put their name on it. Many new students refuse. They go to a few writing groups looking at other students' work, and find out that we talk only about what we like. There's no room for anybody to say they don't like something about a piece of writing, there just isn't room. It doesn't occur. I make it so clear that's not what we're doing. . . . So they're still taking a risk every time they write because all those people are going to read it, but it's a safe risk. It's a risk out of which they're probably going to feel okay. (interview, Salt Spring Island, British Columbia, November/December 1996)

Other instructors commented that this is a nice example of routine, structure, and choice. Students can make the choice to take the risk—to participate—or sit in and see how it works without presenting their own writing for feedback. The clear guidelines ensure that the risk students take is a safe one—they will not be humiliated or shamed.

Literacy workers described a variety of ways to support learners to take the risk of making mistakes. Evelyn Battell talked about using a spelling program regularly, again providing routine, and using it so that students have to shout out the morphographs of each word together. She calls it *spell and yell*. Using the program in this way creates a process where students learn to put their voices out loudly in the room. Similarly, Evelyn talked about having students work on math problems in groups at the blackboard so that they learned to take the risk of making mistakes within a supportive setting:

> Obviously it's risky: "Okay, you five to the board, write this question down, you're all going to do it. You can look at each other, that's one of the reasons we're going to the board, the other reason is you've got erasers." It's risky going to the board but they very soon get to like it and start saying things like "Can we do our tests on the board?" And at first they're really [nervous]. I make a big point of closing the door so it's only those of us in the room, and nobody else in the room. If people are sitting at their desks watching cause there isn't enough board room, they're doing it on paper. And there's a switch over, later on those people are at the board. (interview, Salt Spring Island, British Columbia, November/December 1996)

Evelyn Battell spoke of encouraging the students to risk working on the board; she thinks it is important that they take the risk and physically get up from their desks and move around. Another instructor in a community college spoke of following a similar pattern with English exercises; she thought that, in addition to the risk of doing work that is visible to everyone, they "get to own a little more of the classroom" by taking over the blackboard. In all these examples, students are encouraged to take risks within a structure and with instructors who are careful to make it a safe risk. Instructors recognized that such risk-taking requires students to trust that the instructor will not allow them to be humiliated. For many students, it may take some time to reach that level of trust. Yet careful opportunities for risk-taking may be crucial to help students learn to make choices with more freedom from anxiety about making mistakes.

Making Choices

Many literacy workers talked about the challenge of working with learners who continually asked them how to do something—who wanted to be told whether to take the subway or the bus, to know how to spell every word, and whether they could move onto something else. A community college instructor from British Columbia described a situation where she was unclear what she could do:

> What I'm particularly interested in is—that person goes to talk to the counselor, so half an hour later she comes back to class, or I know that they see the counsellor on a regular basis outside of class, or whatever. But then they come to class, and they still have behaviours in class that interfere, that's one of the things that I'm interested in talking about. I have noticed for example that a woman that I have who is currently being battered won't move in the classroom unless I give her specific permission to do so. So if I don't keep my eye on her all the time, and notice when she needs to move, like when she needs to get up and get the other kind of paper, or when she needs the other pen, or when we're reading around in a group, even though we've been going all around the room and she knows she's the next person, she won't move without looking at me, and I nod at her and then she starts to read. . . . Other people certainly have other behaviours that I don't notice as a result of that kind of thing. . . . I don't know if I should say to her "You don't have to wait for my permission." Well, maybe I should just say that to her. (interview, Salt Spring Island, British Columbia, November/December 1996)

Another instructor found that students who were not used to being in control did not take control themselves easily:

> This woman has a long history of violence in her life and abuse, and no. I've said it lots of times. She's in her seventies and she says "Can I leave a little bit early today?" This is . . . a drop-in, you can come when you like, you can leave when you like. But she [asks] if she wants to leave before four, and I keep telling her, but no, she doesn't change. And I don't expect her to. So now I'm being really gracious and saying yes, you may leave. Cause that's what she wants me to do. (interview, Salt Spring Island, British Columbia, November/December 1996)

These examples illustrate how violence can completely undermine the possibility of taking action. The challenge for instructors—to support such learners to believe they have the freedom to make even the simplest choices—is enormous.

"Never trust someone who has been abused." These are the words of a counselor who was trying to make clear to me the issues of manipulative or passive–aggressive control. She wanted to make sure I recognized the challenges of women who avoid confrontation, but then take on issues in manipulative and indirect ways. I resisted the prescription as judgmental and stereotyping, but I recognized the pattern in both learners and workers. Therapist Lorna Gallant talked about the importance of teaching survivors that manipulation is not the only way to power and of reframing the resourcefulness that led to developing manipulation. Workers may need training in issues of control to be able to work well with learners who are struggling around control.

When literacy workers recognize that some learners will have to learn how to make choices, supporting them to learn the skills to take control of their own lives—through beginning to make even minor or insignificant choices—can become part of literacy classroom learning. Even choosing ideas from a brainstorm or a topic to write about could be a scary or perhaps impossible prospect for many learners. Working on this research has led me to notice language around control. The learner I tutor frequently says "I had to. . . ." Now we talk about whether she *had* to and explore what other choices she had, what limited her choices, and what she might try next time.

Failure to take control or make choices can easily be seen as a symptom of students not taking their learning seriously and not applying themselves. An alternative is to make the challenge of teaching learners to make choices part of literacy learning. Learners who are already skilled in this area might be able to help other learners to explore issues and develop skills. Heather Bain suggested that learners with little experience making choices might need to have choices presented to them and be encouraged to choose randomly so that they can experience making choices without significant consequences. She also suggested that learners might be encouraged to recognize where in their life they do have choices, even extremely minor ones, and to explore what it feels like to make a choice. The experience, difficulties, and feelings could all be part of reading, writing, listening, and speaking exercises.

Creating a place in the program where women can learn to take control may allow learners to begin to take more control in other aspects of their life. One caution: Some literacy workers warned against advising women to take more control in life, especially for outsiders from a different community or culture. These workers suggested that it is crucial for women to know what supports are available to them in case of repercussions arising when they begin to try exerting more control.

CONNECTION

Like control, connection is also central to literacy work; it is similarly complicated and fraught terrain in the face of trauma. Communication—speaking/listening and reading/writing—is about connection to others; it requires trust that it is possible to communicate something. The connection to the tutor or teacher, to others in a group, and to the program as home are all crucial in facilitating learning in the literacy program. Profoundly severed connection creates an immense barriers to literacy learning. Will the interactions in the literacy program enhance connection or leave women who have experienced violence isolated?

The dislocation of connection and isolation resulting from trauma inflicted by another human being is well documented in the literature.

> Traumatized people feel utterly abandoned, utterly alone, cast out of the human and divine systems of care and protection that sustain life. Thereafter, a sense of alienation, of disconnection, pervades every relationship, from the most intimate familial bonds to the most abstract affiliations of community and religion. (Herman, 1992, p. 52)

Herman (1992) went on to suggest that the traumatic event "destroys the belief that one can be oneself in relation to others" (p. 53). Such a breakdown would make it hard to be present and study with a tutor or in a group and also take part in the process of finding shared meaning in text.

Children and adults who are abused can easily feel that they have been singled out because they are bad. They feel different and separate from others. They often lose connection to family, friends, and community:

> Trauma permanently changes one's personal construction of reality . . . people may begin to appear less benevolent, events less random, and living more encumbered. . . . (Root, 1992, p. 229)

> Traumatic events call into question basic human relationships. They breach the attachments of family, friendship, love, and community. They shatter the construction of the self that is formed and sustained in relation to others. (Herman, 1992, p. 51)

When children are abused, they frequently feel that they have changed as a result and are no longer the same as others. The learner I tutor was convinced that she was the only person who had ever been abused and was amazed when we read about other people's experiences.

Batterers frequently actively isolate women, cutting them off from the world at large to make them more vulnerable and limit the possibilities of access to support resources:

> Virtually any social contact can serve as an occasion for the abuser to become pathologically jealous. Any time the woman is away from home, the abuser may obsessively imagine that she is having an affair. Thus jealousy,

overpossessiveness, and intrusiveness tend to lead to the isolation of the battered woman. She may cease normal social activities, stop seeing her friends and family, and become a prisoner in her own home, sometimes without ever needing to actually lock the door, although it is not unusual for the batterer to lock her in the house without easy access to a telephone. (Walker, 1994, p. 60)

For immigrant and refugee women, the isolation may be particularly acute:

Isolation is a fact of life for all women who are battered. For immigrant and refugee women, however, the isolation of abuse is compounded by language and cultural barriers, racism and the fact that many immigrant and refuge women are far from their friends and their extended families. (McLeod & Shin, 1990, p. 7)

Citing the numerous systemic barriers, McLeod and Shin (1990) suggested that immigrant women are likely to remain trapped with a violent spouse and so remain terrifyingly isolated:

. . . most immigrant or refugee women conclude that living with abuse at the hands of their husbands could be prefereable to the abuse, uncertainty and bureaucratic obstacles they would endure if they leave. (p. 10)

Women who attend a literacy program while living with a violent husband or boyfriend may have particular difficulty because of the threat of increased violence posed by connections made within the program. Yet the program may provide a rare opportunity to decrease the isolation. One literacy worker explained:

Literacy programs are a potentially powerful place to support women survivors. For women whose movement is so tightly controlled by the men in their lives, a literacy program may be the one place that they are allowed to go (it's more likely than counselling, for instance). And we get to see them (sometimes) over a longer period of time. I was so often struck by how our centre was the safest place that many of my students had in their lives.

Therapist Clarissa Chandler explained that trauma says, "I don't belong, I should not be connected." For those who experience many losses, their reflection on their life is on disconnection rather than connection. That sense of disconnection reinforces the sense of having "no value and no meaning." She explained:

> Every time I experience another loss and another disconnection every other loss and death and disconnection is revisited and it says that I am primarily disconnected. And connection is what gives us meaning and understanding of our value. (n.d., *Weaving the Story*).

In journal writings, Lewis (1998) spoke of her desire for connection and her resistance to connecting:

> Feb. 12, 1997
> How subtle the erasures of self are: withdrawal rather than speech, compromise, rationalize, facilitate for others. How deep is my hatred of my need, my longing for connection. My capacity to adjust silently to the conditions of my life frightens me. I get glimmers of the depth of my self-hate, the sword it holds in judgment over my everyday actions not to be an imposition, not to let the past explode all over the present, not to expose who and what I am, not to deserve the life I want. (p. 152)

Clearly connection is important, yet complicated and fraught.

Connections in Literacy Learning

In many literacy programs, much emphasis is placed on the creation of community and an assumption that the shared experience of difficulty with reading and writing will create commonality between literacy learners. In the light of these insights about the profound complexity of connection, it is not surprising that more often there is competition and tension between learners. Sometimes the difficulty may be because students know each other prior to the program:

> Literacy students in Duncan tend to have lived in Duncan for a long time. They all know each other. They have histories from the street, and from the food bank, and they all know each other. (interview, Salt Spring Island, British Columbia, November/December 1996)

Similarly, the student I tutor has a complicated history with many of the learners in her program; she knows many of their stories and does not like them. Workers often seek to create community, knowing nothing of these inside stories that may limit desire for connection between learners.

Most essential, perhaps, for literacy learning is the ability to connect to the self. To connect to others, a woman has to connect to herself. If she experiences herself as only fragments, she will struggle even to connect with herself. Ability to connect with the whole self, "with all of oneself in the same place at the same time, unified" (Markova, 1994, p. 68), may be

a challenge for many women who have experienced trauma. The therapeutic literature talks at length about the fragmentation of knowledge,
memory, and emotion (Herman, 1992) and change to the self brought
about by the experience of trauma. Chronic trauma, Herman suggested,
may cause a woman to "lose the sense that she has any self at all" (p. 86).
The process of writing may help in the process of reintegration—of rein-
venting a self. As Bass and Davis (1988) suggested:

> By going back and writing about what happened, you also re-experience
> feelings and are able to grieve. You excavate the sites in which you've bur-
> ied memory and pain, dread and fury. You relive your history. (p. 27)

Holistic learning supports women to reintegrate themselves. Bringing
their whole selves to the learning process might also enhance learning.

A woman cannot learn to read and write unless she can make a connection between a word and its meaning. The ability to connect words to
experience, to find meaning in print, to make connections between this
word and that word, between experience and meanings, between experiences and the connections of causality (this happened because that happened) are all connections essential to finding meaning in written stories
or descriptions. Questioning how this difficulty might be an element of
disconnection, rather than framing the trouble learners often have with
taking meaning from print and following a story as poor memory or lack
of concentration, makes me curious about whether exploring such dimensions of connection further might be valuable to enhance literacy
learning.

In a women's group I ran many years ago, I had a vision that women
would work together and support each other. The reality was quite different. Women seemed to find little common ground. They wanted to speak
about their experience, but did not want to listen to each other speaking;
they wanted my attention, but had little interest in getting the attention
of the other women. Although all the women in the group had been
marginalized and most, I now realize, had experienced profound trauma,
their differences—of race, ability, age, educational experience, and
role—seemed more marked than their similarities. A white woman with
mental health issues had been sterilized; a woman from the Caribbean
was first a mother and a grandmother; a white woman with intellectual
disabilities who grew up in Canada had been mistreated in school; a
woman who grew up in the Caribbean had had no opportunity to attend
school; a woman with physical disabilities and speech difficulties wanted
to tell her story, but few had the patience to listen to her; a woman who

had experienced abuse throughout her life was terrified to reveal anything. Most often, rather than connection, there was competition for
each learner's needs to be met. The strongest connection between the
group was when they were furious at me for betraying their trust—when I
did not return to the group after the previously mentioned summer away.

With new insights about the complexity of connection, I would now
explore the commonalities and differences—the shared and conflicting
needs—more actively with a group. For example, I might try doing varied
exercises around identifying commonalities and differences. I would get
women writing about what they think is unique about themselves and
what is the same as others in the group. Perhaps I would ask women to
interview each other and give the group a description of the other person.
As a whole group, we might create a character that had some characteris-
tic of each of the women and together tell stories and write about her ad-
ventures. We could play with writing, where each woman writes a line, or
even a word, and the paper is folded over and the next person adds a
line, and so on, until strange stories are created. As I reflect, I know that
many fine ideas are hard to carry out in practice as each participant jos-
tles for attention and has difficulty attending to others. However, I believe that consciously focusing on building connection and testing out
ideas with connection as a primary goal would create different possibilities for connections within a group.

I led a learner leadership group composed of many learners, volunteers, and paid workers who had experienced trauma. Rather than this
leading to connection and solidarity, the experience of trauma seemed to
lead to a pattern of competing needs. One learner said that she thought
many learners "have never had enough attention" so are always trying to
gain the attention of the facilitators. A literacy administrator I spoke to
thought support groups for learners who start in a program at the same
time might help learners stay connected to each other and to the program. I found that an interesting idea, but it also made me reflect on the
difficulties so many learners have listening to each other and connecting.
Learning to listen to and support others is a challenge that takes time and
practice. One participant in the online seminar said, "connecting, trusting, working as a group has to be learned." She added that such learning
makes a difference to other learning. I agree and am curious to explore
how much of a difference it might make to all aspects of learning.

During a learner leadership project, taking on a common task together
built a sense of shared purpose by the end of our process of working together. Several connections have been developed subsequently; more often along the way, however, it seemed to me that the tensions and ani-

mosities within the group were increasing rather than decreasing. In the future, I would stop and spend time along the way to explore this perception carefully and to build solidarity, rather than assuming that connections would naturally happen (Horsman, in press).

Learners often speak of having common cause with other learners against staff. Although I have problems with this divide, it does speak to the sense that learners often have of being *different*. It perhaps leads to the conviction some learners hold that learners should be able to find common cause:

> We have let the big THEY have the right to direct us because we haven't worked together to learn and change the old ways of dependency. . . .
>
> As long as we continue in this divided, dependent and self-destructive way the established literacy community will continue to use the "we know what's best for you" attitude and our voices will never be heard.
>
> A united voice will be heard.
>
> I would like to see a solely run coalition of students with a united voice funded by the government and employing consumers only. (Lovell, 1996, p. 79)

Perhaps the belief that learners must share common cause against the rest leaves learners few options to explain the divisions between them except self-blame and criticism of learners' failure to work together. The language that *all learners are in it together* assumes there will be connection. Experience shows me that this is not necessarily so and may be a dangerous assumption that fuels future disappointment and blame. My future approach would be to offer a wide range of activities designed to build connections between learners, including exploring their commonalities and differences and examining the factors that create divisions and competition among learners.

Building Possible Connections

When I asked about the issue of connection during the online seminar, Lynda Toews, a literacy worker from British Columbia, suggested that taking on a task together is key to building connections. She also drew attention to the danger of individualized learning as a divisive process:

> It seems to me that the most successful groups I have shared in have been groups in which the focus became a joint initiative of some kind. I've done everything from writing a cookbook, to raising money for a microwave in the lunchroom, to helping a student move, to playing sports, to planning a

field trip, to running a food bank drive. Even if the effort is of short dura-
tion, the benefits in terms of group connection have been long term.

Incidentally, I think that too much emphasis on individual self-paced
learning can isolate learners, impoverish their learning experience and ruin
their chances for success. (Alphaplus Literacy & Violence Online Seminar, February–April 1998)

Individualized learning is often offered as a solution to the problem of
learners' different and competing needs in a group. However, the loss of
any possibility for building connection, along with difficulties with control
and meaning when learners work in isolation, make it an extremely problematic solution.

Another worker, Janet Isserlis from Rhode Island, drew attention to
the importance of sufficient time for learners to build trust and develop
connections:

. . . thinking about connection—about building community and trust—
makes me re-realize that a huge piece of this is simply time. I'm not suggesting that an unsafe place will enable people to feel any closer to one another or more trusting over time, but I am reminding myself that even very
supportive and caring facilitators/co-learners can not expect that trust will
necessarily develop in any particular time period simply because time has
passed. I do believe that as learners experience different ways of being
around one another—discussing a range of topics, engaging in all kinds of
literacy work—that trust does stand an excellent chance of growing.
(Alphaplus Literacy & Violence Online Seminar, February–April 1998)

Judy Hofer, a literacy worker in rural Massachusetts, described some of
the factors that built connection in her group in the online seminar:

1. Making our lives beautiful, creating a space.
They literally created a room of their own in the back of our Center and
made it beautiful: Painted it, hung up their favorite sayings and their own
art work.

2. We ate a lot (donuts) and drank a lot of coffee. (Not so great for the
physical health, but wonderful for health reaped from just hanging out together.)

3. The women made Tshirts for themselves that said, "together we bloom"
and had painted them with flowers.

4. A sense of purpose: We are making a video! (Alphaplus Literacy & Violence Online Seminar, February–April 1998)

She went on to describe factors that she felt hindered connection between the learners in the group she led:

1. Lots of confusion about the commitment to the group: the women wanted to give each other "permission" to not come on a particular day if they weren't in the right frame of mind. Yet, they were so disappointed and frustrated when others didn't show. This became especially problematic when we faced deadlines with our project. Agreeing to and holding one another accountable to a common set of ground rules was one of the most difficult things for me as the facilitator. (I can so understand what many of you have been saying about the need to respect and uphold one's boundaries and limits. The flip side is to also "challenge" one another to follow through on commitments both to oneself and the whole group.)

2. Difficulty for the women to deal with their differences. It was especially hard for some of the white women to also see how they are in the one-up position relative to the women of color in the group. (Alphaplus Literacy & Violence Online Seminar, February–April 1998)

Judy reminded us of the factors that make connection difficult. There may be many limits and challenges to building connections in programs, particularly where the gap between worker and learners is hard to bridge—where structures do not allow for creating a beautiful space where learners can feel ownership, hang out together, or take on creative and challenging tasks together. Many programs are shaped by a range of requirements, such as a limited time span, a narrow focus on a curriculum, or demands of the achievement of particular goals such as passing tests or gaining employment. Such demands can get in the way of building connections.

Connecting Around Trauma

During the course of my research, several learners talked about the *smiling face* as a way to hide the pain they were experiencing. This necessary hiding creates a barrier to communication. Listening to students talk, it became clear how many of the connections around shared experience of violence cannot easily be drawn on because of the profound shame and silence around violence.

When I interviewed a group of learners at Malaspina College in British Columbia, all of whom had experienced violence and agreed to talk to me about the impact this had on their learning, one learner did not want to be part of the group. She seemed scared to participate. However, she had come to talk to me at the group time by mistake and was quickly drawn in by the other students. She began to tell her story and they told pieces of their stories to help her believe that she, too, would come through and could cope alone with small children. By the end of the session, they had exchanged phone numbers and agreed to babysit each others' children and offer whatever support was needed. Several women talked about having chosen people in their life to replace families that had not supported them. I had a sense that this group might lead to more adopted grandmothers and mothers.

These women showed the value of connection for support to help each other hang in there when school, parenting alone, living on welfare, and dealing with stalkers and memories felt too hard. This group of women were all adamant that if the college were to run a support group for survivors they would not attend because they would not want to be seen attending it. They told me that they had been scared to be seen coming to my room and had each ducked in quickly hoping no one would see them. Yet the value of connecting with others with a shared experience was clear as they quickly stopped talking to me and began talking to and supporting each other. I wonder whether greater visibility of issues of violence in the college or program that makes clear that violence is a social and political issue, rather than private and shameful, might help shift some of this burden and foster greater connections around shared experience.

Women at the Learning Center in Alberta spoke of not telling about their abuse in the program because they wanted to protect those who did not know about it and because they were afraid that they might be judged. One learner, Lilian Gallant, spoke to me and fellow students about the abuse she had experienced in her life in the group interview. She said it was the first time she had spoken about this in the program. At the end, she talked about how good she felt to have shared in that way. Then she wrote about it and gave me a copy. After she had described her experience in her marriage, she ended by saying:

> Today in the Women's Group it was good to talk about what happened and not be afraid any more to tell people that I was an abused wife with children and I don't have to feel ashamed about it as it was not my fault. It took a lot of years before I could say that it wasn't my fault. I wasn't to blame, put the blame on the abuser that's who did this. I truly hope he feels guilty because that is how he made me feel for all those years. I often wonder how could you do this to someone you love. I wonder if there is an answer. (Gallant, unpublished writing, 1996)

Later she wrote a piece about her experience, which she made public in a collection of writings from her program (Gallant, 1997). The interview session with a group of women who had already worked together for some time, and naming violence and learning as the topic of the meeting, allowed this woman to break a long silence about her experience.

During the Learning Centre session, there was much talk about how hard it is to share such stories in the program. As I thought about the sensitive discussion in this women's group, where a learner was now ready to trust the response she would get, I was reminded of a comment made online by Karen Ritchie from New South Wales, Australia, that brought home the type of reaction this student had been cautious to avoid:

> There is often a sense of "they deserve it," "they should know better," "what do they expect," when discussing issues of women and violence. In a class recently, one woman laughingly announced that her sister wouldn't be in class today as she had been beaten by her husband, but it was her own fault, she should have known better. (Alphaplus Literacy & Violence Online Seminar, February–April 1998)

Ritchie commented that "women are often guilty of 'keeping other women in the snake pit.' " In the Learning Centre group, one of the staff questioned what the program could do to make it easier for women to name their experiences of violence and expect to get a supportive hearing from others in the program. The group concluded that educating those who have not experienced abuse so that they would understand the issues, be less likely to judge, and less likely to say, "why don't you or why didn't you just leave" might make a major change in the atmosphere in the program. Such a shift of attitude might encourage women who have experienced violence to feel less ashamed or responsible, which could be crucial to their sense of self and whether they choose to tell their story.

Judy Hofer, whose insights on building connections were included earlier, described how questions of violence were opened up in her program:

> Commonality between students and teachers in terms of issues of class and being a survivor—the amazing day that started our effort began when a teacher facilitated my class and she shared her own story of growing up poor and being a survivor. Her disclosure inspired the other women to then share with each other the stories that they had either been discussing with each other outside of class (during breaks) or one-on-one with me. Having a teacher who shared their histories and openly discussed her experiences in class was a radical, transforming act. Finally the class was turned upside down in terms of being a place where people brought their real lives to the table. I realized how important it is for programs to have teachers from similar backgrounds as students. I must say that I doubt that

I, as a middle-class white woman who's not a survivor, could ever have brought the discussion to the table . . . and not in this kind of liberating way in which students aren't inadvertently made to feel ashamed of their own lives. (Alphaplus Literacy & Violence Online Seminar, February–April 1998)

Such an opening might not always be possible in a program and might not be desirable in all situations. A worker's disclosure might put pressure on learners with poor boundaries to disclose even if they are not ready, do not feel safe, or have no one to support them as they begin to take on this reality. Nevertheless, it worked in this instance. Care to ensure that supports are available and encourage learners to think about their own boundaries and limits ahead of time might help learners take care of themselves or make use of the available resources where they are needed.

Judy Hofer also wrote about the importance of workers making connections and finding supports. She dove straight into the discussion because of her own sense of isolation as she tried to understand how to address the issues of violence in adult education:

This work of addressing issues of violence in women's lives in ways that are thorough, respectful, responsible is so incredibly difficult. So many times I knew I was "in" over my head. (Women's lives were sometimes further jeopardized as their partners were increasingly threatened; after discussions which brought their rage to the surface, a few of the woman took that anger out on their own children; I heard a rumor in the community that we were seen as a "bunch of dykes" and I questioned our safety as well as that of all my students.) The obvious answer of our getting support and making referrals was not so easy in our context. We were in a rural area, without public transportation and without immediate support services other than a counseling organization which did not have a good reputation among the women. Eventually, we were able to get organizations from other towns to support us. I can't emphasize enough how important it is to not do this work alone! (Alphaplus Literacy & Violence Online Seminar, February–April 1998)

Like the woman who originally experiences trauma, the literacy worker who learns second-hand about trauma can easily become isolated. Preserving and building new connections is important for workers. Connections that literacy workers and programs might make with other services that can support addressing issues of violence in literacy programs, and a variety of supports for literacy workers, are discussed later in detail (chap. 7).

When literacy programming is carried out in recognition of the complex terrain that connection represents (rather than on the assumption that connections will inevitably occur) and in a context of visibility of issues of violence, connections that support learning could be built, new insights might be recognized, and new possibilities explored.

MEANING

Meaning and connection are clearly intertwined. Where shared meaning cannot be located, connection is diminished. Isolation and disconnection also inhibit possibilities for exploring shared meaning. Literacy learners often have difficulty dreaming of possibilities or imagining goals—difficulty in finding meaning, in life and in print. They may also have difficulty trusting their own knowledge. Many learners have enormous difficulty finding meaning in a text even when they are able to decipher the words. Much of this difficulty may be about limited vocabulary and lack of experience with a variety of words. However, the concept of traumatic loss of *meaning* may also be relevant and suggests new questions.

The therapeutic literature often talks about the loss of meaning resulting from trauma. Herman (1992) stated that traumatic events "undermine the belief systems that give meaning to human experience" (p. 51). Agger (1994) further described the profoundly shattering effect of experiences of violence:

> In the confrontation with violence and assault, we meet universal, existential questions which Geertz (1973, pp. 87–141) calls the "problem with evil," "the problem of suffering"—in the final sense, "the problem about meaning." It is not a coincidence that researchers (and therapists) who work within this area often end their presentations of the problem by raising existential questions. This is also the case for the direct victims of violence: the meaningless suffering and evil are unbearable. Everyone seeks meaning, understanding, a larger context. (p. 19)

Agger also asserted that out of the serious anxiety created by loss of meaning can come new meaning:

> . . . if we succeed in giving a new meaning to chaos and cleanse ourselves of shame and impurity, then this can also be the beginning of a revision of the traditional patterns of meaning. In this way, a traumatic experience can also become a transforming experience of great positive value. (p. 14)

Loss of meaning in life in the literacy context seems to connect to the profound difficulties many learners have with imagining goals or dreaming of possibilities for change. Kali Tal (1996) explained more about how the problem with loss of meaning complicates conveying experience:

> On the surface, language appears unchanged—survivors still use the word terror, non traumatized audiences read and understand the word terror, and the dislocation of meaning is invisible until one pays attention to the cry of survivors, "What can we do to share our visions? Our words can only evoke the incomprehensible. Hunger, thirst, fear, humiliation, waiting, death; for us these words hold different realities. This is the ultimate tragedy of the victims." (p. 16)

From such a place of inadequacy of shared meaning, both reading and writing may be challenging. I am reminded of the learner I described earlier who had not dared to speak or write of her experience of violence, fearing the reactions of her listeners. I realize now that wariness also entailed fears about the lack of shared meaning. She could not risk that listeners might interpret her story and give it a meaning that shamed or blamed her until she was confident of an interpretation that blamed the abuser and not herself. Similarly, the learner I worked with could recognize that she was not to blame for the abuse she experienced, but quickly slid back into feeling ashamed and guilty. Only recently, after many years, has she reached a place where she could write about our work together and read it in public. She wrote: "I'm not different, I'm a valuable person. I don't feel I'm the world's worst, I no longer have to hide the abuse" (Garrity, 1998). She also described the value of learning that she was not the only one to have experienced abuse:

> [Jenny] brings books and poems and reads them. We read stories of other people who have gone through this. This really help me a great deal. She's read things to show me that I'm not the only one who has been abused. There are lots, so I shouldn't feel ashamed. (Garrity, 1998)

It is harder in isolation, without the support of shared meaning with others, to become confident about placing the blame for violence firmly on the perpetrator, especially in a society that often shifts the blame to the victim.

Many literacy learners experience difficulty finding meaning in the reading process. In particular, writing a personal story may seem impossible. Lewis (1998) spoke of pleasure in reading while detailing her difficulties with writing:

> I remember waiting to answer the spelling quiz or the times tables, hoping I would get it right, fearing humiliation. My printing was smudged and messy. Pleased I could read like the other children, it quickly became my

salvation, a way to live that required only inactivity and solitary silence. I could live out my desires without once making a mistake, being laughed at or punished. For once there was only one message (not two or three) to decipher and negotiate. Through books I could think, feel and know I was alive. That has shaped who I have become, my "normal."

Writing was a problem. Like my mother, it seemed to require routine. I would sit and wonder how, in a sentence or a paragraph or a page, I could convey the wholeness, the beauty of what I could see in my mind. Each sentence seemed to negate or deny part of that picture. With the shattering of a sense of self before I had language, it is not surprising that expression presented a puzzle. Who was left to weave meaning between the shattered parts? Expression could also penetrate the mask of the terrorised child who knew too much. My survival depended on her disguise. I thought much and wrote little. (p. 70)

"Weaving meaning between the shattered parts" is a powerful phrase, suggestive of the difficulties literacy learners may have finding meaning, particularly as they try to write about their life experiences. Despite the difficulty with this task, Tal (1996) asserted the value of the attempt to tell the personal story:

> Literature of trauma is written from the need to tell and retell the story of the traumatic experience, to make it "real" both to the victim and to the community. Such writing serves both as validation and cathartic vehicle for the traumatized author. (p. 21)
>
> Each one [authors of autobiographies of experiences of abuse] also affirms the process of storytelling as a personally reconstitutive act—changing the order of things as they are, and working to prevent the enactment of similar horrors in the future. (p. 121)

Such bearing witness can be a way to give "meaning to meaninglessness" (Tal, 1996, p. 120). In literacy programs—where women have the possibility to speak and write about their experiences—this may be a valuable step in their struggle to put their experience outside themselves, find perspective, create meaning, and make connections with similar experiences of others.

Contested Meaning

Learners I have worked with often seem to have difficulty trusting their own knowledge or their own understanding of their experience. Elly Danica (1996) wrote about "learn[ing] to hide from the truth." She had learned early that telling about her experience only created conflict; instead she learned to lie to herself. As she explained:

> I learned to ignore how I really felt and feel as I was told I ought to feel. I began to live on two levels: the level of responding to the abusers', my mother's and my teachers' expectations; and the level of my denied inner life. I soon found I was happier if I did not acknowledge that inner life, and I abandoned it in favour of the image that other people wanted of me— of a devout and obedient Catholic child—which seemed so much safer. (p. 17)

The denial of any connection with their own feelings and thoughts, and of the possibility of holding to their own judgments, may contribute to the difficulty that those who have been abused experience holding onto meaning. Lack of support in society for the meanings that learners might make from their standpoint may also contribute to this difficulty. The learner I tutor often tells me *facts* according to everybody to whom she has spoken. Only with much prompting do I learn sometimes that she puts a different meaning on the event herself. Holding onto her own interpretation or finding a balance among a variety of interpretations is something she seems to find extremely difficult.

In a 1988 article, Elaine Gaber-Katz and I quoted Dale Spender on the male reference point to meaning in language. We added our own perspective about the need for poor women to have the opportunity to speak and write their own meanings:

> Males, as the dominant group, have produced language, thought and reality. Historically it has been the structures, the categories and the meanings which have been invented by males—though not of course all males—and they have then been validated by references to other males. In this process women have played little or no part. It has been male subjectivity which has been the source of those meanings, including the meaning that their own subjectivity is objectivity. (Spender, 1980, p. 143)
>
> Many literacy practitioners recognize language also excludes those who are poor . . .
>
> We know that it is "crazy-making" if our experiences are misnamed or if there are no names for our experiences. Chris Weedon says that, "What an event means to an individual depends on the ways of interpreting the world, on the discourses available to her at any particular moment." (1987, p. 79)
>
> This experience of going through life and not finding your experiences represented is what literacy learners experience. It is powerful when liter-

acy learners get together in groups and name their experience. (Gaber-
Katz & Horsman, 1988, p. 64)

At that time, we were writing about poor women in general. My research has helped me to see that the silence and exclusion can be compounded—for women who have also experienced violence, who also
have mental health issues, who are also racialized, who also have disabilities, or any combination of such factors—by the difficulties of naming experience and finding language that speaks the complexities already
named differently from outside the experience. Thinking about women
who have experienced violence, I can now see that it is crucial that they
have opportunities to find language to name their own experiences, to
develop and articulate their own meanings of their lives, to have those
meanings read or heard, and to learn that they are not alone and that
shared meaning is possible.

In the online seminar literacy worker, Beth Sauerhaft talked about her
experience supporting a learner to hang onto her own meaning of her experience in the face of redefinition by her emotionally violent husband.
The student had been to the library to try to solve a problem:

> [She] wanted to improve her "intimate" relationship with her husband so
> she went to the library (where her literacy class meets) and read some ma-
> terials about "communication" in sexual relationships with partners and as
> she put it "changed some of her ways with her husband." Her husband no-
> ticed the changes and immediately accused her of sleeping around for how
> else could she know about such things!!! (Alphaplus Literacy & Violence
> Online Seminar, February–April 1998)

This worker described the reassurance she gave the student as a way to
"do what we can to give someone back to themselves." That is a powerful
image. It implies that being denied your own meaning is a process of being denied your own self. In this case, the literacy worker helped the student contest the damaging meaning her husband assigned to her changes.
Without support, her husband's meaning might have held sway and the
process of disconnection with self could be relentless.

An example of the different meanings that simple everyday words can
hold was described by two academics, Sheryl Gowen and Carol Bartlett
(1997), in an article about workplace literacy. They begin their article
with these words:

> Ms. Taylor: I tell my girls, when they have a fight, to go into the kitchen,
> their friends are in the kitchen.

Carol: You mean the knife?
Ms. Taylor: Yes, the knife, the ice pick, the boiling water, the scissors. (p. 141)

Ms. Taylor may be one of the African-American working poor women students in the literacy program who the authors explained taught "two white, middle-class academics . . . that their notions about women and literacy were reductive and naive." These academic women—Gowen and Bartlett—described how their notions of literacy and change were radically challenged by women's stories of the violence in their lives, which escalated when they joined a GED class:

> About two years ago a young woman with two small boys and a "live-in man" came to a GED program at a local technical school in the metro-Atlanta area. She was very bright and wanted to get her GED, but the closer she got the more her man beat her. She confided all of this to her teacher, who encouraged her to get her man to come with her to classes, but he refused and the beatings escalated. Finally she got tired of it all and shot him one night. She is now serving time for murder and her children are in foster care. She does have her GED, but she has 12 more years of prison time to serve as well. (p. 153)

This story, along with one from another woman whose ex-husband told her his violence was "because of her GED class support group," sobered the authors and forced them "to reflect upon the particular consequences of literacy for women who are poor and undereducated and who are caught in abusive relationships" (1997, p. 153). I am left thinking with horror about the inadequacy of the instructor's suggestion that the woman should get her man to come to class. I wonder whether the instructor's assumption is that literacy will transform this violent man or whether she thinks that if the man is in class he will see what is happening and that it is no threat to his control. Literacy can have many different meanings, but for women in violent situations, the meaning can be danger.

In this article, Gowen and Bartlett (1997) contrasted Ms. Taylor's meaning of kitchen with their own experience. For them, the kitchen is "central to family and community"; they have never had to think of what weapons it might contain:

> It is where we perform the food rituals associated with holidays, birthdays, weddings, child-birth, anniversaries, illnesses, and funerals. It is where we have nurtured and taught our children and where we still share chores with our husbands. It is where we tell our stories at the end of the day, a

place to reconnect. It has witnessed some of our families' most spectacular fights. It has also mistakenly been a place for trying to fill the deepest of hungers with mere food. The kitchen has defined our roles as homemakers, mothers, and community members, but it has never once in either of our lives been a place where we thought about how we could use its tools to defend ourselves from the violence of the men we have lived with. (p. 154)

A student I know has another meaning for the kitchen. For her it is the place where the knives will forever remind her of the violence that has been used against her. For the Toronto women raped by the "balcony rapist" who found the knife he threatened each woman with in her own kitchen, the kitchen may have become a stark reminder that they were not safe—in bed in their own home—in the place they might previously have felt safest from the world (*Jane Doe* v. *Toronto Commissioners of Police*, 1998). For these women, the meaning of *kitchen* and *knives* was changed, and the connections between the concepts of *home* and *safety* were also irreparably severed.

These same crimes are also a reminder that the different meaning made of incidents is not insignificant and can even be life threatening. The Toronto police force judged that the rapes perpetrated by the balcony rapist were not violent because there was no additional violence beyond the rape and that women would become hysterical if warned that they were vulnerable to attack. This led to low priority for police resources and no warning to be given to women in the neighborhood. Like the judgment that women who have experienced trauma are *overreacting* to subsequent trauma, meaning is often made by those outside the experience; when it is those outside the experience who have the power to assert that theirs is the true meaning, it can be dangerous. It is unlikely that the women raped by the balcony rapist would have believed that it was wiser not to warn them or that the rape they experienced was not violent. Questioning dominant meanings of violence and the concept of *normal*, pervasive in society, is fundamental if literacy programs are to be places where trauma survivors can explore their own meanings of their experiences, free from labeling, medical diagnoses, or demands to *get back to normal*.

Lynda Toews, a participant in the online seminar from British Columbia, suggested that the denial of the reality of abuse (e.g., "abuse doesn't happen, or at least doesn't happen to 'nice' people, or 'good' people, or to people in 'my culture' ") makes it harder for women who have experienced abuse to insist on meaning for the experience. She thought texts that "speak directly to their situation," their own writing, or the writing of those in similar circumstances are crucial to help learners create their own meanings. She suggested that:

> . . . if a learner is having difficulty finding meaning in a text, it might work to concentrate for a while on reading her own meaning (that is her own journal writing), and using that as a bridge to finding meaning in other readings. (Alphaplus Literacy & Violence Online Seminar, February–April 1998)

This worker wondered whether second language learners also need read about the reality of violence in their own language to help them believe that it does happen in their own home country and that the experience can be named even in their own language.

Another worker, Ann Unterreiner from Arizona, suggested:

> STORY STORY STORY . . . Literature is a powerful way to move the personal in to a public arena for discussion and reflection. Adolescent literature is wonderful . . . reading to students is also wonderful. (Alphaplus Literacy & Violence Online Seminar, February–April 1998)

It is not easy to know what material will be helpful for each learner. Learners have told me that they found it valuable to read experiences similar to their own and that it was too hard to read similar experiences, even more so when they knew the stories were true.

Exploring Meaning

Literacy programs can be a place where meaning is explored. Rather than simply assuming that students can find meaning in text, in their own stories, or in life, many aspects of the struggle for meaning could be taken up and problematized. Playing with multiple possible meanings of a text or an oral account might help learners explore different readings and understand that the meaning is not simply in the text and eluding them, but is something they create in reading. Learning that meaning is being made by the reader, not the writer alone, and that any piece of writing has many potential meanings is crucial to allowing people who have always had their meanings contested or denied to begin to see the possibility for making their own meaning.

A variety of ways to explore multiple meanings could be used in literacy work. Learners could tell a story from many different locations to explore multiple accounts of an event. They could read different versions of the same history or event and then tell new stories that were omitted. Work of this sort contrasts with the more common comprehension work, which tends to focus on the truth about a story.[3] Traditional comprehension work—where students are required to find the *right* answer to questions about the meaning of the text—can form a part of the process of denying learners their own meaning making, particularly when stories make no sense in learners' worlds. For example, I remember a workbook I looked at long ago:

> One story is about a Vietnamese couple. In the illustrations they are shown sitting in comfortable chairs either side of a fireplace. The story is about them hearing a strange noise outside which makes them very worried about burglars. Finally they look out the door to discover that the noise is only a cat which wants to get in. The story tells us that the cat is friendly like American people. (Atkinson & Horsman, 1989)

Such a story would make it hard for immigrants to speak of their experiences of being immigrants in a strange country. This may include feeling at risk of violence, experiencing Americans as unfriendly, and having troubling memories of the oppression and violence they have fled. If material of this sort has a place at all in literacy, it must be taken apart and compared with the many different stories that could be told, making space for a variety of more realistic meanings of the immigrant experience.

Another story in the same book described a man who was going to the store to pick up something. Before he leaves, his wife asks him to buy an item of food as well. Each time he is about to leave, she adds another item to the list until finally he suggests that when she is going shopping she might like to buy the item he needs. The message of the story is clear: Shopping for food is a woman's job; men are reasonable, nice, and patient, whereas women are silly. Such a story used uncritically offers no space for women to question the embedded assumptions about men and women and their respective roles. In the face of such clear meanings, it would be hard for a woman to speak about her husband's anger, irrationality, or violence or her own anger at his expectations that she perform all work he judges as women's work. Such exercises make it harder for learners to imagine meanings embedded in their own lives, let alone articulate them in writing or speech in the literacy classroom.

---

[3]*Reading Stories* takes up somewhat difficult literary short stories to offer multiple readings and "encourage students to explore the stories and their readings of them for themselves" (1987, p. 120).

Creative literacy workers can design a multitude of learning activities that would enable learners to explore multiple meanings, play with the possibilities of conflicting meanings, and create new meaning through telling and reading different versions of stories. Such activities would support learners to create, or hold onto their own meanings of experience, and reconnect to meaning in their own lives.

INTEGRATE CONTROL, CONNECTION, AND MEANING

Journal Writing

Over and over again during my interviewing, literacy workers spoke about their use of journal writing. Therapists and counselors also spoke of the value of journal writing. Gradually I began to see that journals may be a tool for exploring control, connection, and meaning and can act as a bridge to goal setting in literacy programs. Journal writing can be a way to connect with the self and with others. The journal can provide a private place for writing that the learner can control. Initially the journal might be completely private; control over whether anyone else may see that writing would rest with the writer alone. Eventually a woman might choose to share sections with her instructor or other students.

Writing in a journal can also be a way to create meaning—to put an experience outside the self and find new meaning—as well as new understandings through gaining distance and from the responses of readers. Journal writing is a tool recommended not only to literacy learners, but also to anyone who wants to think through an experience:

> One handy thing about writing is that it's almost always available. At three in the morning, when you're alone or you don't want to wake your partner, when your friend's out of town, when your counselor's answering machine is on and even the cat is out prowling, your journal is there. It's quiet, cheap, and portable. A journal can help you figure out how you feel, what you think, what you need, what you want to say, how you want to handle a situation, just by writing it through. (Bass & Davis, 1988, p. 27)

Sheryl Gowen and Carol Bartlett (1997) described the journal writing process in the workers' literacy class they studied:

> The stories of abuse all came out as class members wrote in their personal journals, which Carol has used since the beginning of the classes. Carol has read and responded to these journals only when the women in the class

have wanted to open a written dialogue. Carol has encouraged but not forced this dialogue, and many of the women in the class did not initially want to share what they had written with anyone. Ms. Colbert is a good example. She began writing in her journal, held it very privately, and said that no one could look at it. Several months went by with Ms. Colbert writing in her journal privately and quietly. Then one day, Ms. Colbert told Carol she wanted to share what she had written with Carol. The story in the journal was about Ms. Colbert's sexual abuse as a child by her stepfather and her mother's refusal to protect her. She finally was rescued by her grandmother. As Carol pointed out, "it was finally a story of love and support." During all the months of private work in her journal, she had been writing the same story over and over, improving it and making it more explicit with each revision. When Carol eventually read the story, she suggested to Ms. Colbert that her story might have real value to others and asked her if she might want to share it. Finally, she wrote it anonymously for the literary magazine (called a newsletter) Carol publishes for every one in the Physical Plant. Ms. Colbert also began writing poetry as she continued writing her story. She also began publishing her poetry in the "newsletter" under her own name. Then she became interested in math, and she figured out that she could move out of public housing and into an apartment in a much better school district for only $2.00 more a month in rent. And she kept on writing her story. She began to talk to Carol about all of this, but it took months of writing and establishing trust first. These conversations were always private. No one else in the class knew about the abuse until she published it in the newsletter, but then it was still a secret of sorts because the writing was anonymous. When she and Carol talked about goals, she finally explained, "Before I didn't have any goals. The secret took up all my space for goals. Now I don't have a secret and I have goals." (pp. 146–147)

Journals can be a place for writing that learners control. Encouraging learners to keep the journal private or make their own choice about whether they want others to read the journal, or sections of it, can offer learners an opportunity to explore making choices and take control over their own writing. Joy So, when working at a literacy program in Winnipeg, Manitoba, set up a system where much of the learners' writing is private unless they mark on it that she may read it. In this way, she extends learners control, creating a situation where they practice making choices and experience having those choices respected:

There are a lot of reflective writing exercises we do as well, such as "think about this," talk alouds, etc. Since very personal pieces of writing are usually kept in their journal, for certain reflective pieces I will instruct learners to mark "ok" at the top of the paper if it's alright for me to read them. If I see an "ok," I'll read it. If I don't, then I won't read it even though we go through the portfolios. Their journals are kept in their portfolios which are in a big box right at the front of the classroom. In this way learners see for themselves that everything is not "just all talk," "She does it." This leads to the trust and the feeling of safety they have with us (tutors and instructors) in the program. This is especially important because they are accustomed to being with men who always say one thing and then do another. I know that the instructors and I are very conscious about saying something and then following through on it—and the importance of such actions. (interview, Winnipeg, Manitoba, December 1996)

Journal writing can also provide a way for a woman to connect with herself, writing initially for herself alone as reader. Then when she is ready, she may feel able to connect with her teacher and perhaps finally with others in her class or, like Ms. Colbert, with a wider public through publishing in a newsletter. In the novel *Push*, narrator Precious Jones writes her own journal in a literacy program and through it comes to an understanding of herself and her life. She begins with a dialogue journal with her teacher:

> You know how you write to teacher'n she write back to you in the same journal book like you talkin' on paper and you could SEE your talk coming back to you when the teacher answer you back. I mean thas what had made me really like writing in the beginning, knowing my teacher gonna write me back when I talk to her. (Sapphire, 1996, p. 94)

This novel provides a vivid account of the journal as a way for a literacy student to create a connection with herself and her teacher. The idea that writing is a way of making talk visible was important for this student and helped make her journal a place where she could give new meaning to her experience—seeing it outside herself and through her teacher's eyes.

Andres Muro, who coordinates a literacy program at a community college in El Paso, Texas, which serves mostly women immigrants from Mexico, wrote about recognizing the value of journal writing:

> Regarding the issue of control and connection, we discovered a few years ago (by accident) that journal writing was one means for the students to gain some sense of control and connection. In a particular class, the instructor would encourage the students to write anything they wanted in a journal. The rule was that they should write anything that came to mind without thinking about grammar, spelling or punctuation. Nobody would check this. Eventually, the instructor began to ask if the students wanted

to share their writings with the rest of the class (purely voluntarily). At first they were reluctant, but eventually, everybody started reading out of their journals. The students began sharing their own personal stories, discussing them together and crying every single class. The students loved this period of class time and demanded that it be included in their daily sessions. Attrition was very low in this particular class. (Alphaplus Literacy & Violence Online Seminar, February–April 1998)

This is a lovely example of creating a space for learners to gradually connect, beginning with connecting with themselves, then with the instructor, and finally with the whole group when they are ready for a wider audience. This approach might be exciting to try while watching the effect on individuals and the group, observing the connections to see if they gradually develop and change.

Andres Muro also drew attention to a problem with such journals:

While the instructor controlled the class and expected the emotional content during "journal sharing" time, he began to feel worn down by many of the traumatic stories. We never explore these issues in much detail when they originally emerge. However, I have stressed to my staff that they ought to incorporate a journal time in their classes. (Alphaplus Literacy & Violence Online Seminar, February–April 1998)

I am tempted to agree that workers need to incorporate journal time into classes. However, I was concerned that the demand that staff *should* include journal writing could create pressure on literacy workers, preventing them from honoring their own limits. They might feel they have no option but to use journal writing even when they feel unable to cope with listening to traumatic stories. If workers feel worn down, that needs to be addressed in some way. Support should be provided to help them release the pain they hear and renew their energy. This may be especially acute in a small community where no one is a stranger. Just as I believe that it is crucial not to expect learners to override their own feelings from experience, or to just trust that someone else has the answer, as workers we need to respect each other's limits and our own.

For many learners, telling experiences in a journal may also make new space for the possibilities of imagining a future and setting goals. Elly Danica (1996) illustrated how a journal can serve as a tool to recognize change and the possibility of movement when it is hard to see day to day:

The best way for me to keep track of my progress is to look back and see how far I have come. This is why I keep a journal. When I know where I have been, I feel less anxiety about my current struggles and difficulties. . . .

> I use my journal to remind me of the importance of always moving forward in the healing process, for if I stray from the path, I find myself investing in stasis. . . . (p. 20)

Journal writing could be a place for reflection that can lead toward the possibility of creating goals. Many literacy workers already use journal writing in their practice. An awareness of the importance of working with the complexity of control, connection, and meaning might encourage instructors to explore the potential of journal writing and use it in diverse creative ways. The possibility of using journal writing as a process through which students can build connections, explore taking control, and assert and construct meaning for their experience suggests diverse ways to use journal writing.

Setting Goals

More and more in adult literacy work, the discourse of identifying measurable outcomes, or at least observable outcomes, and organizing learning around learners' goals organizes literacy practice. It is hard to question such an approach. Who does not want learners to shape their goals and learn material that will help them meet their goals? Yet for survivors of trauma working with the complexity of control, connection, and meaning, goal setting may be a challenging, if not impossible, demand. To set goals, a woman has to believe that she has some possibility of having control and connection at least to herself, and she must believe that life can have meaning.

Therapist Kathleen O'Connell talked about women's difficulties with setting goals:

> . . . If a woman, if a girl, has been abused, has had very little control and power in her life, then this idea that she can set goals, that she could have some control over her life, first of all has not been part of her experience. It may not have been part of her socialization, it may have been more connected to roles, this is what you're expected to do, and then you get married or have children and that kind of thing. And there hasn't been room for her to really think about what does she want? What would make her life more meaningful? And how does it connect to what's expected in her community and what she really wants, cause maybe there is a big difference between those things or maybe they are closer.
>
> So again this idea that a woman could have some control, could in fact plan, set goals in place . . . and even have resources to help in setting goals or following through, and have opportunities it hasn't been there so much.

I've certainly noticed in myself that sometimes I might have a sense of frustration around a woman not setting goals, but then I usually have to sit
back and go, of course, this makes perfect sense. That maybe even, the
dreams this woman had as a younger person weren't articulated or if they
were put out, it was "Too bad this is not going to happen;" "You know
you're not smart enough for that;" "Our family doesn't allow that;" "Our
community doesn't. . . . " And I think there is kind of a giving up on and a
closing down of that woman's wishes, interests, and her passions. . . .
    . . . For some women it can kind of lead to hopelessness and passivity,
this deep sense of . . . "I don't have power, things won't go my way, this is
all I deserve, and when I've tried to make things better I've been slapped
down again, I've been assaulted again." (interview, Toronto, November
1996)

Educational programs expecting women to walk in the door and set
their goals as part of the prerequisite to beginning the program may become one more experience of feeling controlled and helpless. Rather
than helping women imagine a future, such demands may leave women
feeling more completely powerless—less likely to even imagine the possibility of becoming an *actor* able to make change in their own lives.

In a study of children who have experienced trauma, Lenore Terr
(1990) looked at changed belief in the future. She argued that "a sense of
a limited future" appeared to be a good indicator of childhood psychic
trauma:

> An untraumatized child is able to plan far into the future for a career, lov-
> ing relationships, and a long life. Children come to the conclusion that pa-
> tient work will bring happy rewards. Children expect good futures even
> when their current life's circumstances are not so good. They hope to do
> better than their parents did. For most youngsters, therefore, psychic
> trauma destroys an already comfortable trust in the future. Something
> snaps. The world turns topsy-turvy. Time goes "out of joint." (p. 165)

Later, speaking about three girls who experienced trauma, Terr (1990)
suggested that their early school leaving, when other members of their
family had not left early, was an indicator of their lack of goals:

> The girls themselves appeared to have lost the ability to pursue a lifelong
> goal or to become committed to a series of life-enhancing projects. Their
> sense of futurelessness had taken material form. (p. 290)

Terr spoke of the belief that "patient work will bring happy rewards."
Several therapists talked about how that belief evaporates for abuse survi-

vors. This has major implications for setting goals. To believe in the possibility of attaining a goal, a belief in the future and faith that change can be achieved by regular work is essential.

I have noticed that the learner I work with will often say "I don't care." Recently we have begun to explore what she means. It appears that she senses she has no possibility for control and so feels there is no point in "caring" because she cannot exert her will. Lewis (1998) wrote about her lack of practice with developing and acting on any goals beyond those for survival:

> In very concrete ways I have little experience in acting to achieve my desires unless they are connected to my survival. Realizing my projects within the world requires practice connecting my body, feelings and thoughts in action. (p. 54)

For women whose energy has gone into survival, a process of learning—including practice formulating desires and working toward them—may be essential to educational programs if learners are to be able to set meaningful goals and work toward them. It cannot be assumed that goal-setting ability is something all serious students know when they enter a program.

Trauma can destroy all sense of hope that anything can ever be different. Ann Unterreiner drew attention to the importance of hope during the online seminar:

> There are organizations of support that have members who are willing to come to share their experience strength and HOPE. . . . Hope is very important. The soul is wounded and needs the healing of hope!!!! (Alphaplus Literacy & Violence Online Seminar, February–April 1998)

Literacy worker Judy Rose of British Columbia commented on the role that other students who have made changes can play in supporting learners:

> I also acquaint students with others who have some similar experiences to share information and provide some peer support. That level of support works well with people who are looking actively for ways to move ahead. (Alphaplus Literacy & Violence Online Seminar, February–April 1998)

Role models who can help instill hope may be a crucial element for those who have learned well how to endure, rather than believe in the possibility of change.

Beth Crowther wrote about an experience that clearly revealed problems with assumptions that women can just *get their act together* and make choices:

> The class I taught was for women on welfare, a GED track class. Most of them were very low level and had a long way to go. One day, when the class had only been meeting six or so months a guest speaker from the Department of Human Service came and delivered a fire and brimstone lecture on taking control of your education and your lives, and no one can do it but you, your responsibility etc., etc. After about twenty minutes of this I heard the smallest, most tired little voice I have ever heard say "how?" (Alphaplus Literacy & Violence Online Seminar, February–April 1998)

Beth Crowther went on to talk about how, after they had asked the guest speaker to leave, they settled in as a group to explore taking control. After I read that comment, I found myself hearing that tired little voice asking, "how?" That voice captured a tension. How in literacy work do we help literacy learners, and sometimes ourselves, explore taking control and setting goals without getting into a blaming mode—a "you should know that you can make choices" approach? A central issue is educators learning to truly respect how thoroughly a person has learned that she has no control and no choice, no possibility of change, and at the same time help her to learn to explore the possibilities of control and choice and imagine a future.

That learner's tired little voice suggests that, rather than feeling some hope of possibility, she was experiencing being told she had choices as disrespectful. Yet the value of supporting her to reach a place where she can begin to discover some choices and some possibility, however small, of making changes seems absolutely crucial. Supporting learners to imagine a future—to imagine the possibilities of change—is an important piece in literacy. That may be necessary for a woman to believe that she can learn and improve her reading, as well as make any other change, such as moving toward employment.

I am not advocating that literacy workers simply teach skills of planning, goal setting, and problem solving, although those may be part of what a woman may want to learn. Opportunities to play or experiment with gaining control, making connections, and finding meaning—as discussed—may be more central to the ability to imagine new possibilities. Government-initiated discourse around outcomes approaches and simplistic versions of teaching goals and making choices as simply skills—ignoring the sensitivity needed to open up possibilities for survivors of trauma—will leave too many women feeling undermined and condemned for failing to make choices and act on them to improve their life.

Those who have not experienced captivity often ask, Why would a woman stay in a violent relationship? That question haunts the media and tends to blame women for staying. There are a myriad of complex answers to why women can or cannot leave—some in the woman's beliefs about what is possible and some in the practical circumstances of the material and emotional support that may or more often may not be available. The therapeutic literature contains many vivid descriptions of the effect of captivity on the psyche. Herman (1992) argued that *learned helplessness* is an inadequate description of the "constriction in the capacities for active engagement with the world," which even a single trauma can create. Chronic trauma creates a sense of timelessness and "constriction of initiative and planning" (p. 90). Living with a batterer, a woman learns:

> That every action will be watched, that most actions will be thwarted, and that she will pay dearly for failure. To the extent that the perpetrator has succeeded in enforcing his demand for total submission, she will perceive any exercise of her own initiative as insubordination. (p. 91)

Women struggling to leave a batterer do not fail to make the choice to leave because they lack skill in decision making. Similarly, women who have experienced trauma of any sort confront a complex reality that cannot be simply addressed by skill development in decision making and goal setting when they seek to make changes in their life through participating in a literacy program.

A recognition of lack of belief in a future and consequent lack of goals or even dreams, and what it would look like to dream and imagine a future, could become part of curriculum in literacy programming. Such an exploration might include work with fantasy, metaphor, and storytelling to support learners to imagine alternative futures. However, it is crucial that any imaginative work around setting goals must balance dreaming of possibilities with acknowledging the multiple limitations too often present in women's lives.

While recognizing limitations, creative work to help women begin to connect their past and their present with new possibilities for the future also need to be imagined. Journey metaphors might help make those connections. Work using art and life charts, music and sound, movement and role play, storytelling, readers' theater, and writing and rewriting stories are all possibilities to explore. Learners could begin to learn to dream and to create both short- and long-term goals through exploring possibilities for control, connection, and meaning within the literacy program. A woman has to feel she can have some control and some sense of meaning to dream—to even imagine a future for herself.

This work is painful, often painfully slow, but essential. It is not work that quickly leads to visible changes, and funders may not be prepared to recognize the work as part of literacy learning. Limitations within programs—limits on number of staff, individual tutoring, lack of physical space and resources for creative work, lack of training, or even understanding the necessity—may frustrate the possibilities for this crucial work along with the limitations set on women outside literacy programs.

The limitations set on the time learners can participate in programs, including the expectation of visible outcomes in impossibly short time, form an enormous barrier to the creation of new creative approaches to assist women to explore the possibilities of making choices. Just as we begin to recognize the work involved for many women to learn to set goals and the supports necessary to help them move toward them, just as literacy workers begin to look at designing program activities that would support women in developing this ability, government initiatives focusing on *observable* outcomes may eliminate any possibility for innovative programming. Yet the importance of respecting learners' own experiences and knowledge of their own situations, of understanding women's difficulties with making choices and setting goals, of supporting women to learn to make choices, and of recognizing that such a process will take extensive time will not evaporate. Although this may not quickly produce observable change, if women are given opportunities to explore goal setting, in the long term, their potential to make meaningful change in their lives will be immeasurably enhanced.

6

Bringing the Whole Person to Learning

When I began to analyze the information gathered in my interviews, I found I was reading and listening to repeated mentions of the ways trauma experiences affected aspects of the person, especially the body, mind, and emotion. I also noticed occasional mentions of the spirit or the soul. Initially, I began to organize groups of data describing *damage* in each of these areas—body, mind, emotion, and spirit—and to look at how each area could be addressed in literacy programming. As I thought and re-thought the material, I began to reframe it. *Damage* illustrates the range of violence and its relevance to literacy learning. The impacts of trauma—is-sues of presence, all or nothing, trust and boundaries, telling the pain and finding space for joy, creating safety in literacy programs, as well as control, connection, and meaning—create challenges for literacy learning. Conse-quently, how to enhance literacy learning is a different discussion. For the woman who has experienced trauma, engaging all aspects of the self in a creative learning process can support integration and connection within the whole person and so facilitate literacy learning. Dawna Markova (1994) drew attention to why these connections are so important:

> Milton Erickson believed that people who are traumatized get stuck in one frame of reference, in one way of thinking about the world, themselves, and their difficulties. It is that "stuckness" that imprisons us, because it knocks us out of connection with our bodies and sense. We feel as if we have lost the spirit from our lives. (p. 35)

Engaging the whole person in creative learning processes can open possibilities for learners to move from the *stuck* place of trauma, and of being unable to read, and create more effective programming for literacy learning.

> Trauma is holistic assault, which is why we "learn" or are affected so deeply from it. Healing from trauma is a slow process of re-connecting those wounded parts. (Joyce, 1993, p. 44)

If trauma is holistic in its impact, then it is crucial to address the impact through an equally holistic approach. Considering each aspect of the person, becoming aware of the impact of trauma on all aspects of the person, and recognizing gains and shifts of sensitivity can create a holistic approach to literacy learning for survivors of trauma.

Not everyone who signs on for literacy learning or teaching wants to participate in fully holistic programming. It might be difficult or inappropriate to try to include body, mind, emotion, and spirit extensively in every program. However, minimal acknowledgment of all aspects of the person is crucial in all programming. Recognition of all elements can take place through minor changes in approach. For example, the freedom to get up and go out of the room or fetch a cup of coffee may be a valuable physical movement to lessen stress and discomfort. Including talk about fear and how to cope with literacy learning in the face of terror as part of class work might make literacy learning possible.

Literacy programs do not always have to take on all aspects of building a stronger sense of self. Instructors need to be aware that learners may be working on aspects of themselves outside the literacy program. Offering support may enhance the literacy learning in the program. For example, a First Nation student taking part in traditional ceremonies outside the literacy program may be rekindling spirit crucial to her literacy learning. This could be enhanced by an instructor who acknowledges such work and creates space for the learner to write or speak about it in the program if she chooses. At the least, instructors need to recognize that this work complements literacy learning, rather than seeing any resulting infringement on attendance as indicating that the student is not serious about her studies.

Traditionally, much education, including literacy learning, invites only the *severed head* to participate in the process. Exploring how possible it is to include all aspects of the person in all types of literacy programming will enhance learning possibilities. Focus cannot be only on the mind. Restoration of balance is crucial for successful learning. Literacy cannot be seen only as a set of skills to be learned while the whole person is ignored. Balance between a narrow focus on literacy learning and a broader inclusion of the whole person is essential for many to learn successfully. Opening up to include the whole person must not become a focus solely on pathology and damage to each aspect of the person. Instead, balance is needed between recognizing possible damage and drawing on strengths and every aspect of the person to enhance all learning.

SPIRIT

In my reading, I came across the concept of *soul murder* (Shengold, 1989) used to describe people who have been severely abused and brutalized. Initially I found this concept disturbing—it seemed like another description of *damage*, another way to make people *other* and outside. However, the concept stayed with me because it seemed to capture the way in which some people who have been severely abused seem to see themselves as outside the human compact. This concept begins to reveal the depths of loss of meaning in life and the hopelessness that many theorists and practitioners spoke to me about.

When a First Nation group of instructors talked about students whose "spirit has left," I realized that this talk about the soul, or spirit, was important. Yet I struggled with a sense that I would be laughed at by non-Aboriginal people if I tried to say that literacy work and the spirit had anything to do with each other. I was pleasantly surprised when I dared to mention this idea in a workshop with few Aboriginal participants. One white participant said, "I was excited when you wrote spirit up there." She also said that she would be criticized as being too *touchy feely* if she talked about spirit in her program—"Here we go I'm going to be in trouble again." In various workshops, several other participants picked up the concept and talked about their own sense that it is crucial to recognize the spirit when teaching literacy. One literacy worker, Beth Sauerhaft, the Jewish daughter of a holocaust survivor who has also had close personal relationships with survivors of political torture said that she too had come to the

> unusually sad conclusion that has to do with being able to acknowledge that in many cases the perpetrators succeeded in destroying or murdering souls, and unfortunately this includes the souls of very young children as well as adults. (Alphaplus Literacy & Violence Online Seminar, February–April 1998)

This understanding has led her to believe that:

. . . literacy work and spirit have much to do with each other, for they are both about the ways we make meaning of our lives, and I [try] to practice this connection in my work and my being. (Alphaplus Literacy & Violence Online Seminar, February–April 1998)

First Nation instructors in Toronto also talked about the link between literacy and spirit:

I think Edna Manatawabi said, when we're talking about literacy we're talking about expressing the spirit within, birth, you know trying to find that spirit to let it out. . . . (interview, First Nation Instructors, Toronto, January 1997)

The suggestion is not simply that rekindling spirit is crucial to literacy learning, but that literacy may be part of the self-expression and meaning making that supports the rekindling of spirit.

Breaking the Spirit

In her audiotape lecture entitled *Body Terror*, Clarissa Chandler (n.d.) said that power is the connection between the body and spirit and that terror separates them. Agger (1994) drew on Foucault to spell out more about the connection between the body and soul:

Power can use different languages, different techniques, but all are aimed at making the body docile. According to Foucault, in modern industrial-ized societies, the techniques are aimed at the soul rather than the body, but the goal both of the deliberate and conscious use of violence that oc-curs under some dictatorships, and the hidden and unconscious use of vio-lence that occurs under more "refined" dictatorships, is the same: a psy-chological process in which the power relationship is internalized. One weapon in the resistance to these strategies is to expose them. By publicly denouncing the techniques of those in power, the psychological internal-ization of the power relationship is counteracted. The inner psychic mech-anism that allows power to function automatically, so that the oppressed "becomes the principal of his own subjection," as Foucault expresses it, is challenged. (p. 56)

In literacy programming, how can we expose the ways in which power relationships that diminish women who are survivors of violence are in-ternalized? Through the sense of worthlessness, the feeling of being *bad* and generally terrified to make mistakes, which many literacy learners speak about as following from trauma, a psychological process where the oppressed become part of their own oppression is created. *I am bad* seems like a leap of desperation for the abused child trying to make sense of an otherwise impossible situation. Either her parents must be bad or she must be. If they are bad, she has no possibility of hope and meaning. Judith Herman (1992) described this in detail:

> Though she perceives herself as abandoned to a power without mercy, she must find a way to preserve hope and meaning. The alternative is utter despair something no child can bear. To preserve her faith in her parents she must reject the first and most obvious conclusion that something is terribly wrong with them. She will go to any lengths to construct an explanation for her fate that absolves her parents of all blame and responsibility. . . . (p. 101)

This explanation perhaps helps show how the sense of being worthless and bad can be so hard to shift for an adult who used it as a strategy for survival in childhood. It has become a deeply ingrained element of who she is.

Several learners talked about what it meant to negotiate a situation where they did not know when they would be punished or for what. When adult learners talk about beatings, shaming, and humiliation, it is not surprising that a terror of making mistakes accompanies many of them in their adult learning experience. The following comments were made by two groups of learners; several were made by one student as she thought through what her own experience had meant and joined in with others:

A: Being called stupid all the time (in tears).

B: Being called stupid as you are being whipped with a nice little leather strap in front of people. . . . or even you can do better, you don't feel like you can do better, but they keep telling you I know you can do better. They are not willing to look at why you're not doing better. Having somewhat uneducated parents, the mixed messages I could never figure them out . . . they wanted me to excel, they wanted this amount from me, but when I brought it to them and showed them they would ridicule it.

C: I always thought what am I doing wrong. I always thought I was doing something wrong. So you're feeling stupid . . . maybe it belongs to teachers to really be aware. . . .

B: I'd get a detention for breathing and live in fear that they would be told that. That would be an excuse to break out the leather strap, go to your room and I'm going to whack you wherever I like. I remember waiting on the bed. . . .

D: . . . need to be aware of terror. . . .

E: Where did these teachers learn about humiliation . . . ?

C: Some teachers still do it. . . .

B: Where do you think they learned it, same place we learned it—at home. . . . (interviews, Horizons & Malaspina, British Columbia, November 1996)

These learners' words speak about the loss of their power and sense of themselves through ways they were shamed at home and at school. They bring this legacy and all the terror it entails to their adult learning. They remind all teachers how crucial it is that we examine ourselves to avoid unthinkingly reproducing abusive educational practices that we have experienced ourselves.

Children in abusive homes are beaten and beaten down and come to believe they must deserve what is happening to them. Pat Capponi (1997) talked about how in school, in her other contacts, and at home everything confirmed that she and her siblings were responsible for the violence inflicted on them:

There would have been no violent beatings if we hadn't brought them on ourselves: whether five months old or seventeen years, we were responsible, we deserved what we got. We weren't good enough, quiet enough, clean enough, smart enough, invisible enough to make our presence tolerable. . . .

In eighteen years, I don't remember a day that didn't begin and end in fear. It would have taken a much stronger person than me not to internalize all that blame and guilt for being alive, and a much wiser individual to understand exactly how those feelings would affect my later life.

It wasn't surprising, then, that I spent most of my time wishing I didn't exist, feeling I had to constantly justify being alive. (pp. 8–9)

Capponi also talked briefly about that legacy of destruction on her ability to learn in stressful situations as an adult. She talked about how this limits the jobs she can take on because she quickly slips into a suicidal depression when trying to learn new tasks that are supposed to be easy:

I might have been able to flip burgers, if only I could have flipped them competently. But I freeze up when trying to learn new things in that kind of work situation, as though my body and mind are in some kind of time warp, anticipating the violence of fists or accusations of stupidity. I have tried, in the past, factory work, collections, dish-washing, cleaning, waitressing—I was pathetic. And I felt pathetic, which usually contributed to yet another hospital admission. (p. 13)

An awareness that, for many women, feeling pathetic may lead into a time warp directly back to terror may help reveal the difficulties some women have with all learning. It is not new to literacy workers to talk about learners feeling stupid, but the depths of feeling pathetic or worthless, of shame and guilt, and how firmly that might block literacy learning is something we have not spoken about nor adequately addressed.

Teaching to Strength

I found hope for the possibility of change, despite such oppression, embedded in accounts that showed that the total belief of being bad, or worthless, could be shifted at least a little by even a single person's respectful treatment. Many survivors have written about how absolutely essential it was to their survival to be treated as a worthy person by somebody in their life. For those who experienced extreme trauma, survival can rest on that valuing. As an adult, even the slightest hint of disregard or disrespect can take a person straight back to the depths of feeling worthless. Every instructor has a responsibility to support learners to come to value themselves and discover their own knowledge:

Many students end up feeling they have no faith in their own abilities, and instructors really need to acknowledge that lack of belief in themselves and honour students' knowledge and work with that. Stress what students know . . . validate what they are knowledgeable about. (interview/personal correspondence, 1996/1999)

Having described the unbearable horrors of her childhood that continue to haunt her so thoroughly she is always vulnerable, ready to slide into despair and the temptation of suicide, Pat Capponi (1992) talked about how much it meant to have *one* school teacher believe in her:

My fortunes turned dramatically the day I was stopped in the hall by an English teacher. He'd heard about my writing from another teacher, who had enjoyed my essays and encouraged me to write for the school paper. . . . He'd looked at me with interest and respect; he'd asked for my help. This was quite at odds with how I was treated at home. (p. 58)

Later, as she reflected on why she was able to get out of the psychiatric system while so many others lose themselves there, she referred again to the value of this interaction:

> I've mentioned the high school teacher who stopped me in the hall to ask for my assistance in a school performance. Before that man, whose name is Stan Asher, no one had ever looked at me or spoken to me as though I had value. For that's the key. Otherwise, I probably would have gone on believing that I was intrinsically bad, with nothing to offer. (p. 207)

She spoke about being *offered a positive image* of oneself as absolutely essential for survival. Similarly, Elly Danica (1996) talked about surviving soul-destroying abuse in her childhood because of her grandmother's absolute belief in her and her grandmother's intervention, which failed to protect Elly from her father's violence, but still sent a powerful message:

> I knew that she had tried to stop him and, more important, that what he had done to me was wrong. If I had not known this, had not had the memory of a grandmother who I knew loved me, but whom I did not see again until thirty-eight years later, I do not think I would have survived. Too much was against me, too much effort was made to break and destroy me. (p. 30)

Making the unacceptability of abuse and other violence visible—shameful only to the perpetrator—and offering each learner a positive image of herself may make an incalculable difference. This suggests the crucial importance of every respectful interaction in the educational setting that implicitly or explicitly offers the message that the learner is valuable and has worth.

These stories help confirm for me the wisdom of Clarissa Chandler's reminder that women who have survived trauma have done so because of their strength and the positive aspects in their life, however limited and few and far between those positive aspects may be, whatever unbearable horrors they have endured.

> . . . when I think about any time I'm working with somebody and I think about how the trauma effects them I ask myself what are the resources that they are drawing on to exist and the fundamental thing that I don't want to do is to squash or diminish or humiliate or limit any of the things that they are drawing from. . . .
>
> When I think about something like teaching them how to go on with their lives, or how to read, or how to do a task that they really want to do,

I don't look at their victimization at all. I don't see their victimization or their traumatic experiences as . . . [they are] things that might interrupt it, delay it, slow it down—but it is not the thing that is going to create it. So I want [them] to be able to not be paralysed when they have their reaction right? As a traumatic, as a trauma survivor and I want to be able to understand that and contextualize it for them so they don't lose me as a resource out of shame or humiliation. So I want to also project what I think of as a positive presence, because that is the thing that they are most likely to have not have had, so I want to be providing and contextualizing this warm experience that the trauma is most likely to have limited or constricted in some way in their lives. I want to be able to acknowledge, contextualize, neutralize and not get connected or attached to the shame or humiliation and disrespect associated with the trauma and be able to build and connect to the part of them that is alive and able to go on. (interview, Toronto, November 1996)

Her advice to literacy workers is to teach to that strength, be careful not to connect to the shame or humiliation that forms part of abuse, and support the vision of growth and change. Pat Capponi's teacher, Stan Asher, may never have known what value his assumption of her worth had for Pat, yet it seems his treatment changed her life.

In literacy work, there are often debates about self-esteem and literacy and which comes first, whether work on improving literacy skills improves self-esteem, and whether work on self-esteem is needed to enable literacy learning to take place. Self-esteem and literacy are intertwined and need to be addressed together for learners who have been traumatized to have a sense of being able to learn. Thinking in terms of the spirit can help us notice approaches different from traditional self-esteem work. We need to look at what helps a person believe she is worth something and how specific beliefs that block learning—like "I'm stupid," "I mustn't make mistakes," "I'm worthless"—can be turned around. How can we, in literacy, help people to believe they are not stupid, to accept it is okay to make mistakes, to believe in their ability to learn, and to move from feeling badly about themselves?

One answer was offered by a learner at Malaspina College in British Columbia, who talked about the value of having others believe in you until you can believe in yourself. For her, the model of an AA sponsor helped her begin to believe in herself:

What I needed was for somebody to believe that I could do it until I came to believe it myself . . . now I'm beginning to believe it myself. . . . (interview, Malaspina College, Duncan, British Columbia, November 1996)

I listened to this learner provide support to and show her belief in another learner. In the interview group at her college, a learner who had just left an abusive husband and was terrified that she could not cope alone came to the session. The learner who recommended the AA idea had left her own marriage and survived. She shared her belief that the other would also be able to manage, although it would be hard. This was obviously important encouragement. She and other learners also talked about the value of a support group, although they did not think it would work if others knew that those who were part of it were survivors. There is a tension here between the value of the common ground of shared experience and the problems of shared stigma. More opportunities to build a strong sense of solidarity between learners might help each learner feel others respect her and believe in her when she has difficulty believing in herself.

A learner in the Horizons Program in British Columbia added another layer of complexity to the challenging task of supporting a learner to build a stronger sense of her ability to learn. She said that an instructor telling her she is not stupid would not help her shift her negative belief about herself:

> The hardest thing in this class was reading notes saying I was intelligent, untapped intelligence and then having a one-on-one very deep conversation who also said that to me, you're so intelligent, I just shut it down. I couldn't hear her say that. Because I shut down being called stupid, I also shut down being told you're intelligent, so I don't quite know where you tap into that. What would bandage the stupid but allow you to believe the intelligence? (interview, Horizons Program, Duncan, British Columbia, November 1996)

Her instructor responded to her comment:

> If you're told you're stupid and intelligent, when you're told you're intelligent you expect the stupid message. So it's about figuring out—am I in a different place? It's about trust—can I trust this person? I couldn't trust those people I was supposed to trust. (interview, Horizons Program, Duncan, British Columbia, November 1996)

Perhaps her instructor is right—the issue is trust. If she can begin to trust her instructors, she will trust them even when they tell her she is smart. Perhaps she also needs to believe in herself enough to believe that it is possible that she is smart, capable, and worthy of success. It may be that, once she can trust her instructors' encouraging words, they will give her support to reach the place where she can trust herself. Many learners talked about the ways they were spoken to during their childhood and adulthood: "Who do you think you are?" (when they tried to do something well) and "You thought you were so smart" (whenever they made a mistake). No wonder it is crucial, yet not enough, for instructors to create supportive and encouraging learning environments.

Although much of this discussion could simply be seen as psychological effects of trauma, I hold to a sense that the concept of spirit helps us see a person as a whole and focus on something bigger and more momentous than what is captured by self-esteem. It leads us to think of *rekindling, fanning the flames,* or even *resurrection.* Literacy worker Christina Patterson from British Columbia explained her own approach:

> I have to say how much I believe in resurrection. For my thinking it's like a seed, buried how long, scratch the soil and add water and it still creates the beautiful original. I understand escaping reality for survival purposes. I believe in the possibility of healing anything, otherwise I wouldn't be doing this kind of work. (Alphaplus Literacy & Violence Online Seminar, February–April 1998)

The challenge in literacy work is to add the *water* and *nutrients* that help the seed in the learner to grow again.

Fanning the Flames

For First Nation literacy programs, a focus on culture-based curriculum and traditional spiritual practices can create a space that builds cultural pride, supports understanding oppression, and leads to a sense of personal self-worth. First Nation educators across the spectrum—from children to adult—have created innovative educational practices structured around the medicine wheel and the teacher as healer:

> [T]he "teacher as healer" is one who, infused with spiritual understanding, seeks to make things whole . . . seeks to respect and foster interconnections—between herself, her students, and the subject matter; between the school, the community and the universe at large—while respecting each part of these interconnected webs (Katz & St. Denis, 1991, p. 24)

This approach, of respectfully building connections to *heal* not an individual in isolation but a community broadly, is being followed in many First Nation-run literacy programs. A group of First Nation educators described how they work in their programs:

A: Usually, the beginning of class, when we do check-in—after we do a smudge to encourage that trust in the circle—when we have a check-in, that check-in is always really very personal. Usually the whole group—it's that time that people empathize with each other. So they might not necessarily be healing in that moment—like in a sense when I say healing, they might not be confronting any real issues—but just talking, letting it out, and then the group empathizes with them, and there is that feeling of empathy in the room.

B: That's one of the things we always do, no matter where we go. We go around the room and say hi, my name is Nancy, I'm from Rama, I grew up here, and the next person, hi, I'm Sally. And you go out into other programs and workshops in the non-Native community, that almost never happens. Except maybe in the feminist community. And so you're left with a feeling of, I don't know any of these people, they don't know my name, and that's really important for any learning to take place, is to be recognized as an individual. So we do those things like ritual: smudge, talking circle, whatever, before anything happens around learning. . . .

C: You allow that person to talk and take whatever amount of time it takes for them to share. And they will share whatever they're comfortable sharing. Some of it will be strictly from the head if they're not used to doing it. Some of it will be here, from here [the heart], the pain. . . .

A: . . . in the check-in—whether you're passing a feather or something, where as long as you're holding that you can talk. And if you pass it to somebody they don't have to talk, they can just say "I'm going to pass." What happens also is that in that check-in those people, because the main central thing of it is empathy, they won't turn around and then grab that feather and then say "So you know what, Dede, I'm gonna tell you now what I think." They'll look and say "You know, I really feel for you, Dede, because of what you're saying today. That happened to me a year ago, and I just want you to know that I feel for you." And then they'll say something about themselves, they'll say "This happened to me," and they'll tell a similar experience. So it's sharing, it's not anything about teaching, it's sharing and that's where I see a big difference between people who all of a sudden think they're going to broaden your horizon by explaining something to you. That's how it's done differently I think. (interview, First Nation Instructors, Toronto, January 1997)

After listening to First Nation instructors talk about smudging and talking circles, I wrote a note to Priscilla George about the value of ritual. She responded, clarifying:

To us, it's more than ritual. With the smudge, we are acknowledging and calling on the spirit world to be with us. When Nancy talked about work-

ing with the whole person, that means addressing the mental (which educational programs do recognize), physical, emotional and spiritual aspects
of the person. (personal correspondence, March 1997)

Native educators have no doubt that they need to dig deeply within their
own traditional practices and approaches to design appropriate literacy
programs. Robert Beaton and Nancy Cooper made connections between
the oppression of Aboriginal people and the importance of creating holistic educational practices that support learning:

> Aboriginal peoples are in the process of healing themselves in spirit, body
> and mind. Many aboriginal peoples have begun to remember and redis-
> cover, and build upon, the strength of their traditions and cultures. Much
> is known about racist government policies toward the indigenous peoples
> of the Americas over the past several hundred years. These misguided gov-
> ernment policies have pervaded all areas of life for aboriginal people. The
> policies of colonialism have brought about forced relocations, residential
> schools, economic deprivation, dispossession and the loss of land. Many
> aboriginal people know little about their own languages, histories and
> cultures. This lack of understanding and awareness has contributed to low
> self-esteem for a majority of aboriginal people, and has nurtured resentment
> and feelings of inferiority which all too often have been expressed through
> substance abuse, violence and suicide. This desperate situation has re-
> sulted in First Nations peoples having the highest illiteracy in Canada.
> A pervasive collusion between church and state worked until very re-
> cently against the best interests of aboriginal peoples, leading to losses of
> identity that are only now beginning to be retrieved. One way in which
> this retrieval may be fostered is through the recovery of aboriginal methods
> of teaching, the honouring of aboriginal methods of learning and to have
> these values respected, valued and implemented wherever and whenever
> necessary. We must recognize the fact that First Nations people cannot af-
> ford to lose another generation to policies that convince them that they
> cannot learn and have nothing to contribute to their own or other com-
> munities (pp. 2–3).

Nancy Cooper and Robert Beaton drew on the wisdom of the medicine
wheel to clarify that literacy programming cannot be disconnected from
processes of growth and change for individuals and communities: ". . .
[H]ealthy adult literacy programs are not separate, isolated 'skills development' classes but rather programs that help adults on their path to recovery, growth and positive change" (p. 10)

For literacy programs that serve students of a variety of ethnicities, the
challenge to create literacy programming that feeds the spirit will be different. Yet I think many lessons can be learned from the example of these First

Nation programs. Check-ins, supportive rounds, and regular ritual could all be appropriate. Even the simple repetition of some activity at the beginning or end of sessions—such as reading a poem, lighting a candle, or an opening or closing round—can create a ritual that honors the work students and instructor are doing together, marks off their time and space, and lends importance. Where participants' spiritual beliefs and practices are more varied, shared spiritual practice would not be appropriate, but inviting students to draw on the strength of their own spiritual beliefs may still be important. Christina Patterson wrote about her approach:

> I ask learners if they practice any particular spiritual rituals, like church or like lighting a candle in their bedroom. At least that brings the language into our conversations and something may come of that. I encourage learners to get their hands into the earth, literally into the earth in their backyard or somewhere. I do believe in the healing qualities of the planet mother earth. (Alphaplus Literacy & Violence Online Seminar, February–April 1998)

Encouraging students to reflect on their own spiritual beliefs and look at how they can draw on these to support their sense of themselves and a sense of their brilliance could be valuable if taken on with care. It is always crucial that learners not feel pressure to share what is not comfortable or participate in or feel excluded by any ritual that is not part of their own spiritual practice. As literacy workers begin to conceptualize relevant curriculum and learning processes, they may need to explore broadly outside the literacy field. Resources might include art, music, or dance therapists; First Nation healers; spiritual writing of all forms; as well as a broad range of creative arts.

Many ideas could be taken from existing curriculum and assembled to help women understand how they lost belief in themselves and rebuild hope. Material on building self-esteem may also be useful. Ideas that focus on supporting learners to reflect on themselves as learners and begin to change the messages they learned as children would support learners to build a stronger sense of themselves and their potential. For example, Christina Patterson described using an exercise I wrote for *Making Connections* (Canadian Congress for Learning Opportunities for Women, 1996)

> We did the series of activities which are described in Chapter #2—Exploring Learning and Identity. This was an excellent activity for learners to work with their own language and writing (printing) skills at the same time as we were discussing issues that are important for self-esteem and learner identity. . . . Most students had to really work at remembering how they

had formed their own opinion about themselves as learners. Every student loved the section of the activities where we went back and changed any negative messages received from friends, family, teachers, anyone. We changed the negative messages, literally covered a huge bulletin board with positive messages and kept using that board all the rest of the term as a reference for the kinds of messages we thought would be encouraging to a learner. (Alphaplus Literacy & Violence Online Seminar, February–April 1998)

Other exercises in *Making Connections* look at the learners' voice as children and the ways they were supported to speak out or silenced. They help learners look at their own knowledge and how they learn best. These may all support women who have experienced trauma to rebuild a stronger image of themselves.

Kathleen O'Connell talked about the importance of helping learners develop compassion for themselves. Priscilla George added the importance of learners seeing themselves as a spirit. O'Connell proposed exercises that help learners develop understanding of the social pressures of racism, sexism, ableism, and classism. Exploring how these oppressions undermine how we see ourselves and others and how we present ourselves and react to others could be varied and creative. Work with images from magazines, television, advertising, and popular songs could be entertaining ways to develop a sophisticated analysis that would help rebuild community, connection, and meaning. Exploring some of society's myths about people who are poor, illiterate, intellectually disabled, or labeled in any other marginalized category and changing the messages could lead to greater clarity about the forces that have undermined learners' sense of self. Developing an understanding of the social context of individual messages can support women to place their own individual experiences in a broader context.

Work to develop understanding of the broader issues could also lead learners to become ready to take on these forces and engage in political activism. Beth Sauerhaft suggested that this focus is central:

I think that these struggles must also be fought as part of social and political movements for human rights—a collective struggle against the daily murder of body, soul and spirit. It is really important that we acknowledge the ways social, political and economic violence are sanctioned in our cultures and to connect our literacy work with efforts for change. (Alphaplus Literacy & Violence Online Seminar, February–April 1998)

Groups of learners have taken on activities on the issue of violence against women such as creating a video, assessing existing curriculum, writing curriculum, making presentations, leading workshops, and writing pamphlets to educate others on the issue.[1] Some of the women involved in creating the video, *Together We Bloom: Women Speaking Out Against Domestic Violence*, wrote about what it meant to them to move from telling their own stories to each other to creating a video for others. The facilitator wrote about the "power of doing, of sharing with the intention of making a difference for others; and the pride we felt in having accomplished such a monumental task" (Hofer, 1999, p. 10). Mary, a participant in the group, spoke of how engaging in the process changed her:

> I have become a stronger woman due to the making of our video, because a couple of years ago I might not have been strong enough to take a stand on my beliefs. I am self-confident, and I'm more aware of and recognize the cycle of violence in other people's relationships. It is difficult for me to witness physical abuse. I still feel threatened, and my first response is to flee. But when I see verbal abuse, I now speak up rather than keep silent. They might not want to hear it, but I know it's what we all need to do for each other to end the violence. We have to point it out and say it's wrong and that we're there to help if they need it. (The Literacy Project, 1998, p. 30)

Such activities can be valuable for the individual—helping to build a sense of worth—and valuable socially, helping to break silences and shift perceptions on issues of violence. Finding a balance between the individual and society can be an ongoing challenge.

Ideas that help women recognize the support of others and draw on the positive ways others see them may also be valuable. Judy Swekla, a participant in the video project, spoke of the value of the trust and friendship developed in their group:

---

[1]I have heard about a variety of projects, but not all have produced published materials. A few interesting ones follow, and many more may have materials available locally. A video and guide is available from a video project in Massachusetts: Together We Bloom: Speaking Out Against Domestic Violence video (available from: Laubach Literacy Action, Box 131, Syracuse, NY 13210-0131). The students and coordinator, Anson Green, in La COCINA de Vida in San Antonio, Texas, have produced curriculum on domestic violence. (Available from: La COCINA Curriculum Development Project, Northside ISD Adult Education, 6632, Bandera Road, San Antonio, TX 78238. Three books were published from an action research study where each program created a "woman-positive" activity (Lloyd et al., 1994a, 1994b, & 1994c). Several programs' activities included the creation of resource booklets. Descriptions are included in Lloyd et al. (1994b). *Listen to Women in Literacy* (Lloyd et al., 1994c) is written for literacy learners. It describes what women in a variety of programs did and what they learned from the process. It could be a good jumping off point for programs that want to take on an activity.

They hold me accountable from my actions and challenge me in what I believe; they do this while giving me support and the love of friends that will stand by me no matter what may come my way. The growth of each one of us might go unnoticed if it weren't for the group's acknowledgment. (The Literacy Project, 1998, p. 33)

One exercise in *Making Connections* asks students to bring in a photo of someone they would like to remind themselves is with them in spirit as they learn so that they can feel the strength of their support (Canadian Congress for Learning Opportunities for Women, 1996). In another unpublished exercise, each learner writes about herself as someone who values her would describe her. This sort of work can help learners begin to stretch from the *stuck* place of devaluing themselves and draw on others' belief in them—even those who are not present in the class—to begin to believe in themselves and their ability to learn.

A variety of creative approaches might be appropriate to play with concepts of being seen and heard and valuing oneself. Learning to play with voice, song, shouting, breathing, making different sorts of noise, drumming, and percussion, and learning to echo others' sounds, are among a wide variety of exercises that can help learners to put themselves *out there* and listen to others. Talking or writing about what I see, hear, think, and feel from where I stand, and listening to each others' writings from where they stand, might help explore commonality and difference. Actively focusing on listening to others, learning to hear, and exploring where learners have closed down hearing might help each participant see and hear others, building connection and community.

Exploration around change—as each learner looks at her past and the ways she has changed and considers what has helped and hindered it—could be taken on in creative ways. The metaphor of a journey (e.g., playing with the idea of climbing up and down mountains—"What can you see when you are at the top of each new mountain?" "What can you see when you are in the valley?") could help women move their thinking and imagine the possibility of reaching a place where learning and change seem possible. Elly Danica (1996) used the metaphor of preparing for a physical journey for her own healing work:

I found it was easier to accept the work that had to be done if I compared my inner struggle to a physical challenge. If you plan to climb a mountain, you undergo a training period before you begin (awareness of the issues you are facing), and you start with easy short climbs (a slow letting go of denial and negative behaviours) with experienced guides (sharing experiences with others). You outfit yourself with harness, ropes, pick, helmet and companions, whatever will keep you safe and enable you to make progress. Continuing this metaphor, I find comfort in the image of the Goddess of the Mountain as a guide for this climb. (p. 19)

In the northern town of Iqaluit, women talked about the *kometek*, or sled, as a symbol for a journey. They suggested working with the idea of what you need to pack in the *kometek* to prepare for a journey as a useful metaphor for helping women imagine and prepare for change. I imagine using the physical challenge of a journey as an extended metaphor for curriculum that would focus on rekindling the spirit and making more concrete the emotional and spiritual support and the belief in self that might enable women to learn successfully.

Learning to dream can have enormous impact. An exercise reading and writing about dreams inspired by Maxine Tynes' (1993) poem *The Woman I Am in My Dreams* led to regular readings of that poem and re-written versions in one women's group every Friday afternoon (Canadian Congress for Learning Opportunities for Women, 1996). One woman's version ended:

> The woman I am in my dreams
> avoids nothing and is willing
> to meet challenges with
> strength and courage
> The woman I am in my dreams
> knows the difference between
> aggressive, assertive and abusive
> behaviours and when she's using
> them
> The woman I am in my dreams
> believes dreams come true. (cited in Leroux, 1998b, p. 15)

Kathie Leroux (1998a) explained that reading these poems about dreams aloud became a treasured ritual in the *Women's Success* group she ran. The women created a motto to symbolize their sense of an ongoing journey:

> By the end of the first session, they had established a motto based on their reflection of the past and their hopes for the future. Each session would be-gin or end with that motto which soon became a daily affirmation: . . . "WE WILL NOT GO BACKWARDS." (p. 7)

Building some sense of being a whole person and feeding the spirit so that the sense of feeling worthless is not the strongest sense a woman has

when trying to learn can begin to open up the possibility of bringing emotions, body, and mind actively into the literacy learning process. Although embracing the concept of spirit may be challenging for literacy
workers who have not previously recognized this aspect of the learner,
the enhanced potential for learning may offer startling results.

EMOTIONS

A sense of worthlessness leaves a spiritual hole, and the feelings connected with it—sadness, anger, and fear—will be present in the literacy
class. Feelings of fear and anxiety, and sometimes also the efforts to block
expression of them, may be taking up enormous energy for many learners.
Questions about who and what to trust, fear of another betrayal, that
boundaries will not be respected, that by speaking about the experiences
of trauma and issues they struggle with as a consequence they will be
judged as *less than* can all take learners' attention away from other aspects
of learning. Through the turmoil of living with crises and struggling with
control, isolation, and the terrifying possibility of creating connection,
through the despair that there is no meaning and no possibility of hope,
emotions such as fear, sadness, and anger can become a central presence
in the literacy classroom. Yet many literacy programs do not allow a lot of
space for emotions.

A literacy worker described a situation when one woman in her program
was upset by the way one of the men in the program teased her. His teasing
brought up this woman's history with teasing and "dirty talk" and distracted
her from her literacy learning: "And she herself says that restricts her learning. She can't concentrate. She's too busy being upset" (interview, December 1996). That felt very familiar to me. I knew what she was talking about. I
have seen many learners I would describe as too upset to learn. Therapist
Heather Bain explained more about emotions and difficulties with feelings.
She said many survivors fear feelings while they struggle internally with intense sadness, vulnerability, and enormous anger. This complex mix may
make it easier to bypass feelings of sadness and fear and go straight to anger.
This can mean that, for a time, a survivor suppresses her feelings, showing
nothing, and then suddenly blows up. This pattern can lead to a survivor being described as *overreacting*. Feelings are a response to past, as well as present, issues. Learning how to respond respectfully to such a complex mix of
emotions may be hard. It requires not dismissing emotions that seem childlike, not getting hooked into one's own problematic patterns, not being offended or hurt and overreacting in response, and avoiding shaming or blam-

ing while recognizing that the emotions may not all be in relation to the current situation.

When the feelings become too much, many learners will *leave* emotionally or in terms of attention. They are no longer present to learn. I discussed presence earlier, but here I want to draw attention to the paralysis and complete absence of thought that result from extreme fear or panic. Learners in Prince Edward Island said: "Fear will make you lift the end of a car. . . . Fear paralyses you or it can give you super-human strength and you don't control that" (interview, Charlottetown, PEI, March 1997).

Recently, I was learning to white water canoe and was terrified that I would panic when I was in the middle of the current and forget everything I had learned about where to put my paddle to turn the canoe. When I finally plucked up courage to tell the instructor that I was terrified, he did not seem surprised. He made no comment that made me feel foolish. Instead he seemed pleased to have a chance to offer his strategy for panic. His approach was not to worry about putting my paddle anywhere if I blanked. Instead, he suggested if I just lean in the direction of the turn, we would not tip over. I was encouraged by that advice, did not blank out, always managed to put my paddle somewhere (although not always, or even often, the right place at first), and I remembered to lean. His lack of surprise and clear strategy helped reduce my fear that I would do it wrong or, perhaps more important, look stupid for doing it wrong. Consequently, the panic receded. He did not tell me not to be afraid, reassure me that I would not panic, tell me it would not hurt me to get it wrong and fall in, or make any other comment that would surely have increased the likelihood that I would feel unheard and shamed, add fear and block learning.

I think about literacy learners I have worked with. I question whether we routinely make enough openings in literacy for talking about fear, for exploring the fears learners are dealing with and validating them, and for generating practical strategies for when fear becomes overwhelming and the mind blanks. Christina Patterson wrote about beginning "random check-ins for math anxiety" saying: "We've had fantastic conversations about what happens when you hold your breath for a while or draw a blank for $3 \times 2 = .$" Openings of this sort could help reduce a learner's anxiety and help develop new strategies for learning in the context of fear and shame.

A learner from Prince Edward Island told me that in her program they are told to leave their emotions at the door. She stressed that approach did not work for her or for many other learners in her program. Learners (and workers) need space for feelings within the program and places to go outside the program when the feelings are *too much* for others to deal with in the class. As part of literacy work, learners could work with their feelings, learn to recognize them, and draw, talk, and write about them. Exercises that help learners free themselves from their fears may help. Lorna Gallant suggested that writing or drawing with the nondominant hand might free learners from their own judgment of themselves and form the basis for thinking and writing about their fears and the ways they judge themselves. A variety of creative strategies may be needed to support explorations of what to do when feelings are so strong that they block literacy learning.

Working With Feeling

Priscilla George, a First Nation literacy consultant, reminded me that validating women's feelings can be very important for women who have never had their feelings validated:

> I also wanted to reiterate the importance of validating the feelings of women who have experienced violence. Too long, they have been taught to hide them, or deny them. . . . They need to know it's okay to have those feelings—it's human, it's normal, it's not wrong—the Creator gave them to us for a reason. Particularly with tears—I tell them it's okay to cry. I tell them that water is one of the important elements in tears and that water is a life giving element in the universe. Tears cleanse and release, and help growth, the same as water does. (personal correspondence, March 1997)

Too many people have been told that they are not feeling what they are, that they should not feel what they do, or that they should just get over it and get on with work. In another note, Priscilla George[2] clarified further: "Feelings are ok—it's what we do with the feelings that may not be ok—people need to understand this. . . . Processing and releasing is necessary for growth." She also suggested that charting emotions hourly might be a way to help some see that emotions come and go and that is okay too. Her words reminded me of the description of feelings offered by Thich Nhat Hanh (1991):

---

[2]I thank Priscilla George for her immense generosity in engaging in a wonderful, detailed, written conversation with my manuscript and many stimulating e-mail notes and conversations in person. Through all of these, she has helped me gain new understandings of her community and offered many insights that have enriched this book. Gichi Miigwech Priscilla.

Our feelings play a very important part in directing all of our thoughts and actions. In us, there is a river of feelings, in which every drop of water is a different feeling, and each feeling relies on all the others for its existence. To observe it, we just sit on the bank of the river and identify each feeling as it surfaces, flows by, and disappears. (p. 51)

Keeping pain at a distance may have also kept feeling at a distance. Learning to explore feelings and having support to recognize their place in blocking or enabling learning may be crucial. Being heard and acknowledged, free of shame and blame, can be an enormous support for a learner beginning to tentatively explore her own feelings.

Learners bring their emotional experiences to literacy learning situation even when programs seek to exclude them. Talking about experiences and sharing with others is crucial. Chan Lean Heng (1997), speaking about her work with women workers in Malaysia, described the importance she now places on workers' emotional subjectivity, not only the material circumstances of their lives. She argued that attention to emotions is necessary if "we are concerned with education for empowerment":

Addressing conscious and unconscious thoughts, unexpressed feelings and emotions that make up their sense of themselves, their relation to the world (their inability to act) are an essential agenda (but not the only [agenda]) for women. Although emotional suffering is only one dimension of women's subordination, it is a critical agenda in women worker's education. (p. 83)

Chan (1996) designed a workshop process that she calls *talking pain* to create space for these feelings to be articulated and acknowledged:

Sharing their stories in small groups enabled the factory women to experience the commonality of their emotional suffering. "Talking pain" in an interactive small group context enabled the reclamation of suppressed feelings and the reconstruction of lived experience. Group validation of forbidden emotions was powerful in changing perceptions that were guilt-ridden and paralysing. Naming both their own feelings and the ways in which they had been victimized was liberating. . . . (p. 223)

Although in North America it may sometimes be more challenging to find common ground and create a situation where everyone feels heard, the chance to voice forbidden emotions is also extremely important if learners are to be able to shift their sense of themselves.

Therapist Liz White stressed the importance of literacy workers developing the "capacity to witness." She reminded me that women who have experienced trauma may often be depressed and suicidal. Observing such desperate feelings can be hard. She suggested two ways workers can be helpful. Workers can hold onto a belief that things will get better—hold onto hope—and share that hope with the learner. They can also support her to find ways to be with herself in despair that are not harmful. This might include helping her strategize safe alternatives to look after herself at such times, perhaps creating a list of ways to support herself, and a list of people who might be a resource. As discussed earlier, Liz White also stressed the value of creating the literacy program as a place of joy, not only a place to speak of pain. Creating a precious space for enjoying moments of pleasure and silliness can have great value in rebuilding hope and the capacity to learn.

Where learners feel sure that they will fail and make mistakes, or that they cannot learn, literacy learning is blocked. If they believe they can never make it, they can sabotage themselves. When the situation helps learners feel good about themselves and recognize what they can do, they may be helped to learn. Ways of working that help learners see their successes and help them feel good about each increment of achievement enhance literacy learning. For some learners, the smallest criticism may be felt as major and cause them to give up. Hence, supportive critique that helps learners see their strengths as well as areas for development are crucial.

Disguising fear with a pretense of disinterest is a defense mechanism that can be misread by instructors. Instructors may simply assume the learner is not motivated when she is actually hiding a terror of failing. Nancy Cooper, a First Nation instructor in Toronto, described her own learning when a student bolted from the room:

> I think too when, people in the class can sense that the instructor is expecting more of that them then they have ever expected of themselves because they've been so beaten down, that's when some of them will walk from the room. . . . I was instructing and this woman bolted out . . . and the rest of the class turned on me: "You should know better then to hurt her feelings like that." And it was a really important lesson for all of us to learn, about how important someone's feelings are in a literacy class. . . . (interview, First Nation Instructors, Toronto, January 1997)

That learning about the importance of feelings influenced Nancy Cooper's teaching:

> We talked a lot more about feelings from then on because this one learner she is in her fifties and right from the time she was born no one ever loved

her . . . lived by herself . . . she had a cat, really sad, sad kind of stories. So here she finally had a little bit of a community and everyone really liked each other, and cared about each other, what was happening to each other, they'd call each other up. Immediately, we started more of a feeling-based . . . we would have check-ins in the morning, but that [incident] was kind of a break in that facade . . . and [from] then on people would come and say this is what happened to me last night, this is what happened to me four years ago and that kind of thing. . . . (interview, First Nation Instructors, Toronto, January 1997)

Believing in students and their ability to learn, and not being fooled by a facade of indifference, may be terrifying for students and lead to more explosions and anger. However, it may also be a key factor in helping them rebuild a sense of self-worth and begin to have faith in themselves.

Thinking back to the earlier discussion of presence and Tanya Lewis' suggestion that simply taking on a difficult task may bring back the endurance and shame of the experience of abuse reminds me that developing tolerance for difficulty and learning to recognize the risk in a current activity may be part of the challenge of learning to manage fear. Looking at safety and risks, supports, and asking for what you need; learning ways of controlling defense mechanisms rather than having them control us; and learning to stay grounded would all be useful for learning how to learn, how to speak out, and take on challenges in the face of fear. One workshop, held as part of a learner leadership project, looked at all these issues. This workshop was quite remarkable in helping learners with the challenging task of teaching others what they had learned from an activity to increase learner leadership in their programs. Learners talked about their defensive activities and explored their fears and the things they would take on if they dared. The metaphor of rock climbing and the protection used to safely climb a rock face (helmet, rope, person at the other end of the rope, etc.) provided a concrete way to talk about dangers and the supports needed to surmount them (Metro Toronto Movement for Literacy, 1996).

Not all emotions can be safely shared in a literacy program. Making the class safe for all may mean a difficult balance between expressing and restraining emotions. An instructor from British Columbia described a time when she was away and one of the men in her class was apparently in a "foul mood". All the women complained to her when she returned that, because she was not there, they had to "experience this violence." Finding the balance that recognizes and makes space for learners' feelings, while also maintaining limits on expression that ensures the classroom remains safe for all learners, is a challenging role for literacy workers. Recognizing that finding a balance of this sort is a key first step.

Reacting to Anger

Anger can present a complex problem. Women are often trained to suppress anger. Different cultural styles, as well as past experiences with anger, can mean that students have different standards of what feels comfortable. When a lot of anger surfaced on a listserv about violence, I was interested to hear women's varied reactions. Some suggested that different personality types were more or less comfortable with anger. Others suggested that our differences were dictated more by culture and race. Others said that many women are afraid of their own and other people's anger. One woman suggested that for women who have been the recipients of violent anger, anger can evoke terror. For women, the *good girl* mythos can make it seem unacceptable to let anger out. Literacy workers from Prince Edward Island talked about learners who cannot learn because they are so angry they want to kill everyone, but they mask the anger under being *sweet*. One participant in the listserv suggested that if you are used to suppressing anger, when you first release it, you can feel frighteningly out of control. Exploring this complexity can help build connections and avoid some of the tension and unease that could otherwise surface as learners struggle with their own and other learners' anger.

Many years ago in a learner leadership course, I included a session exploring anger and how people dealt with it. This was not a skill session—not about anger management—but rather about exploration and shared reflection about feelings. It was a surprising, but popular and moving piece as learners looked at the source of their anger and talked about what to do with their anger (Ontario Literacy Coalition, 1992). Neither workers nor learners should have to deal with the anger of a worker or learner who is out of control. Exploration about how to deal with anger and group ground rules could provide a way to avoid this danger.

Therapist Liz White talked about anger and rage. She said one of the things that literacy workers need to do, if they are to work with survivors, is to learn to *metabolize negative transference*. She explained the term this way: As a person in a position of authority, you will inevitably find that a lot of anger and negative emotions, much of which may have been generated by other situations, will land on you. She talked about how important it is to have processes to address complaints and be prepared to acknowledge mistakes and apologize. She suggested that the worker needs a way to work through the impact of such anger so that it works through the body and so a worker can absorb the negative emotion without retaliating. She also recommended that workers set boundaries, rather than feeling that they have to simply receive any level of anger or rage. Her limit was that she was not prepared to be unseen—to be the object of rage. She would seek some distance and wait for the woman to be able to see her and engage with her directly. Workers need to learn how to avoid getting caught by emotions that are transference and retaliating, or feeling bad. Recognizing the complex position of being in authority might help workers keep distance and get less entangled in the dynamics of anger.

Although I discuss more fully literacy workers, their feelings, and their need for support in a later chapter, a discussion of emotions would not be complete without acknowledging the burden of workers' feelings. Several therapists talked about the importance of workers recognizing their own feelings. Counselors suggested that workers need to notice when they are feeling angry, put upon, resentful, or overworked. They need a place to check what is happening, to question whether they need to reset their own limits, and to see if they are getting hooked into their own problematic patterns by the learner's behavior. For example, I eventually realized that the reason I felt so irritated when the learner I tutor often asked me on the phone what I was doing, what I was having for dinner, whether I was cooking, and so on was that it reminded me of well-intentioned questioning that I experienced as invasive in the past. Once I realized the source of irritation, feelings defused.

To escape and avoid dysfunctional dynamics, it is important for workers to have somewhere to explore the feelings that get stirred. Literacy workers may be challenged to do our own *work* so that we know when it is our own *stuff* that is engaged and have our own strategies to address the problems. As Priscilla George suggested:

> Doing holistic literacy requires that literacy workers be willing to examine themselves—What are their issues? Where are they coming from? What can they do to resolve them? In doing so, they not only make better quality literacy workers, they make for themselves a better quality of life. (personal correspondence, September 1998)

I believe she is right, but I am not sure that literacy programs could ask that underpaid, overworked literacy workers also take on their own therapy and personal healing processes, although my own experience tells me that the personal gain can be as great as the gain for them as workers. Liz White suggested that workers need to learn to trust their own instincts and to consult with others. She suggested that it was important for workers not to just try harder when someone was driving them crazy. Instead, she advised learning to confront and challenge clearly and in a nonjudgmental way. Such confrontation creates a clear boundary and keeps a space for the worker to be clear about what he or she needs, which is also important.

Emotions can be a barrier or an aid to learning. Although many learners may be too upset to learn, emotions cannot be excluded from the literacy classroom. A balance of emotion and safety is crucial. Where anger is allowed free reign, women's fears will be increased. Exploring fear, risk, safety, and anger can help learners create strategies to deal with these emotions and avoid creating blocks to learning. Workers as well as learners must explore their feelings and avoid getting hooked into old patterns.

BODY

It is easy to recognize that the body, too, may be severely affected by violence. Over and over again in my interviews, I heard about women's physical injuries from experiences of violence. Women could not attend class because they were injured and were ashamed to be seen. Women were so badly injured that they could not get to or sit in class. Women may be in class with invisible injuries—bad backs, shoulders, and necks; headaches; and visual and hearing problems. They may be uncomfortable sitting especially for any length of time; they may have difficulties seeing or hearing the work in the class. Injuries and ill health may make it hard for women to get to class, to sit and pay attention, and to learn. I heard one particularly stark example from a learner before I began the research. She spoke casually one day of having had epilepsy ever since her father threw her against a wall when she was a baby. I was horrified, but the group of women learners she was talking to were not surprised. They each had their own story of ongoing health problems as a result of the violence in their lives. When violence is viewed as unspeakable, only rare occasions allow for the possibility of talk about these issues. At other times, women cannot easily talk about their physical problems or their difficulties paying attention and sitting still to study.

During the research, I heard about myriad health problems that can result from childhood or adult violence. Therapists described a process of *somatizing trauma*, where the trauma is absorbed into the body and results in a wide array of ailments. Clarissa Chandler discussed somatization and the way the body is taken away as a comfortable place to be in one of her taped lectures:

> But what these assaults do is say we should not be in that place, we should be on guard. Part of what happens is with every assault, our body contracts. . . . (Chandler, n.d., *Being an Ally to Children*)

Clarissa Chandler explained that physical and emotional hits all help the body to grow or contract. The body stores what is *too much, too toxic* until it is safe to discard it. That negative energy leads to somatization. In interviews, I was told that by the time women leave abusive men they are likely to be taking antidepressants, drugs to sleep, to deal with anxiety, for nausea, for stomach ulcers. They also may be using alcohol or drugs to numb them. Women who were abused as children, particularly, may have developed addictions to drugs or alcohol to "keep the memories down, to numb feeling" (Bass & Davis, 1988, p. 49). Women who continually have yet another health problem may seem to be avoiding literacy learning or, like other continual crises, may be judged as somehow responsible. A Toronto-based literacy worker, Michele Kuhlmann, described a volunteer's description of the situation of a learner in the group she was leading:

> One really bright woman comes to the group and always defends herself with her ailments. It is hard to get to the learning because of the shield she puts up to defend herself. . . . This woman uses her physical ailments/sickness as a defence and can't have normal conversation. She gives a litany of what's wrong with her. The tutor lets her go. She feels the woman is using this to say "Don't hurt me." The tutor feels she is having success with her by listening and not judging her. (Tutor's Notes, 1996)

This volunteer's judgment may be exactly right, but it may also be that the enormous litany of ailments is the woman's experience of her body. Because her body is uncomfortable and demanding her attention, it is hard for her to focus on her literacy learning or anything else without distraction.

Dawna Markova (1994) included a description by "a young woman who was recovering from a history of abuse" as part of her explanation of how adults are disconnected from awareness. Betsy, the young woman, says:

> I'm beginning to see how inhabiting my body is a choice I make, and how being fully human does, in the end, require me to inhabit my body. A question I have had since I began my healing, and one I still have, is: Who is in my body when I'm not? Who has been controlling, making decisions about, for instance, my pelvis, all these years that I haven't been there? The fear, as I re-enter, is like returning to one's village after a bombing—not knowing what atrocities one will discover what violence, what destruction. Yet it is one's home, my home, so return I must or stay a refugee. (pp. 36–37)

The concept of being a refugee from your own body is elaborated further by Clarissa Chandler. She argued that if we do not occupy our bodies, "we are either dead or we have been co-opted as a resource" (*Body Terror*). She further argued that terror is the most potent tool to stop people from occupying their bodies. Oppression works to deny people comfort in their own bodies.

Clarissa Chandler drew connections among all oppressions, seeing racial oppression and other forms of oppression as attacks on the body, similar to sexual and physical abuse:

> Trauma is sexual abuse, trauma is physical abuse, but the reality is any one of those things—heterosexism, sexism, racism, adultism—all of those things are about placing someone else in a position where they would not be backed up by society and they would be given freedom to be used by others without intervention. That has to do with placement. That has a very potent and powerful impact on the body. (Chandler, n.d., *Being an Ally to Children*)

In another lecture, Chandler stressed that the experience of racism that tells women of African descent that their skin color is wrong and their hair texture is wrong, like trauma, denies women pleasure in their own body. It tells them not to listen to their body, but to focus outside and respond to others to survive (*Weaving the Story*). Dorothy Allison (1995) described how working class, poor white women's bodies are judged unacceptable and girls are denied pleasure in their bodies:

> Let me tell you about what I have never been allowed to be. Beautiful and female. Sexed and sexual. I was born trash in a land where the people all believe themselves natural aristocrats. . . . My family has a history of death and murder, grief and denial, rage and ugliness—the women of my family most of all.
>
> The women of my family were measured, manlike, sexless, bearers of babies, burdens, and contempt. My family? The women of my family? We are the ones in all those photos taken at mining disasters, floods, fires. We are the ones in the background with our mouths open, in print dresses or drawstring pants and collarless smocks, ugly and old and exhausted. Solid, stolid, wide-hipped baby machines. We were all wide-hipped and predestined. Wide-faced meant stupid. Wide hands marked workhorses with dull hair and tired eyes, thumbing through magazines full of women so different from us they could have been another species. (pp. 32–33)

> We were not beautiful. We were hard and ugly and trying to be proud of it. The poor are plain, virtuous if humble and hardworking, but mostly ugly. Almost always ugly. (p. 37)

When she talked about her sister's beauty, she described how that only increased the contempt with which she was viewed and left her more vulnerable:

> My beautiful sister had been dogged by contempt just like her less beautiful sisters—more, for she dared to be different yet again, to hope when she was supposed to have given up hope, to dream when she was not the one they saved dreams for. Her days were full of boys sneaking over to pinch her breasts and whisper threats into her ears. . . . (p. 79)

Allison talked about how hard she found it when she tried to do karate and why she kept going back even though it was immensely difficult: "What I wanted from karate was some echo of love for my body and the spirit it houses" (p. 65). In the process, she gained a glimpse of a "sense of my body as my own," which she saw as a miracle.

Chandler stressed that being forced to stay in the place of terror breaks down health and prevents those who are oppressed from having the energy to make other decisions. When she asked participants in her workshop what attitudes those who have been abused have about their bodies, a variety of comments were called out:

- body belongs to perpetrator
- something is wrong with my body
- no one else will love my body
- because of my body this happened to me
- my body is not the real me
- my body is a tool
- my body has been trashed, soiled, used up, is a betrayer
- I can't trust my body, it's ugly (Chandler, n.d., *Weaving the Story*)

This list strongly conveys the distrust of the body and the separation from it that follows abuse and violence. Clarissa Chandler summed up by commenting that you cannot expect basic functioning of the body to be healthy after such an onslaught. Those who are oppressed are unable to pay attention to the functioning of their own body. Instead they must be attuned to danger, to the perpetrator's body, because "survival depends on paying attention to them." She suggested that we need the "ability to comfort each other, to empower each other to occupy our own bodies any way we can" if we are to find our own power (*Body Terror*). Allison (1995) asserted that one of the things she knows "for sure . . . is that if we are not beautiful to each other, we cannot know beauty in any form" (p. 86).

Commonly in educational settings, there is little to support a woman in the challenging task of learning to occupy her own body. Sylvia Fraser (1987) described how during her university studies, rather than being empowered to live fully in her own body, she felt she was only *a severed head*:

> . . . only my head went to college. My severed head. That was how I rid myself forever of the red-shoed mannequin I invented to hide my other self—I chopped off her head and registered it in Honors English and Philosophy. (p. 120)

During her studies, Fraser was able to hold herself together with: "I think, therefore I have worth." It was a long time before she was able to learn to *go home* to her body and feel whole. For literacy learners, that option of being *in the mind* may not be there. Yet I think literacy programs do not often recognize the body or the difficulties learners may have because of the pain in their bodies or because of their disconnections from their body, spirit, and their own power.

Women who were abused as children have learned that their body is not their own. It is not theirs to take care of, nurture, provide food, rest, and watch out for:

> The child who experiences incest learns that her body is not hers. She learns that touch is not affection, but violation. (Blume, 1990, p. 192)

> One way to separate from the violation of incest is not to be with one's body: my body is not my self, is not me. This may manifest itself in a variety of ways. Some incest survivors may not pay attention to the pains or other signals of an illness. . . . Often they feel no wholeness with their physical selves, no continuity between the experiences of their physical feelings and their bodies. (Blume, 1990, p. 198)

Such disconnection from the body creates many ongoing health problems, a lack of general ongoing care, as well as a continuing sense of fragmentation and powerlessness.

When children are sexually abused, they are told implicitly and frequently explicitly as well that they are only good for sex, they are only a body, and that body is not their own. Some children escape into their mind and into excellence in school. Others, perhaps particularly where school is also violent or where the self is too shattered at an early age, have nowhere to go. Even as children, they may feel abnormal and wrong. As adults, that feeling may continue. Elly Danica (1996) talked of the way she grew up believing that women's bodies were wrong:

> . . . what mattered most of all was that women not burden men or society with what they perceived as our messy bodies and our even messier, diffuse and illogical minds. I grew up thinking that weak women were subject to physical processes such as menstruation and pregnancy, which they could not control and were required to deny and hide. (p. 21)

As a child, Elly Danica wanted to be like her father and brothers, who seemed to lead a life free of all the messy processes that constrained women. She did not want to be in her messy woman's body. She had no opportunity to grow in self-worth and personal power as a woman. Instead she was fragmented and alienated from her own body. Such profound separation hinders full presence in the learning process.

Janet Liebman Jacobs (1994) described the objectification of the female body:

> Victimized daughters, like all women in Western industrial societies, develop their sense of self in a culture dominated by images of the sexually objectified female. For the sexually abused child, the cultural portrayals of female objectification and degradation merge with internal representations of the self that have been shaped by the experience of traumatic sexualization. As the shame of her private humiliation is mirrored in the social construction woman as body, the abused child's sense of self becomes tied to her identity as sexual object. (p. 119)

Tension around the body for those whose bodies are devalued and judged in terms of race, ability, and class may be layered in complex patterns of trauma. Maria Root (1992) drew attention to the importance of recognizing that the "normal" experiences of being devalued are traumatic:

> . . . insidious trauma is an experience of trauma that has been totally neglected. While its impact shapes a worldview rather than shatters assumptions about the world, over time it may result in a picture of symptomatology similar to that of direct or indirect trauma, particularly involving anxiety, depression, paranoia, and substance abuse. Insidious trauma is usually associated with the social status of an individual being devalued because a characteristic intrinsic to their identity is different from what is valued by those in power for example, gender, color, sexual orientations, physical ability. As a result, it is often present throughout a lifetime and may start at birth. (p. 240)

For many women, the experience of *being in the body* is one where the body is devalued and stigmatized, whether in terms of race, ability, class, age, size, or looks. It is judged to be wrong or not satisfactory. When such experiences are compounded with body memories, pains, discomforts, and ill health, the desire to be present in the body is diminished still further. The issues of presence discussed earlier can also be seen as a "flight from the body" (Jacobs, 1994, p. 132) because it is the site where chaos, pain, shame, and vulnerability are experienced. Yet as Clarissa Chandler revealed, to leave the body behind is to live in exile. The ongoing challenge to reclaim the body is also a process of regaining a sense of personal power.

Reclaiming the Body

Si Transken (1995) talked in terms of *reclaiming body territory*, speaking of abuse as a way in which others projected their needs onto her body. Over the years, she worked to reclaim her body for her own use and her own needs:

> I take up space because it is my right to take up space. My mind is open and my body is open and I am trying. I want to reclaim one-hundred percent of my health and my knowledge of my body. I will reclaim all of my body from my father and his collaborators. (p. 29)

Her words bring to mind Maria Nguen, project manager in the Stepping-Up Program for Immigrant Women, in British Columbia, who spoke of participants in her program—all survivors of abuse. She said the women often hunch, have their head bent, or hide their head. She sees that as a physical effect of put-downs and abuse. In her program, they do energizers to help the women learn to be in their body differently. The exercises include focusing on breathing and dealing with the stress in their lives. She described the changes in the women, which resulted from the work that brings them back in to their bodies as crucial to support learning.

More often in educational programs, I think of the lack of notice taken of the body. I think of the limited and make-do space that literacy programs often use and wonder whether these programs tend to confirm women's sense that they have no right to take up space. What does it do to women who already struggle to occupy the space of their own bodies when there seems to be little space for them in the program? When the programs also seem to have no right to suitable space and, in times of financial cut backs, perhaps no right to exist at all? Can we create the sort of literacy learning spaces that will help students feel a right to exist and supported to claim space—claim the power of their own bodies and claim their full potential to learn?

I can only speculate about how literacy programming might look if the priorities were to make the center or classroom a place where learners could feel their right reclaim their bodies, to take up space, to feel physically comfortable and safe. Of course there is an enormous range of spaces where literacy programs take place, and many programs are constrained by the way space is organized in the larger institution. Some space priorities might include enough room between students to feel comfortable and unintimidated, with freedom from people walking in or overhearing discussions. Space for learners to store their own work, particularly confidential journals, might also be important. A setting that feels warm and comforting, unlike a traditional school classroom, might also be valuable for those who experienced violence in the school setting.

Learners I met at the Horizons Program in British Columbia sat in easy chairs with a coffee table in the middle. This was obviously the setting where they did a lot of their work. In the Chapters Program, in small-town Alberta, I learned that taking on the task of making the room pleasant so that learners feel good about the room is one of the ways they begin to think about what things help them feel good about themselves and build self-esteem. The students and staff had taken on creating a space together. They had managed to get old easy chairs and a quilt, as well as a large table they could all sit around to write. They talked about how important their sense of comfort and safety in the space was. The room certainly did not feel like a classroom and was obviously a space the group had a lot of ownership over.

If programs were more aware of the injuries, health problems, and importance of taking up space, would we be able to do things differently? Would we use the space of the literacy program in ways that are more likely to be comfortable? Would we recognize bodily needs more and take regular breaks or include more movement in classes? Would we be able to support learners in bringing the whole person to class, reclaiming their bodies and claiming the right to take up space? How would such claiming of space support learning?

In community programs, it is challenging to think about how recognition of students' bodily needs could make much difference because so much about such programs is not by choice, but *making do* with whatever is available. Consequently, programs are frequently run in small, airless, windowless rooms. The furniture used is often old, uncomfortable, or even broken. The space is often shared with a variety of groups or different organizations. Privacy is hard to maintain. Anne Moore described the endless frustrations she experienced when she tried to find space in her community-based program for a women's group to function:

> When I started the group for Action Read, my first challenge was to find a suitable location for the women's group. At the time, Action Read was on the fourth floor of a building where the "elevator man" was known to be abusive, especially to women who were poor. Complaints were made but nothing changed. I had no choice but to look for alternative space. With very little money, it was difficult to find a place. . . .
>
> Even when it began, the group just barely fit in the space we chose. However, we were aware that our conversations disrupted the staff and at times theirs disrupted us. . . .
>
> As hard as it was for the staff, the cramped quarters also had a major impact on the group's development. At one point we thought about doing a play but postponed it because there wasn't enough room to move—a wave of the arm might knock into someone. . . . Our physical space was just too limited. Our emotional space was limited as well. Confidentiality for women in the group was a joke at best. Male tutors and learners overhead many of our most intimate discussions. . . .
>
> As staff, we were caught in the middle and left blaming ourselves while trying to cope. . . . (Moore, 1994, pp. 95–97)

Clearly the costs for learners and workers alike must be recognized and widely talked about as a first step if such issues as space are to be understood as fundamental to learning, not merely inconsequential window dressing, and for any possibility of programs obtaining adequate resources.

Engaging the Body in Learning

It is equally challenging to think about how it might be possible not merely to accommodate the body, but also to actively involve it in the literacy learning process. It would be exciting to imagine including access to outdoor courses such as the Canadian Outward Bound School Women of Courage courses because outdoor adventure clearly offers the experience of profound physical learning. These are week-long courses that:

> centre around an expedition that includes canoeing, camping and 24 hours of reflection time, alone or with another. Through these activities, participants engage in a series of increasingly difficult challenges. The progression of these challenges is geared to the social and emotional resources of the individual and the group. Stress is kept to a reasonable level and challenges are met with success rather than frustration of failure. This is

the meaning behind "challenge by choice," each woman determines the level of risk she will take to meet each challenge. (Joyce, 1995, p. 51)

Ruth Goldman (n.d.) wrote in more detail about the program's focus on the body:

The second theme is that of body-consciousness. Abused women are often extremely disconnected from their bodies after experiencing physical and/or sexual abuse. It is very difficult for survivors to feel good about or believe in/trust their bodies. The work that women do at recovering and owning their bodies is a great physical metaphor for the process of self-recovery. As the women do all the physical Outward Bound activities they initially thought were impossible, they physically "take back" control of themselves. We ask them to be aware of bodily sensations and spend an evening discussing pleasurable body experiences. The body is an important place of self-recovery for women and something that feminist education rarely explores. Most of us are disconnected from our bodies in some way and it is hard to feel good about the world when we don't like what we live in. (pp. 65–66)

Stories I have heard of women rock climbing and facing the terror of being on the rock face and trusting that others are holding the rope securely suggest that such learning is profound. Joyce (1995) described the effect: "When a woman accomplishes what a day earlier she thought was impossible, she sees the world anew. She develops the courage to take risks and the confidence to try again" (p. 52). This new learning becomes a part of the self, bringing new possibilities to other learning situations.

Although wilderness trips may not often be possible in literacy programs, exploring the possibilities for incorporating physical adventure as part of literacy learning would be very valuable in transforming women's sense of themselves. Staff at the Learning Centre in Alberta now hold a regular exercise session for learners who choose to participate, which grew out of a health project. They are now planning to work toward a physically challenging expedition. Mary Norton wrote recently:

We are thinking about introducing a "challenge" program next fall for people who are keen about learning and want structure, challenge, etc. We're thinking of suggesting an "outdoor" component—as a treat but also as a challenge (e.g., a hike in Jasper). (personal correspondence, July 1999)

I will be very interested to see the impact of this new project on learning in the program.

Even where dramatic physical activity cannot take place, recognizing the body in more minor ways and incorporating that aspect into literacy learning can have major impact. Instructor Christina Patterson has tried various physical activities and plans her work with a belief in the value of creating new physical patterns:

I have been designing and teaching a course for fundamental level English learners which gives them physical experiences in the classroom. Some activities are simple sounding like moving huge piles of oranges from one table to another with a team of people you choose from your classmates. Or, building stand-alone structures from Tinkertoy to answer the questions "what do you need to make something stand as tall as possible on it's own?" Then changing the question to "What do you need to make someone stand as tall as possible on their own?" and going back through the same ideas.

I do things in the classroom that you can't talk about, or if you do talk about them they are reduced by the words. I try to give the learner experience with non-verbal learning. I do truly believe in the body's memory. I teach them to draw mandala and try to get them to understand the idea that the purpose is the process. It is incidental that you have a beautiful drawing at the end.

How this relates to issues of violence and learning is not scientific. If you believe that the body remembers then maybe you can believe that the body stores patterns of response to situations. To give a learner opportunities for physical response puts them in touch with their patterns and gives them an opportunity to re-pattern their responses. If you set-up situations where learners are made to rely on each other, help each other, refuse each other, compete with and against each other or against time or pressure, you give them an opportunity to change their physical response to life, which can change their thinking. (Alphaplus Literacy & Violence Online Seminar, February–April 1998)

This work helped me imagine how women might experience themselves differently and connect to their whole selves and others in the group. Christina Patterson had a wealth of wonderful physical activities she tried. In another message, she described an experience of juggling:

I have done juggling with lemons, limes, oranges and grapefruit. That was a lot of fun. Once we had all had some time to juggle alone and then with a friend, we designed some juggling in one large group. Sort of like dancing with two rows of people moving along until it was their turn to go down the center of the rows. And all the while people were throwing fruit across to their partner. When it was your turn to go down the middle with your partner, you also had to dodge the other people's fruit. We laughed a lot with that one. (Alphaplus Literacy & Violence Online Seminar, February–April 1998)

This activity reminded me again of the value of creating pleasure in the classroom, and that laughing is a physical experience that changes the body and mind.

Recently, I was facilitating a group where we were struggling to accomplish a task that seemed pretty daunting in the time available. When one participant said she needed something to wake her up and get her moving, it was the perfect invitation for my co-facilitator, Moon Joyce, to draw on her Outward Bound experience and initiate an exercise. She had us form a "Gordian knot." We formed a circle and each of us linked hands to two different women across the middle of the group. Then she told us we had to unknot ourselves. With much climbing and maneuvering, much laughter, and many protestations that it could not possibly work, we were eventually standing in a circle unknotted but still linked. By then we were all awake, enlivened, and had shared the experience of achieving something we were sure was impossible. It carried us into our challenging intellectual task. This particular exercise might not work for people with some physical disabilities or in a mixed group, and it might not be a comfortable physical distance for some. However, there are many physical initiative games of this sort that might help learners change the energy and lead to a strengthened sense that they can "do it," which could carry over to literacy learning.

Exercises or activities that get people to experience something—so that they have data—and then draw from that experience for their writing can also give students a different sensation and engage them fully. Students at the Chapters Program talked about some of the activities they tried (e.g., playing on the swings in a children's playground, putting temporary tattoos on their body, going to the city together). These physical activities provided them with pleasurable emotions and physical sensations. When they returned to class, they wrote vividly about these experiences, read them out loud to each other, and sometimes worked on the writing to create a book. Physical activity can be a rich source of material for discussion and written work. Physical activity can also change the energy in the room. There are many physical exercises to draw from that are aimed specifically at warming people up, getting a group of people to know each other, and energizing when the energy slumps. These exercises, or ones adapted specifically to the literacy classroom, might help learners stay fully present.

Caution needs to be exercised to ensure safety so that physical exercises are not too challenging for anyone in the group, remembering how hard any exercise may be for women with health problems, disabilities, or those with little practice at being in their body. It is crucial to always be clear that everyone has a genuine option of sitting out, free from even subtle pressure. One First Nation instructor based in Toronto spoke about her experience:

> . . . as I'm planning, especially anything to do with the body, I notice some women might be uncomfortable with doing that. So I don't push it, I give them a chance, they can opt out, . . . and they can watch and observe and participate in any written thing afterwards. I don't want to push, but usually they are uncomfortable for a while and then they see the other women doing stuff and decide "oh I want to do that too," so they get up and do it, and it's a really good experience, that's another area where I'm aware to be sensitive about where they are at in terms of how they feel about their body. . . . (interview, First Nation Instructors, Toronto, January 1997)

Even minimal movement can play a major role in reconnecting women to their bodies. The simple reminder to breathe can help a group calm themselves, notice their bodies and bodily needs, and take stock of the work they have accomplished. The opportunity to walk across the room may be valuable, as Christina Patterson wrote in the online seminar:

> I sometimes find when learners are not present for thinking well, they are present for doing a stand up exercise. Here's me and physical learning again. Asking a student to come to the chalkboard and do a question engages them differently than asking them to just think in order to be involved. (Alphaplus Literacy & Violence Online Seminar, February–April 1998)

In workshops and trainings, whenever I simply get people standing and moving, I notice that the classroom comes alive again. I often include exercises where participants show where they stand on a question by standing along a line. At one end is one extreme and the other end the other extreme. Then participants have to decide where they want to stand in relation to the others in the group and to the two extremes. They talk to each other to help them decide where to position themselves and then call out, mentioning reasons why they are standing where they are or insights they learned from talking with the others around them. The whole exercise makes an issue visible, gets small-group discussion happening, and energizes people as they move from their seats.

Physical activity can help us draw on the wisdom of our bodies. Denise Nadeau (1996) made strong claims for the value of drawing the body into activist work—claims that I think are equally applicable to literacy work:

> The body is much more than a tool which we must periodically wake up, energize or refuel in the educational process. Rather, it holds some of the keys to both analysis of present circumstances and identification of the future direction women can take to meet their needs and regain control over their daily lives. (p. 58)

She went on to argue that: "Using certain forms of body-work that release energy, and using voice in chants, slogans and yelling, help to build a sense of authority and collective power" (p. 58). Her description makes me think of the possibilities in literacy program for harnessing women's collective power, rather than remaining in individual isolation. Denise Nadeau drew from bioenergetics, developed from the theory that: "held or repressed feelings have power and that when a feeling is freed it becomes possible to liberate not only the energy of the feeling itself but the energy that has been used to repress it" (p. 50).

Bioenergetics, guided meditation, and exercises that get women acting out their experiences, such as how they spend their days, can all draw on the body's knowledge. For women who have been devalued and disconnected from themselves, such work may be particularly important to reconnect emotion and body knowledge to reach a complexity of "rational analysis" that seems impossible when women have learned too thoroughly that they are not smart. Denise Nadeau (1996) argued:

> When education methods focus solely on the mind, the body-self that has been silenced or locked away in denial is not permitted to emerge. That silencing or denial is often at the root of the deep sense of powerlessness which makes women feel unable to act. (p. 51)

I would add that when education methods focus solely on the mind with learners who have been told explicitly and implicitly that their minds do not work well, opportunities to tap women's potential brilliance are lost.

Literacy programming needs to be designed and carried out with an awareness that damage to the body caused by trauma impedes participation—health problems, injuries that making sitting difficult or that make a woman embarrassed to attend class or unable to get there—but this is not enough. We need to think about what happens to literacy programming when we recognize the body more fully. Program planning and facilitation could be enhanced if we take account of the bodily needs of learners. Awareness that learners have bodies that take up space and attention to the physical space within which literacy learning is occurring could be crucial in making learning possible. Opportunities to draw the body into the learning process, for people to move as part of literacy learning, and to explore a wide variety of physical experiences may be extremely challenging for women who have fled their bodies. However, movement may help them find a sense of personal power and enhance learning possibilities, increasing the potential for many learners to stay present and learn. In adult literacy, the extraordinary potential for learning activities that involve the body to tap power to learn has hardly been imagined, let alone mapped out. It is exciting to imagine the difference exploring a variety of ways of involving the body could make for many learners.

MIND

Like my approach to the body, I first began thinking about the mind in terms of damage. However, a group of literacy learners in Charlottetown, Prince Edward Island, were very clear that they did not like the concept. They argued that it suggested no hope and was demeaning. Lillian Mead said eloquently that damage felt like a put-down because it sounded unfixable. She explained that abuse causes so much pain that the mind blocks the pain, and literacy learning may also be blocked at the same time. For her, the way in which the mind protects itself suggested that, far from not working, the mind is working brilliantly. Her mind was filled with reacting to the violence, which takes energy away from new learning: "My mind is already being used, my mind is not damaged, my mind is busy" (interview, Charlottetown, PEI, March 1997).

This understanding of the mind as busy seems particularly helpful. Learners who are in crisis may well have difficulty with literacy learning. Learners and shelter workers suggested that it was important to recognize that, particularly during a crisis, it is unreasonable to expect the mind to work on literacy learning when it is focused on learning how to survive in new circumstances. Lillian Mead told me a story from her own experience. While in the process of leaving a violent husband, she had tried to study math. She had terrible difficulty and thought she just could not do that math. Later, after things had settled down in her life, she looked at the math book and was surprised to find it quite straightforward. We talked about what a difference it would have made if someone had explained to her at the time that it is often hard to think when you are dealing with a crisis, especially when the situation is stressful, so that she would not have felt stupid on top of everything else.

A learner at Malaspina College in British Columbia described a similar experience where crisis blocked her ability to learn:

> Even now I'm in court for my abuse as a child I can't think. I cannot think and things are popping back. I have to deal with it right now. I write about it and tear it up. Right now I am having a real struggle with it . . . I know it has a lot to do with it. It's a lot to deal with it. (interview, Malaspina College, Duncan, British Columbia, November 1996)

Some literacy workers do help learners recognize that when they are having difficulty learning literacy it may be due to the circumstances in their life at the time, whereas others may not realize what the problem is and why their student is having such difficulty. Many learners in crisis are left condemning themselves for their inability to learn or remember. It is important that workers are aware of this possibility; they should encourage students to reflect on their lives and think about what else they may be learning that has more immediate urgency than the learning they are trying to focus on. In this way, learners may at least avoid condemning themselves as stupid.

Many learners struggle with thinking that they are stupid and cannot learn. Sometimes this may be because their mind is busy, for others, it may be that abusers have told them or shown them that they are *stupid*. Pat Capponi (1992) described how her belief in her stupidity was formed:

> I believed what my father had always told me: I was stupid and lazy. I'd heard it so often I couldn't choose to disbelieve it. It seemed I'd always been slow and stubborn. I still couldn't tell time in the fourth grade, couldn't add or subtract, despite my father's nightly tutorials. I couldn't understand why I persisted in my laziness when it always brought me so much grief. I have very few memories of the time I spent in early grade school, and those I have are riddled with beatings and shame. (p. 35)

She went on to describe the nightly sessions where her father would ask her math questions and every failure to answer correctly would expose her to his vicious beatings. She concluded the scene: "Every wrong answer brought pain, causing me to panic so much the few correct answers I could remember scooted right out of my brain, abandoning me to his cruelty" (p. 36).

In such learning conditions, she could not be anything but *stupid*. Terror would have closed her mind down. Now when she tries to learn, a shadow of that earlier terror often recurs, making her feel again that she cannot learn. Many learners have come to believe that they are stupid in similar circumstances and have had that judgment reinforced repeatedly until they, too, have no choice but to believe it must be true. That legacy can be a firm knowledge not easily turned around.

Therapist Lorna Gallant talked about a client now studying in university who still has difficulty remembering anything. She said she thought that feeling stupid was "the strongest thing" going on for this woman. First Nation instructors in Toronto talked about the weight of feeling stupid: ". . . when you're told you're stupid so many times, you start believing you're stupid. Or you can't do anything. Or you're incapable of doing anything" (Interview, First Nation Instructors, Toronto, January 1997).

Several students talked about the messages they received about their stupidity:

> You are stupid, I can't believe it, you have no idea, on and on. . . . The body language I can't believe. . . .
>
> At first I'd fight back . . . but after a while, you can only take it for so long, I'd feel like I was shrinking. I started to believe it. It made me scared to ask for help or try to learn, I thought I couldn't learn. So I didn't even try. . . .

> I was raised basically like that, the men are the breadwinners and the women stay home. Kept home. I heard the same things, you can't do it. . . .
>
> I was scared to open the text book, I was so intimidated. I didn't want to look in it. It took me about seven weeks to open the book. . . . I closed it, I can't do it. . . .

> I felt stupid, how stupid can someone be, not to know. . . . (interview, Malaspina College, Duncan, British Columbia, November 1996

Earlier I discussed strategies for supporting women to move away from feeling worthless and to address fear. Here I want to add the importance of creating a relaxing, playful atmosphere and supporting women in developing new judgments about their ability to use their mind.

My intense reading of therapeutic literature left me overwhelmed by all the possible effects childhood or adulthood violence can have on the mind. I found extracts like the following very disturbing:

> Physiological hyperarousal interferes with the capacity to concentrate and to learn from experience. Aside from amnesias about aspects of the trauma, traumatized people often have trouble remembering ordinary events as well. Easily triggered into hyperarousal by trauma-related stimuli, and beset with difficulties in paying attention, they may display symptoms of attention-deficit/hyperactivity disorder. After a traumatic experience

people often lose some maturational achievements and regress to earlier modes of coping with stress . . . in adults it is expressed as excessive dependence and in a loss of capacity to make thoughtful, autonomous decisions. (van der Kolk et al., 1996, p. 422)

Although I was intrigued and worried about the implications of such research for literacy learning, I am also disturbed by the unproblematic creation of those who have experienced trauma as *other, not normal,* and clearly *less than.* Certainly the description does appear to offer information that I recognize from Mary—the learner I tutor—but the picture also obscures other characteristics. Mary frequently finds it difficult to remember words she has read, but she often has an amazing memory. For example, she remembers the exact words of an interaction that has been significant to her and can rerun some conversations years later. She often has difficulty paying attention and is easily distracted by crises going on in her life. She often has enormous difficulty making decisions, which seems to be part of the complicated dynamic around control discussed earlier. At other times, she is adamant about her judgment.

There is also a growing literature exploring the possibilities that learning disabilities may develop because of exposure to childhood trauma (e.g., Gardner, 1971; van der Kolk et al., 1996). There seems to be some value in exploring these sorts of accounts because they may help learners and instructors understand patterns they experience and help students avoid the label of *stupidity.* However, the danger in such accounts is that they become another label that categorizes literacy learners as *other* and thus behavior that contrasts with the pattern is missed.

There is often enormous debate about the value to survivors of work that suggests that trauma affects the mind. It often surfaces on the listserv on violence previously mentioned, and many argue that the research data do women a disfavor. Rather like the learner I spoke to, they argue that "ascribing deformity" to women and children who have experienced trauma is not helpful. Such studies, they say, suggest a uniformity of impact and that there is no possibility of change. On the other side, many argue that there is value in noting the impacts of trauma on the mind. It can help survivors understand what is going on for them; rather than feeling crazy or stupid, they see how to work with the effects. Sandi Barbero, one participant on the listserv, put it this way:

Those of us who are counselors-psychotherapists know that the impact on the ability to absorb information is significantly impaired. We know that Post Traumatic Stress Disorder usually is concomitant with Major Depression (from violence), a distractive block to absorbing information. . . . In fact since the brain chemistry is often altered, why wouldn't learning be impaired? (FIVERS, April 1997)

Others have difficulty with the medical definitions of *disorder* and *depression*. Some argue that, because all experience impacts on the brain and development, of course trauma would also affect the brain. However, it may not affect functioning. Matthea Smith explained:

> Any life's experience, enjoyable or otherwise, has an effect on brain patterns and personality. My concern is that the evaluation of child abuse and the effects on personality is getting very close to victim blaming.
> There is much research that has shown that, depending on the motivation, the person can heal from the abuse.
> I liken it to a severe burn on the arm. While the area is healing there is much pain, and most times the person will be "overly" careful to make sure that they don't reinjure the area . . . whether their perception of the possible reinjury is real or perceived. But after time the burn heals and leaves a scar. That scar is a memory of what happened in the past, but is not necessarily an indication of how the arm performs normal daily tasks. (FIVERS, April 1997)

This image is an interesting way to suggest that some aspect of the mind may be wounded or scarred, but that it may not affect functioning or the possibility of learning. There may be value in recognizing the wound and then focusing on rebuilding strength. As Priscilla George pointed out, from the experience comes a teaching—greater empathy for others becomes a strength—that should be honored (personal correspondence, September 1998).

Getting "Unstuck"

In the therapeutic literature, there is much discussion of the nature of memory, particularly the memory of the trauma. Some aspects of that debate merge into the popular discourse about false memory and the reliability of previously repressed childhood memories. The questions crucial to literacy learning are not so much about the memory of trauma, but about the impact of trauma and past trauma on ongoing memory formation. A learner in the Horizons Program in Duncan, British Columbia, looked for understanding of her lack of memory. She had a lot of questions about whether the trauma she had experienced as a child had affected her memory and her ability to learn in the present. She is hoping to go to college eventually and wonders whether that makes sense if she still has difficulty remembering and has not done anything to shift the problem, such as working on her memories of trauma. She said:

> I graduated, but don't remember anything . . . for me what I went through from Grade 6 on I don't remember anything. I don't recall anything that I did learn. It concerns me, I can take in the information, and pass the test, but to remember it even two weeks later it is gone. I am wondering if that is common, because it is all repressed from Grade 6 on. I can only remember the bad things that happened.
>
> I am concerned now, I can go there and do the work . . . but I'm concerned am I still in that pattern because I haven't done anything to change the memories that are still there. I am wondering whether it is still going to be there. (interview, Horizons Program, Duncan, British Columbia, November 1996)

Other learners in her program also talked about having a hard time remembering what they learned in school. I am not sure that there are answers to that learner's perceptive questions. I asked various counselors whether they thought past trauma affects current memory and, if so, whether it is permanent. Several said that these were the questions they were currently asking themselves. In response, they referred me to the sort of literature excerpted earlier and drew on their own experience working with survivors. Mary Beth Levan explained that she thinks about the issue of memory in terms of the "nervous system wired for escape" described earlier. She suggested that, in that state, it is hard to retain information; trauma survivors need to learn to leave the trauma behind and become "rewired for calm" so that remembering is easier. Similarly, Lorna Gallant thought that the most effective strategy to help survivors learn and remember was to focus on helping them to stay *present* through reducing their anxiety as far as possible.

Lorna Gallant also thought that women who cannot remember their school years are at a disadvantage in their future learning because they cannot remember the basics and have nothing to build on. She suggested that memory is not repressed selectively—things that were not traumatic are repressed along with the trauma. Perhaps in the process of recovering memories of the trauma, survivors might also recover memories of their childhood and rediscover skills they had previously learned. Similarly, research into amnesia and recall of trauma describes one pattern of amnesia:

> Many reported amnesia not only for the abuse that occurred, but also for whole eras of development (e.g., early or middle childhood) and whole categories of experience (e.g., events inside the home or contacts with specific

family members) as well. Most reported witnessing family violence as well, and many reported abuse by more than one perpetrator. (Harvey & Herman, 1994, pp. 302–303)

Maxine Morris, a mental health therapist, wondered whether going back to the time of learning literacy skills would help survivors who do not remember learning literacy skills in childhood to remember them and then build on that knowledge base. The therapist referred to earlier, Lorna Gallant, suggested that we need to frame literacy work as a creative process—connecting to the past by looking at where a learner "got stuck" and helping her "get unstuck." She believes it is crucial for survivors to have long-term individual, free therapy to help in that process of getting unstuck. However, she was quite pessimistic about the possibility, "saying it doesn't make it available."

Although some research suggests that trauma affects memory generally: "Studies of traumatized people now demonstrate that some have abnormalities not only in trauma-specific memory but also in general memory" (Herman, 1996, pp. 7–8). The literacy worker is offered little help by such pronouncements because it is unclear what the effect of such *abnormalities* might be. Some research has suggested that visual memory is not affected by trauma, but the verbal short-term memory shows *deficits* (Bremner et al., 1995). The main value for literacy of such research might be that it encourages learners and instructors to explore memory, recognizing that some aspects of memory might be affected while others are not. Work that helps a learner to discover how she learns best—to notice, for instance, whether it helps her to see, hear, write, or say a word out loud or to move or be still while she learns—will support learning. Even recognizing that her memory may have been affected by her experience of trauma may free a learner from critical judgments as long as the information is used to help her focus on discovering her strengths, rather than simply documenting her losses.

The academic literature suggests that problems with such areas as narrative sequence, language development and attention may result from childhood experiences of abuse:

Current research among preschool children exposed to both intrafamilial and community violence has indicated interference with this task [narrative coherence], resulting in more chaotic narrative construction. Achievement of this developmental task is essential to subsequent competencies in reading, writing and communication skills. (van der Kolk et al., 1996, p. 342)

I am wary about this simple statement. I wonder what would count as "chaotic narrative construction" and I am also concerned about ethnocentrism in the assumption that everyone orders and creates a similar narrative structure. What might be defined as *chaos* here is order in another culture, class, or race. Nevertheless, this observation does point to work that could be carried out in literacy exploring narrative form. Literacy work frequently includes literacy learners telling autobiographical tales, and many learners have difficulty telling a chronological narrative. Sally McBeth and Vivian Stollmeyer (1988) talked about the difficulty Rose Doiron had remembering things in sequence and illustrated this with Rose's first writing, which later became My *Name is Rose* (Doiron, 1987). With the help of another student, Rose first wrote:

> About my father
> he bet me with his belt
> In My dream, I told him
> leave me alone
> after the dream I take dizzy
> don't touch me
> and Paul had to awak me
> When I was six years old
> My father starting beting
> I have barse om my body
> I had burns on my back
> I was sixteen I left home
> I went to see paul
> My clothes were all ript
> Paul gave me some of his clothes
> Paul clean me up all the blood from the
> noise. . . . (p. 53)

When Rose wrote and rewrote her story, she was able to choose the best order to make what happened to her vividly clear to readers. Exploring narrative order through a variety of exercises (e.g., reordering written stories or series of pictures, creating stories from collections of pictures or photos, completing stories from a series of prompts) might be useful to strengthen literacy learning.

Work with narrative order could offer playful ways to help learners discover they have a mind. The legacy of abuse leaves many women feeling that learning is not for them—that they are only good for sex. However, it is important to remember that some who have experienced severe trauma do extremely well in academic work. This suggests that perhaps a key aspect of the mind that can be addressed in literacy programming is helping learners shift their own sense that they do not have a mind that works or that counts. Some learners have told me that what they needed was a program to help them "learn what a mind is" and learn that they "have a mind."

A layered, integrated curriculum might help learners perceive their mind at work and help them play with learning. Exploring the messages women have been told about their minds and turning these around with work that helps women see their brilliance, such as thinking about something they do really well and teaching it to others, could be part of the process. Priscilla George talked about the impact of getting a student to remember one thing she is good at:

> I remember this one woman that I was working with, and because she had been abused in so many different ways, and always had been put down, she did not honestly think she had ever done anything well. When we were trying to put together her resume, that was so painful for her to think of anything she had done well. And do you know how far back we had to go? Grade four. She made a cake. Because she just kept saying no I haven't done anything, and no I haven't succeeded at anything. It was starting to get painful for me, even, and I thought I should just leave it alone. But then there was something inside me that kept saying there's got to be something. And she finally came up with this cake. And so when she described the cake to me, how she made it and who she gave it to, and how everybody reacted, it was like opening up a dam. She began to realize well, okay, maybe I didn't exactly excel at school, but there are certain other things. It was like we were talking about, there are other things that she can be good at besides being able to read the written word. And so getting them to recognize that there are other skills. (interview, First Nation Instructors, Toronto, January 1997)

Re-reading the quote, Priscilla George reminded me that she had also talked about the importance of remaining calm—not showing any frustration in the long process of seeking out something the woman had done well (personal correspondence, September 1998). Clearly such a process could easily become a diminishing one if it drew attention to the absence of things the learner did well, rather than celebrating that there was something she could do well.

A variety of activities could support women discovering their mind and exploring reasoning and problem solving. For example, a group might collectively take on a problem scenario and think of ways to address it. Groups could play "if . . . then" or "fortunately . . . unfortunately" and tell a variety of fanciful stories of consequences and carry out mind, memory, and problem-solving games of various sorts. Although such activities could make learners feel put down as childlike or vulnerable, if introduced well, could free learners from some of the anxiety associated with trying to read and write and help them explore and believe in the possibilities of their minds.

Learning more about ways of learning and what blocks learning might also be valuable. Creative work to look at *stuckness* (e.g., drawing lifelines) explore when women first got stuck with their literacy learning, and look at why and when could be used to help them find new ways to move forward and get unstuck. In every group I talked to, learners talked about the value of learning about how they learn, of understanding that feeling stupid is a product of abuse, and learning that anxiety prevented concentration. Such learning can help women begin to believe in their ability to think and learn. Then they may find that their minds are able to learn reading and writing better than they could have imagined.

CREATE BALANCE

Looking at people in terms of these four aspects has challenged me to think about new possibilities for literacy work—focused on the body, mind, emotions, and spirit—to fully engage learners in a creative learning process. Some literacy workers' approaches suggest directions that, even within conventional programs, recognize the whole person. Christina Patterson wrote about teaching math while recognizing emotion, body, and mind and using an approach in all her teaching that seeks to rekindle the spirit:

> I also need to add another book to the list of materials you can use with learners. *A New Way to Look at Math* is the title, written by Kate Nonesuch et al., [ABE Fundamental Level Mathematics I, 1994] . . . The first three chapters are 1) Emotions and Learning 2) and 3) Strategies for Dealing with Anxiety Part 1 & 2. I started last term's fundamental math classes with these introductory exercises and it brought the whole idea of fear, doubt and anxiety into the classroom. Throughout the term I checked-in using the vocabulary we had become familiar with and students became accustomed to checking in with themselves about the way they were feeling.
>
> I do a bunch of things in my math class to engage the learners physically. Attendance is a sheet by the front door where they are asked to sign their initials. Test sign-up is on a different wall. Computer discs are in another corner. I set the room up so students have reasons to move around

the room. I just bought a dart board. It's excellent for add, subtract and multiply. Students love it. It wanted to have an element of danger in their hands. Hard to describe but that was part of my purpose. Long ago a young prostitute said she couldn't give up the streets because nothing scared her like tricking and she couldn't give that up. We roll dice for adding, subtracting and multiplying. We sit in a different location each time, random, but I do usually try to make the class come around the one person that day who I feel would feel better if the group came to her instead of her having to move to be part of the group. I observe students working at the board and come to recognize evidence of stress. L's math gets smaller and smaller. T spits on her hand and swipes at mistakes she makes to get them off the chalkboard as soon as possible. Every student should have their own chalk brush. No one likes to have their mistakes written for long. Once a term I take the group as a whole for a tour of the library. My purpose is to move us through the College as a group. It builds glue.

As far as the mind I most often have students who draw a blank. I reassure them time and again, calmly but surely. I identify their own learning for them, talk about their progress, help them remember how they were and where they now are. I try to give them patterns for learning new things. Long division is divide, multiply, subtract, bring down and I sing it to them like a rap song. Pretty soon they're standing at the board mimicking my singing and keeping track of the order of performing the skills. (Alphaplus Literacy & Violence Online Seminar, February–April 1998)

Christina Patterson's description provides a lovely example of what the classroom can look like when body, mind, and emotions are recognized together. She reveals that, even within a structured, formal college program, it is possible to draw in the body and emotions and recognize the part they play in learning.

Similarly, drawing on creative forms such as music can create a balance that involves body, mind, emotion, and spirit. One instructor described singing as *heart-warming*. Singing can create pleasure and ground learners in the present. I have seen how singing a simple round ("Steady as a rock, rooted like a tree, I am here, standing strong in my rightful place"; written by Kim Brodey[3]) affected learners. Over and over again, I have heard and seen the sense of power that singing has given everyone participating. Literacy learners have taken on presenting to a group or writing after singing that song. They have spoken about how they felt able to take on the challenge because of the singing and that they found themselves writing in a new way. Moon Joyce (1996) spoke of the effect of singing on all aspects of the self:

---

[3]This is the first verse of Kim Brodey's song "Steady as a Rock," copyright SOCAN, 1995.

Singing is a very effective enabler for learning generally. As an enabler in experiential learning, singing can be used to support us as we move through the stages of a learning experience. This can be achieved because of the nature of singing itself: it relaxes, refreshes, and energizes, and it encourages and supports lateral thinking and right-brain processes by stirring the imagination through metaphors and imagery, and creating mental space for possibilities. Singing supports creativity by promoting playfulness. As a cognitive process, the structure of singing exercises left-brain functions which assist in sequential patterned thinking, and serves to increase concentration and memory. Singing also connects right- and left-brain functions.

In support of our spiritual capabilities, the process of "giving voice" is sacred work and as such, promotes the full expression of ourselves as spiritual beings. It connects us to our humanity and sacredness; it grounds and centres us to our own power. Singing is a sublime experience that elicits joy, awe, wonder, and reverence—even in the midst of despair and sadness. Singing can also inspire our individual and collective will and desire.

Singing creates an opportunity for us to open up to one another in order to hear each other in a deep and integral way since it crosses differences of class, race, religion, and sexuality, among others, and creates space where differences can be seen and acknowledged in a positive and powerful way. In many dramatic ways, singing takes us into our bodies and puts us in touch with our emotions. Singing can relax our body, release physical tensions, and provide a vehicle for safe emotional release. It generates physical energy and aerates our bodies through deep and sustained breathing. All our physical senses are stimulated by the process of singing which in turn produces heightened states of sensitivity and arousal. . . . (p. 256)

The value of singing collectively to enhance group energy suggests exciting possibilities in the literacy classroom:

Singing can connect us internally to our own complete inventory of learning capabilities. But even greater possibilities exist when a group of individuals sing en masse. While exercising our individual capabilities, particularly the capacity for relational learning, all members of a group contribute to building a synergistic spiralling of collective energy, insight, and creativity which is extremely compelling and effective. (Joyce, 1996, p. 256)

Moon Joyce provided a compelling description of the value of singing. She argued that singing engages body, mind, emotion, and spirit. Her recent work (Joyce, in press) explored ways that singing also marks belonging or exclusion. Singing can be alienating if the singing practice is one of "a dominant group marking the space as culturally theirs, not yours." It is important to be careful with the choice of song and design of the activity to notice who could be excluded, feel like an outsider, or feel that they are being asked to set aside their differences and join in a false sense of unity and harmony. Despite the challenge to use singing carefully, like Christina Patterson's practice, the description of song suggests enormous possibilities for experimenting with new approaches. I believe that if we begin to use singing more fully in literacy work and explore its potential for enhancing literacy learning, the result may lead to surprising success in learning.

In all programs, some approaches that draw in all aspects of the person are possible. In some programs, it may be possible to run a women's group or a special holistic program or create a variety of innovative programming to draw the whole person more fully into the literacy learning process. A fascinating health workbook produced by Julie Devon Dodd in Prince Edward Island for the Women's Network (1998) looked at health in terms of physical, mental, emotional, and spiritual health. This book led me to think about a course that could engage learners to explore themselves, looking at each aspect of the person. The workbook includes exercises to help a literacy learner understand each aspect of the self and experience that aspect. Such exercises could form the starting point for journal writing and further personal reflection. A course in personal exploration could support learners in creating a new identity as a successful learner.[4] Learners could also look at ways to look after all aspects of themselves and strengthen their ability to learn. They could collaborate with instructors in drawing spirit, emotions, body, and mind more fully into the regular literacy classes.

Whether the program situation enables broad, innovative initiatives incorporating the whole person into the learning activity or only minor modifications that draw on all aspects of the person, honoring the presence of spirit, emotion, body, and mind and drawing from the wisdom of each aspect will create the fertile ground for an instructor to discover new creative possibilities. It is not sufficient in literacy to teach only to the mind of the literacy learner. Body, emotions, and spirit can all play a part in preventing learning if they are ignored or, if they are addressed, in making it possible for all women to learn perhaps more effectively than we have previously imagined possible for many literacy learners.

---

[4]In collaboration with Parkdale Project Read, a community-based literacy program in Toronto, I will design and lead such a course during 1999/2000. This has been funded by the former Ontario Provincial Ministry of Education, now Ministry of Training, Colleges and Universities, along with the Federal Ministry of Human Resources, National Literacy Secretariat.

III

BEARING WITNESS

7

Bridging the Divide Between Literacy and Therapy

Traditionally, literacy and therapy have been seen as entirely separate. Frequently, however, literacy workers are called on to carry out a counseling role. Many feel unprepared to do so and unclear whether they should. Both clarity about boundaries between therapy and literacy and acknowledging that a simple division between the two fields is arbitrary are useful understandings for considering appropriate links between literacy and therapy. Creating a variety of bridges between the two disciplines and making therapy and counseling more visible within literacy programs will support the capacity of learners to learn effectively. This shift also interrupts the frame that impacts of trauma are only to be addressed in isolation between a woman and her therapist so that a woman can return to *normal* and resume ordinary life as soon as possible. Unsettling this frame is not only significant theoretically, but enables silences about violence and learning to be broken and frees learners from impossible expectations that they simply put the past behind them. It opens new possibilities for successful learning.

I recognize the value of individual therapy, yet encourage a shift away from assumptions that a woman should heal and come back to literacy when she is better and away from the discourse of the *privatization of pain* that suggests impacts of trauma are only a private medical matter. Through focusing on connections to therapy and counseling, I do not want to suggest that counseling is the only way for a woman to explore her memories of trauma and address the legacies of violence in her life. Rather, I also want to hold an awareness of the varied ways women might be able to address their own issues. Writing a journal is often recommended as part of the healing process. For some, the process of writing may meet their needs to work through issues in their lives. Dorothy

Allison (1988) explained: "I was not the kind of person who could imagine asking for help or talking about my personal business." Instead, she wrote and rewrote her way to her own truths. Initially she wrote for herself:

> Writing it all down was purging. Putting those stories on paper took them out of the nightmare realm and made me almost love myself for being able to finally face them. . . . I did not imagine anyone reading my rambling, ranting stories. I was writing for myself, trying to shape my life outside my terrors and helplessness to make it visible and real in a tangible way. (p. 9)

Elly Danica (1996) also used writing as a way to work through her pain, believing that there was no help besides what she could give herself through her own writing. After 10 years of writing, she said: "Eventually I had more than two thousand journal pages and a growing clarity about the issues" (p. 11). She also provided a reminder that writing is not the only route. As she put it: "I used words as my tools, but there are others" (p. 39). For her, weaving was another valuable tool:

> I began my long, slow healing process through my hands. It made me feel good (and slightly warmer) to be absorbed completely in a weaving project. I taught myself and was soon very skilled at it . . .
> I cannot adequately describe how important the work with my hands was to my healing. Even as I felt ugly and hopeless beyond measure, my hands learned to speak an eloquent beauty and to weave the strands of my future into whole cloth. (p. 37)

It is important that literacy workers not suggest that therapy or counseling is the only way to seriously address impacts of violence. Many women may find more culturally appropriate approaches or prefer to discover creative ways to work through their issues. However, when learners ask teachers and other literacy workers to listen to their disclosures of violence, they may be looking for someone to take on the role of listener or counselor. Many literacy workers will want to make connections with counseling organizations—either to find someone else who can carry out that role more adequately or gain the training and support that will enable them to provide the help themselves.

The challenge of inviting therapists and counselors to build strong connections with literacy work lies in deciding which versions of counseling and therapy should be invited in and in what ways. The danger is that therapeutic practitioners might bring with them traditional conceptions of the divide between literacy and therapy and pathologize learners or judge them within a deficit model. The potential gain is that creative approaches to bridging the divide between literacy and therapy give literacy learners more access to counseling supports. Making these resources visible and accessible would in itself break silences, reduce shame, and ultimately enhance learning.

WHAT COUNSELING? WHICH THERAPY?

The questions of what types of counseling and therapy should be accessed and linked to literacy work and what roles literacy workers should play in relation to counseling are absolutely central. Mary J. Breen, a participant in the online seminar on literacy and violence, asked:

> If as teachers, we are moving towards some kind of therapeutic role, then we have to be really clear about what our goals are. For example, is it to help students learn to behave so as to avoid the blows, or is it to help them figure out their own best answers (answers that may include staying put as well as leaving)? Or is our role to take on the bigger issues of poverty and unemployment that are, if not reasons, then at least triggers for violence? (Alphaplus Literacy & Violence Online Seminar, February–April 1998)

Other seminar participants voiced further concerns about the purposes of therapy and counseling; they pointed to the dangers of seeing the impact of trauma as a medical problem to be addressed privately. They talked about how broader issues of inequality and oppression disappear in the process of focusing on symptoms. In view of all this, sensitivity to the types of counseling and therapy in use and support for students who are not comfortable with any counseling made available to them is crucial. There is danger in handing over therapeutic matters to the experts without assessing which experts and how their therapeutic approach views a woman who has experienced trauma.

Medical approaches tend to pathologize, labeling the woman's problem as a particular personality disorder or syndrome. They ignore the material realities of her life and her experience of trauma and address only the symptoms. Working as a mental health worker in community boarding homes led Kathryn Alexander to question the meaning of *mental illness*:

> I began to wonder if the labels of mental illness should not be renamed "patriarchy effects" because so many of the women—from twenty to seventy-five—were survivors of battering, incest, dehumanizing effects of long-term institutionalization, poverty, neglect, refugees from war and so it went.

What amazed me was how—despite the documentation of admitted battering or sexual abuse from spouses and family members—analysis of violence against women was not brought into the "case management" of these women residents, instead the focus was on the individual's deviance, medication and "acting out behaviours" . . .

I think that we need to be aware of the wide range of therapeutic frameworks that therapists and counselors bring to their understanding of women's lives—because many of them are "professionally" trained—not to see the social/cultural/gender based frameworks that examine the effects of violence, poverty, racism, exploitation that shape the "symptoms" of depression, mental or physical breakdown and illiteracy. (Alphaplus Literacy & Violence Online Seminar, February–April 1998)

Later, while clarifying that she did not want to "condemn the mental health field wholesale," this literacy worker continued to voice her fears about the *othering* that can take place through medical responses to trauma. This is a particularly important caution in literacy, where learners are frequently and easily *othered* and judged as deviant for their limited literacy in highly print-oriented societies. Kathryn Alexander explained:

Women are so easily labelled as "deviant"—within psychiatry—that I worry that we risk adding on even more layers to the "othering" that is experienced—especially if the counseling resources/services do not share a feminist perspective. I think that is so important—that we forget that not all professionals share these beliefs with us—I just remember a woman I worked with saying that her "career" as a mental patient began the day she went to her doctor because she thought she was depressed—he never examined her life as a resilient survivor of poverty. (Alphaplus Literacy & Violence Online Seminar, February–April 1998)

A literacy learner used to feeling looked down on for her limited literacy is particularly vulnerable to feeling put down or judged by a professional counselor. She may feel that her language is being condemned or that she is seen as stupid; she may easily feel that the therapist's language is too full of "big words," meant to silence and make her feel *less than* the professional with "big papers." Literacy workers need to critically look at therapies on offer. Literacy workers may also need to play a role in educating therapists and counselors about literacy issues, support learners to choose between different models of counseling and therapy, and critically analyze the way they are treated by these professionals. Feminist counseling, where it is available, may be more likely to offer a perspective that recognizes the social context and avoids blaming the victim.

It is important to be cautious about approaches that subtly blame the woman and suggest she must have done something wrong to experience violence. Couple or family counseling is often framed around the idea that everyone plays a part in contributing to violence. Helen Dempster, a worker in the shelter movement, stressed the need to recognize the impact of inequalities, oppression, as well as direct violence, and to be cautious that systemic issues are not masked by self-esteem, anger-management, or stress-management courses. She explained the problem:

> . . . then the whole thing about stress too is another interesting thing because, as a feminist, isn't it stressful to live in a homophobic society or a patriarchal, a sexist society? "This is just my stress." I don't think so, I think it is more than that. What if you are a woman of colour and you live in our racist society—that is more than stressful, surely? So I think we have to watch that because oftentimes women from abusive relationships are sent to stress management classes or self-esteem classes and I think that is insulting. Although there is a place for that. . . .
>
> All that stuff then tells the woman that if she were somehow different he wouldn't be abusing her or battering her and you don't want her ever to get that message. You want to get the message to her that he's totally responsible for his behavior because her experience usually is she is damned if she does and damned if she doesn't, that no matter what she tries to do to predict his behavior and ward it off, she is walking on eggshells. . . . (interview, Vancouver, British Columbia, November 1996)

Women who have experienced trauma may easily accept counseling or courses that subtly make them responsible. The legacy of shame and the belief that there must be something wrong with them to have been abused are common. Abusers often actively reinforce this belief, which makes it all the more important that counselors, therapists, and literacy workers do not.

It is important that, through making links to therapy or counseling, literacy programs are also prepared to open therapeutic practices up to critical examination, rather than collude in denial of the layers of violence in society. There is always a danger that adult literacy work is a Band-Aid addressing problems of illiteracy as individual deficit, providing a smokescreen that obscures social inequalities. It is crucial that opening up issues of therapy and counseling does not add another layer of denial to literacy work, which simply addresses the after effects of violence as individual ill health, blames learners who are unable to benefit from existing inappropriate or limited services, and leaves society unquestioned and unchanged.

Over and over again, I heard about how little counseling was available for free or limited cost. What is available is often short term and practical, focused on problem solving. Long-term therapy is rarely available. Even the Band-Aid is worn and small. Shelter workers talked about how overstretched they were; counselors in other settings talked about the cutbacks in their organizations. This limits choices, easily leading to situations where people without financial resources are expected to be thankful for what they get, cannot choose among a range of people or styles of approach, cannot easily switch if unhappy with the treatment, and cannot receive support for as long as necessary. Limited options may lock a woman into the institutionalized mental health system.

During my interviews, some concern was expressed that, although group counseling might be cost-effective, it could be harmful for individuals not ready to work in a group. In particular, counselors talked about the dangers of self-help groups without a leader accountable to the group or an organization. In contrast, one learner spoke with enthusiasm about the value she found in a self-help group. She was pessimistic about the possibility of trusting a counselor, feeling that a counselor was just one more person in authority and that many women would worry about how they would be judged. This learner felt that learners could *get real in a group*—find their own answers and form bonds. The group that had worked for her was an Adult Children of Alcoholics (ACOA) group. These contrasting judgments suggest the value of a wide range of options so that women can try out different alternatives and choose something appropriate.

Cultural Questions

Linda Pemik, a literacy worker originally from southern Canada who has worked in the North West Territories for many years, mentioned an Inuk woman who felt that seeing a counselor was culturally inappropriate. This led Linda Pemik to speculate whether an informal group with women of all ages—where women could tell their stories—might be more culturally appropriate and might allow younger women to dialogue with their elders. She spoke about the bonds that can be developed as women tell their stories about various forms of pain, including the abuse of the colonial system. She suggested that direct approaches to dealing with feelings would be viewed as inappropriate within Inuit culture (Phone Interview, Rankin Inlet, March 1997; and follow up, July 1999). This suggests the value of recognizing different versions of group and the cultural boundaries of both individual therapies and self-help models. Culturally appropriate resource people and models of working may broaden the range of possibilities for many women. For example, Inuit people might value traditional ceremony and the lighting of the qulliq (traditional seal oil lamp).

Many First Nation people may feel affinity for working with a medicine person or an elder and prefer a talking circle to a self-help group model. A group of First Nation instructors talked about how they integrate sharing and talking about pain into their learning practices so that each person can be recognized as an individual:

> You allow that person to talk and take whatever amount of time it takes for them to share. And they will share whatever they're comfortable sharing. Some of it will be strictly from the head if they're not used to doing it, some of it will be from here [the heart], the pain. . . . Whether you're passing a feather or something, as long as you're holding that you can talk, and if you pass it to somebody they don't have to talk. They can just say "I'm going to pass." (interview, First Nation Instructors, Toronto, January 1997)

As well as recognizing various cultural forms of healing, forms of therapy that move away from talk may also be valuable, particularly for women for whom English is not their first language, for those who do not have a lot of facility with language, or those with intellectual disabilities. For many women, body work, art therapy, dance therapy, and other alternatives all may offer potential ways forward if they are available and accessible.

Avoiding the "Normal" Trap

It is important to be cautious about the implicit goal within much therapy of returning to *normal* as soon as possible. To move away from this purely privatized understanding of problems, literacy programs need to make links—not only with individualized therapeutic approaches to violence, but also with grassroots organizations committed to address issues of violence collectively and work toward broader social change. American literacy worker and popular educator, Beth Sauerhaft, whose own work links literacy with health and social justice issues, made the case during the literacy and violence online seminar:

> What can we learn from the social movements that have been led by survivors of trauma, such as the battered women's movements, Mothers of the Disappeared, welfare rights groups and other grassroots human rights campaigns?

How do we individually and programatically link with these groups? I would suggest that we work jointly when possible in creating curriculum and learning environments that contextualize the traumatic experiences that students have and offer access to the voices, analysis, and struggles of others who in some way share their experiences. I have found linking students with peers has been especially important in responding to students who have experienced domestic violence, rape, and political torture. The strengths and knowledge brought to these interactions is part of keeping us away from the "deficit model" of education and building on the strengths in our communities.

If as Ora Avni states, "the problem lies not in the individual but in his or her interaction with society," then I think it is of critical importance that we find ways to acknowledge the multiple realities of our students and their trauma experiences and that we be careful not to put our main emphasis on our one-on-one interactions with students, rather that we offer an environment which recognizes the systematic and structural violence in our societies and the grassroots movements that challenge the different forms of violence that impact all of us. (Alphaplus Literacy & Violence Online Seminar, February–April 1998)

Rooted in popular education, Sauerhaft suggested that a long tradition of literacy practice linked to grassroots social change movements provides examples on which to build. Literacy programs working collaboratively with other grassroots movements can help maintain clear visibility of the social and political nature of violence. Building connections to social movements helps break silences about the public issues around violence and break down assumptions that *normal* is an unproblematic *place* to return to.

When literacy programs make connections to therapeutic services, they have a responsibility to learn about the approach offered. They should not just hand over to the experts. It is important that they talk to learners about the different approaches and support learners to find a way through the maze of different services and find appropriate support. A program making an organizational link with counseling services or other resources needs to ensure that the philosophy of the organization fits with their own. Where limited services make it impossible to find the ideal service, learners may need support to understand the problem as the inadequacy of the resource, not the inappropriateness of their needs. The focus of counseling should not be on returning to normal, but rather on work that enables students to be successful in their learning. Literacy work should not be complicit in medicalizing trauma and privatizing problems. The basis of any approach must build awareness of the public and political nature of violence while also supporting learners' access to services that meet their personal needs.

LINKS AND SEPARATIONS

I talked to many literacy workers, learners, and counselors about the access to counseling or therapy currently available in their programs and communities. I asked whether they thought literacy workers should be trained in counseling and whether counseling should be provided as part of literacy programs. In the process, I learned that a range of different possibilities exists in programs. I heard complete divergence in the views expressed about what is needed. There is no one answer to the question of what access to counseling is needed in literacy programs. Instead, considering a range of possibilities might provoke programs and institutions to assess the adequacy of the services available for survivors in their program and community and consider their options for creating connections and deeper links.

It is useful to draw a continuum of types of counseling and therapy. At one end of the continuum would be life skills work, social skills, and self-help type groups. Next might be supportive, problem-solving type counseling, then short-term issue-based therapy. Finally, at the other end, would be long-term psychotherapy. In this conceptualization, the first end of the continuum might connect more closely and integrally with literacy work, whereas the latter end might be expected to be more separate. Some therapeutic practices might be easily integrated into the classroom, whereas others might always be separate. In between lie the various possible links between literacy and counseling.

Currently many institutional programs and some multiservice centers have counselors on staff, although in some situations literacy workers and counselors were not always satisfied with what was offered. A university college instructor questioned the adequacy of resources offered in her institution to support women in the upheaval precipitated by returning to school:

> I question if we provide enough support and counselling. . . . When you have students who have been subject to oppression, systemically or in their own home, and then you provide them with this other way or additional ways of looking at the world or understanding the world. I often wonder about that . . . I feel concerned . . . if we do this kind of work, are we going to be there to pick up some of the pieces or provide ways of dealing with the feelings that are generated. . . . Anger, resentment, sadness, loss and so on. (interview/personal correspondence, 1996/1999)

Some workers worried that counselors had little understanding of literacy learners or their experiences of poverty or racism, or that learners' only option would be unsympathetic or judgmental counselors. Counselors working within a literacy organization might easily be influenced by other people's judgments of the client and so be less able to provide in-depth therapy.

The fears that some learners expressed of being seen meeting with me, and the concerns expressed by the learner I work with about seeing a counselor in the same community as her literacy program, suggest that learners frequently worry about these issues. I wondered whether a general shift away from a frame that says trauma and impacts of trauma are shameful might be accomplished if issues of violence are addressed in a variety of ways in literacy programs. Perhaps creating greater openness about violence might lead to a lessening of these fears.

Some counselors working in community colleges were frustrated with what they could offer. They were often limited to providing short-term counseling. In some colleges, the counselors focused exclusively, or almost exclusively, on job-related counseling and were not qualified or allowed to provide personal counseling despite the connections between the two. In either case, counselors or instructors would have to refer women dealing with issues of abuse to another therapist or counselor for long-term therapy. Several said that appropriate, free counselors were often not available and that a second referral (first from teacher to counselor, and now to therapist) was problematic for many learners. Their statistics suggest that few women took up the referral. Lorna Gallant, in Prince Edward Island, suggested that it was important to carry out referrals in a way that would feel like another support was being added and avoid contributing to a woman's despair that she is alone, her problems too big, and that no one can give her the support she needs. A suitable process might be a transition period of meetings with both counselors, with the original counselor or instructor continuing to offer support by asking questions about the new therapy and listening.

Counselors Supporting Literacy Workers

Some literacy instructors who had the luxury of on-site counselors regularly referred students to their counseling department. Many spoke of the importance of the support they received when they worked closely with counselors. Diana Twiss, a community college instructor in British Columbia, described that connection as essential to literacy workers providing appropriate support for their students:

We have counselors on staff who work with our students. These counselors are readily available to meet the students' needs. For example, I have a new student who has a series of bruises on her and some new ones every day. She claims that her four-year old is doing this to her, which may very well be true, and if so she definitely has to deal with it. A few days ago, at a teacher's suggestion, the student was taken down to the counselor's office and met with her. She wasn't sent there right away. She was encouraged to go once she felt safe and accepted in class. From the very beginning, I was in touch with our counselor, to fill her in and to get some ideas about ways that I can help with the situation. Our counselor is wonderful and is a vital part of our program. I could not imagine doing this without her as part of our team. (Alphaplus Literacy & Violence Online Seminar, February–April 1998)

Diana Twiss went on to talk about how, in financial crises, counseling is frequently cut back and rarely seen as essential; she suggested this is mistaken:

Adult literacy programs must have trained counselors right on site. They must be readily available and easily accessible. They must be known to the students and accepted by them. Otherwise, we are on our own. I've been there, and it's scary. (Alphaplus Literacy & Violence Online Seminar, February–April 1998)

Reading those words made me think of many literacy workers—some of whom I met during the research—who are on their own and are scared—terrified that they will make a mistake and harm a woman who has already been hurt too much.

In programs with First Nation students, the availability of an elder was also crucial as a resource for both the students and the instructors. An elder in residence, or at least with an ongoing connection to the program, can be especially helpful for non-Native instructors to understand the cultural context and particularities of Native experiences of residential schools and other aspects of racism. Through this research, I have come to see that the availability of counselors and other supports, although valuable to students, is also essential as a resource for workers to check their own responses, seek support, and disentangle the sort of complexity that can develop in the classroom. Workers in a position of power can find themselves participating in complex dances around power and control. They can easily end up on the receiving end of learners projecting earlier struggles around power and control with those who were abusive.

A group in Brandon, Manitoba, talked about what a difference it made in the Samaritan Program to have counselors on staff. Marie Matheson described her own situation when she began to teach:

> But I think the thing that you've got, some counseling background within the realm of your staff makes a real difference. Because there are times when you're in the classroom where what you need to be is a counselor. I think back to when I was in the college, in my first year of being a literacy practitioner, two of my students were raped, one who was in an abusive relationship and constantly went back, and the kids were always in jeopardy, and one person tried to commit suicide, and this is in the first year! By the end of it I was a [wreck]! . . . It would be not unusual to have to go out in the middle of the day's lesson for a few minutes and deal with somebody in crisis. I was exhausted after the first year. It was never dull—but there were times when I don't think I felt like I had the background to cope with some of that. (interview, Samaritan Program, Brandon, Manitoba, December 1996)

Sylvia Provenski from the Samaritan Program described an incident where it made a difference to have a counselor available, although the counselor was not free to work with the student:

> I had an incident last year where I had a fellow come in who was contemplating suicide, and we had to sit down there and then and work with him. It was my first experience with quite that big a crisis. It was nice having . . . [a counselor on staff—she] wasn't in at the time so I couldn't refer him to her, so I dealt with it and then her and I talked about it afterwards. Did I handle it appropriately or not, and what else could we do for him, that kind of stuff. It's nice having that feedback. (interview, Samaritan Program, Brandon, Manitoba, December 1996)

The difficult situation in rural programs may be that they not only have no counselor, but the literacy worker may be the only staff person:

> A: The true luxury that you have here is the supportive staff. In a lot of programs, they're it. They're the coordinator, they're the instructor, they have a working group that's maybe available via telephone call, but not always even that accessible, and they don't have a lot of others, networking comrades, in the same community. So particularly north and small rural centres, I think they really do sense some isolation around that stuff.
>
> B: I don't know how they survive without the support staff. I can't imagine how I'd survive without them.

A: Well, a lot of them pick up the phone—but then there's a lot that don't, so I often wonder the same thing. They may have established [support] within their own communities—a clergy person, or . . .

B: Spouse, friend, whatever. (interview, Samaritan Program, Brandon, Manitoba, December 1996)

For those workers who feel truly alone, the challenge of setting their own boundaries and limits on what they will hear, combined with the absence of any resource where they can check in and get support themselves, creates a real danger that they will lose perspective and balance. That danger must begin to be publicly discussed in the literacy field so that workers seek out appropriate strategies and supports, rather than waiting until they feel in over their heads and embarrassed to ask anyone for help.

The Pressure to Counsel

In programs where counselors were available, some instructors had clear strategies to ensure that they did not take on a counseling role; instead they made a smooth transfer to the counselors. Two instructors spoke clearly of how they encouraged students to talk to the counselor rather than to them. They both spoke of affirming a student's desire to speak to someone while clearly stating that they were not the right someone. Kate Nonesuch described her approach:

> I teach groups of students. I spend from quarter to nine till three fifteen with a group, and I don't have very much time to talk to people individually, but people will disclose to me and I try to make it possible for people to disclose to me. When they disclose, I'll say "It sounds like you really need somebody to talk to. Do you have somebody to talk to?" "Well, I'm talking to you." By this time I may have gone into the hall with them, if they're crying or something. I say "I have fourteen people in there waiting for me to tell them what the answer is to question forty-two, and so I have to go and do that. But you really need somebody to talk to, so can I walk you down to the counseling office and we'll see if there's somebody there?" And so we do that. I avoid as much as possible being that kind of counselor—partly because I don't want to do it, what I want to do is teach. I don't have time to do both, and I don't have the training to be a counselor. My follow-up is usually in the same vein "Did you see the counselor? Was it helpful? Are you going to see her again?" I get to be side support, not the main support. (interview, Salt Spring Island, November/December 1996)

Kate Nonesuch also said that when a student disclosed in writing, she encouraged her to take the writing with her to the counselor. Evelyn Battell explained that she could not hear the stories and return to her teaching:

> I don't want to be a counselor, I'm no good at it. I can't stand to hear that much of it. I said to a student the other week, you know I can see this is horrific, and I'm gonna just cry as hard as you. Let's go find a counselor. I'm not gonna be any use to you here. I'm so upset already, if you tell me any more, you'll have to take care of me. That cracked her up, you know. So she agreed to go find a counselor.
>
> I can't take it, I can't take it and then go back in the classroom and pretend it didn't happen. That's the other thing, 'cause I'm finished, I'm worn out. (interview, Salt Spring Island, November/December 1996)

Both these descriptions provide honest clarity about the limits and boundaries these instructors need to maintain while also affirming the student's right to tell as well as her right to tell a witness who can fully attend to her needs.

These instructors contrast with others who expressed more ambiguity about whether to bear witness to the students who chose to disclose to them, even when there were counselors on staff or in local organizations. Several spoke of feeling trapped at the end of a class when they felt they should hear the student, but were tired, unprepared, or unclear what they might best do. Often they felt students had made a connection and built trust with them and that a referral would not meet the students' needs. Dee Goforth, a college instructor in Northern Ontario, wrote her reflections in the online seminar:

> Learners tend to bond with their classroom teachers and depending how teachers define their role in the classroom (some are much more comfortable in a counseling role), many will attempt to work with their learners before referring them to the college counselor. In situations where I have suggested that a learner meet with a counselor, [the learner] is often reluctant. She knows me. She trusts me. I, however, don't always feel qualified or confident in helping some of the women in my program who are hurting from extreme emotional or physical abuse. The dilemma for me is that I don't know how much I should encourage learners to seek other counseling either inside or outside the college as this often doesn't work for them either. (Alphaplus Literacy & Violence Online Seminar, February–April 1998)

The trust already developed in the relationship is a powerful draw for learners and workers alike. Crisis counseling is an area that many workers can easily be drawn into even when they work in an institution that has counselors available because the needs and connection are so immediate. Janine Luce, of Street Haven in Toronto, described her experience:

> You wouldn't believe how much suicide counseling I did last fall. It's because women connect. In our organization women may connect with other staff for other issues, but if they're feeling like they need to connect with you, then that's who they're going to connect with. And you can't say "My job isn't counseling so I'm going to pass you on to somebody else." You know, you just can't do that. Especially when it erupts in the middle of a writing group. "I'm gonna go down to the lake and throw myself in." "Well, let's not do that tonight!" (interview, Community and Street Program Literacy Workers, Toronto, February 1997)

The tension between seeking to meet the immediate need and feeling unable to offer adequate counseling leaves many workers struggling for an appropriate response. This is particularly difficult when a learner is in crisis or where the worker is doubtful about how to balance her or his own needs in the face of the enormous needs of another.

Connecting With Counseling

Many instructors I interviewed had not made a strong connection to their counseling department. Particularly newer instructors, or those working in larger institutions, often had not had opportunities to get to know the counselors, learn what they offered or when they were available, and become familiar enough to confidently recommend them. Current clear-cut divisions in programs, combined with long teaching hours and general overload for both teachers and counselors, often contributed to the separation of these two areas. After discussions in interviews, several instructors talked about various ways of trying to bridge the divide. Some began to consider inviting counselors into their classes regularly so that students would have a chance to become familiar with the counselors and services offered by the counseling department. Others suggested jointly sponsored courses that would allow learners to address some of the personal barriers to learning in a supportive setting. Both of these alternatives might mean that learners get to know the counselor, have an opportunity to build trust, and are then ready to talk to a counselor, instead of preferring the teacher with whom a relationship has been developed. As workers in Prince Edward Island suggested, thinking of school children, if the counselor has a presence in the classroom, then this suggests, "Here we are. Two adults you can approach."

One literacy program for Deaf students had counselors available on site, but there was little connection between the counseling and teaching departments. During our discussions, the worker, Deanne Bradley, began to consider the value of inviting counselors into her classes (Interview, Toronto, February 1998). I questioned the possibility of going further and reconceptualizing the literacy work to include students spending class time in counseling where it seemed appropriate. This would mean that students could leave a full-time program to attend a counseling session without being registered as absent from the program. This shift would serve a bureaucratic need. Students' financial support would not be affected by their attendance at counseling during program time. It also suggests an important reconception of the literacy and counseling, where counseling is understood as an integral aspect of literacy learning.

The possibility of creating such connections raises practical questions. How easily a student could switch between the different types of demands of counseling and class might depend on the depth of work she was seeking to do with the counselor. Whether she would be able to return to class after an intense counseling or therapy session or whether she would need to take time off when necessary might need to remain an open question. The educators in Prince Edward Island thought flexibility within the program and from funders was crucial:

> I think it's really important for the programs to be flexible enough to permit that person to go out at ten o'clock on Wednesday mornings and perhaps not come back for the rest of the day if it has been a particularly upsetting counseling session. They shouldn't be expected. . . . That's sometimes difficult when the funder is saying "That person has missed a half-day every week." (interview, Charlottetown, PEI, March 1997)

They even wondered why learners would be expected to go to counseling instead of counselors coming to the school. The possibility of such rethinking raises questions about the value of these links for literacy learning. This research suggests that such connections would create possibilities for new interconnections between literacy learning and overt work on "healing" from issues of trauma. In that way, it would increase learners' likelihood of improving literacy skills.

Many literacy programs, particularly most community programs, do not currently offer access to counseling as part of the program. Most of these programs could develop links with various services in their community that might provide counseling to literacy students. In some remote areas, such as communities in the North West Territories, I was told that no counseling service was available in the community. Some of these small communities did have counselors in the school system or access to telephone crisis lines. Generally, few programs knew exactly what was available in the community, had explored the ways such services could be a resource, or made any substantial links. One counselor in Iqaluit, Nunavut, talked about going into people's classes *if* she were welcome. She clearly had not previously made an assumption that she would be welcome. She seemed to have been prompted to suggest going into classes only as a result of participating in an interview session where instructors sounded interested in making more of a link with her work. Janet Isserlis, who runs a resource center for literacy workers in Rhode Island, tentatively began to explore possible links in her community:

> We're trying to set up a meeting to see how the women doing the work in shelters can teach and learn with women doing literacy work—trying to broaden everyone's knowledge base, at least a little. (Alphaplus Literacy & Violence Online Seminar, February–April 1998)

Focusing on Learning

A literacy learner in Prince Edward Island talked about how there were no counseling resources available even in the holistic literacy course she was part of. She and other students were told they should not let their issues get in the way of their literacy learning (Interview, Charlottetown, PEI, March 1997). A group of workers from British Columbia mused about the contrast between learners who suggest that setting issues aside is the answer and those who see that as impossible:

> A: I know people've got things on their mind, maybe just aren't able to put those things aside.
>
> B: 'Cause there's always people—there's women who say "Can I talk to you later?" "Do you need to talk now?" "No, lunchtime's fine." So they know they're gonna talk and they set it aside.
>
> C: It's true. I have students who come in and announce to all and sundry "I say leave your problems at the door when you come to class. That's what I do!" And they do, and it's fine, but the advice that they give is not well taken. (interview, Salt Spring Island, British Columbia, November/December 1996)

Workers suggested that perhaps these were simply different styles. Some learners could not put their issues on one side even temporarily and focus on their learning, whereas others were comfortable leaving their issues aside while they learn. The learner from Prince Edward Island who was frustrated with her holistic program argued that there had to be support to learn how to "leave their junk at the door" and places to go when their need to address the issues was too urgent. She argued for a link to counseling of some form. When students found that working in the literacy program brought up issues they needed to attend to, this learner thought it was crucial they have somewhere to go to work on the issues.

In my teaching, I have found value in briefly listening to an individual student who is struggling with current crises and asking her directly whether, given what is happening, she feels able to participate in the group. If she wants to try to remain, I ask what support she needs to help her leave the issues aside temporarily. I have been surprised how often that has helped a learner refocus on the present. If I am prepared to address the question of what a learner needs—rather than avoiding the question for fear her need will be too great—and if I am simultaneously clear about my own limits so I am not drawn into listening to the full story when I have no time, crises that might have proved insurmountable barriers have often been set aside while learning continues. The learner may be able to return to work after something quite simple: a hug, a few moments on her own, a chance to write in her journal or draw, or a walk. She may recognize that she will not be able to learn if she remains in class. Instead of trying to work, she leaves to look after herself in some other way. There seems to be value simply in naming the issue so that the learner is reminded to actively refocus or decide that refocusing is not possible. Such a process can enhance everyone's presence and focus on learning. The availability of a counselor, of course, would make this negotiation process easier. Most important, such negotiation needs to be carried without judging or shaming a learner who is struggling with crises or unable to learn.

Connection Through Referral

Although *referral* may sound like separating the issues of violence from the literacy program, this research led me to see that even referral can occur in a way that does not silence issues of violence in literacy or imply that they do not belong in literacy programs. Referral can form a link between learning and other approaches to addressing impacts of violence. Issues of violence must be frequently talked about and become part of curriculum; referral information about a wide range of resources should be on display and talked about. Literacy workers need to know enough about the options and the people in different agencies to be able to talk knowledgeably about choices, and at least some staff members need to be able to offer ongoing support while learners are accessing counseling elsewhere.

For referral to be an integration of different resources, not a passing off of the problem, it takes work—work that few literacy workers have spare time for, that may stir up their own issues, and that few funders understand as part of literacy. It takes time to learn in detail about what options exist either within an institution or outside, to know whether there are waiting lists, whether the service is completely free, or whether the counseling offered is short or long term, individual or group, problem-solving or in-depth psychotherapy. It takes even more time to make the personal connections to know first hand what the organization and counselors are like—to know enough to be able to demystify the available services and the concepts of counseling or therapy for literacy students. Will the organization and individual counselors be sensitive to literacy learners, to racialized groups, to First Nation learners, to different cultural styles, or to those with intellectual disabilities? Does the literacy program need to teach the counseling service something about literacy issues? Can they learn from the counselors something about how the issues play out in the classroom? Where literacy staff choose to invite counselors into the literacy program, so that learners can meet them and learn about the services offered and the contrasts between different organizations, arranging such visits and planning how to make them useful is also time-consuming.

I wondered if some of that work could be done—not in individual programs, but through literacy networks or other organizations. In many areas, a phone line provides referral information about the range of literacy programs available in the area and helps learners and volunteers find an appropriate program. If counseling is seen as a related resource, relevant to literacy learning, a literacy information line could also provide information about the full range of counseling services available in the area. Such a resource would not replace the need for knowledge of resources within the programs, but would make the task of keeping up to date with changes in programs, lengths of waiting lists, and current staff quicker, easier, and more possible. Links of this sort would also help strengthen awareness of the interconnections of learning and counseling.

Jeanette Austin-Odina, a counselor in an ESL program in Edmonton, stressed the importance of literacy workers both encouraging referral and offering support in the literacy program. Jeanette Austin-Odina thought it was important not to separate counseling and teaching arbitrarily, although boundaries are important. This counselor thought learning from counseling could help a literacy worker focus on the learner's strengths and on creating positive relationships that help her see something other than abuse (Interview, Edmonton, Alberta, December 1996).

During our interview sessions, Joyce Cameron, a British Columbian college literacy instructor, began to see possibilities for how to be more proactive about links to issues of violence. She suggested there were options to take more initiative rather than waiting for disclosures:

> I've been trying to think about . . . more proactive work. If literacy work went on, and then there was another place that people could go where that stuff got dealt with. So we all knew that that stuff got dealt with, and we could say when something came up "Well, that's something you could raise in that group." And then they could also be learning things that spill in a positive way into the classroom.
>
> [A group] might be one way to approach it. If there was a proactive place where women who were dealing with stuff [had] . . . connections to counseling when that's needed, or individual work when that's needed. (interview, Salt Spring Island, November/December 1996)

At that time, Cameron was just beginning to think about possibilities for creative connections to counseling and other resources so that women could have somewhere outside the literacy class to address their issues. Focusing on what proactive work might look like, not tying it only to a group, suggests creative possibilities. Her idea later took shape as a group entitled Women's Success, now running for a second time. The initial group still meets at the Women's Center, although their formal sessions have ended. They invite anyone who comes to the center to join in. Even prospective students who drop by receive support from this group (Leroux, 1998c, p. 11). I wonder whether the Women's Center is becoming exactly the sort of alternative place, besides the classroom, that Joyce Cameron imagined might support learning. The Women's Success group is one exciting model described later in this chapter.

Valuable Separations

Ideas about possible links between literacy and therapy also suggest areas of separation. For example, Joyce Cameron's suggestion is to have somewhere outside the literacy program to take the issues of impacts of violence so that they are neither silenced nor totally enmeshed in the literacy work. Although this may seem contradictory at first glance, it may also be that clear links between literacy and counseling offer valuable separations. Several literacy workers talked about the value of focusing on the literacy skill and pleasure many women find in having a space where they are not working directly on their issues. Instructors, mostly from community colleges in British Columbia, discussed their experience:

> A: I have this skill they can build [on] . . . this step they can use to make a change in their life, other than all the ones that they're already aware they need to work on. And so it's always been key to me that however it is one offers that, with whatever kind of supports and mixed with life skills, and in whatever kind of sensitive way, some of the students really want to be actively working forward on that skill, specifically. For some of them, it's the only relief they get in their week from dealing with all of the shit in their world, is they get to focus down,' practice reading and writing, notice that they're getting better at it, practice math, notice that they learned something. It's a very tangible, forward skill thing, that they can then see themselves equipped with another tool they didn't have before, the next time they go to deal with X or Y.
>
> And I certainly have students that have said to me. . . . I'll say, they're obviously in a mess, or they just missed a week, or god knows what, and somehow in our conversation it comes out that they're dealing with yet another stage of whatever misery—stalking, or violence, or whatever. And I'll say "Are you okay to be here?" and they'll say "Oh, yeah. I want to be here. I want to just do this for a bit." And . . . they don't want to talk about it in the group. And there's some people in the group that don't know, and there's even a few people in the group for whom none of it's happening. They really want to be part of that, a place where it is not the focus.
>
> B: That's been my experience as well. There's just been so much reflective learning—I guess that's what I'm calling this "how are you feeling today?" stuff—that my students will tolerate. And the message is pretty strong and clear, that "I want to know about something that's not in my experience, something—history! Or something in science, or geography. Get out of this reflective, what's going on inside me all the time, because I'm living with that anyway. There's where having a counseling department, if you're lucky enough, can get that emotional need taken care of. (interview, Salt Spring Island, British Columbia, November/December 1996)

Although the *it* that is being referred to may not be the same for all learners, sometimes a space that is free of focus on issues in their lives, where the instructor is not a counselor, may help learners experience a sense of accomplishment. This may then, in turn, contribute to taking on personal issues effectively elsewhere. Priscilla George offered another possible model, where a talking circle can provide the space for learners to unburden so that they can focus on accomplishing the work, having been heard (personal correspondence, September 1998). One of the workers in British Columbia said:

> I think that for at least some people it's important to have somebody with whom they do something quite different. . . . Even if I were to have the skills and the time and the energy to take on all of that [counseling], then [the literacy class] . . . would be one of those places, and they'd have to find another place . . . one of the students had done a lot of writing, and she was working with a tutor on it, and the tutor said to her (god, I cannot believe this) "Can't you say something positive? because people aren't going to want to read it." And the woman said "You know, the only positive thing in my life is going to school. What can I say?" I'm afraid that she would lose that little bit. (interview, Salt Spring Island, British Columbia, November/December 1996)

For many learners, some version of separation may be important to help them achieve success as long as suitable places to explore the issues are also available and there is no silencing or invisibility of the issues within the literacy program.

Links to and separations from counseling and other services are crucial in literacy programs. Literacy workers need to assess the counseling and other resources available within their programs and in the broader community. This assessment should lead to developing clear links and connections with these services that reveal the integration between literacy and such support services. Literacy workers need access to appropriate supports for the complex work of doing literacy with those who have experienced trauma.

Although some learners are happy to leave personal issues aside and focus on learning, others may not be able to or may not choose to. Those learners who cannot set their issues aside, but want to continue to focus on reading and writing, may need immediate support. With students who do not want to set personal issues aside, the challenge may be for literacy workers to honor the learning they are doing while exploring their personal issues. Referral to counseling services is an important aspect of literacy work. Referral needs to be done in a way that preserves the visibility of issues of violence within literacy programs. The work involved in making connections with counseling organizations and counselors needs to be recognized and carried out in programs, networks, and referral services.

A key challenge in literacy programs is to create clear links and strong visibility for issues of violence, as well as clear boundaries, separations, and times when those issues are definitely not the focus. Where specific services have been identified and links created—counselors on site regularly, detailed referral information easily available, support groups or courses taking place—it is more possible to have a clear separation of the issues. This enables learners to experience times of freedom from focus on these issues without leading to the implication that disclosures should be silenced or that issues of violence are only a private matter.

EXPLORING MODELS

In many places, I spoke to counselors who were eager to make greater links with literacy programs, but who had severe limits on their time and resources. Literacy workers were also interested in greater links, but talked about the limits on their time and energy and difficulties with envisaging how such links could be structured. However, I did hear about some interesting models that had been tried. Each model offered exciting possibilities, and the range made it clear that innovative alternatives could fit each situation, particularly if funding and program structures offered possibilities rather than constraints.

In one community program, the Learning Centre in Edmonton, Alberta, Mary Norton had made links with a mental health counselor who visited the program once in a while so that she would become a familiar face to students; she worked individually with several women who were also students in the program. She was also available as a resource to the program staff. In another program, directed at women leaving violent relationships, personal counselors were always available for learners if their class work brought up issues.

One short-term project, in Hay River in the North West Territories, was a summer course funded as a Job Re-entry program. The first stage focused on personal development led by a trained facilitator. During this time, links with counselors working at the local shelter and women's center were created. During this phase, the Adult Basic Education (ABE) instructor sat in the class. A second stage was led by the ABE instructor, with counselors still available for individual counseling when necessary. A third stage involved students carrying out work placements in the community. This frame allowed for a discussion of issues that the group chose, including issues of violence and inequality. The facilitator, Mary Beth Levan, thought it was crucial to provide students with a framework for analysis, as well as the opportunity to talk about their own experiences and feelings (Interview, Yellowknife, March 1998). During the second stage, the focus was on upgrading literacy and basic education skills.

At the end of the whole process, the students would be ready to assess what further preparation they needed before they would be ready to find jobs. Cate Sills explained the project and its value a little further:

> Mary Beth [Levan] provided a critical link between the participants and the shelter workers by inviting them to do mini-workshops as part of her month-long personal development piece of the project. This helped the women develop a sense of who the shelter counsellors were and break down some of the fears the women may have had about coming forward to get some support through the women's centre. Women were allowed time off from the program to attend counselling sessions if they requested it.
>
> All in all, it broke down a lot of barriers and developed a greater under-standing of issues of violence and the power of women to support one an-other. What was most interesting to me was the ways in which the group supported each other. Many of the participants were feeling very isolated and it was a revelation for many of them that their experiences of violence and powerlessness were shared by others in the group . . . having permis-sion to talk about their lives and examining their experiences from a criti-cal perspective in a supportive environment was the most important fea-ture of the project . . . everything else flowed from there. (personal correspondence, July 1999)

This course was a fascinating and innovative interweaving of the re-sources of literacy and counseling. It illustrated the value of moving vio-lence from a private issue to a shared concern to support women to envis-age and move toward change in their lives.

I had an opportunity to learn about another interesting link when I gave a workshop at a regional training event in Southern Ontario. I was fascinated to meet a counselor who was offering a workshop in self-esteem for literacy learners. She had been working with a community literacy program offering workshops. As learners got to know her, they were able to meet with her in-dividually for counseling. The program hired her using short-term project money. When I met her, the project was over, but the program was trying to find further funds to continue. A student I met from the program thought there was a crucial need for the counselor to continue with the program. She talked about the difference the workshops and counseling had made to her sense of self and her ability to learn.

A therapist in Prince Edward Island suggested that she would be inter-ested in going into literacy classes as an observer to assist the instructor with exploring impacts of trauma visible in the classroom. A therapist in Ontario said she would love to explore the possibility of co-leading a lit-eracy class. This interest from therapists encouraged me to imagine various creative possibilities for how a counselor and literacy worker could work creatively together. Classes co-led by a literacy worker and counselor might make it possible for reading, writing, talking, and listening to become, not the end goal of the course, but the means for personal reflection and healing work. The presence of a counselor might make it easier for the literacy worker to invite learners to write about their lives and for the students to tell their stories knowing that counseling supports are available. The chance to reflect on early learning experiences and critique the limitations of the school system might be a therapeutic process for many literacy learners.

A similar experimental program was started recently in a British Columbia College, Women's Success, referred to earlier. It was not co-led by a literacy worker and counselor. Rather, it offers another model for collaborative work and effective links between therapeutic work and literacy learning. Instructor Kathie Leroux explained how the program came into being in the provincial literacy magazine:

> We sought out help from other women and resources in the college and formed an advisory committee, consisting of women from the counseling department, the Douglas College Women's Centre, the IBT (Institutional Basic Training) program and other pertinent areas that had an interest in women being successful. During that process, we spent time defining what the course was not going to be, i.e. a therapy group, and we discussed what it was to be. The underlying principle comprised three components: it would be participatory, experiential, and feminist. . . . The process would be determined by the women themselves, what they needed to learn, what they would identify as the barriers and obstacles in their process and where they envisioned themselves in the future. The course would have to have an instructor who was not only sensitive to women's issues, but who also was experienced in teaching literacy level students.
>
> The course was scheduled to cover seven weeks—beginning half way through the fourteen week semester to enable instructors to identify potential candidates. Habits and patterns were observed in the first weeks of the semester or where an instructor noticed an unmotivated student and a candidate was selected on the basis of the instructors' "sense" that there was an on-going obstacle preventing that student from succeeding. Some students were easier to invite into the course because they had disclosed past physical, mental, sexual or emotional abuse. The course was described as a pilot program called "Women's Success Course" and we scheduled it for Mondays and Fridays to provide a sort of weekly check-in and check-out process. Finally, ten students were identified, invited and interviewed, and we were all set to go. As the instructor, I think I was as scared as the students. None of us knew what to expect. The pressure was on!

The meeting place for our course was the Douglas College Women's Centre, a place that was closed and deemed "safe" and which provided us with a comfortable living-room setting. (Leroux, 1998a, pp. 5–6)

In a later article, the instructor provided more detail about the course, illustrating how the link with the expertise of a counselor was made and integrated into the program:

One of the major areas that the women wanted to learn was the topic of borders and boundaries. At the dinner on International Women's Day, I brought my dearest and oldest friend, Patricia Spear, with me so she could meet the women. Patricia has been working with those issues in her work with clients for years. The women were able to get to know her in a social context, which made the work ahead much easier in that the women felt they "knew" her and trusted her to lead a workshop in an area that they were keen to explore. We spent a few weeks exploring that topic and recognizing the way they had learned in the past, so they could "unlearn" behavior they were uncomfortable with. (Leroux, 1998b, p. 13)

Karin Thompson, one of the learners in the Women's Success program, made absolutely clear the impact of such work and support on her ability to stay in a program and have success with her learning. She wrote about the importance of the support the group gave her when previously she had only "a small circle of support, almost none, and was feeling alone and out of place" starting at Douglas College. Karin was able to address issues that might otherwise have blocked her learning:

Another topic that has helped me grow is boundaries. I have been able to take my life back from people who owned it before. I am able to put my own commitments to what I need above the needs and wants of others. So, instead of being guilted to spend every weekend with certain friends, I have said "no," and done my homework and assignments. School is my priority and if my friends can't respect that, they're out of here! Many of the exercises we did brought back memories that I have avoided to deal with and it is these memories that have kept me from being a whole healthy person and in turn threatened my life as a student. Once these memories were acknowledged in this course, avoidance wasn't so pleasant, so I am dealing with them now. (cited in Leroux 1998b, p. 13)

If, at some point, Karin Thompson chooses to see an individual counselor to continue her process of dealing with those memories, she will do so from a place of strength—where the connections between impacts of trauma and learning have already been made, where the silences have already been broken, and the commonality of her issues with other women has already been established.

Another experimental and innovative program, called GOAL, was offered in Prince Edward Island to men and women full time for 2 years. The program continued during the summer when students' children were included in the plan. The course was intended to give students a chance to *address their personal baggage* before taking on their education. A wide range of courses and projects included life management, healthy exercise, nutrition counseling, a community kitchen, computer training, and a wealth of different resource people to provide information on legal issues, safe sex, child care, and many other areas. Although the course was judged to have been extremely successful, like other creative options, it was no longer running when I visited.[1]

I talked to several students who had participated in GOAL. One signed her name, adding "survivor and grateful for GOAL." Learners in the PEI interview group debated the value of offering life skills or life management courses before other educational programs or integrating those issues alongside other educational aspects. One learner said that some learners felt they were "being treated like little kids again" in GOAL when they were taught about how to do their lives better, but also pointed out that she thought those who were most critical of the course were often those who needed it most. She said that, although she and many others saw the course as an opportunity to make changes, others experienced it "as part of the criticism that they'd lived with all their lives." Some workers felt that there is a tension between the value of life management course content and the implication that participants do not know how to cope (Interviews, Charlottetown, PEI, March 1997). Yet, according to the course developer, the intention of the course was to provide an opportunity for participants to surmount barriers:

> Both the men and women were in the program because they were considered to be high potential but were struggling with things that were stand-

---

[1]A representative of the Department of Education explained that money was not available to continue GOAL because the Federal funding SARS (Social Assistance Recipients) was discontinued. She said: "There was agreement across the board about its value. That is exactly why there has been an all out effort to ensure province-wide accessibility to literacy based programs free of charge to any adult islander. This year for example we had 650 islanders in a variety of programs, no time limitations, no financial requirements." She described men and women in the GOAL program as "devastated when they realized others would not have the same opportunity," but said that "bits and pieces of GOAL are incorporated into programs on an as needed basis and, of course, are included in the costs of those programs" (personal correspondence, July 1999).

ing in their way of getting to where they felt they wanted to be . . . no coercion . . . no threat of being cut off from financial support . . . they knew they wanted to make some changes while at the same time attain academic requirements for courses they eventually wanted. (personal correspondence, July 1999)

Several learners spoke eloquently about the value of this course to help them imagine a different reality than the one they were living when they began; one said that it "saved her life."

There is often a tension around any version of life skills courses. Life skills type programs can be a supportive learning place for the whole person—a place for a woman to work through a wide range of practical and emotional issues likely to block her learning. However, despite best intentions and preparation, life skills courses may be experienced as ignoring the myriad of skills a woman has already developed for surviving her life. Unfortunately, the value of innovative course content can easily be lost if students feel patronized or feel a lack of recognition of their capabilities. Some life skills courses are designed to teach how to live *better* and teach middle-class values as the underpinnings for a successful life. One literacy worker explained the danger:

Life skills gets turned into "I will teach you how to be a middle-class person, the ideal middle-class person" which none of us even are, with our middle-class background. That's when life skills gets to be really ugly. When it's done without a class perspective. (interview, Salt Spring Island, British Columbia, November/December 1996)

Yet life skills courses—where assumptions and values are questioned and explored—can create a space where participants enjoy excellent opportunities to explore possibilities, work through personal issues, and gain new confidence and skills.

The interview group of literacy workers that met on Salt Spring Island spoke about a program at Nicola Valley Native Vocational Institute, which they thought had been highly successful and believed had avoided the dangers of patronizing students. They described one model where learners did alternate days of life skills and academics—where the life skills work included a strong focus on how learners were coping with being a student and the pressure of academic work. Another model included an intensive 3 weeks of life skills counseling followed by an English and Math course, during which a half day at the beginning and end of each week were devoted to life skills. This model also included further intensive blocks of 2 weeks and 1 week to continue the in-depth life skills work. These versions, which intertwined life skills and academics, were praised for helping keep students focused and making progress. Although all students might not want to take part in such a program, and some might find it daunting to take life skills while working on literacy or other academic skills, it could provide a useful support for many students who otherwise might struggle with the course they have chosen, fail, or quit, believing they are not capable of such study.

I was inspired by all the models and ideas I heard about during interviews. Every one seemed an enormous step forward from the silence and disconnection from counseling issues more common in literacy programs. A wide variety of models might be appropriate for different types of programs and different regions. Ideally various models would be available in each area so that learners could make choices about what they were able or wanted to participate in. Yet that seems an impossible dream when only a few models have even been piloted and those have usually only run once despite praise for their potential. A major barrier to the creation of new models has been the lack of funding. Funders must often be convinced that such programs are not costly luxuries appropriate only as an occasional special program, but necessary ongoing aspects of literacy programs that build essential connections and strengthen learning. Test running a variety of links between services offering counseling and literacy programs would enable more options to be explored and fully assessed so that every program could discover models appropriate to their situation.

LITERACY WORK AS THERAPY?

In interweaving literacy and therapy, a key tension arises between the appeal of literacy workers learning more about counseling and taking it on more in literacy programs and the concern that in literacy we have a tendency to try to do everything—to continually stretch a little further—and sometimes let literacy learning slide from the center of our attention. During my interviews, it was clear that the presence of some literacy workers with a background in counseling in a program meant there was less fear and more openness to considering diverse ways to address impacts of violence within the program. This greater openness provides fertile soil for new creative possibilities.

Some literacy workers I talked to argued that it was impossible to separate counseling and therapy from literacy work. The educators group in Prince Edward Island debated what was counseling and what was simply teaching. Several thought that "listening well enough to be able to ask

. . . a question" was definitely something that belonged in education. Several workers suggested therapy is an integral part of literacy work, and workers should learn more about what they are doing and how to work with survivors of trauma. The PEI educators said "a little bit of knowledge is a very dangerous thing" to bolster their argument that adult educators need training in counseling.

British Columbia instructor Diana Twiss argued that literacy workers are therapists:

> I think part of the problem is that literacy instructors are in fact therapists, and I can't see any way around that. We are the front line. We are the ones who develop the trust, the connections with the students. A new student just started with me yesterday. . . . I spent the morning talking to her and then the afternoon talking with the counselor. Now I go back to the student and communicate all that stuff to her. My head is spinning and I am so afraid to do something wrong. But I'm only a teacher!

I responded with a worry that we should not be therapists—that our work should be therapeutic, but not therapy. Diana Twiss replied:

> I hear you. I do not think that I am a therapist, but I often feel that I am put in the position of one. After working with a student like the one I spoke about earlier, my first thought was, I need to do more reading about this, maybe a degree in counseling. (As if I have the time). I am speaking out of frustration that I constantly feel like I am making it up as I go along, but then again, of course I am. All of this is new, society's realization of the effects of abuse and neglect are hopefully bringing more of this into the foreground, out in the classroom. I know that the longer I do this, the better I get at it. But my improvements are due to a deeper understanding of counseling issues. (Alphaplus Literacy & Violence Online Seminar, February–April 1998)

This worker argues for the value of learning more about counseling to shift from feeling "ill-equipped . . . to do what truly needs to be done." This is a concern many workers voiced. The recognition of the interconnections of literacy and counseling, and the learning possible from understanding more about counseling, is valuable in literacy.

First Nation instructors said that a rigid separation between literacy and counseling is in conflict with their cultural values. Nancy Cooper talked about her approach when students disclose abuse:

I listen respectfully because for many people (as most of you well know) this is the first time they have felt safe to disclose and discuss these things. It's really hard for me and my colleagues to do the work that we do because all of these atrocities are never far away in our minds. Many of us have been taught that all First Nations people are our family, not just clients or learners. This is not something I can compartmentalize and send the learner over to the counselor or the medicine person to deal with. They are there to learn, we have many time out sessions and we laugh a lot. We also cry together and smudge. I am lucky to have such a giving family. (Alphaplus Literacy & Violence Online Seminar, February–April 1998)

Memories of violence within the educational system is particularly likely to be present in the literacy class and need to be taken up there. This resistance to compartmentalizing was strongly reiterated by another First Nation worker:

But to me it's violence, even, to say that that's not something we can deal with here. That's kind of like cloaking it in shame, we don't talk about that, that's something that you need to go and discuss in confidentiality with your counselor. (interview, First Nation Instructors, Toronto, January 1997)

First Nation women are clear about the dangers of silencing the issues in the classroom and the value of having further resources available for a student to access. One First Nation woman in the interview group explained:

I always talk about the importance of combining therapy with literacy. And I always let them know that I'm not trained to provide therapy, that I only have my own experiences. I can share what I've had with them but that I'm not a certified therapist. I encourage them to go see an elder or go to therapy or go to a circle outside of the class and deal with stuff there but also we talk about things in the class if they feel comfortable. (interview, First Nation Instructors, Toronto, January 1997)

It is challenging to make further resources available without giving the impression that issues of violence are shameful and not to be addressed in the literacy program. However, providing extra resources for women who choose to draw on them can increase options and support to enhance instructors' work.

Therapist Liz White thought that it was important for educators not to see themselves as counselors. She suggested the importance of avoiding being pulled away from the task at hand—the educational focus—into the therapeutic issues. She argued that some success in the educational pursuit would be of great value for a survivor; she encourages literacy workers to focus on boundaries and the educational task of literacy learning:

> . . . watching your boundaries—boundaries clear and stuck to, developing an ability to tolerate people who continue in self-destructive behaviors. I think the most painful aspect of working with people who are traumatized is that they continue to do things . . . here and now that are really self-destructive and to be able to not get caught in it, and not get crisis oriented, to know that and to just stay on what is your task.
>
> Because I think it's another way for them to defeat your processes, which are healing and healthy processes, it's another way to get you all occupied and then they won't be able to read and it'll just be more of the same. In counseling or in therapy. . . . they'll be doing prostitution, they'll be doing this that and the other . . . and you'll begin to focus on that. My task as a therapist is to do the memory work and to support other parts of self that are healing. Your task is NOT to do the memory work. Your task is to do the literacy, so it's like not selling out what it is we're here for.
>
> So it's very clearly staying with your focus. And you can stretch this far but after that you end up resenting it and . . . it's not fair to the rest of the group. . . . Part of it is establishing that . . . we are a literacy program, this is an education. (interview, Toronto, November 1996)

This argument—that it is important to maintain a clear focus on the literacy work—is similar to the literacy instructors from British Columbia, quoted earlier, who mused on the value of having a space free of therapy and stressed the satisfaction for learners of accomplishing the task of improving reading, writing, or math skills. One survivor reminded me that a place where you are treated as an adult—where you are able to be in the present, separate from the memory work, to be treated respectfully as an adult, with an expectation that you can and will function—is a gift. I found myself fascinated with the value of clear boundaries, but concerned that even with the most educational focus the work of literacy includes self-expression and the presence of a range of stories. Some aspects of counseling should not be moved entirely outside the frame of literacy work. It is useful to both recognize the value of not getting diverted from achieving success in the task at hand and ensure that this focus is not accomplished at the cost of creating a false separation that silences issues of violence within the literacy program.

It is particularly important to recognize that counseling cannot always be carried out elsewhere. Therapy or counseling may not be an option for many women. Some women feel it is not acceptable to spend time on their own healing and think it is not acceptable to concentrate on themselves—viewing that as selfish. Some cultural contexts may reinforce that judgment. Many women may believe, or are pressured by family and society more broadly to believe, that they should focus on being a good wife, mother, and daughter. They feel only guilt if they focus on their own needs. This makes it crucial that they are not given the same message to *get over it* and get on with the task at hand in the literacy program.

Some learners may have no appropriate counseling or therapeutic options available in their community. In small communities, there are often few options; or those that exist have enormous waiting lists or are sexist, classist, ableist, racist, or culturally inappropriate. I was reminded by a group of Deaf literacy workers that hearing people often forget how completely unavailable confidential resources are to many Deaf people. Deaf people cannot go to the local shelter, their general practitioner, or a counselor or therapist and operate in their own language unless they can arrange for an interpreter. If they can get an interpreter, there is always a third person sharing in the interaction and they work within the limitations of bridging linguistic and cultural distance. Perhaps some will get by with a hearing aid and lip reading, but then they must put energy into simply trying to follow the communication and may suffer the cultural insensitivity or ableism of the hearing practitioner. These added difficulties put more pressure on literacy workers to learn counseling skills and literacy programs to include counselors on staff.[2]

Women of various cultures and ethnicities may face a lack of counselors who speak their language or understand their culture and experiences. This lack of choice may be particularly true in small communities. Although many people spoke about the lack of resources in small communities in the North West Territories, they also suggested that outsiders, who will leave the community sooner or later, should be careful not to become a lifeline, but instead should refer to local supports. When women are unable to access appropriate alternative counseling, the pressure on literacy workers to counsel and be familiar with different forms of listening, counseling, and therapy increases.

The argument that literacy work is therapy and that issues of violence cannot be separated out from the classroom may seem to be completely

---

[2]Deanne Bradley reminded me that the Deaf community is small, with few qualified counselors, so even those fortunate enough to be able to work with a Deaf counselor may feel uncomfortable because they will likely meet at social events. This can be awkward for both counselor and client.

in opposition to the suggestion that literacy workers should focus on the literacy work and maintain good boundaries. However, both are valuable observations. In literacy, we need to be clearly focused on the task of literacy teaching and to recognize the interconnections so that learners can access all the resources that can support and enhance their learning. In some situations, it may be necessary for literacy programs to take on counseling as a resource for literacy work. In other situations, they can advocate for better resources outside the program and make good links to these. Whatever the situation, more understanding of counseling improves literacy teaching.

TRAINING IN COUNSELING

Several literacy workers I talked to were already looking for opportunities to take training in counseling. They either felt it would help them develop as literacy teachers of women who have experienced trauma or they recognized that they already took on a counseling role and should know how to do it better. Diana Twiss explained why she felt that teachers need training in counseling:

> The more I learn about the behaviours that come out of abusive experiences from childhood, and all the other issues that people are struggling with, the better I am at helping them get on the road to learning. The vast majority of people that I work with have issues that are getting in the way of their learning. Because of past experiences they can't sit in a classroom for a long period of time, they don't function well in a group, or their behaviours are too disruptive for the others in the class. I can't separate the "literacy instruction" from the other deeper issues that I know they are struggling with. (personal correspondence, July 1999)

A couple of literacy workers did have some training and talked about how valuable it was in helping them understand what might be going on for learners in their program and simply in life. In contrast, other literacy workers I talked to were clear that they did not want to learn counseling skills. They did not think counseling was something they would do well, but they were extremely committed to strategizing how to serve survivors better through their literacy teaching and through access to counselors.

One group of instructors talked about the expertise they thought that counselors would have and that counselors would know better how to support learners struggling with the impacts of trauma in their lives. An instructor who was asked about flashbacks and felt unable to give a good answer said:

> That sort of experience leaves me feeling quite inept and I think that perhaps that happens for other people too, who are literacy instructors, that you have these things, and you just know there's something that you should be doing but you don't know what it is. And when you get them often enough, as we probably are getting them more and more often these days, I kind of worry about the build up of feeling inept at your job. I think there's a real need here for some training that we could get, or we could maybe give each other, or get some experts in, some counselors. Just how do you deal with that sort of thing? Because I'm sure that there is a way to deal with that that's much more satisfactory than the way I dealt with that situation. (interview, Salt Spring Island, British Columbia, November/December 1996)

Literacy workers seeking more counseling expertise, rather than only referring the learners to the expert (counselors or therapists), can provide relief from the discomfort of feeling inept and the confidence of knowing what is offered by different forms of counseling.

A variety of training might be useful to help literacy workers develop more comfort, knowledge, and sensitivity for working with women who have experienced trauma. One counselor I talked to thought that all educators should have training in counseling because their work is inevitably therapeutic. Similarly, in PEI, some workers thought that:

> Absolutely everyone in adult education should have a counseling course. Because if they don't, it's going to happen. We're always told: "Make sure you get them to the right people, get them on the right track, get them to the counselor, the professional." Yeah but . . . a person seems to have a crisis at four o'clock on the afternoon the counselor's not around. . . . Or use [the local counseling center]. Fine, there's only a four month waiting list, and in the mean time, we have somebody in the midst of a crisis. So I think there has to be a way of working through the problems as they arise. (interview, Charlottetown, PEI, March 1997)

In Germany, I was told, it is commonplace for literacy workers to have training in counseling. The assumption is that any adult who has not learned to read as a child will have issues to address even if they have not experienced any other trauma. Training focusing on responding to crises, recognizing limits, and seeing the demands and dangers of working directly on issues of violence might be particularly useful for literacy workers and volunteers who are not planning to become counselors. They might become more effective teachers if they understand more about the terrain in which they are involved.

Training offered to crisis line volunteers or shelter volunteers might be a useful model. Training should focus on learning not to rescue, but rather to respect boundaries, help empower and keep the power with the person seeking support, listen well, bear witness to another's pain, look after oneself well, and understand suicide prevention. Information sessions to help literacy workers be clear about the contrasts between different forms and approaches to counseling, therapy, and other related services would also be valuable to help literacy workers with appropriate referrals.

For literacy workers more interested in using counseling skills, fuller training in all aspects of counseling might also be useful. Recognizing the range of approaches within the field, this raises the question of which experts should be asked to give literacy workers training. Gradually, as the literacy movement gains more understanding of the complexity of impacts of violence on learning and more self-consciously tries new approaches to support learning, literacy workers might be able to offer each other varied and rich training, as well as drawing from resources outside the field.

The suggestion that literacy workers might do literacy work differently if they had training in counseling is interesting. Mary Carlisle, a literacy worker from British Columbia, described talking to a therapist and realizing that the therapist's perspective gave her some useful insights. Mary wanted to know more:

> And she told me about secondary posttrauma stress disorder, it really impressed on me the need to take care of myself. I have always known I should have some counseling skills in order to be an ABE instructor. And now I'm totally convinced of it. I don't really want to go near a job teaching ABE without some counseling skills, some training. Because I just feel, like I probably have the skills but I can't articulate what they are. And I think there's also an approach to teaching ABE which people who have some counseling skills or training or background have, that is protective. And I don't have it, because I've come from a teaching background. So I feel really strongly that this is very essential for literacy workers.
>
> I know that counselors have rules for how many clients you take in a day, how many days you work in a week, and the counselor that I see, she's very impressed by the amount of energy it takes to be a teacher. (interview, Salt Spring Island, British Columbia, November/December 1996)

Counselors might be able to help literacy workers set limits, feel more comfortable with their choices, and even open up questions about how much literacy workers can take on. Addressing these questions might enable literacy workers to be less caught up in what Priscilla George called a "dialogue of doubt," which distracts them and limits their full presence and attention to the students in the classroom (personal correspondence, September 1998).

A shelter worker in Nunavut felt that counseling skills were no mystery and at their heart were listening skills—skills that literacy instructors should already know (Interview, Iqaluit, March 1997). Others suggested that it was important not to obscure all the complexities of issues that may be present in the classroom, such as transference and countertransference. When I read the following article in a literacy program newsletter at the beginning of this research process, I was delighted to see that someone else was suggesting that it was important to offer counseling in literacy programs:

> I'm not a trained therapist, counselor or psychiatrist, but I give it my best shot. I'm honored that our students trust me enough to turn to me for guidance or support. I'm flattered that they think I have the answers or solutions to their problems. I wonder, however, how many opportunities adult literacy students have just to talk to someone. Do public literacy programs offer holistic counseling services? Do students in your programs have the opportunity to speak with you on matters other than literacy and education? . . . The kind of counseling to which I am referring involves advice on matters other than literacy and education. (Kroll, 1996)

But when I re-read it later, having carried out most of my interviews, I was disturbed. I recognized several dangers in the description. The writer gives the impression that counseling is largely about giving advice. The idea that the worker will be flattered by the implication that they have answers and do their best to offer advice suggests that the worker will not be supporting learners in recognizing their own wisdom and supporting them in developing their own strategies, but instead will be offering answers. This article confirmed the value of training in deep listening and in recognition of some of the dangers of sliding into giving advice or becoming a rescuer.

Complex Listening

Dori Laub (1992) provided a clear description of the complexities of listening to trauma, revealing tension for both the speaker and listener. For the speaker, the very act of telling moves the experience of trauma from an overwhelming shock to a narrative to be witnessed:

... the listener to trauma comes to be a participant and a co-owner of the traumatic event: through his very listening, he comes to partially experience trauma in himself. The relation of the victim to the event of the trauma, therefore, impacts on the relation of the listener to it, and the latter comes to feel the bewilderment, injury, confusion, dread and the conflicts that the trauma victim feels. He has to address all these, if he is to carry out his function as a listener, and if trauma is to emerge, so that its henceforth impossible witnessing can indeed take place. The listener, therefore, by definition partakes of the struggle of the victim with the memories and residues of his or her traumatic past. The listener has to feel the victim's victories, defeats and silences, know them from within, so that they can assume the form of testimony.

The listener, however, is also a separate human being and will experience hazards and struggles of his own, while carrying out his function of a witness to the trauma witness. While overlapping, to a degree with the experience of the victim, he nonetheless does not become the victim—he preserves his own separate place, position and perspective; a battleground for forces raging in himself, to which he has to pay attention and respect if he is properly to carry out his task. (pp. 57–58)

Re-reading these words reminds me that bearing witness is an active role and by no means simple. It draws the listener into her or his own story as well as into what he or she is witnessing. Dori Laub also spoke of tension between historical truth and testimony, suggesting that the historians interested in fact can lead away from the felt truth of the teller and away from the struggle to hear the elusive words and respond to them in a way that shows they have been understood: ". . . we both share the knowledge of the trauma, the knowledge of what facing it and living in its shadow are really about" (p. 64).

In contrast, Laub (1992) suggested that, instead of the flash of recognition and understanding, telling can be simply traumatizing—a reliving that retraumatizes. Clarissa Chandler also spoke of the importance of the empathic listener to ensure that the telling is not merely reliving pain, but a creation of connection. Laub clarified the danger of the failure to connect:

> The absence of an empathic listener, or more radically, the absence of an *addressable other*, an other who can hear the anguish of one's memories and thus affirm and recognize their realness, annihilates the story. And it is, precisely, this ultimate annihilation of a narrative that, fundamentally, *cannot be heard* and of a story that *cannot be witnessed*, which constitutes the mortal eighty-first blow (the ultimately fateful blow, beyond the eighty blows that a man, in Jewish tradition, can sustain and survive.) (p. 68)

The importance of listening well or being clear that you cannot listen seemed even more important after reading Dori Laub's words—a half listener, a reluctant listener not truly able to hear may be worse than no listener at all. Literacy workers must learn how to say when they cannot listen. When a literacy worker cannot listen, she needs to support a learner to find someone who can hear her—counselor, therapist, or another literacy worker. If she can listen to the learner's stories of what it was like to tell and be heard, or how she feels as she continues in counseling, offering, as Kate Nonesuch called it, the *side support*, can preserve an important connection. If educators are clear that they do not have to be able to listen at all times, or even at all, they are more likely to remain in contact by finding another listener and continuing as a side support, rather than becoming paralyzed with guilt and avoiding any further reference to the issue. Such behavior may inadvertently give a learner the message that nobody can listen—that she should not ask anyone to listen or provide support and confirm an expectation that she should remain silent.

Training Questions

Some counselors and literacy workers were concerned that instructors stepped into counseling without realizing they were doing so or, even worse, they stepped into providing advice, thinking they were doing the best they could in the absence of trained counselors. They suggested that what was needed was not so much for literacy workers to learn to be counselors, but to learn *not* to be counselors—in particular to learn how to maintain clear boundaries and how to say no when they cannot hear in ways that do not blame the teller for wanting to be heard. I think every literacy worker should have at least this minimal training, even those who are not interested in taking on the role of counselor in any way.

Some literacy workers looked for the opportunity to go farther in their learning and explore fully what it would mean to be a counselor. Those who felt this was something they could incorporate into their approach to teaching might also be able to do more actual counseling with literacy learners in appropriate situations. Some literacy workers and counselors thought all literacy workers must be trained in counseling; even if they are only doing referrals, they will still do some counseling and need to know what to do. I believe it is important for such training to be available. However, to respect workers' limits, it should not be an expectation. We should not expect all workers to be trained as counselors. For those who know it is not an area they are comfortable with or ready to enter, training should be offered in how not to counsel.

During the research process, I wondered about the value of literacy workers with counseling skills spending at least some of their work time explicitly doing counseling. One worker I suggested that to, based in downtown Toronto, surprised me by saying that she did not think that was useful. Although her counseling skills helped her provide a transition between the literacy program and counselors outside the program, she felt the separation that kept her primarily a literacy worker was valuable.

Although the possibilities for literacy workers to obtain some training in counseling are exciting, training is not a panacea that enables all literacy workers to become skilled and sensitive in responding to disclosures. In one small group of literacy workers, a literacy worker who had no counseling training spoke with great sensitivity about the ways in which learners' experiences of trauma got in the way of their learning. Her sense of responsibility as part of her literacy work was to support them in addressing these issues. She was also careful to be clear about her own boundaries about when she could hear and support them and when she could not. Although I find the commonly used frame of trauma *getting in the way* of learning problematic, suggesting that the experiences can be got out of the way and the student will learn normally again, this instructor has found a way to include some careful listening to her students' experiences in her work (Interview, Yellowknife, NWT, March 1997).

In contrast, another literacy worker seemed less sensitive. She had training in counseling that she felt had been quite helpful. However, she talked about students wasting her time if they just wanted to talk to her and were not prepared to do anything about their problems. Her tone seemed quite critical of students who were unable to continue in the program. These interactions reminded me that some instructors may be excellent, nonjudgmental listeners and clear about their limits without training; others, despite training, may be less able to support learners in an open and nonjudgmental fashion. Of course, this is in a sense obvious. Many literacy workers spoke of trained counselors they were not comfortable referring students to. There is obviously both a range of approaches among counselors and a range of levels of sensitivity and empathy however well trained a person may be.

One factor that may affect the ability to develop empathy and understanding may be whether a person has done *their own work*. Several counselors and workers talked about the importance of workers having addressed their own issues. They suggested that a person is more likely to be empathetic if she is not fleeing from her own issues. Some counselors suggested that when people have not done their own work, they either do not want to believe the dreadful stories, insisting that they cannot be true, or they need to be needed and find their own value through helping others and so are more inclined to rescue. One therapeutic text stated the case strongly:

> Clinical work has taught us that the ability to tolerate the plight of victims is, at least in part, a function of how well people have dealt with their own misfortunes. When they have confronted the reality of their own hurt and suffering, and accepted their own pain, this generally is translated into tolerance and sometimes even compassion for others. Conversely, as long as people deny the impact of their own personal trauma and pretend that it did not matter, that it was not so bad, or that excuses can be made for their abusers, they are likely to identify with the aggressors and treat others with the same harshness with which they treat the wounded parts of themselves. Identification with the aggressor makes it possible to bypass empathy for themselves and secondarily for others. (van der Kolk et al., 1996, p. 36)

bell hooks (1994) stressed the importance of the university professor being self-actualized if she is to support students in becoming more fully self-actualized. She drew from Thich Nhat Hanh's work to suggest that the teacher is a healer who must also heal herself:

> The practice of a healer, therapist, teacher or any helping professional should be directed toward his or herself first, because if the helper is unhappy, he or she cannot help many people. (p. 15)

Many people enter the literacy field wanting to help others and make change. This incentive may make it challenging for literacy workers to recognize that we cannot fix everything—we cannot solve things by "rushing out and getting a hold of a whole new set of skills." Only so much success may be possible. Susan Goodfellow, a counselor in a women's shelter, and I wondered in conversation whether perhaps when someone is doing their own work, they have less belief that they can fix themselves, or anyone else, and more faith that everyone has to travel their own road—no one knows the answer for someone else. Perhaps this leads to less need to offer solutions—that it makes more sense to just hear, offer support, and encouragement. Of course, even when a person is doing their own work and aware of the importance of maintaining boundaries, it is still an enormous challenge to hold onto the value of keeping clear boundaries. Although we might all be better literacy workers if we do our own healing work, not to mention the value it may hold for us personally, several literacy workers suggested that it would be unreasonable to expect literacy workers to add that requirement to everything else demanded of literacy workers—all for little pay, recognition, or acknowledgment. Yet the value of such work was convincing to many of those I interviewed.

Recognizing aptitudes and interests of literacy workers will mean that some workers will want to focus more on the area of counseling, take more extensive training and design, and lead innovative and collaborative courses. However, it is important for all workers to know something about the issues so that counseling is not pushed off to one worker and outside the literacy frame. It is important that every program considers how it can serve the needs of women who have experienced trauma and support their learning, but the issue should not be one only for individual programs. Literacy networks, counseling organizations, and funders must all play a part in supporting access to counseling for individual learners and creative collaborations between the literacy and counseling fields, which maintain the visibility of the issues within literacy programs.

ASSESS APPROPRIATE CONNECTIONS AND INITIATE NEW PROGRAM MODELS

Listening to the range of options currently available inside and outside literacy programs, it was obvious that no single answer would address the questions of appropriate links with counseling organizations or whether literacy workers need to be trained in counseling. Literacy workers and their situations are so diverse. Yet listening to the voices of literacy workers and learners makes it clear that we cannot simply take refuge in saying "but I'm not a therapist" when issues of violence emerge in literacy teaching. Nor should we simply send learners to counselors and preserve the implication that impacts of violence are shameful and addressed only in private with a counselor. Whatever the context of a particular program, it is crucial that all programs recognize that learners will be dealing with issues of trauma and many will want access to culturally appropriate counseling or other resources. To assist them, programs must have a solid knowledge of the range of counseling services available in their community. They should also assess what capacity is needed within the programs to make good links and provide support for learners continuing with their learning in the program while seeking counseling.

Some knowledge of counseling within a program and strong links with counseling services, whether offered internally or by another organization or organizations, will enable the program to function more effectively. Where few appropriate resources are available in the community, literacy workers will need a broader range of counseling training and may also want to become advocates for better resources to be made available. Few programs currently explore the links they might be able to generate with programs that offer counseling or with counseling departments in their institution—links that could build greater visibility and more creative alternative possibilities for counseling support to learners. Some exciting models have been tried, but these have usually been cut short due to lack of funds. Models that interweave counseling or more holistic literacy work with regular literacy teaching, such as the Women's Success course in British Columbia, provide exciting examples. The centrality of this work to literacy programs must be recognized or learners will be left frustrated with their inability to learn, trying again and again to complete courses, but despairing at their limited success.

8

Examining the Costs
of Bearing Witness

Literacy workers experience major challenges in their work. The contradictory pressures silence talk about the extent of violence that workers
and learners experience while leading many workers to believe they
should be able to listen to anything learners want to share, provide ex-
haustive support to learners, and successfully teach everyone to read in
record time. Alongside such tension is continual pressure for workers to
do enormous amounts of work of all sorts, often for little pay, benefits, or
appreciation. Workers are frequently exhausted and frustrated. They
question whether their work makes a difference as they operate with the
demand to work a little harder, show more student progress, and justify
their program. Paid workers who work alongside volunteers may feel they
should to take on volunteer hours themselves to ensure that volunteer tutors receive adequate training and support. Encouraging, guiding, appreci-
ating, and listening to volunteers may take substantial time and energy.

The eagerness with which literacy workers came to my interview sessions, and their concerns about telling the stories they had heard and the
limits on their ability to change the situation for women struggling with
trauma, suggested a need not being met elsewhere. Frequently literacy
workers spoke about how rarely the many issues of violence were discussed in their programs or local networks. The group of workers in British Columbia all agreed when one woman said: "I think it's time we blew
the cover on this in the ABE Association" (Interview, Salt Spring Island,
British Columbia, November/December 1996). However, taking up these
issues in networks and programs creates more work for literacy workers.

The commitment of literacy workers to the challenges of literacy work
in general, and of working with survivors of trauma in particular, is incredible. Although many leave the field suffering from exhaustion and

burnout, particularly in provinces with low pay, poor working conditions, limited benefits, and no structure for advancement, many also try to continue in the field. They are carried by their commitment to redress inequality, to work with those who are marginalized, and to teach those who have been labeled—or who label themselves—*stupid*. A long-term instructor spoke about the value she sees in literacy:

> I used to do community work, including work with survivors, and work with women in prison, and work with women on the street, and work with women in housing . . . then I found literacy work, and in literacy work I have a thing I can offer. I have this skill they can build, this step they can use to make a change in their life, other than all the ones that they're already aware they need to work on. (interview, Salt Spring Island, British Columbia, November/December 1996)

One temporary instructor spoke of her eagerness to find a permanent position in the field:

> I plan to teach literacy students for the rest of my life because I care about helping them see some success in their lives and I feel good when I'm part of their growing and that helps me grow. . . . I see how crucial teacher attitude is to the whole range of possibilities for learner growth. I see I have to keep my eyes open and ears attuned for clues from learners. I believe trauma survivors want to be seen and heard to validate their thinking so they can know they're not just crazy or lazy. I believe people know how to heal themselves but we all need an environment to try new things. (Patterson, personal correspondence)

Literacy work is challenging, but it is also enormously rewarding. Literacy workers need a wide range of supports and recognition of the work involved in literacy teaching to enable them to gain more satisfaction and feel less frustration from the work.

HAVE YOU GOT A MINUTE?

During my interviews, one counselor in an interview group in Yellowknife spoke of *door knob* disclosures made when the woman was on the point of departure—her hand on the door knob. Many literacy workers agreed that this description fit their experience and spoke of disclosures prefaced by the question, Have you got a minute? They explained how hard it was to say they did not have a minute and, once the disclosure began, how hard it was to put an end to the telling even if they did not have time or energy to listen. Christina Patterson spoke of the difficulty of being approached when she had other work to do:

> It also reminds me of other learners who come before or after class starts if they need to talk to me. They need for me to know what's going on in their lives in terms of things that interfere with their learning or attending, but they do that kind of talking out of class. I don't always like that part of my job, partly because I need the time before class to get ready and partly because I have trouble hearing a lot of "stuff" before class and keeping my own grounding in place. Somehow hearing the same information in a group in the classroom instead of one-on-one in private before or after class makes it easier to hear the "stuff." Maybe I feel less responsible when the information is shared amongst many people. (Alphaplus Literacy & Violence Online Seminar, February–April 1998)

This instructor suggested that she might try taking time at the beginning of each class for learners to check in and share what is happening to them. She hoped that might reduce the demand on her to listen privately before or after class. However, she also recognized that the very learners who might benefit most from such a check-in are the ones who are most likely to arrive late, which reflects their difficulty with being *present*. It is also important to acknowledge that learning to check in and share honestly may take practice, and only with time will the trust that enables sharing be built up (Priscilla George, personal correspondence, September 1998).

Many instructors spoke about the difficulties of knowing how to respond to horrific stories shared during class or in writing assignments. One university instructor described her experience:

> I have a lot of disclosures through writing also. I often ask students to do journals in my courses. The journal assignments relate to the assigned readings, and I might also give them questions that ask them to relate to the materials to their own lives. These disclosures, could occur in class or in a private discussion with me, depending on how intimate and supportive the classroom environment is and how well everyone knows each other. I've had some night classes where disclosures did occur because of the high level of respect and trust there was in those groups. Sometimes it can be really overwhelming. And I also feel is listening enough? What else should you be doing, other than to validate and listen? (interview/personal correspondence, 1996/1999)

The question of whether listening is enough can be an enormous burden. It can be compounded by the dilemma of how to respond to written disclosures, particularly in assignments that must be graded.

Some counselors suggested that literacy workers who hear about trauma, like women who experience trauma, also face the challenge of regaining a sense of control, meaning, and connection for themselves. A growing literature exists about counselors' experience of vicarious trauma. For literacy workers, the impact might even be more severe than for counselors because workers have less control of the listening process. Literacy workers have little control over when they hear stories and fewer boundaries limiting how much they will hear and what to expect. A literacy worker may read a horrifying story in a journal or she may hear one from a learner when she is preparing for class or at the end of the day when she is hurrying home. Or the disclosure may be dropped abruptly into the classroom bringing the best-planned session to an abrupt halt. Two instructors in British Columbia spoke of the strain:

> A: It's that unpredictableness . . . that made me want to withdraw into the dark safe warm room at night, 'cause when you're dealing with that, never knowing what's going to be told to us or when you're going to hear it. . . .

> B: Counselors at least know when they make an appointment with someone. . . . (interview, Salt Spring Island, British Columbia, November/December 1996)

Counselors and therapists set clear time limits and a designated location for hearing disclosures. They also have training and experience in being engaged and attentive, yet also detached. They have fixed appointments in their office; they know who they will see, when, and what that person's central issues are in an ongoing relationship. They are able to set up the environment and do not have other interactions with the person. Listening is their only relationship. The story is not sprung on them, with the potential of continuation at any time in any spare moment before, during, or after a class or as they carry out some other aspect of their work.

The unexpectedness of the disclosures and the sense that listening to them is essential but not legitimate work for a literacy worker leaves many literacy workers exhausted, but unclear why they are quite so shattered. For example, when they have only been working with a small group of students, it is hard to pin point exactly what was so exhausting. Perhaps, too, the sense that the pain and stories are an unavoidable aspect of adult literacy work but not legitimate makes it harder for each worker to take control, to decide on appropriate limits for herself, to assess ahead of time what she can cope with, and what options she has available for referral and other resources. The worker may not even be able to name the best time for her to listen or be clear about at what times listening makes her work impossible (such as just before she teaches).

Choosing to Respond, Choosing How to Respond

Although the profound impact of hearing about the horrors inflicted by humans on each other is not spoken about in literacy, it is under discussion elsewhere. Dori Laub (1992) described the impact on listeners of hearing about the nightmare of the holocaust. He argued that all the biggest questions in life are opened up by bearing witness to such tragedy. Such questioning is profoundly terrifying:

> The listener can no longer ignore the question of facing death; of facing time and its passage; of the meaning and purpose of living; of the limits of one's omnipotence; of losing the ones that are close to us; the great questions of our ultimate aloneness; our otherness from any other; our responsibility to and for our destiny; the question of loving and its limits; of parents and children and so on. (pp. 72–73)

The level of human tragedy many literacy workers hear about daily must open up similar questions or lead to responses, such as numbness or closing down, which avoid the impact of hearing. Laub (1992) described in detail the dangers of defenses against listening and being disturbed by existential questions. These defenses limit the possibility of bearing witness:

> To maintain a sense of safety in the face of the upheaval of such questions and the onslaught of the images of trauma, the listener experiences a range of defensive feelings, which he needs to control and of which he needs to be aware, if he is to carry out his tasks. These listening defences may include the following:
>
> - A sense of total paralysis, brought about by the threat of flooding—by the fear of merger with the atrocities being recounted.
> - A sense of outrage and of anger, unwittingly directed at the victim—the narrator. When we meet a friend who has a malignant disease, we often feel angry at that person. We are torn apart by the inadequacy of our ability to properly respond, and inadvertently wish for the illness to be the patient's responsibility and wrongdoing.
> - A sense of total withdrawal and numbness.
> - A flood of awe and fear; we endow the survivor with a kind of sanctity, both to pay our tribute to him and to keep him at a distance, to avoid the intimacy entailed in knowing.

- Foreclosure through facts, through an obsession with factfinding; an absorbing interest in the factual details of the account which serve to circumvent the human experience. Another version of this foreclosure, of this obsession with factfinding is a listener who already "knows it all," ahead of time, leaving little space for the survivor's story.
- Hyperemotionally which superficially looks like compassion and caring. The testifier is simply flooded, drowned and lost in the listener's defensive affectivity. (pp. 72–73)

Recognizing these responses as defenses may not make them disappear, but may allow a literacy worker struggling with reaction to learn to control her response and understand that these are barriers to witnessing that prevent the one who seeks to tell her experience from being heard. This chilling description of the defenses we put up to preserve a sense of safety and avoid facing the impossible questions triggered by violence makes it clear that if we are to listen adequately we must know that we have supports. Rather than slipping unknowingly into reaction, a worker needs resources to learn how to listen and to know that she has options—she may not always be able to listen. At the end of a lengthy group session, one worker said:

I have been finding myself getting a little hysterical recently because of the feeling that somebody has to do something about it, and clearly I'm the only one who knows that somebody has to do something about it. (interview, Salt Spring Island, British Columbia, November/December 1996)

Priscilla George also reminded me that, in small communities, "we often know the person who is the perpetrator and it adds another dimension when we encounter him or her at the store" (personal correspondence, September 1998). Workers need adequate places to take these feelings and learn to maintain a balance that is self-protective, but also supportive of the individual and politically meaningful:

The researcher/therapist therefore also needs a place where she or he can tell the story about the meeting. In other words, a forum to express the difficult and conflict-ridden story and gain insight as to how to protect oneself. (Agger, 1994, p. 19)

For literacy workers, the challenge of being with people who are in pain is enormous. Therapist Liz White talked about the need to learn how to tolerate self-destructive behavior without getting caught up, becoming crisis-oriented, and losing focus on the work. That demand takes a strong toll on the worker. Yet Liz White stressed that the worker needs to hang onto hope and firmly continue to convey this belief, even when the learner seems to have lost hope herself, despairing of the possibility that anything will ever change:

> I think that the literacy worker must learn the capacity to witness, to just bear witness. [For example] to read poetry that has to do with moments—that describe the desperateness of people at times—not to take them into it, but to mirror back to them, just to witness and to trust. To witness and to trust that it often feels like a choice, and to focus that the desire to kill yourself is the desire to get peace, to get relief, because there is no belief that I'd ever get a rest from this. . . . I just think sometimes we desperately need a rest. So it is the capacity to witness—to know that people feel that. "It is painful to see you in this place I wish it were otherwise for you, but I can imagine that it will be, and it's hard for you to see it. So it's like I have a vision—it's hard for you to see around the corner. I can see around the corner, I see around the corner for you and I wish you could come over here to see around the corner, but you have to go around the corner in your own way. But I have lots of visions for you, I can imagine a time when you are able to do this . . . it's not pie in the sky, it's real. . . ." (interview, Toronto, November 1996)

Women's shelter counselor Susan Goodfellow suggested that the key to literacy workers being able to instill hope in others is to maintain a sense of hope themselves. To maintain this hope, workers need to have opportunities to, in Susan's words, "stay full." They must be able to maintain a sense of their own knowing. Susan suggested that, rather than building our own sense of knowing, we often go in search of someone else who knows (e.g., a course that will tell us the answer). She argued the importance of recognizing our own knowledge.

The insights offered by Liz White and Susan Goodfellow remind me of the importance of finding balance. Although it is valuable for instructors to learn new skills and knowledge, such as the information offered earlier by Liz White about learning to bear witness, it is also important for instructors to recognize, as Susan Goodfellow observed, that a hectic search for a new set of skills is not what is needed. We need to look for a balance between learning more and drawing on our own wisdom to hold onto hope. After a lengthy session discussing these issues, one literacy worker concluded that what she had learned from discussion and reflection was:

> We are not responsible, we don't have to fix it. It's not a matter of getting a new set of skills—there may be only so much success. (interview, Salt Spring Island, British Columbia, November/December 1996)

This conclusion may not sound hopeful, but it does move a worker away from the frustration of self-blame and make it easier to make her own choice about what she needs to learn and what she can listen to.

Liz White added an extra thought when she read her own words about the need for literacy workers to learn to witness, as she wrote about the power of the writer observing herself:

> When women write about their despair they are also joining you as a witness to themselves. It is often empowering for the writer/observer to see that this time they are watching and caring for themselves even as they are living—and sharing it, putting it into words. This is the beginning of mastery. (Personal correspondence, June 1999)

This recognition that the writer or teller is also witness to his or her own story is important. In the literacy class, the instructor bears witness, but the person writing bears witness also to her own story and to the responses of those who witness. Christina Patterson also explored these interconnections:

> I need to add how embarrassing it is for students to have no better control than to display these physically clumsy movements. The body is worse than the mind in terms of not being able to hide it's expression or true feelings. I try to be as gentle as possible when a student is looking at me looking at them being clumsy.
>
> At the same time, I've been thinking about my role as a witness. I think we all need witnesses to our "good" behaviour and our "bad" behaviour. When a student sees me seeing their body out of control there is some moment of them non-verbally saying to me "see what I have to put up with?" (personal correspondence, July 1999)

This insight reminded me of an earlier comment by literacy worker who also spoke of being witnessed by her student. This instructor reported that when she checked in with a woman student to see if a male student's behavior was bothering her, the woman remarked that she had seen the instructor watching the interaction. The student said that, because the instructor did nothing immediately, she had assumed that meant that the instructor thought the man's behavior was acceptable. This is a powerful reminder that if an instructor does not take action when she sees violence—such as harassment in the classroom or a woman's bruises—students witness that silence and lack of action and take a message from it.

Numbing Out

Staff from programs in Toronto that serve people on the street were particularly worried about the volunteers in their program. They were concerned that the position of volunteer had more blurred boundaries than that of paid staff person or counselor and easily merged into friendship. They feared that blurred boundary could mean that learners would disclose more than the tutor could handle. I also think the implication was that staff people had learned not to be shocked, whereas volunteers might be more vulnerable and isolated. Janine Luce, a worker at Street Haven, explained the problem:

> I think sometimes I worry with our tutors about shock—learning things about people that are shocking. If you feel close to somebody, you're not going to worry about that, you're not going to worry about shocking them. Sometimes I worry about tutors finding something out that they find really difficult to take and then disappearing. Feeling that they can't work with somebody because of one thing or another about that person. Lowering those boundaries, or creating more of a friendship, can sometimes make that really difficult—what you share and what you don't share. . . . When women are working with a volunteer, there are certain things that are appropriate to share and there are certain things that maybe aren't. And it's part of women's own boundaries as learners, to define what's okay to share with this person and what isn't. Because they're not a staff, a social worker, a counselor, they don't have as much [institutional] power, but I also think in a learner's mind they're not [seen as] separate . . . the same way that a staff [person] is . . . and a counselor is. (interview, Community and Street Program Literacy Workers, Toronto, February 1997)

This group implied that perhaps the learner did not make a distinction between tutor and paid staff or even said more because the boundaries were less distinct with a tutor. It was interesting that these workers were very concerned about the cost to tutors, but focused less on what it cost them as workers to have acquired an expectation of hearing horrors to the level where they were no longer shocked.

The tension for workers—about whether it was good to learn some distance from the stories they heard or whether that suggested they had become numb and uncaring—was vividly illustrated in a conversation between several instructors.

> A: I can't take it, I can't take it and then go back in the classroom and pretend it didn't happen. That's the other thing. 'Cause I'm finished, I'm worn out. I'm gonna go home, pet the cat and play mah-jong.

B: See, I used to be much better at doing that kind of switch. I can remember having somebody on the phone threatening to commit suicide, and I had to send another student to get the counselor up and transfer the call over to him, and then went back in and continued teaching. And the counselor was saying afterward, I couldn't believe that you could do that. I used to be a lot better at doing that. But as I've gotten more in touch with my own feelings—

C: That's interesting, 'cause it takes me back to what we were talking about earlier with the people who can learn and be in crisis at the same time, which is maybe something some of us learned, that I know I can do, because it's something I did as a child. I think I was reading before life became hard, and I think that helped me, because then I could escape into books. But maybe it depends where the violence occurs in your life. . . .

D: Sometimes I surprise myself that people tell me stuff, and I—I took some counseling courses—try to do what I learned about doing, but I'm surprised at how much I separate myself from that experience and don't get [caught up]. I know that it's a horrible thing, but also it's not mine.

A: I'm notoriously good at not separating myself from anything.

D: I wonder what's wrong with me, if I don't—you know?

E: Or perhaps you have learned to keep boundaries?

D: Well, like you said, you're not going to be any good if you're right in there too.

F: But the problem is, sometimes you think you've kept your boundaries, and then you don't. Like at the end of the day you find you're just exhausted. Where did that come from?

A: You think about it all night long.

F: Was it somebody who talked to you at ten-thirty or twelve-thirty, or what?

B: A counselor I was talking to said that—I was commenting on how little social stuff I did, I found I just didn't have the energy to do anything or go anywhere or see anybody—and she said that's really common for people who do anything like the kind of work that I do. You just can't respond anymore. I find it hard going home with kids sometimes, they are wanting stuff from me, and I just want to sit in a room with all the lights off for a while. (interview, Salt Spring Island, British Columbia, November/December 1996)

The conversation suggested that being able to go right back into the classroom after hearing something horrifying might mean that you were not in touch with your feelings. However, being able to set some bound-aries and not be completely drawn into the pain might be useful and something that could be learned, although trying to maintain boundaries is recognized as never simple. The ability to hear a horror and return to class as if nothing has happened may be an approach to dealing with hor-ror learned in childhood; it is a reminder that each worker brings their own memories and coping methods to their literacy work. The group broke into much hilarity at this point, suggesting that they should set up a support group because the desire to sit in a room with all the lights off sounded like a cry for help. Although that worker explained that she meant it metaphorically, the thought prompted a rich discussion about the cost of bearing witness to so much pain at work:

> D: I know that as I have started to increase my circle of friends, I've made an active—an almost conscious choice to have well friends. Because at the end of the day, I try to spend time with people—people who are fairly mentally healthy. I was just thinking about that recently. I don't have a re-ally big circle of friends, but that's been important. And we had a person living with us in the summertime who I knew was—well, I felt she was just really needy, and I just avoided it. I didn't need to come home at the end of the week, and—

> B: That's actually what I was talking about [with the counselor], just hav-ing a small circle of friends, was that odd? And she said it was actually re-ally common.

> G: Well, it makes sense.

> H: Not to want to go places where you're going to run into people that, there's gonna be situations where you're going to have to handle it. To go out with people that you know are okay, where you know you're not going to be surprised suddenly by one of them getting drunk and breaking down and telling you all. 'Cause you don't want it, so you can keep yourself safe by not going into places where there's lots of people that you don't know. Lots of potential for anything to happen.

> B: That's a real price to pay. (interview, Salt Spring Island, British Colum-bia, November/December 1996)

DOING IT WRONG

Many literacy workers talked at length about the tension of not knowing how to work best with the impacts of trauma they saw in the classroom. Several workers spoke about times when they felt particularly in-

ept—when a learner asked how long her flashbacks would last or if the
fact that she had forgotten much of the trauma of her childhood meant
that she would continue to have gaps in her memory. Because in literacy
the possibilities of disclosure are unspoken and the impacts of trauma in
the classroom are rarely mentioned, workers may also feel unable to seek
support. There may be a sense that she is wrong to be hearing disclosures
or wrong to need help. She may feel unable to speak about the effect that
being with so much pain is having on her.

One therapist (Hellmut, 1992) wrote an account of a situation where
he was working with somebody outside his mandate: His way of working
was outside the acceptable approaches in his field and his diagnosis was
widely seen as an error. His description of how that contributed to his
failure to keep good boundaries or seek out appropriate supervision to
help him monitor his own approach made me question experiences
within the literacy field. Because his approach, and even that he was
working with this particular client, was unacceptable, he could not
expect critical insights and challenging support from his colleagues. As
he described the situation where he was "effectively quite alone," I was
reminded of my own sense of isolation when I first began to tutor a survivor. I did not feel I could ask for support from other literacy workers because when I sought to speak about my experiences I felt only disapproval. Either I should not be doing such work because I was not a
therapist or what was my problem—everyone else deals with this stuff every day and copes. Judith Herman (1992) spoke about the denial within
the therapy community:

> Therapists who work with traumatized patients have to struggle to over-
> come their own denial. When they encounter the same denial in col-
> leagues, they often feel discredited and silenced, just as victims do. (p.
> 151)

Herman argued against allowing this isolation to continue because the
tendency for the therapist to be left alone, believing only she understands
her *patient*, will lead her to make serious errors. Literacy workers have
told me that they have seen this tendency all too often. Those who bear
witness to trauma need places for connection, like those who experience
it. Isolated literacy workers are no less at risk than counselors. This isolation will continue in literacy unless there are more opportunities for talk
about the ways in which literacy workers frequently become entangled in
learners' disclosures of abuse and more possibilities for support. Workers
need opportunities to explore their own limits as well as issues that come

up, and they need to check out the adequacy of their responses to each student.

Literacy workers are often alone with the stories they hear. Learners often request confidentiality—not an unreasonable request—which leave many believing that they must not tell anybody anything they have heard. The worker is often alone, wondering whether she said the right thing, whether she could have done anymore, whether the learner is safe, and whether she must now hear whatever horrors the learner wants to tell. Some programs are clear that there is no confidentiality between staff. If you tell one staff member, others will be told, but that too creates problems for workers who question whether they are being untrustworthy when they tell others. Betsy Trumpener, a Toronto-based literacy worker, described the model used in her program:

> . . . among the drop-in staff, it's a staff team model. . . . We have a daily—actually, this might be sort of a strategy thing—a daily debriefing, and sort of that same thing. So that it's not on each individual that you're carrying the burden of what everyone's told you, so that it gets discussed. I mean, on the other hand, it can take on it's own weird dynamic too, that you've gotta sit around talking about everyone for hours.
>
> That whole concept of secrets and trust, if someone discloses something, and may not give you the warning, then what? Then you say "Oh, by the way, I have to share this with staff?" . . . People kind of feel, "Oh, you're all gossiping about us." That kind of works against trust. (interview, Community and Street Program Literacy Workers, Toronto, February 1997)

Many program workers might benefit from in-depth discussions about confidentiality and what that should mean in terms of what can be shared in different situations. For example, stories, without names, might be shared outside the agency or with certain people, but perhaps some stories must lead to reports to Children's Aid. Sometimes a learner may be happy to have the story shared with other staff members so that they will understand what is going on. I wonder whether an assumption that confidentiality must always be required is part of a societal response that assumes silence and shame are the appropriate legacy of violence. Perhaps we should be asking if a person wants his or her story to be kept confidential and exploring why, recognizing the importance of maintaining safety, but avoiding the implication that the victim of violence should feel any shame. Such talk might challenge, rather than preserve, silence about violence. If workers know ahead of time what they might do in a variety of situations and what supports they can obtain both for the teller and for themselves, they are likely to be less burdened by disclosures or by guilt that they have betrayed a trust.

Sometimes the telling is less of a direct disclosure, but nevertheless, a cry for help. An Adult Basic Education instructor from British Columbia described a student in her class:

> To me, she's somebody who—it's almost like a suicide note, I feel like she's trying to tell me something. I have this generic exercise that I have students do when they don't want to do what the group is doing or whatever, and if they can handle it at that level—it's a fairly high-level one—they take a look at the *Province* newspaper and choose an article that they like, and they choose one of the generic exercises and do that. So she was doing that. One of the articles that she chose—and they were small, like I had a hard time finding them in the newspaper when I went to read them and to look at her work—one of them was "Boy Kills Babysitter" and the other one was "Sex With Teen Admitted." I mean, is she trying to tell me something, or what? And I don't know what to do with this. I mean there isn't really a mechanism set up as part of [the program]. She hasn't said to me, "I want counseling." But there's clearly—lots of stuff [that] needs to be dealt with. Exactly what you were saying, she knows something one day, and she doesn't know it the next day. And when she did the assessment, she said "Oh, I'm really surprised by how well I could do. Some days I can't understand anything." (interview, Salt Spring Island, British Columbia, November/December 1996)

The concern instructors lives with—wondering what to do and what such behavior means—is mitigated in a program where instructors have access to counselors to consult with and can ask the student whether she would like to meet with a counselor. Where counselors are in and out of the program and known to the students, a student may be more likely to talk directly to a counselor rather than make direct or indirect pleas to the instructor for help.

Hard Choices

Workers also spoke about other tensions around the best way to address a problem. In programs with clear rules about use of violent language, workers struggled with enforcing these regulations. Janine Luce, a worker from Street Haven, a program serving marginalized women, said:

> I always have a lot of conflict, I think just around guilt, when I have to—'cause we don't allow language, too. You know, it's not okay to tell a computer to fuck off, it's not okay to tell another person to fuck off, there

are certain rules. Not even the computer, in a really aggressive way. You know, if you're just joking it's one thing, but if you're getting very angry and aggressive and paranoid—because we do work with a lot of people who are paranoid schizophrenic, that certainly comes up, and you have to tell them to leave. I hate doing that, because I know it's like this side of them that they almost—that they don't have control over. It doesn't feel like they're doing it on purpose. So it's hard, to do that because I wish we could accommodate this in some way. But because it makes the other people in the room really nervous, because this person's getting very aggressive, and they're swearing at the computer. . . . (interview, Community and Street Program Literacy Workers, Toronto, February 1997)

Other workers shared some of this sense of tension. Although they felt such rules made a place safer for all learners, they felt conflict about rejecting anyone especially those with the most problems. A worker in another program serving people on the street explained:

It's this kind of weird thing if you look at it holistically, because it's the kind of really angry, disturbed people that likely, you know, sexist, racist, misogynist—that we kind of push out, and then they're on the street. You know what I mean? We create safe space, but what happens. . . . (interview, Community and Street Program Literacy Workers, Toronto, February 1997)

Workers in programs serving people on the street put out enormous energy and risk their own safety to create a space that they hope will be safer and allow for learning. However, rather than satisfaction with their achievement of relative safety in the program, they are left with doubts and questions. The program is supposed to be empowering, but enforcing rules cannot seem empowering for the person thrown out; the power imbalance is simply reinforced and some are told that there is no place for them in the program. This seems to be in opposition to everything most literacy workers believe in. One worker from a Toronto-based street program explained, and others agreed:

Yeah, I think there's—sort of the empowerment thing. People don't have anywhere to go, it's winter, it's cold, who the fuck are you to say "You can't come in here 'cause you're sexist." Right? You're sending them out there to die on the street. On the other hand, not having safe space means women aren't coming in at all, or—you know, come to the front, kind of look and go "Oh, I don't think this is a place for women" or come in protected by their boyfriends. (interview, Community and Street Program Literacy Workers, Toronto, February 1997)

This tension, combined with concern that whatever choice they make will fail some potential learners, leaves many workers always questioning whether they are doing something wrong and whether they could find a way to meet everyone's needs if they just tried harder. Priscilla George offered a valuable suggestion to help in the process of letting go of self-blame. She suggested that "we just have to keep reminding ourselves we're doing the best that we can. It's hard and really requires discipline—ritual almost—'What I did well today' instead of . . . those critical messages we often give ourselves" (personal correspondence, September 1998).

Feeling Helpless: The Dangers of Rescuing

Much of the therapeutic literature I read talked about the dangers of the therapist feeling helpless in response to the experiences she hears about. The therapist absorbs the client's own experience of helplessness and may come to doubt the value of the help she can provide:

> This may lead the therapist to underestimate the value of her own knowledge and skill or to lose sight of the patient's strengths and resources. Under the sway of countertransference helplessness, the therapist may lose confidence in the power of the psychotherapy relationship. It is not uncommon for experienced therapists to feel suddenly incompetent and hopeless in the face of a traumatized patient. (Herman, 1992, p. 141)

Judith Herman continued this account with a story of a therapist who begins to share her client's sense of helplessness and feel that psychotherapy has nothing to offer. Instead, the therapist begins to offer practical advice, rather than listen to the client's experiences. During her supervision sessions, she comes to understand that she has lost faith in the value of listening and gone off course, so she goes back to her client to offer to hear the story in full. Gradually, as the woman is truly heard, the symptoms of the woman's condition lessen. One therapist I interviewed offered a similar story of beginning to doubt the value of listening and doing therapy in her work with a prostitute to whom she gradually began to offer more and more practical help. She began to go with her client to a resource service for prostitutes to help her get off the street. When the therapist realized that she was no longer doing work she was competent to do, she too went back to the therapeutic relationship. She found that by doing the work that was the intended focus of their interaction, rather than trying to *fix* things for the client, the client was able to get off the streets herself. I wonder whether there is a parallel in literacy work, when we lose belief in the value of the educational process and concentrate instead on the other issues in the learner's life. These stories suggest that it is particularly important for therapists and, I would argue, literacy workers to get support that will enable them to notice their own patterns and prevent the sense of helplessness from undermining belief in the value of the work they are contracted to do and lead into trying to fix things.

In the absence of support, worker's hopelessness may lead to a tendency to rescue the survivor. Herman (1992) suggested that a key element when a therapist assumes the role of rescuer and takes on an advocacy role is that she "implies that the patient is not capable of acting for herself" and so "disempowers the patient" (p. 142). The problem of rescuing was discussed earlier in terms of the cost to the learner. Here I am concerned particularly with the cost to the worker of getting caught in the *rescue trap*.

The appeal to the therapist or literacy worker—that only he or she can help the survivor—can be seductive. Kathleen O'Connell, a counselor at a community health center, described the implication that "no one else could be as good as you" as a trap. She suggested that it is problematic when a worker is flattered by the suggestion that only she is a good listener, only she can be trusted, only she can help enough. Instead, she encouraged workers to find ways to help the woman looking for support to trust herself and believe that if she were able to find one person she judged trustworthy, she will also find others. O'Connell advised workers to remind a woman to trust her own judgment to find other appropriate people to give her support, just as she did the first time, rather than stretching to meet all needs. O'Connell said keeping a balance can be challenging:

> . . . how to actually be gracious, about someone valuing your work, and say thank you about that, not either saying oh, it's all you, but saying "Thank you for that, I really appreciate that, I enjoy working with you, we're doing good work." But also be mindful of the goal to, I think always with the learners and [anyone] . . . , it needs to be decreasing their dependence and increasing their resources, their contacts in the community, their trust in themselves, increasing their sense of competency, as opposed to them . . . almost putting you on a pedestal. . . . (interview, Toronto, November 1996)

Accepting the pedestal can be appealing especially if a worker is not getting enough appreciation for her work in other ways. It may be tempting to bask in the praise, but it is hazardous for both worker and learner. The literacy worker, no less than the therapist, needs adequate supports for her own sake and for the sake of those with whom she works. To learn to bear feelings of helplessness and maintain belief in both the student's power and her own, she needs a place to take the pain, the issues brought up for her, and to check out the appropriateness of her reactions.

Hellmut (1992) also wrote about how easily therapists can take on a client or perhaps take more responsibility for a client than they should based on a feeling of being flattered. He describes his own reaction:

> Much less consciously, however, I had reacted to the implicit appeal for help. I *wanted* to help her, and this desire—better *need*—inside me had overridden my usual caution. . . . I was reacting as much on the basis of my own needs, wishes, and fantasies as on a foundation of professional judgement. The flattery implicit in her appeal for help from *me* no doubt also played a part. (p. 276)

Later he said: "It gives one a warm feeling to be reflected in the client's eyes as a thoroughly good and properly appreciated carer, but it is a feeling which must be monitored carefully" (p. 278). He and others remind therapists that they must avoid the appeal of being the best or only rescuer because they can only fail to meet that huge need and will undermine the survivor's potential to develop a sense of her own power and ability to look after herself without rescue by another. These cautions apply and are just as crucial in the literacy context.

DEALING WITH ANGER: FEELING LIKE TOXIC WASTE

In situations of power imbalance—like the relationship between therapist and client or between instructor and student—counselors suggest that survivors are inclined to transfer feelings, like anger toward those in power who abused them or failed to protect them, to the current situation. Such transference can lead to countertransference, where the worker responds to the emotion projected onto them. Therapist Liz White talked about how important it is for the literacy worker not to retaliate in response to the rage they receive and to find a way not to absorb the rage in her own body:

> I think you also need to know that you will have to metabolize the negative transference. You will have to recognize and be prepared for negativity coming toward you as a teacher, as a person, as a caring person. You need to have supports to help you to deal with that. . . .

You have to work it through so you don't carry it [in your body]. So it's sorting out what is the legitimate complaint that she has about me, not just dismissing it as total transference, but if someone is disrespectful to you, is rageful, that you are clear that that is unacceptable, that there is a certain standard. I don't know if this comes up that often, but often there is an idealizing followed by a strong negative transference and projection on you and somehow you need to be able to absorb without retaliating. But they need something to come up against that is not punitive, but also will not accept rage.

There's a difference between anger that is coming at you and rage which obliterates you and it doesn't see you and it doesn't acknowledge what you have given. (interview, Toronto, November 1996)

Several counselors spoke of asking their clients how old they are when their reaction seems to be beyond what might be expected in a particular situation. They use this as a way of getting the woman to think about whether her reaction derives from a past situation instead of the current one. I am wary of how such a technique could be used insensitively and become a process that invalidates a woman's response. However, I can also see value in checking where a reaction is coming from and helping a woman develop her own sense of what is going on for her. The woman I tutor has found it valuable to understand the basis for her well of anger and to be able to explain to herself and others what is happening when she feels her anger is more than she wants. Where there is no awareness that transference may be happening, literacy workers may easily be drawn into responding to the anger, or other feelings, as they are directed at them. Several counselors and therapists advised literacy workers to be aware of this possibility and keep a detachment that would help them avoid getting drawn into retaliating. They suggested workers need a place to check out how they are feeling. Are they getting hooked? What is getting stirred up for them? These check-ins can help literacy workers learn detachment. If workers do not have the opportunity for such checks, then the transference from past abuses of power and consistent mistrustfulness could lead workers into behaving in ways that replicate the abuse. Judith Herman (1992) described the issue. Although she referred to therapists, literacy workers too face the same risks:

> Engagement in this work thus poses some risk to the therapist's own psychological health. The therapist's adverse reactions, unless understood and contained, also predictably lead to disruptions in the therapeutic alliance with patients and to conflict with professional colleagues. Therapists who

work with traumatized people require an on-going support system to deal with these intense reactions. Just as no survivor can recover alone, no therapist can work with trauma alone. (p. 141)

Workers can find themselves identifying with the learner's helplessness, rage, or grief. One worker spoke about her own awareness of the level of rage she carries and questions what she should do with it:

I have a real well of rage, and I have to be careful not only to take care of myself and that kind of stuff, but there's something very explosive for me personally. I have to learn to be able to both take things on in ways that take care of me, but to deal with that well of rage, and I don't know what that means. I don't know if that means finding some vent for it, or if it means keeping the lid on it. But there have been occasions when I know that that is there. (interview, Salt Spring Island, British Columbia, November/December 1996)

Workers need a place to deal with the exhaustion of being on the receiving end of anger, and they also need ways to address their own anger.

Women workers who have a heavy load of hearing disclosures of violence and are frequent targets of anger are often enraged at the unequal loads that different workers carry. A few male literacy workers came to interview sessions and participated in the online seminar, questioning their own role and potential to support women in their classes. Women workers were aware that they frequently carry a disproportionate emotional load in relation to trauma and learners. Some workers rarely hear disclosures. Male workers, in particular, are less likely than women to be chosen as confidants and less likely to be the recipients of learners' rage, especially male learners' rage. The group of women instructors in British Columbia complained:

A: I've been in . . . gatherings of ABE instructors, and the men know that this stuff is going on. They're not doing anything about it except muttering something. "Oh, that was sure awful," some little comment, they know that it's going on, but I don't know of any of them who are actively doing anything to resolve it, alleviate it, deal with it.

B: You mean, the violence from male students?

A: Yeah, they're aware that women are being subjected to violence, women in their programs, and they don't feel very good about it, but they're not doing anything about it. And I don't think it's appropriate for

women to be the instructors [who] take on the male ABE students who
may be violent. It seems to me, there are all these guys out there who make
just as much money, and why can't they do some [of the work]? Men are
going to listen to men before they listen to one more woman telling them
to clean up their act. I just feel that there aren't many men out there who
are doing very much about it, even though they know it's going on. (interview, Salt Spring Island, British Columbia, November/December 1996)

These workers are angry that this imbalance in the work is not acknowledged or addressed in any way in their workplaces or in the literacy
movement.

Violence in the Program

Some women who have taken on the task of trying to make their program a safer place for women to learn to question whether they should
also be seeking to educate the male learners in the program:

People appreciate a safe space, but in order to create a safe space—there's
a lot of conflict, 'cause you're kicking people out and you're confronting
people. I think of a safe place as peaceful. Everyone just knows how to be-
have, does the appropriate thing. Working with predominantly men, my
first inclination is [to] kind of shut up that sexist remark, shut them down,
I don't want to hear it. On the other hand, what is the process of change
for them? Have they ever had an opportunity to engage with a feminist on
this topic? And I think the ideal is a men's group with a male facilitator,
and they're questioning each other. But a lot of men who need to go to a
men's group wouldn't go to a men's group, so just kind of what is the process of challenging men's sexism in a way that promotes their change? And
is that our job? In addition to protecting the women, we'll be educating the
men. . . . (interview, Community and Street Program Literacy Workers,
Toronto, February 1997)

Women literacy workers are weary of work that seems never ending and
question how far their role should extend. Despite their efforts, they
never seem to reach the desired goal of a peaceful place where women
and men can learn.

Women who regularly take on abusive men in street programs told me
they "make jokes about feeling like toxic waste." They spoke about the
exhaustion of the daily attempt to maintain nonviolence in their program. The brunt of violence they bear directly is shocking. Yet although
it seemed to be something they take for granted as the daily reality of
their workplace, the cost is not widely recognized. Staff from Beat the
Street in downtown Toronto spoke about their experience:

It depends on the individual incident, if it was just inappropriate, or if it was a real attack on someone. It depends on how many things they threw at us before they got out the door. I mean literally, it happens—I'm sure it happens where you are. Chairs fly, and coffee cups fly and so a lot of that stuff depends on how violent they were. (Interview, Community and Street Program Literacy Workers, Toronto, February 1997)

These workers spoke of looking out for each other—never closing a door or meeting with a learner alone. Some staff had been physically attacked, all had received death threats, and all knew they were in danger of assault. They worked daily with the knowledge of that danger. It is hard to know what that reality means to the workers because there is so little talk about the impacts on the workers. I was left wondering how long women could feel like toxic waste before they became ill or had to leave the program. Staff from several street programs in Toronto talked together about the threat they felt in their programs and where it could lead:

A: I think we do a lot more preventive than reactive now. We've taken a whole different approach. So it's preventive. Like, we ask people for their weapons at the door. [B. We hope that they'll give them to us.] We don't wait to find out if they've got one in the building. . . .

C: Those issues around barring people, in our case . . . it's a decision that's shared by the team, however that person's anger is still directed at the person they had the altercation with, right? And I leave at the end of the day, and I. . . .

D: Who's waiting for you at the door?

A: Oh, we know about that.

C: Yeah. So—my phone number's listed—all that kind of stuff. . . . [Walking] between work and home, I'd see everyone I saw during the day. So a feeling of being pretty vulnerable, and pretty out there.

A: We try really hard to leave together. It doesn't always happen. It's not always possible. Coming to work is a lot more dangerous for us. I threw someone out, they got really mad at me, came back and hit me with a two-by-four the next morning.

E: Actually hit you?

A: Oh yeah. Gave me a concussion, knocked me out cold. This person was very ill, that's part of why I'm not as angry as I would have been. He was very ill, it was apparent that he was not well as soon as he hit the front door. Got in as far as the front door, I said "I'm sorry, we're closed." We were. He saw a couple of volunteers in the building and said "Well, how come they're welcome?" I tried to be nice. He obviously had some psychiatric issues and was not in good shape. . . . It was pouring rain, he was wet, he was angry at the rain, he was angry—he said to me "I need housing," I said "I'm sorry, I can't help you, if you want to call this afternoon, we can make an appointment" I thought by then either he'd forget or we could set up something that's a little safer. He came back later in the afternoon and I still wouldn't let him in, so the next morning, he just got really angry. (interview, Community and Street Program Literacy Workers, Toronto, February 1997)

As I listened to these accounts of danger, I had a sense that these workers did not believe that anyone outside their situation could fully understand the reality of the daily threat or recognize the extent of the work they do to address the tensions and brewing violence. In these vivid accounts, I heard a tension between powerful energetic descriptions of actively taking on maintaining safety in the program and exhaustion and fear in the descriptions of vulnerability to individual men's violent anger. Perhaps together they feel like a powerful team because they enforce the rules of the program, whereas alone in the street they experience not only the risk that all women know walking through a particularly dangerous area of the city, but the added knowledge that men they have excluded from the program could choose to take out their anger in a violent attack.

A worker from another program serving mostly men on the street spoke of her exhaustion at the never-ending work of trying to address the issues and prevent abusive language or violence from erupting:

I think it's really hard, the pressure and responsibility on the staff of a program like ours to make the space safe for women. How that in itself can be an all-consuming role, how exhausting that is, and how that constantly puts you in conflict with men. You sit down to play cards with people, and every round there's some anti-woman comment, and you're just constantly going "Okay, okay, okay guys." And it just becomes exhausting. I think that's how I feel, as a staff person who has the power to kick someone out of the program. How can a woman in that situation who relies on these guys for safety and support on the street confront that? (interview, Community and Street Program Literacy Workers, Toronto, February 1997)

Although workers could understand that it is difficult for the women students to confront the men in their lives, they clearly found it tortuous to stand by while some women seemed "almost [to] make themselves as vulnerable as they can" so they can be rescued. As one worker said ironically:

Isn't that what men do, if they love you, they protect you and rescue you and beat up other men? I mean, that's what they do in the schoolyard, and lots of other places. That aggressiveness is about protection and caring. (interview, Community and Street Program Literacy Workers, Toronto, February 1997)

Woman who experienced no loving attention as children were prepared to accept control by their male partner as a sign that he cared. Workers spoke of how hard they found it not to intervene as women continued to accept violent and controlling behavior from the men in their lives. Disentangling care and control and learning self-care may be important for workers and learners alike. Workers suggested that, although they can create a safer space in the program, they cannot create "mental and emotional space":

I think that even though the women often feel safe with what's going on, especially if they're doing something together, their mental space is not with their learning. Their mental space is over where their partner is, or over where the guys are. It's almost as if they feel that's what they should be doing, that's what they should be paying attention to. . . . (interview, Community and Street Program Literacy Workers, Toronto, February 1997)

One worker described a situation where a learner quit the program when her abuser was excluded from the program after beating her in the building:

He battered her every week for at least a year and a half for attending the woman's group. Finally he did it in the building. Finally he took an action where I could say "This isn't based on her, this is based on you broke our rules." And then would not allow him back in the building so she quit, and was very angry with me, because I should have forgiven him. At this point she's so angry that [when] I've seen her on the street, or at drop-ins in the community—she won't look at me. You know, [I say] just pleasant hellos and it's like—ugh. I offended her so much by taking that stand against her partner. If he wasn't welcome, then she didn't want to be there. She really didn't want to be a part of the program.

And we would have phone conversations—I would have to have repeated phone conversations with this person where he would verify, "Did she attend, what time was she there? I'd like to see her grades." And she wanted us to do that for him. She insisted. And he controlled her diet, and what she ate, she had a health issue. So he told her when she was eating properly and even tested her blood sugar for her. So this was like

"AAAGH." But that made her feel valued to him. That really made her feel valued. He cared enough to tell her what she should eat and when she should eat, and to look at her blood every time she tested it. And I think the hardest part for me was to understand why it made her feel so valuable, I think I spent a long time trying to sort that one out, 'cause I guess I was looking at it from a different place. But it did make her feel valued. And as she shared other things with us, it was so apparent that as a child, no one had ever paid attention to her. There had never been any attention, especially from a male in her life. So whatever kind of attention this was, this was very valuable "You're important, I want to know everything about you, and I want to help you, and I want you to go to school and be smart, and I'll tell you what you should do there. 'Cause I'm smarter than you." Of course. And that was very clear, and she believed it. (interview, Community and Street Program Literacy Workers, Toronto, February 1997)

As the workers described this situation, their frustration was evident. Staff understood why this woman and so many others accept control and violence from their partners, yet found it hard to watch learners accept men's violence and even appreciate violent and controlling behavior. Workers in other programs also talked about how challenging they found it to stand by unable to help a woman to safety when she remained with a violent partner or returned after having left. Although the women I spoke to knew that each woman must follow her own path, feeling powerless wore them down. Later one of these workers said that participating in a discussion about violence and learning helped her recognize her feelings and their impact and so to:

Give "ammunition" for getting mental health days at [the program] reminding ourselves that the stress and craziness is real—burnout is real—and being able to clearly articulate why and what causes it is very useful. (Alphaplus Literacy & Violence Online Seminar, February–April 1998)

Without talk to remind and help them clarify the causes of their exhaustion, workers find it hard to see the cost to themselves as real or address these costs in terms of self-care and supports. Too often workers are so caught up supporting and nurturing others that they forget that they too need support and nurturing. This research process and the online seminar on literacy and violence offered a rare opportunity for such talk. More space must be created in the literacy field for workers to recognize the costs to themselves—to identify a range of sources of support and possibilities to take care of themselves.

VICARIOUS TRAUMA

Counselor Susan Goodfellow was particularly concerned about *vicarious trauma*. She explained that someone who hears the story of another person's traumatic experience experiences *secondary trauma*—absorbing something that needs to be released, similar to the person who experienced the original trauma. Hearing repeated accounts of trauma, as counselors and many literacy workers do, can have a profound effect. Judith Herman (1992) explained:

> Trauma is contagious. In the role of witness to disaster or atrocity, the therapist at times is emotionally overwhelmed. She experiences, to a lesser degree, the same terror, rage, and despair as the patient. This phenomenon is known as "traumatic counter transference" or "vicarious traumatization." The therapist may begin to experience symptoms of post-traumatic stress disorder. Hearing the patient's trauma story is bound to revive any personal traumatic experiences that the therapist may have suffered in the past. (p. 140)

Places that support literacy workers to recognize the physiological and emotional effects, including reviving their own experiences, and find help to address those issues outside the literacy context are crucial.

Susan Goodfellow (1995) drew on the literature on vicarious trauma to elaborate a problem she has seen through her involvement as a counselor in a shelter. The parallels for literacy workers are powerful:

> If the therapist is not a survivor of abuse herself, she is likely to go through a similar process to that of her client. The steady diet of traumatic material and the energy required to continually witness leads to the therapist's deconstruction of her own world view. She may be haunted with images she has heard from her clients of their abuse and she may find herself unable to allow herself to experience pleasure and safety with this knowledge (Pearlman & Saakvitne, 1995, p. 293). She may not be able to find comfort and she may feel rageful at and betrayed by God. She may become cynical, embittered and withdrawn. Despair may take her over and she may find it increasingly difficult to convey hope to her clients. She may feel isolated from her co-workers and friends, particularly due to restraints imposed by confidentiality, but also she may participate in the belief that therapists do not require help from others. She can't talk about what she has heard so she can't get support, if indeed others could tolerate hearing this information. Fears of being alone and anxieties over interactions with strange men may increase for her. In fact, she may begin to believe that all men are perpetrators and suspect most men she sees as possibly violating

the women they know and incesting their children. She may choose to use and sometimes abuse drugs and alcohol to help with this increasing discomfort. With the growing despair and the volume of stories she keeps hearing, her feelings of helplessness and powerlessness increase. It becomes easy to see that self-neglect (ie. not eating properly, not exercising adequately) would follow. Her fatigue and exhaustion may intensify and she may believe that what she really needs is just a good vacation. If she is fortunate enough to be able to do this, after she returns, it will not be long before these symptoms reoccur. She may then become physically ill. (pp. 5–6)

Susan Goodfellow also added that if the therapist is a survivor, there is a higher risk that she will reexperience trauma. Thus, it is even more crucial that she has the opportunity to do her own therapeutic work generally and particularly to address issues triggered for her. When Susan Goodfellow examined her own experience and that of her coworkers, she saw extensive evidence of the phenomena she had described:

I realize now that numbers of us have suffered from depression, insomnia, irritability, relationship breakdown, eating disorders, physical illnesses, hypertension, anxiety, substance abuse and exhaustion. Yet, when such symptoms are named, they are placed in the context of overwork, lack of structural support by the organization, lack of funding, increased workload, needing a vacation, lack of personal support at home, parenting pressures or mid-life crisis. It is very true that these and other situations increase our sense of difficulty with this work, but the impact of being exposed to the horrors of trauma, on a daily basis, year after year, is rarely mentioned. . . . We do not often even allow ourselves to feel the horror of what we are hearing and so do not realize how that horror impacts us. (pp. 8–9)

Reading Susan Goodfellow's account of vicarious trauma, and of the lack of acknowledgment of the impact of the work the counselors do, I recognize much that we see in literacy programs. Experienced literacy workers frequently leave the field complaining of overwork and exhaustion. Sickness and exhaustion is blamed on overwork and organizational problems, without mention of the impact of hearing horrors and feeling helpless to make change.

Recently I heard a story of a wonderful literacy teacher who had quit because she felt that teaching literacy was like standing at a horrendous car wreck with only Band-Aids to hand out. Literacy workers must have places to take their despair and sense of helplessness. We need to have a strong and varied support network. Susan Goodfellow stressed the importance of therapeutic supervision, training, and discussion with coworkers to break down isolation. In the literacy field, we need a greater recognition that literacy workers also hear disclosures and, like counselors and therapists, experience vicarious trauma. Then perhaps as a field we can begin to envisage appropriate supports, training, and other opportunities for in-depth discussion; conceptualize creative ways to take care of ourselves; and fight for the funding and structures that recognize these needs.

GETTING HELP

Peer Support and Supervision

Two literacy workers disagreed about whether they were doing counseling in literacy, but both were sure they needed supports:

> A: I know that counselors do this sort of thing, they get together and they have support groups for each other, and they all have their own therapist, and that's the way they operate. And yet—so much of what we do is really counseling. We call it teaching and we're resistant to the idea that we're counseling because we think of ourselves as teachers, but what we're really doing is counseling and the sensitivity we bring to it is the sensitivity that counselors have.

> B: Well, whether I successfully bring to it counseling or not, I hear disclosures. All day every day. I listen to people's pain all day every day. Whatever I successfully do for them, that's what I get. So I certainly hear that part of the argument. That I need to know how to protect myself in the situation, and I need to know how to feel not inept, coming out. 'Cause that piles up on me. (interviews, Salt Spring Island, British Columbia, November/December 1996)

When I first began to hear about the forms of support that therapists and counselors make use of, I was fascinated with the possibilities for the literacy field. Counselors participate in peer support groups and work under supervision. In peer support, counselors or therapists support each other by listening to concerns about each other's cases and helping each other think about how else they might have dealt with issues or how they might continue in the next session with a client. Supervision, I gather, is a similar process, except that rather than being between peers it is with a senior or more experienced person. The counselor sees another therapist or counselor to discuss the issues raised for her by the clients she sees and seeks help in how to work with them. Almost like her own therapy, these sessions focus on the way her work with clients sparks her own issues and hooks her. She receives help to identify ways to proceed with her client. Hellmut (1992) described his understanding of supervision:

> The term "supervision" has a somewhat specialized meaning in this context. The supervisor's principal task is to support the therapist, and especially to expose and clarify the therapist's own reactions in the course of the therapy, and so ensure as far as possible that the personal reactions—especially feelings—do not intrude into and distort or block the therapist's understanding of what is going on in the therapy. (p. 284)

I read repeatedly that it is particularly important that counselors have these supports when they are working with trauma survivors. Judith Herman (1992) said: "It cannot be reiterated too often: no one can face trauma alone" (p. 153). She stressed the importance of support of all sorts:

> The therapist should expect to lose her balance from time to time with such patients. She is not infallible. The guarantee of her integrity is not her omnipotence but her capacity to trust others. The work of recovery requires a secure and reliable support system for the therapist. (p. 151)

I have since talked more to counselors and learned that not all counselors have access to such supports, but that those who do not often struggle to put them in place. In the era of cutbacks in shelter provision and other services, this is difficult to fight for, but more acutely necessary. In literacy, too, some supports are crucial.

For the sake of the literacy workers and the learners we serve, programs must ask questions about what supports and supervision are needed by both paid and unpaid workers. Each program needs to do its own assessment of what is possible within and outside the program. Opening up that question with a program serving street youth caused them to start to consider the cost of arranging with a therapist to offer supervision when staff felt they needed it. I was surprised to hear that the cost did not seem as if it would be a big barrier. The shift needed was primarily a program-wide recognition of the importance and value of such a commitment.

A few programs already have a variety of structures in place; others appeared to have none. In a Toronto program, one staff member said that they all meet individually with the program coordinator every 3 weeks and that they have a check-in at their staff meeting each week that allows space for discussion of difficult issues and how they are affecting the worker. That program also seeks to support tutors with regular support nights and includes issues of setting limits in the tutor training. Other staff, even in that program, might not consider these structures adequate, but many other programs did not have any places that could be used to address the need for support and supervision. In some programs, a staff member or regular visitor from the network may informally take on the role of listener and offer support to colleagues. Usually this work will go unrecognized, perhaps even by the person who is offering support.

Literacy programs carried out in community colleges and multiservice agencies with counselors on staff often have access to informal consultation as discussed earlier. This resource can be crucial in reducing the literacy worker's isolation as she tries to support learners who are in crisis. Rarely is there any more formal support in place. I was fascinated to read a description of the structures in place in an organization serving women in crisis:

> We do this support work with each other every single week. The direct support staff have an hour of clinical supervision, two hours with me [the coordinator], and a few hours of private time with each other to process their feelings. They pay special attention to the things that trigger them about the women they see and we discuss this. The feelings are real and must be processed, they won't just go away, they can't be argued away, whether they are justified, victim-blaming or a result of "burnout." (FIVERS, May 1997)

I believe that some structure of this type would provide a significant support for all literacy workers and thus strengthen the field.

Recently I heard from Cherie Miller, a clinical social worker, about a structure in place in her workplace that provides counseling. I immediately began to think about how it could be modified for use in literacy programs. The process offers a combination of peer support and supervision. All staff meet every other week, during their paid work time, with an outside supervisor. For each session, one person brings a problem. To prepare, she pulls together a 10-minute transcript, or notes, of an interaction with a client, adds her own description of what was happening, and lists key questions. This material is given to the supervisor and colleagues to read and consider about a week ahead of the session. In the meeting, the supervisor reads the material aloud, adding commentary and reactions, and opens the discussion up for everyone to join and add their analyses and suggestions. This structure, carried out with a counselor, would provide literacy workers with an enormous amount of support, as well as an opportunity to reflect and develop nuanced understandings and practical strategies.

Peer support and supervision, or a combination of the two, are models from counseling and therapy that would be beneficial to the literacy field. Yet to even begin to imagine how to construct versions of these approaches appropriate to different types of programs, we need to raise awareness in the field about the prevalence of issues of violence and the cost to workers as well as learners. We need far more talk about violence, its impact on learning, and the enormous complexity of literacy work in the face of these impacts. Only then will a climate be created in which literacy workers can make a case for support and the financial cost of these support services being incorporated into the basic cost of providing literacy tuition. Recognizing that many literacy learners (and workers) have experienced trauma and that literacy workers need supports in place is vital if literacy programs are to serve all learners well.

A Chance to Talk

Even the simple opportunity to talk can provide critical support for literacy workers. Several participants in group interviews commented on the value of getting together to talk and suggested that they should be getting together regularly, not only when I arranged it. An ABE instructor from British Columbia explained:

> I think this kind of process that we're going through here, is really important and valuable. And I would like to see it as something that was available to people on a regular basis, not just something that happens because Jenny's doing a research project. . . . It seems to me it would make the programs better, it would have a positive effect on the participants, and it would help the instructors. (interview, Salt Spring Island, British Columbia, November/December 1996)

It was clear that discussion in interview sessions and the online seminar prompted many workers to see their students differently, and that new view sometimes offered new possibilities for practical approaches. When Christina Patterson was evaluating the online seminar, she said:

> The workshop and the visit from Jenny Horsman was the first time it ever occurred to me that trauma survivors were bringing their survival response behavior into the classroom. I've talked in terms of people growing up with a "hard life" but the specifics make the whole picture much more clear to me. I need to add that it doesn't make the individual behaviors any more

homogeneous. Each finds their own way to cope and keeps the tools that work, but my vision has opened up in terms of being able to see trauma behavior in the classroom. This helps me set a safe space more easily, a space for growing and trying, with each student having personal control, comfortable timing and real support. (Evaluation of Alphaplus Literacy & Violence Online Seminar, February–April 1998)

As Priscilla George questioned, "I wonder how many of us don't recognize this [survival response behavior] and consequently react, inappropriately for us and the learner" (personal correspondence, September 1998). This is an important reminder. The vital importance of more opportunities to talk about what we see in the classroom, share ideas, and develop new insights was mentioned repeatedly in interviews.

Many literacy workers talked about the need to have somewhere to talk about their experiences and the stories they heard. Women who team teach or who work in some form of group often talked about the value of being able to debrief at the end of the day at work, and so leave the pain of their work behind them a little. Workers in two different programs disagreed about what that talk at the end of the day offered them:

A: But partly those safety issues are the staff sharing at the end of the day, so that you can check in with other people.

B: I don't think of that as safety. I don't know if our talks at the end of the day provide any safety for us. They provide a place for us to vent toxic waste, and that's exactly how it feels, but it doesn't provide any safety. (interview, Community and Street Program Literacy Workers, Toronto, February 1997)

Although talking might not provide safety, venting may serve a purpose. Other women talked about the importance of having someone outside their place of work to whom they could talk without any risk that the person knew whom they were speaking about. I heard this concern especially from First Nation women, who knew that in their community everyone knows everyone else and confidentiality was difficult to maintain.

A few members of a group that came together for an interview session have continued to meet. Although they felt that they would like to tell the horrors they hear, they all felt they did not want to listen to anymore horrors. Instead, they have begun to seek to tell the story, not of what they heard, but of the impact of the hearing on themselves and to support each other in looking for ways to change that story and create new ways of letting go of the horrors and new reactions. First Nation instructors have also been discussing the idea of a regular meeting, perhaps a talking circle once a month and sweats sometimes to take care of themselves (Priscilla George, personal correspondence, September 1998)

The online seminar, an 8-week moderated discussion focused on material from the research, also provided a space for workers to talk about the issues they experience in their work and to get feedback from others on how to address them. As Beth Sauerhaft said:

> Just want to quickly add that I think that this online conversation can be a way of taking care of ourselves. I have found myself carving out odd times of the day and night to add a little something to our discussion and value knowing that often something I write resonates with another. This can be an important way to express and/or release some of the trauma we hold inside us and which has little or no space for expression in our work lives, depending on the contexts we work in. (Though of course it would be ideal to consciously make this space, it doesn't always happen) . . . we continually need to find and build [community] among ourselves both in up-close and personal ways and even here in cyberspace. (Alphaplus Literacy & Violence Online Seminar, February–April 1998)

The value of talking to others and creating a community of people searching for appropriate ways to address these issues in literacy cannot be overstated. Although cyberspace has its limitations, it is one way to create a conversation even when no one is free at the same time or even works in the same program or location. In literacy, a whole range of places and ways to talk about the issues and their impact on workers is critical to reduce isolation. A chance to talk at the program level, in local and regional networks, and even national and international discussions on the internet, could all begin to meet literacy workers' need for support and opportunities for essential reflection on practice.

Taking Care of Ourselves

Thich Nhat Hanh, a Vietnamese Buddhist teacher, provided a clear reminder about the importance of taking care of ourselves. Dawna Markova (1994) reported what he said during a retreat:

> He told us how important it is to notice what he called "the un-toothache"—those moments when we are not in pain or danger—to drink them in deeply, down to the parched places in our histories. . . .
> "If you are going to work with suffering, it is essential that you balance it out with joy. If you have listened to suffering for three hours, go walk in the woods and hug a tree until you come back in balance again. You owe it

to yourself, to the people you work with, and to your family. People can't help relieve suffering if they don't have a broad base of joy." (p. 86)

But do we know when we are out of balance and what it looks to get back into balance? If we have spent a lifetime not listening to the messages our bodies send us, do we even know where to begin to change that pattern? If we are avoiding our own pain, maybe we do not stop anything—work, play, caring for others—long enough to nurture ourselves. Our own pain may be waiting in those peaceful moments. Opening the conversation with ourselves to begin to think about self-care may be an essential first step.

Susan Goodfellow suggested that therapists and counselors need to be aware of several aspects if they are to address the dangers of vicarious trauma. Her advice seems equally applicable to literacy workers. She suggested that it is important for counselors to be engaged in their own therapy, "working on our own sense of helplessness, fear, rage and disillusionment." She encouraged counselors to take their own physical needs seriously and the need for time with family and friends to receive support and nourishment. She also stressed the importance of meeting spiritual needs to find meaning in their lives in whatever way works for them. Finally, she talked about the importance of limiting the violence they are exposed to outside their work. Time alone enjoying music, herbal baths, meditating, reading, working out, or gardening may also be ways to come back into balance (Priscilla George, personal correspondence, September 1998).

In each of the sessions I held with literacy workers, I asked them to share how they look after themselves. Some women were quite taken aback by the question and could not find an answer; others had clearly thought a lot about this need and worked hard to find ways to care for themselves that worked for them. I heard from one shelter worker that her program allotted an amount of money for each worker's self-care. Each staff person has to explain to the collective how she plans to use that money—she might join a health club, have regular massages, take a weekend away, do a pottery course—whatever she can describe as something that is purely for herself to help her relax and recover from the burden of the work. That idea fascinated me. I mentioned it to various literacy workers and was struck by what an enormous difference it seemed it would make, and what an impossible dream it appeared, to many literacy workers. Yet $1,000 per staff person annually would hardly be an outrageous budget. Making such an amount available explicitly for taking care, rather than simply as an element of salary or even professional development—although that might be a way to slide it into the budget—would make the need to take care more visible.

I heard about a wide range of approaches to self-care. Many women talked about the importance of learning to know their own limits—to know when to say *enough is enough*. To some, the talk of the possibility of limits or boundaries was completely new and an amazing concept. However, most, for whom it was new, left excited with the idea of trying to work through the concept of recognizing their own limits and their right to even *think* enough is enough. I was disturbed by one worker who reiterated later that we have to learn to listen when the student needs it regardless of whether we have the emotional energy. I wondered how often workers feel there is just no other option.

Some women talked about their need for time alone with their own rituals and in their own space. Women talked of meditation, prayer, drawing on their personal philosophy from their own culture or faith. The creation of a particular place to meditate, pray, or reflect was important to many women. They described how they created a place in their home or in the outdoors that represented safety and their own special place. They spoke of creating a separation between themselves and the rest of their lives and their work. Even taking a long way home could be a way of creating a space that helped the worker to leave work behind. Finally, women talked about a variety of ways in which they play, physically and emotionally, to "let off steam" and let go of their frustration and anger. Many women used some combination of these approaches to help them take care of themselves in the face of the trauma and danger they listened to and experienced.

When I asked questions about how we take care of ourselves during the online seminar, I received a variety of responses similar to those I had heard on my travels. Although I was somewhat disturbed by those who, perhaps in jest, suggested drugs, alcohol, and cynicism, more often there was a commonality of nurturing examples, including, bread baking, gardening, reading, knitting, and spending time with friends. I was particularly taken with Diana Twiss' description of quilting:

> I am a quilter. I cut up fabric, old and new, and assemble it into pieces which I then quilt into three layers. It is an activity which is a long process from the first idea to the finished project. It has many stages and because it takes a long time, it has its ups and downs. It is my therapy. During the actual process of quilting, I have the time and space to meditate a bit as I do the same actions over and over again. The fact that I am creating a functional object of beauty which will cover one of my sleeping children or my husband and me keeps me motivated when the going gets rough. Sometimes I quilt with other women, but most often I do it alone. (Alphaplus Literacy & Violence Seminar Online, February–April 1998)

This description prompted me to suggest online that it could be used with a women's group, "with everyone bringing in scraps and telling stories while it is created—the end result could be a lovely quilt for anyone to snuggle under on a day they were feeling not quite so 'present.' " Although this may be a good idea, looking back I noticed with a chuckle the place I most easily go—thinking about how to use an idea to help others. The online discussion helped me realize that while I was traveling from community to community for the initial research, even when I was asking other literacy workers to reflect on how they took care of themselves, I was not taking care of myself. By the time I came back from 3 weeks of interviews, I could barely move my head. My neck and back had seized up. The crisis started me on a search to find body or exercise work that actually gave me pleasure, rather than something that would be good for me. Now I do yoga regularly and have learned to listen to my body much better. However, I still find it interesting to notice that the old patterns of ignoring my needs—the urge to just stretch a little further—is always present, never far in the background. Similarly, Priscilla George commented:

> I keep thinking of the session in which I realized, "I'm a spirit, too." I'd been seeing everybody's spirit that had to be nurtured—and I forgot my own! (personal correspondence, September 1998)

I continually have to remember to take ongoing care of myself, and I am sure that many other women have to be equally vigilant if they are to balance caring for others with that all-important care of the self.

ACKNOWLEDGE THE VALUE AND COST OF BEARING WITNESS—CREATE A RANGE OF SUPPORTS

Women working in literacy take on a level of bearing witness to the violence in learners' lives. Sometimes they also experience an increased threat of violence in their own lives because of the role they play to create a safer space for literacy learning. Many literacy workers feel they have little option but to hear disclosures of violence when learners ask it of them. Regardless of whether workers are experienced at setting boundaries, there is a cost to themselves and a limit to what else they can take on in their lives as a consequence of their work in literacy. The day-to-day violence in some programs and the level of anger vented on workers are toxic. In other programs, workers may be less aware of what causes the exhaustion they feel at the end of the day. Workers deal with witnessing pain through disclosures and observing learners' lives. They also frequently struggle with the cost of feeling helpless or inept. They frequently wonder whether they are doing it wrong as they make hard choices about how to do their work or decide to exclude some learners from a program to create safety for others.

Workers must establish a variety of places to talk to develop a recognition of the depth and complexity of these issues. The availability of training that will assist workers to recognize their own limits and explore alternative approaches is vital. The silence in the literacy field about demands on workers to listen and bear witness reinforces a sense that, although it is not legitimate work, workers cannot refuse to listen. Workers need to know that they can choose when and if they will listen. Workers need access to training and support to learn to listen in ways that are supportive to the learner, but do not demand too much of the worker. Peer support and supervision offer possible models to assist workers in developing good practice and could provide a resource that would enable workers to talk through the issues they experience in their work. Support to recognize when feelings of helplessness, anger, or grief are blocking the worker's ability to give learners support that reinforce learners' sense of power and resourcefulness is key. Literacy workers need support and encouragement to recognize their own needs and to look after themselves with care. Recognizing the pervasiveness of trauma issues in literacy learning is the essential first step.

IV

PULLING IT ALL TOGETHER

9

Rethinking Change

"There should be 60 million more women in the world today but they have been killed or have died through violence directed at their gender," said a spokesman [sic] for the United Nations Children's Fund (UNICEF). Along with the 60 million "missing," UNICEF said millions more in every country and from every class, live under the daily threat of physical abuse. "This chronic condition of violence amounts to the most pervasive human rights violation in the world today," said Carol Bellamy, UNICEF's executive director. "In today's world, to be born female is to be born high risk. Every girl grows up under the threat of violence."

(Griffiths, 1997)

Carrying out the research that led to this book, I was increasingly disturbed as the horrifying extent of violence against women and children became clearer. I felt that, given such shocking rates of violence, rather than simply addressing the aftermath in terms of its effect on learning, I should be drawing attention to violence and doing something to stop it. Like the literacy worker I quoted at the start of this book, who said at the end of a weekend-long group interview: "I keep thinking, I just have to tell them, because if I tell them they'll do something about it," I wanted to just tell everyone. Having grasped a glimmer of the extent of violence, I felt if I could get everyone else to see the levels of violence, then they would surely see that this prevalence is intolerable.

Yet the more I read, the more I realized that the extent of violence has been described again and again. Elly Danica's (1996) words, quoted earlier, describe it well: "[We] have been breaking the silence over and over again, only to have it subsequently swallow us up again moments after we speak" (p. 141).

The report of the *Canadian Panel on Violence Against Women* (1993) argued not only that violence against women is widespread, but that violence is enormously significant for all women. The report stated:

> Violence against women is pervasive in Canada. We each have a story to tell: a girl molested by her uncles, a best friend whose ex-boyfriend is stalking her, an older woman who can't explain the bruises. These incidents affect us profoundly. They make us fearful for our children, wary about our own activities and often distrustful of men.
>
> The connection between these acts of violence and the inequality of women is clear. All women in Canada are vulnerable to male violence. Race, class, age, sexual orientation, level of ability and other objective characteristics, alone or in combination, compound the risk. Until all women achieve equality they will remain vulnerable to violence and until women are free from violence, they cannot be equal. (p. 101)

This panel's demand that governments, institutions, and individuals must take action has had no discernible effect. Telling is not enough to end violence. The information about violence implicates everyone in society. Perhaps the suggestion that we are all at risk of being violated or violent, or both, is too much of an enormity to face and respond to with any real commitment. Instead, we move rapidly to deny any possibility that it could be true.

The assumption tends to be that the major reports and horrifying statistics are overstatements. Insignificant and trivial violence must be included in the definitions if the figures are so high. An article by Margaret Wente (1994) illustrates this sort of dismissal:

> The most common form of violence, says the survey, is wife assault. But in calculating the rate of wife assault it classifies many domestic encounters as violent that most people would not. These include behaviours that don't involve physical contact, such as threats and throwing things. Then comes minor contact, pushing, grabbing and shoving. The survey's summary (which is as far as most reporters read) lumps all these things together with actions that anyone would agree are clearly violent: beating up, hitting with an object, choking, sexual assault or using a knife or gun to threaten or injure. So throwing a plate has the same weight as a knife attack. (p. A2)

She rejected the statistics, insisting we must all agree they are obviously absurd:

The Statscan report, and the media coverage of it, painted a powerful portrait of millions of women cowering behind closed doors, living in fear of violent and abusive husbands. The picture is false. (p. A2)

Yet I notice that Margaret Wente was writing 1 year after these statistics were released and the outrageously exaggerated media picture hit the headlines. Although her outrage implies that an entirely unnecessary amount of attention was given to the statistic—even a federal cabinet minister "pledged to meet with women's groups to launch a national campaign to combat violence against women"—a year later she was not able to report that such extravagent attention had radically changed the situation for women.

Knowing that violence is widespread is clearly not enough. The more I look at the impacts of violence, the more I believe violence serves society. I can only begin to ask disjointed fragments of the question: Does it serve a purpose if the experience of violence numbs people? Do people need to be numb to endure boring, monotonous jobs year in, year out? Does it serve a purpose if the experience of violence creates great sensitivities? Are those sensitivities valuable for teaching, facilitating, or many other types of work wherever an acute awareness of others' feelings and needs is a valuable asset? Does the presence of coercive violence help to maintain illusions of choice so fundamental to democracy? Does the violation of children teach them about powerlessness and power over others from an early age? Does it teach the value of a distorted creed—Do unto others before they do unto you? Joanna Kadi (1996) suggested:

Child sexual abuse teaches children about social/cultural hierarchies in ways that ensure we'll remember the gist of it (if not the details). Stamping information on bodies and imprinting it into body memory guarantees a high retention rate. This information necessarily covers more than sexism, since sexism isn't the sole source of oppression, racism, classism, ableism, and the systematic oppression of children also figure into these lessons. (p. 74)

Does sexual abuse of girls help reinforce other social messages of inferiority and dependency? I repeat Elly Danica's (1996) words here as a reminder:

I believe child sexual abuse and violence against women are an integral structural part of patriarchal society and culture. They are how we—especially, but not only, women—are socialized to accept powerlessness. (p. 50)

I will not retreat into simplistic arguments that violence preserves patriarchy, ignoring the existence of violence against men or by women. However, I do recognize that violence against girls and women diminishes women's power and ability to focus on themselves.[1] Some portion of our energy is always taken up in vigilance and attention to the possibility of danger, to focus on the other—the potential abuser—although that vigilance has been learned so young that we may often be unaware of its existence.

I do not want to imply that only men are violent or only women and girls are violated. There is far too much evidence that horrific numbers of boys are abused as children, along with evidence that their experience of violence in turn contributes to their later role of abusers. There is evidence too that women are also abusive, particularly against children in their care. However, I do question what preserves and supports the continuation of violence in society. Experiencing abuse as children, or witnessing violence against others (most frequently by men against women) appears to contribute to the continuation of abuse. Evidence suggests that girls who witness or experience violence if they become abusive, more commonly self-abuse. Whereas boys who witness or experience violence more commonly grow up to be men who are violent toward others.[2] Societal attitudes and expectations, and minimizing responses of legal and other institutions, create a climate where male violence and female self-erasure is condoned.

I also believe that the theoretical frameworks through which violence is conceptualized support the process of minimizing and silencing evidence of violence. The fragmented view that considers different types of violence—child abuse, domestic violence, rape, torture, war—all separately, and the obscuring of the role played by racism, ableism, classism, and other forms of systemic discrimination, disguise the enormity that might be visible if we viewed all forms of violence together. Framing trauma as outside *normal* helps preserve silence about individual acts of

---

[1]The cumulative power of Clarissa Chandler's excellent taped presentations (all undated) enabled me to see past my own socialization. She eloquently made the point that women who are devalued or have experienced abuse are unable to listen to their own bodies and instead must always be alert, reading the messages of the other—the abuser or potential abuser's body.

[2]Recently I have learned that activists in the field argue that the idea of a cycle of violence is problematic because it is easily used to blame victims for "choosing" violent men and to avoid holding violent men accountable for their behavior—"he couldn't help himself, he was abused as a child." In this way attention is turned to the individual and away from societal supports for male violence. Research has tended to ignore both men and women who experience or witnessed abuse as children and who grew up to be neither abusive nor abused.

violence and their aftermath. Focusing on reconceptualizing the impact of violence, shifting from private, individualizing, medical approaches to a public recognition of all forms of violence and their effect on learning, can serve to change our awareness of violence and its impact.

Making violence visible in new ways may enable a new recognition that levels are intolerable. Challenging concepts of *normal* and revealing that trauma is the experience of many, if not most, women; demonstrating the commonality between everyday violence and *unspeakable* extremes of violence usually defined as outside normal; and supporting women to redefine their own experiences and become successful learners may have a profound impact not only on individuals, but also more broadly on society. Educators can make a difference, both in the lives of individual learners and in shifting conceptions of violence. It is crucial that our focus not be on supporting the individual's attempt to learn in isolation from the social context and the layers of violence that continue to operate. We must continue to address violence as a social problem, as well as addressing the impact of violence on learning and helping survivors to learn successfully.

In September 1998, I stood at a podium in Cairns, Australia, to speak at the 20th Anniversary Reclaim the Night event. Speaker after speaker had already explained how widespread violence against women is—they had given the statistics and driven home the horror. Of course, many of the women there already knew about violence from their own experiences or those of friends and family. I wanted to stress the links between everyday insidious violence and extremes of trauma experienced by so many women. I spoke about the case in Toronto discussed earlier, where a police officer returned a phone call to a woman who had reported that she had been raped that morning in her bed at home by an intruder who threatened her with a knife from her own kitchen. The policeman asked her why she had taken so long to answer the phone; when she explained that she had been in the shower, he apparently remarked that he "should have been there." There was a shocked intake of breath from the audience as I read his words. I imagine they were thinking about how invasive such sexual innuendo would feel for someone so recently raped; perhaps some were jarred into remembering their own violation. *Shocking* was the word Justice MacFarland used in her judgment against the police force (Doe v. Toronto Commissioners of Police, 1998). However, the point I wanted to make was that, although in juxtaposition we find the comment chilling, we would barely have paused if we had heard such a comment in any other context. In most situations, women who dare to complain about a sexual innuendo of that sort are simply dismissed as humorless.

On that warm evening in Cairns, I questioned the taken-for-granted concept of *normal*. Similarly, in this book, I want to reveal the links between all forms of violence. I question the violence that we take so much for granted that we barely see it as violent and challenge the idea of normal life. Women who have experienced traumatic violence are often exhorted to *get over it*, and therapeutic interventions, not surprisingly, are aimed at supporting women to get back to *normal*. However, normal life includes the risk of further violence and everyday reminders of risk. I do not want to celebrate normal life. *Normal life*, as presently defined, is not good enough. Trauma survivors are the canaries in the mine who remind us that violence is toxic to us all.

As educators working with trauma survivors, we should not muffle their discomforts and be complicit, through our words or our silences, with the demand to erase the evidence of violence and its aftermath. We must make violence and its frequency, and the effect of violence on the person violated, visible. If we do not, we force those struggling to "live beside violation" and to do so alone, or in private with their therapist, because to reveal the depths of struggle is to be shamed and judged. That night in Cairns, we marched loudly down the street shaking home-made rattles, hoping to draw attention to women's lack of safety, drawing puzzled looks from tourists and other passersby.

As we marched, one woman who had listened to me speak came up to thank me and say that the pressure to *get over it* fast enough and *get back to normal* is a weighty burden. She suggested that thinking of herself as a canary rather than as damaged goods could make a real difference. Many women choose education when they want to make changes, hoping to explore experience and learn new possibilities—to combine reflection with analysis. Whether experiences in education are ones that build community, develop analyses, and promote healing, or are places of silence, isolation, and further pain may open or close possibilities for how each woman is able to live the rest of her life. Educators can make a difference.

SUPPORTING CHANGE

Women's experience of educational programs depends not only on teachers, but also on the policies and administrative structures that either create spaces or close them down and set the context for education. As a sad example of current trends, in Ontario, where I live, a wide range of spaces and supports are currently disappearing. Services for women seeking to escape violent relationships and organizations offering violence prevention education have had their government funding reduced or cut off entirely. These cuts have occurred even in the wake of an enormous amount of media attention to the inquest into the death of Arlene May, mentioned earlier, who accessed all available shelter and court systems, yet was stalked and murdered by her former spouse. Clearly publicity about violence is not enough to lead to provision of adequate services. Women seeking to go back to school as part of an attempt to make changes in their lives—whether to escape a violent partner or move on from violence in their past—may find that the resources they need to support the transition from living with a violent spouse, to address a past experience of abuse or protect them from further violence, are unavailable.

Widespread cutbacks to education and training limit the options and possibilities for women seeking to participate in educational programs. In times of cutbacks, courses become more expensive and less accessible in every way, instructors' ability to connect with students is diminished, counselors are laid off, and all manner of supports and resources are reduced or disappear. When welfare is cut and women are pressured to get rapidly into the workforce, instead of being offered the space to pursue education and training, women feel further controlled and punished. They may be forced to accept abusive employment conditions.

Everywhere I have traveled talking about this research—Canada, the United States, and Australia—I have been reminded that current directions in education are the opposite of those I am proposing. Rather than an educational process that honors the whole person, programs and staff are cut back and pressured to serve so many "units" for minimum cost and move people through in the shortest possible time. More and more, curriculum is becoming tightly delineated and frequent assessment is required. Such pressures make it more difficult for teachers and administrators in literacy programs and other training and education courses to respond to the challenge to serve survivors better.

Where instructors are offered only minimal resources, they will be unlikely to have the energy or resources to question their own practice; try new approaches; test out new models for courses; explore collaboration with counseling programs, therapists, and those in the creative arts; learn about a range of supports and resources that might benefit learners; or take training or access supports that enable them to become more resourceful teachers—better prepared to teach survivors of trauma. Where education is controlling and punitive, it is likely to be experienced as a site of further violence. Neither learners nor teachers can be whole in a system that fragments, punishes, and demands immediate progress (Joyce, personal correspondence, July 1999).

Policy frameworks and funding structures can make it less possible for educational programs to be sensitive to the needs of trauma survivors. As mentioned earlier, a woman may need to explore control by starting, stopping, and restarting a course repeatedly, or she may be absent because she has been injured by her spouse or is suffering from the health problems of the aftermath of violence. She may need immediately accessible counseling to help her continue in class when issues arise during her studies. Yet women are increasingly expected to move rapidly through time-limited literacy or training programs. Irregular attendance leads to a woman being judged as unmotivated or not committed. If adequate progress cannot be demonstrated, students are likely to be labeled *unable to learn*, be dropped from the program, or find their funding discontinued.

If space is to be made for trauma survivors to prepare to improve literacy skills or take on training, they may first need to learn about such things as their own degree of presence. They may need to learn to recognize when they cannot be present enough to pay attention to learning the subject of the class or what helps them to stay present despite their fears and challenges. Women who have experienced trauma may be learning many things not revealed by tests or demonstrations of outcomes. They need to be allowed adequate time in the classroom to build on that learning and achieve visible progress in the course, free from the threatening demand that they demonstrate immediate progress.

One hope I have held on to as I have offered workshops to literacy workers, teachers of English, and upgrading instructors is that, despite the limitations in their workplaces, for the most part these educators know that violence is a major issue affecting learning. They are eager to learn more about it to help their students succeed. If necessary, most will stretch far beyond the work they are paid for to offer students help that might make a difference. In the cost-effective terms so popular today, policymakers and funders need to see that, unless the impact of violence on learning is recognized, investment in education will be wasted: Too many educators will become burned out and frustrated with their limited success and too many women will try to learn, fail, and then conclude they are too stupid to try again. Services, resources, curriculum, course lengths, terms of attendance, teacher training, and many more elements must be radically changed for survivors to learn successfully.

Education is not set up to take on issues of violence; it is often not even designed to address the whole person. In times of cutbacks and reductions of service, instructors and counselors—in the rare places where they are present—are often already pushed to their limits. Clearly the answer to addressing issues of violence is not that workers push a little harder, perhaps beyond their own boundaries and limitations. Instead issues of violence and their connection to learning need to be made public: Funders and policymakers must be pressured to open up spaces for creative programming possibilities and essential resources for workers and learners. Opening talk about new opportunities for successful learning might begin to open new frameworks for conceptualizing education and new structures for programming.

CHANGING CONCEPTUAL FRAMEWORKS

Question "Normal"

"The status quo is intolerable," Bellamy said. "We must insist that violence against girls and women be viewed as a shocking aberration, not an invisible norm." (Griffiths, July 1997)

A first step for all educators is to question the concept of *normal*. We face the challenge of how to make the shocking levels of violence more fully visible in educational programs and more broadly in society. If we see violence as the norm, the implication is that it is acceptable. However, if we view it as an aberration, then it seems to suggest that it is abnormal, not most women's experience, not so widespread that it must raise fundamental questions about societal forms and organization. In one recent workshop, a participant commented that violence is just ordinary and expected. By the end of the workshop, she had decided to draw attention to violence and make the unacceptability of violence visible in her program.

Violence—even extreme violence—is so widespread in all women's lives[3] that it is commonplace. This does not mean it should be accepted or tolerated. The value of exploring the meaning of *normal*, rather than simply avoiding the term, is to challenge the concept of *normal* itself, not just to question whether violence is normal. We often speak as if there is a common understanding of normal. We speak of *getting back to normal*. I question the divisions between normal and other because this division maintains the status quo.

Defining *trauma* as "generally outside the range of usual human experience" (Tal, 1996) gives the impression that it is a rarity and divides everyday violence from some level of violence that is extreme. This classification preserves a version of normal. The assumption about what is

---

[3]In particular, women who are racialized, poor, undereducated, disabled, or experience any other additional marginalization.

normal contributes to women who have experienced trauma being judged unless they can act as if they have not. This divide severs connections between the impacts of all degrees of violence. Women accept everyday violence as normal, but if they experience severe violence, they think of themselves as the exception and keep silent. The connotations of normal disguise the fact that normal life is toxic.

By accepting the concept of *normal* as unproblematic, educators participate in the silencing processes and in the preservation of the status quo. When I led one workshop, many of the participants were teachers of English to speakers of other languages. They had learned about trauma and its effects, and whatever I said, they continued to hear it within a medical framework. Over and over again, they would speak about learners getting back to normal. When I pointed out that I was trying to challenge that concept, they would say that they understood and then again speak about normal. They reminded me how firmly that understanding is ingrained.

If, as educators, we question that notion in every way, we can begin to open the possibilities for rethinking violence. Literacy workers and other teachers can begin to notice issues of violence, to question the impacts in the classroom, and to notice how complex an issue it is. We can draw learners' attention to these issues. It is important that workers not preserve the myth that violence is not normal or pressure students to get over it and to return to normal. We can shift thinking by making connections between violences, rather than seeing some as normal and others as not. Jane Field, literacy worker, member of the advisory committee, and disabled activist, who must daily negotiate the pressures of what is viewed as normal articulated the complexity of challenging concepts of violence and normal life:

> What we need to do is see [violence] as a visible norm, not an invisible one. . . . Of course, we have to acknowledge its ubiquitousness and prevalence, but not become blasé and passively accepting of it. Violence is, and must still be, shocking. Therefore, it's a shocking norm. As a shockingly normal thing, we have to make dealing with its effects a less shocking, normal thing to do. Acknowledging and accepting the pervasiveness of the effects of violence on learners should become a normal part of the teaching/learning process. In other words, we accept what must be done as normal, without accepting the normalcy of the reason for it. (Field, personal correspondence, July 1999)

She complained at the end of her note that she had not been very clear. I thought that she had captured precisely the difficulty of questioning such fundamental concepts, a brainteaser and even a tongue-twister, when we try to express the problem.

Avoid Medicalizing

The conception of violence as a private medical issue separate from education is a major barrier to programs and instructors recognizing issues of violence. One danger we face, as we begin to increase awareness of the prevalence of violence and its impact on learning, is the tendency to take on medical diagnoses without problematizing them adequately. For example, in the only article I have seen on teaching literacy and trauma, the authors refer to the medical framework as fact and take its truth for granted:

> Literacy teachers are not psychologists. However, as informed observers we can play an essential role as members on a treatment team. Teachers who suspect symptoms of trauma—and thus, of potential PTSD—in their students should look for three different, yet often overlapping categories of behavior: (a) hyperarousal, (b) intrusion, and (c) constriction (Herman, 1992). (Wolpow & Askov, 1998, p. 52)

The danger here is that literacy workers will be encouraged to diagnose who among the learners has experienced trauma and whether they are suffering from posttraumatic stress disorder. Although medical conceptualizations of trauma and its aftereffects can offer useful clues for understanding the impacts of trauma, educators should be careful to avoid operating within the medical framework. By sliding headlong toward diagnosis, we try to separate out those who have *really* experienced trauma from those who have not. Thus, we miss the opportunity to reconceptualize learning for all students and spend our energy actively colluding in separating out those who are not normal. We divert attention away from the strengths and sensitivities learned through trauma and run the risk of adding to the stigmatization of trauma survivors and the silence and shame around the experience of trauma. If learners fear that, by revealing their experience of trauma they will be categorized as having a disorder and seen as poor damaged creatures, they will be unlikely to speak of the struggles they may be having around learning.

Because the medicalizing discourse is so pervasive that it is hard even to notice when we are using it or operating within its framework, beginning to pay attention and notice how it structures our thinking will be an important task for educators. Noticing how teachers and learners speak about trauma and opening up frameworks can help avoid the slide into deficit models and seeing trauma as solely an individual health problem. This shift is important to allow us to move away from assumptions about a simple separation between literacy and therapy. If the impact of trauma creates a health problem, it is easy to suggest that survivors should address that health problem and return when they are ready to learn. However, impacts of trauma will always be present in the classroom and need to be recognized. We teach whole people even when our educational practices ignore the presence of anything but the mind, and many learners will bring to class a legacy, or present reality, of violence. Violence and its aftermath do not go away because we say it is inappropriate in the literacy class. We need to recognize this as a public aspect of all education. There is no place that is free of violence in which to heal, and no state exists where the experience of violence will not be part of who we are.

Medical models delineate a pattern of problems resulting from the experience of trauma. To see the complexity of the picture and avoiding condemning those who have experienced trauma, it is crucial that we reframe the picture. The image of survivors as canaries in the mine stays with me, helps me hold to an awareness of strengths and greater sensitivity, and let go of a demand to return to an ill-defined state called *normal*.

Create Visibility

Making the issue of violence and its impact on learning visible in literacy programs is crucial. I am not arguing that the goal of literacy programming is to have learners disclose their stories of abuse and violence. Rather, a climate that recognizes the presence of violence in many learners and instructors lives, but declares violence unacceptable, may lead a learner either to talk about her own experiences or choose not to speak. More important, it can help her be aware that she is not alone in experiencing violence, that the violence she lives with or has lived through should not have to be endured, and that she has options if she wants to make changes in her life. Most relevant here, she can learn that she does not need to be ashamed of the violence she has endured or of the impact of her experience on her learning. She will need to know what support is available outside and inside the program to help her identify how she can best learn. In a climate of openness, a learner can more easily begin to explore her own learning challenges and develop strategies without feeling at risk.

A variety of simple changes can make violence visible in a program and create a climate that says it is unacceptable. For example, antiviolence posters showing men and women of different ethnicities and abilities can visually make the statement that violence is something that affects many people and can be spoken about. It can give the message that violence is not something about which the victim need feel ashamed. Visible referral information for shelters, hotlines, and other resources, as well as flyers or cards a student can take away, are also important. Notice of which staff member to approach for further information, or for referrals to other services, would also make it easier for a student who wants to follow up on the possibility of accessing other resources. Where possible, resource people giving presentations in classes can help break the ice and make resources more familiar. Beginning to make change can be a terrifying process. The opportunity to discuss alternatives—to learn a little about the services available and even the details of how the process would work—might support a student who wants to begin to make change. Knowing there is someone in the program who might be able to offer ongoing encouragement might also make it easier to take the first step of approaching a stranger at another service.

Visibility might also include the visibility of "success stories, anecdotes, role models of women who have fought back and escaped violence" (Joyce, personal correspondence, July 1999). Visibility might include talks by women who have been through their own change process. Support groups or peer support approaches help to make change appear possible. I watched one learner listen to another talk about how she had managed to take on her education and survive as a single parent after leaving a violent partner, although he continued to stalk her. The learner, who had just left her husband and was clearly terrified that she would be unable to cope, was obviously encouraged by the stories she heard and the practical information she was given.

Programs could make resistance to violence and successful strategies part of what learners see and hear around them. Women and men who have refused violence and worked to change society in a variety of ways would also be interesting visitors or role models through posters and stories. Judy Cairns, a literacy worker from Nova Scotia, reported enthusiastically in the online seminar about the effect on her literacy class of participating in violence awareness activities:

> We were amazed at the quiet support felt in the session we had on family violence a few weeks ago. We talked about the "normalness" of family violence. We kept it simple while talking about the many issues that accompany violence (blame, fear, anger, hopelessness, helplessness)—we ended with simple solutions—what is available in our communities, and who would be interested in having guest speakers on specific issues to support people who want help, who are living in violent situations or who are sur-

vivors/victims of family violence (in particular children and women). As a result of that one session we have already had one guest speaker, and a community meeting of agencies who support men/women/children/families at risk. This is quite an accomplishment in a rural community. (Alphaplus Literacy & Violence Online Seminar, February–April 1998).

Violence could become visible within the daily practice of literacy education as part of the content of the curriculum. Domestic violence curriculum, as well as autobiographical and fictional readings speaking of experiences of violence, could open discussion about what counts as violence and why it occurs. For material that might be hard to read or might remind learners of their own experience, learners need to know what to expect ahead of time, allowing them to opt out of any activity that they find too disturbing or unsettling.

A whole range of approaches might help create the program as a safe or safer place. Workshops for learners, tutors, and staff on issues of violence can help make the issues visible and help everyone explore what a safe program would look like. Learners in one program explained that learning about what counts as violence and understanding cycles of violence had been important to them. In another program, learners said they would not talk about their past for fear they would be judged or their experience would be too shocking to other learners. Educational workshops and talks might help address these concerns.

For a program to offer a safer place, policies need to be created to delineate what behavior is unacceptable and when somebody would be excluded permanently or temporarily from the program. A focus on language (e.g., commonly used words such as *hit, struck, deadly*) could help everyone begin to notice the violence in everyday language and begin to make the taken-for-granted visible. A recognition of the violence in many jokes and the way in which sexual innuendo can be experienced as threatening and demeaning could emerge from a focus on commonly accepted language.

During workshops and presentations to literacy workers and other instructors about this research, I have often been met by concerns that it is wiser simply not to open up discussion of issues of violence—not to make the violence visible—because it is too volatile or sensitive a subject. I have been asked time and again: What if talking about violence, making the presence of violence and its impacts on learning visible in the classroom, breaks down a learner's "defenses" and causes them to disclose issues they would rather not speak about? It is important to be sensitive to that possibility.

Yet what if our silence gives the message that violence is acceptable and should be endured, not spoken about, anywhere? I do not think that educators should focus on encouraging people to disclose the details of their violation, as if that is the goal of educational programs. I do believe instructors should always be clear about supports for themselves and for learners because whenever topics that even touch on issues of violence are opened up some learners will choose to tell what happened to them. Enormous care should be taken to ensure that disclosure is never the goal of making violence visible. The goal is to make the unacceptability of violence clear—to indicate the acceptability of struggling with consequences of violence so that its impacts on learning become simply one aspect of education.

Although shifting conceptions of violence and learning, and recognition of the presence of impacts of violence in all educational settings, is an enormous and challenging task, it is only in this way that adequate change to educational programs can begin to be envisaged. Shifting conceptions will require constant vigilance because it is all too easy to slide back into taken-for-granted conceptual frameworks. Exploring new conceptions will offer exciting ideas for regenerating practice.

CHANGING EDUCATIONAL PROGRAMS

Each conceptual shift leads to changes to practice. Throughout this book, I have indicated possible practical changes that might be carried out as a consequence of changing conceptual frameworks. Overall, I believe it is not simply individual practical changes that are required, but rather a complete reconceptualization of literacy education. To attain such a place of substantial change, many small practical steps are needed. I have suggested a series of themes for training, the value of new connections with counselors, and new possibilities that could be created by the organization of the classroom. A myriad of new teaching approaches and curriculum content must follow the recognition of the needs of survivors. Although many changes can be carried out within existing programs, there are also possible models for types of courses that could be offered before and alongside existing educational programs.

An important first step to changing programs is for educators to develop an acute awareness—a continual questioning about the possible impacts of trauma on learning. A stance of exploration allows us to try small changes, observe their effects, and develop a more nuanced understanding of how a range of learners respond to impacts of trauma in their particular learning context. We need more talk, writing, and workshops.

Educators need to draw more widely on information about the complexity of impacts of violence on learning and to understand how to create changes to address them. Opportunities to strategize our way through barriers to making change and explore our resistances to change are essential. Every educator can be part of the process of becoming more sensitive to the impact of violence on learning, exploring changes needed in educational programs, strategizing how to translate new conceptions into day-to-day practice, and sharing these understandings with others.

One danger of redesigning educational programs to address impacts of violence on learning could be an assumption that everyone will then be capable of learning quickly. Susan Heald, survivor, advisor to the project and women's studies professor, alerted me to this problem. She suggested that if someone is unable to learn even in a redesigned program, he or she might easily be judged to be at fault yet again. It is important that educators not assume that there is a list of correct practices that will allow learners to respond appropriately. This will diminish space instead of creating it, if learners are no longer expected to have issues and difficulties with learning. Opening up issues of trauma can make learning easier for some, but it will not be a panacea. As Susan Heald said: "They haven't been repressing people in educational settings all these years for nothing." She cautioned us to recognize that difficulties and complexity will remain present despite our best intentions (personal correspondence, September 1998). This is why reconceptualization—a new model of thinking—and not merely individual practical changes, is crucial.

During my workshops on these issues, many literacy workers have quickly begun to imagine what they could take on in their own location. Perhaps they can begin to make violence more visible in their program, they want to read more and think through the conceptualization of violence, or they can see minor changes they can make as they work with a group. Some people have contacted me afterward and talked about seeing a situation differently now that they are thinking about it in the light of issues of violence. One literacy worker, for example, talked about noticing that a learner often wandered off when the group was reading intense material. Prior to the workshop, she had thought this learner had a short attention span. Now she realized the material could be triggering something and planned to talk to the student about what was going on for her. As instructors, groups, and individual learners explore the complexity of the impact of violence on learning in a variety of settings, we begin to discover a range of ways to support each learner.

Changes to practice must include new training opportunities. Training for learners, tutors, instructors, and administrators—either together or in separate groupings—could offer insights into how, whatever their location, each person can move the issues forward in their own setting. Training for educators offered by counselors and therapists might offer new insights to the literacy field. I attended a wonderful workshop recently by Heather Bain, an experienced psychologist and counseling educator, entitled "*The Balancing act. Listening, Enabling, and Looking After Ourselves.*" The workshop description was inviting:

> Those of us whose work involves skills such as listening, helping or instructing often struggle with remembering to listen to ourselves when the focus of work is on the needs of others. We frequently forget to include ourselves and our needs in our 'helping' relationships. This workshop addresses questions of balance. How do we listen to ourselves and others simultaneously? How do we respond to a situation that touches our heart and calls us to action, but urges us beyond the limits of our expertise, energy or work mandate? Together we will explore various ways of listening and communicating. discuss boundary issues, ethical responsibilities, concerns, self-care, burnout and various traumatizations. (workshop flyer, The Learning Centre, Edmonton, April 1999)

This workshop was set up by one literacy program, but open to staff and volunteers from all programs in the city. It engaged us all in the experience of exploring balance—learning to find the balance of listening both to ourselves and others. It gave us the possibility of carrying out our literacy work from a more grounded place. Such a workshop is a wonderful example of the learning possibilities that occur when we begin to draw on resources outside the literacy field.

Exploring links with local counseling resources to ensure supports for both learners and workers may be a daunting task where options are limited and inadequate. Researching local options for counseling, group work, and long-term therapy for survivors of trauma as well as negotiating possibilities for support and supervision for instructors is essential. Educators may face a lack of appropriate resources that are available free or even for a limited charge. Yet learning about what is available, the variations between the different resources, and the limitations and possibilities of each resource could lead to exciting collaborative possibilities and support learners and workers to make use of these options.

Shifting the type of setting where learning is taking place can be an important factor in changing learning potential. Rather than a traditional classroom set-up—settings that provide comfort, support students building connections, create space and delight, recognizing that the body, spirit, and emotions are all part of the learning process—may be important. For example, as suggested earlier, a room set-up that enables students to be *present* but also separate from the class may model middle ground as an alternative to *all or nothing*. Shifting from the proper look of a classroom, providing a beautiful quilt and an easy chair where a student can curl up, might seem outrageous in a formal educational setting, but might help a student feel safe and comfortable enough to learn.

New Approaches and Curriculum

New teaching approaches and new curriculum must be developed in the light of understandings about the impact of trauma on learning. New program structures and procedures might also follow from rethinking. For example, thinking about presence might lead to intake procedures that mentioned staying present as an issue everyone struggles with, a regular check-in at the start of a class, and curriculum that focuses on what helps and hinders staying present. Curriculum focusing on how to learn, explore taking control, and enable the whole person to support learning might all strengthen learning. Making use of existing curriculum, which brings women's real lives into the classroom, might also support making violence visible and assist learners in the task of learning about their own learning.[4] As literacy workers and other educators reconceptualize education and violence, many new approaches will be envisaged. The choice of where to begin to make change and what is possible in any particular setting will vary depending on factors such as existing curriculum, length of the course, or setting. Making whatever changes to program structure, course content, and teaching approaches are feasible within a particular context could begin to shift possibilities for learning.

New courses can offer new alternatives for learning. In some areas, interesting programs have been tried as preliteracy courses. In others, a part-time program alongside literacy or other coursework has helped women find success. The Women's Success Course described earlier was well named:

> The pilot of Douglas College's "Women's Success Course" was the liberating step that both the College and students took in the winter and spring of 1997. For the first time, a small group of women had a glimpse and a sense of the possibility that they were able to be successful. What unfolded in the next three semesters linked that sense of possibility with their personal experiences and educational activities. With the College's acknowledgement of the realities of violence in their lives, these women were able

---

[4]*Making Connections* (CCLOW, 1996) is a good example of this sort of curriculum.

to have the courage to take the steps they needed to be successful. (Leroux, 1998c, p. 11)

While the first group of women continued to meet together to support each other, a whole new group of participants were enrolled in the next course. Options such as this, and many new creations suitable for different settings and circumstances, can be designed once the impact of violence on learning is acknowledged.

Among my next steps will be an intensive women's group in a community-based literacy program, exploring what happens when we recognize that the whole person is affected by trauma and that body, emotion, spirit, and mind can all be drawn creatively into the learning process. A variety of resource people will bring this program to life. A Native elder, a musician, a yoga teacher, an artist, and a body work specialist who might teach grounding and help students explore their identity through mask-making are some of the people I hope to bring wisdom and imagination to the process. I will work with a counselor who will lead workshops, be available for individual counseling when learners need the support, and be available for advice when I need to debrief. Through such a creative and innovative process, I believe learners will discover the strength to envisage future possibilities and become ready to delineate and take on new goals. Putting these plans into practice will offer new data about the potential of this type of model.

Despite factors such as program structure, course length, and funding limitations that may hamper educators in their goal to support women's learning, when educators shift conceptual frameworks, there are many ways to make a difference—from minor changes, such as the way they speak about violence, to the creation of new programs. Despite the immense challenges for literacy workers and other educators to translate this research into practice with few additional resources or supports in place, practitioners are taking it on. Literacy workers, teachers of English to speakers of other languages, and adult basic education instructors are talking about issues and planning new approaches. Each time I speak at conferences or offer workshops about my research, instructors are clearly excited to connect with others who are naming this work as important and to hear that work they know is urgently needed is happening. Educators are seeking funding to try out possible changes in their program or region and to explore what addressing issues of violence in their setting might look like.

Throughout this book, the examples I have used have been primarily from adult literacy programs. However, the impacts of violence are present in all educational programs and must be recognized if a wide range of learners are to have a chance of success. Literacy may be a particularly acute site of complexity around issues of violence, but instructors at all levels of education must learn to address these issues. More research is needed to explore the details of how other levels of education must change. The rethinking offered here suggests ways forward for all educational settings.

This book is one step in the exploration of how experiences of violence impact on learning. The research process I engaged in brought perspectives developed by counselors and therapists who have specialized in issues of violence to groups of educators. Interweaving the knowledge from different locations, I have developed and described new insights for rethinking educational work. With the help of the ideas and experience of many educators, I have offered a myriad of clues to how we might proceed as we begin to rethink educational practice. Much has yet to be tested in practice. That is the next step for all educators.

CHANGING SOCIETY

Changing conceptions of violence in educational programs, challenging the meaning of normal and of medicalizing discourse, making the existence of violence and its impacts on learning constantly visible in the educational classroom, and profoundly changing educational practice will reverberate throughout society. Such all-encompassing change can have a larger social impact that contributes to a process of fundamental social change.

In the literacy field, and more broadly in education, we need to envisage changes, implement them, observe what happens, and question what works for learners in the program. We need to keep demanding change in every forum, talking about the issues of violence, insisting that there is too much violence, and demanding that the needs of survivors be taken into account in all educational sites. We need to shift conceptions of literacy and of education more broadly. It is not just the mind that goes to school—it is the whole person. For far too many learners, the experience of trauma may form part of that whole. If we operate as if only the mind has to be attended to and ignore experiences of trauma, too many students will continue to fail and too many women and children will continue to be exposed to violence and silenced and shamed about its consequences in all aspects of their lives.

Each educational program has to discover its own starting point for change. In different regions and countries, the context for change and the possibilities may vary. There are different starting points and different ways forward depending on what a program has already taken on, what the context is, and what resources are available to support adaptations or new programs. Change can happen at all levels, initiated by program administrators, classroom teachers, students, funders, and policymakers. There is no one first step. Each person can make a conceptual shift in understandings of violence and change each element of practice as a consequence.

Fully recognizing the prevalence of survivors in all educational settings and the shifts necessary to provide education that meets their needs demands nothing less than a complete rethinking of literacy education and, by implication, of all other education. We cannot ignore the need to change simply because it makes many uncomfortable. We need to begin with whatever step is possible—today.

The Research Journey

Fall 1996: Learning From the Therapeutic Field
An 8-month research grant allowed me to begin the research.
Reading, reading, reading. . . .
Interviews with therapists in Toronto.
Pulling out themes to take to literacy workers and learners.

Winter 1996/1997: Learning From the Literacy Field
Interviews in British Columbia, Alberta, and Manitoba—focusing on impacts of violence on learning and bringing themes from therapists to educators and learners.
Two-day retreat with educators from Alberta and British Columbia on Salt Spring Island a highlight.
Back in Toronto, interviews with literacy workers with particular knowledge or focus: First Nation instructors, workers from programs serving people on the street, workers from programs serving those with intellectual disabilities, checking experiences of different groups.
Organizing data into themes, preparing to tell a coherent story.

Spring 1997: Trying Out an Analysis and Collecting More Data
Workshops in Quebec and in the North West Territories allowed me to check out what I had learned and find out more about different situations. Interviews in Prince Edward Island added new dimensions and nuances.

Presentations and workshops in Canada and to an international group of educators in Hamburg, Germany, enabled further rethinking.

Fall/Winter 1997/1998: Going Public

Wrote a discussion paper and sent it out to all the interviewees, contacts from Hamburg, and everyone else I could think of, asking for feedback. Ran an online seminar, more than 100 administrators, teachers of English to speakers of other languages (TESOL), and literacy workers enrolled, and insightful discussion based on the paper followed as practitioners shared their experiences.

Spring/Summer 1998: Writing, Writing, Writing

A new grant to cover 4 months to write and publish allowed me to go back to the analysis and reanalyze, rethink, and write.

Critical readers from different regions and perspectives read the draft manuscript and gave loads of feedback to send me back to rewriting.

Fall 1998–Spring 1999: Making the Next Stage Public

Workshops and presentations in Australia, at a women and literacy conference in Georgia, and at a TESOL conference in New York all allowed me to check out my analysis with new groups of instructors and academics.

Summer 1999: The Final Writing!

One more intense stage of writing to integrate feedback. Requesting permission to include each quote led to new comments and further insights to incorporate.

Interview List

Interviews include a range of types of contact: online comments and phone, individual, group, and informal interviews as I hunted for resources and further contacts. Some participants in most locations chose not to be named, others to be identified only by a first name. Although many are not named in the body of the book, all offered valuable wisdom for the research.

Initial Toronto Interviews
  Clarissa Chandler
  Susan Goodfellow
  Kathleen O'Connell
  Christina Pike
  Liz White
  Marie Barton
  Miriam Ticoll
  Melanie Panitch

West Coast
British Columbia
  Maria Nguen
  Helen Dempster
  Bridget Wall-Bruneski
  Gillian Reece
  Vern White
  Judith Jeffery

Phyllis Cann
Donna Wilson
Henrietta Dessombes
Joanie Sass
Evelyn Battell
C. B. Patterson
Ruth Kroek
Manon
Cathy MacGillvary
Faith Jones
Theresa Pilnasek
B. Maria Hiles
Suzanne
Leanna
Pam Alcorn
Susan
Kathleen Skovgaard
Laura
Terri
Judy Rose
Mary Norton
Sally Gellard
Joyce Cameron
Mary Carlisle
Kate Nonesuch
Evelyn Battell

Prairies
Alberta
  Lil
  Edna
  Betty
  Mary
  Pat Campbell
  Mary Norton
  Deborah Morgan

Judy Murphy
Jeanette Austin-Odina
Moira Hooton
Sharon Skage
Evie Gilmour
Maxine Morris
Heather Bain
Barbara McTavish
Sharon Szott
Terry McGuire
Alice Kneeland

Manitoba
Diane Eastman
Gail Cullen
Ken Norquay
Sheila K.
Marie Matheson
Sylvia Provenski
Janet Smith
Jennifer Howard
Wynn Fordyce
Eileen Cable
Joy H. T. So
Robin Millar

Central Canada
Ontario
Priscilla George
Jennifer Wemigwans
Sally Gaikezheyongai
Nancy Cooper
Beth Bourgeois
Deanne Bradley
Jackie Gignac
Cheryl Wilson-Lum

Dharini Abeysekera
Jayne Caldwell
Nancy Friday-Cockburn
Susan Macdonald
Janice Salsbury
Betsy Trumpener
Pat MacNeil
Michele Kuhlmann
Janine Luce
Lurana Kruchten

Quebec
Vivian Wiseman
Aileen Shattuck-Ezzy
Louyse Lussier
Jennie Peters
Lorna Yates
Elizabeth Garbish
Nancy Garbish
Merryl Hammond
Abigail Anderson
Christina Torsein
Pat Winston
G. Laferriere
Miriam Packer

Atlantic Provinces
PEI
Judy Matheson
Lillian Mead
Mona Bariault
Ermelinda Guerara
Agnes Sashee
Wendy Crawford
Janet MacLeod

Velda Crane
Ruth Rogerson
Karen Chandler
Vianne Timmons
Margaret Cernigoj
Cathy Cotton
Norma McQuarrie
Julie Devon-Dodd
Faye M. Martin
Barbara MacNutt
Joanne Ings
Lorna Gallant

North
Nunavut
Janice Beddard
Lorraine MacCormack
Mary Ellen Thomas
Yvonne Earle
Dorothee Komangapik
Kate Bishop
Agnes B. Ansong
Sheila Knowlton-MacRury
Judy Anilniliak
Darlene Nuqingaq
Geela Giroux
Catherine Acomba
Diane Dilbey
Lynn Johnson
Craig Clark
Sharon Doyle
Maureen Doherty
Sheila Levy
Pitsula Akavak
Linda Pemik

North West Territories
    Debra King
    Verona Winsor
    Glenys Dawson
    Carla Bullinger
    Mary Goldsmith
    Camilla Vandal
    Marci Bulloch
    Cate Sills
    Gabrielle Mackenzie-Scott
    Krystine Hogan
    Joyce Gilchrist
    Sharon Morrison
    Aline LaFlamme
    Mary Beth Levan
    Arlene Haché

References

Agger, I. (1994). *The blue room: Trauma and testimony among refugee women. A psycho-social exploration.* London: Zed Books.

Ahern, W. H. (1978). Assimilation racism: The case of the "Friends of the Indian." In R. W. Nelson & D. A. Nock (Eds.), *Reading, writing and riches: Education and the socio-economic order in North America* (pp. 251–261). Kitchener, Ontario: Between the Lines.

Alcoff, L., & Gray, L. (1993). Survivor discourse: Transgression or recuperation? *Signs,* 18(21), 260–290.

Alleyne, V. (1997). *There were times I thought I was crazy: A Black woman's story of incest.* Toronto: Sister Vision; Black Woman and Woman of Colour Press.

Allison, D. (1995). *Two or three things I know for sure.* New York: Plume.

Allison, D. (1994). *Skin: Talking about sex, class & literature.* New York: Firebrand Books.

Allison, D. (1988). *Trash.* New York: Firebrand Books.

Armstrong, L. (1987). *Kiss Daddy goodnight: Ten years later.* New York: Pocket Books.

Alphaplus Literacy & Violence Online Seminar, Archives. February–April 1998.

Atkinson, T., & Horsman, J. (1989). *Telling our own stories.* Unpublished manuscript, Adult Basic Education Unit, Continuing Education Department, Toronto Board of Education.

Avni, O. (1995). Beyond psychoanalysis: Elie Wiesel's night in historical perspective. In L. D. Kitzman (Ed.), *Aushwitz and after: Race, culture and "the Jewish question" in France.* London & New York: Routledge.

Badgley Report. (1984). *Report of the Committee on Sexual Offences Against Children and Youth* (Chairman Robin Badgley). Ottawa: Ministry of Supply and Services Canada.

Bass, E., & Davis, L. (1988). *The courage to heal: A guide for women survivors of child sexual abuse.* New York: Harper & Row.

Bass, E., & Thornton, L. (Eds.). (1983). *I never told anyone: Writings by women survivors of child sexual abuse.* New York: Harper & Row.

Battell, E., & Nonesuch, K. (Eds.). (1996). *If you could see me now: Stories by women who survived abusive relationships.* British Columbia: Key Consulting.

Beaton, R., & Cooper, N. (1997). *A culture-based approach to learning: Addressing the needs of first nations adult learners in Toronto* (Draft Document). Toronto: Adult Basic Education Unit.

Blume, S. E. (1990). *Secret survivors: Uncovering incest and its after effects in women*. New York: Ballantine.

Bremner, J. D., Randall, P., Scott, T. M., Capelli, S., Delaney, R., McCarthy, G., & Charney, D. S. (1995). Deficits in short-term memory in adult survivors of childhood abuse. *Psychiatry Research, 59*, 97–107.

Brock, D. (1993). Talkin' ' bout a revelation: Feminist popular discourse on sexual abuse. In L. Carty (Ed.), *And still we rise: Feminist political mobilizing in contemporary Canada* (pp. 109–116). Toronto: Women's Press.

Brookes, A.-L. (1992). *Feminist pedagogy: An autobiographical approach*. Halifax: Fernwood.

Brown, L. (1986). *Diagnosis and the Zeitgeist: The politics of masochism in the DSM–III–R*. Paper prepared for the convention of the American Psychological Association, Washington, DC.

Brown, L. (1995). Not outside the range: One feminist perspective on psychic trauma. In C. Caruth (Ed.), *Trauma explorations in memory* (pp. 100–112). Baltimore, MD: Johns Hopkins University Press.

Butler, S. (1992, March). *Centre for Christian Studies*. Notes from public lecture and workshops. Toronto.

Butler, S. (1994, October). *Breaking and entering shattered trust*. Taped workshop presentation from the "It's Never OK" conference, Toronto.

Byrnes, J. (1977). *Never in a loving way*. Manchester, England: Gatehouse Books.

Canadian Congress for Learning Opportunities for Women. (1996). *Making connections: Literacy and EAL curriculum from a feminist perspective*. Toronto: CCLOW/CCPEF.

Canadian Panel on Violence Against Women. (1993). *Changing the landscape: Ending violence—achieving equality*. Executive Summary/National Action Plan. Ottawa: Ministry of Supply and Services Canada.

Canadian Congress for Learning Opportunities for Women. (1996). *Literacy work with survivors of abuse: A research proposal*. Unpublished finding proposal.

Capponi, P. (1992). *Upstairs in the crazy house: The life of a psychiatric survivor*. Toronto: Viking.

Capponi, P. (1997). *Dispatches from the poverty line*. Toronto: Penguin Books.

Chan, L. H. (1996). Talking pain: Educational work with factory women in Malaysia. In S. Walters & L. Manicom (Eds.), *Gender in popular education: Methods for empowerment* (pp. 202–228). London: Zed Books.

Chan, L. H. (1997). Women worker's education in Malaysia. In C. Medel-Añonuevo (Ed.), *Negotiating and creating spaces of power: Women's educational practices amidst crisis* (pp. 75–84). Hamburg: UNESCO Institute for Education.

Chandler, C. (n.d.). *Being an ally to children* (Cassette Recording). Toronto: LCC Consulting, P.O. Box 65215, Toronto, Ontario M4L 2Y9.

Chandler, C. (n.d.). *Body terror* (Cassette Recording) Toronto: LCC Consulting, P.O. Box 65215, Toronto, Ontario M4L 2Y9.

Chandler, C. (n.d.). *Flashback management* (Cassette Recording). Toronto: LCC Consulting, P.O. Box 65215, Toronto, Ontario M4L 2Y9.

Chandler, C. (n.d.). *Weaving the story* (Cassette Recording). Toronto: LCC Consulting, P.O. Box 65215, Toronto, Ontario M4L 2Y9.

City University of New York. (n.d.). *In their own eyes: Self portraits of adult students*. New York: City University of New York.

Code, L. (1987). *Epistemic responsibility*. Hanover, NH: University Press of New England.

Dancu, C. V., Riggs, D. S., Hearst-Ikeda, D., Shoyer, B. G. & Foa, E. B. (1996). Dissociative experiences and post-traumatic stress disorder among female victims of criminal assault and rape. *Journal of Traumatic Stress, 9*(2), 253–267.

Danica, E. (1988). *Don't: A woman's world.* Charlottetown: Gynergy.

Danica, E. (1996). *Beyond don't: Dreaming past the dark.* Charlottetown: Gynergy.

Dinsmore, C. (1991). *From surviving to thriving: Incest, feminism and recovery.* Albany: State University of New York Press.

Doiron, R. (1987). *My name is Rose.* Toronto: East End Literacy Press.

Dosanjh, R., Deo, S., & Sidhu, S. (1994). *Spousal abuse: Experiences of 15 Canadian South Asian women.* Vancouver: India Mahila Association.

Dueno, A., Santiago, A., & De Simone, R.-M. (1993). *It should be told: Oral histories from the open book.* Brooklyn, NY: The Open Book.

Emerson, J. (n.d.). The social construction of literacy with particular regard to rural working class women. In *Through the eyes of teachers: Portraits of adult students* (a publication of the New York State Literacy Resource Centre) (pp. 32–43). New York: Division of Adult and Continuing Education Office of Academic Affairs City University of New York.

Ennis, F., Hickey, S., Biddiscombe, B., Cadwell, S., Jackson, B., Short, C., & Rabbittown Learners Program, St. John's, Newfoundland: (1994). Uncovering fear and isolation in Rabbittown: A woman positive literacy project. In B.-A. Lloyd, F. Ennis, & T. Atkinson (Eds.), *Women in literacy speak: The power of woman- positive literacy work* (pp. 72–83). Toronto: CCLOW and Halifax: Fernwood.

Fay. (1989). *Listen to me: Talking to survival.* Manchester: Gatehouse.

Felman, S., & Laub, D. (1992). *Testimony: Crises of witnessing in literature, psychoanalysis, and history.* New York: Routledge.

Figley, C. R. (1988). Post-traumatic family therapy. In F. M. Ochberg (Ed.), *Post-traumatic therapy and victims of violence* (pp. 83–109). New York: Brunner/Mazel.

Fraser, S. (1987). *My father's house: A memoir of incent and of healing.* Toronto: Doubleday.

Fraser, S. (1994, March). Freud's final seduction. *Saturday Night,* 19–59.

Fraser, S. (1997, January 25). Abuse wars: Whose memory matters? *Globe and Mail,* p. D14.

Freyd, J. J. (1997). *Betrayal trauma: The logic of forgetting childhood.* Cambridge: Harvard University Press.

Gaber-Katz, E., & Horsman, J. (1988). Is it her voice if she speaks their words? *Canadian Woman Studies, 9*(3 & 4), 117–120. Reprinted in *Canadian Woman Studies, 11*(3), 1991.

Gallant, L. (1997). Abuse. In *The writer: Stories poems and muses by writers at the learning centre* (p. 9). Edmonton, AL: The Learning Centre Literacy Association.

Gardner, G. E. (1971). Aggression and violence—the enemies of precision learning in children. *American Journal of Psychiatry, 128*(4), 77–82.

Garrity, C. (1998, June 22). *The greatest women in my life.* Unpublished winning entry to Bread and Roses Contest.

Geertz, C. (1973). *The interpretation of cultures: Selected essays.* New York: Basic Books.

Goldman, R. (n.d.). Canadian Outward Bound Wilderness School and the "Women of Courage" Program.

Goodfellow, S. (1995). *Vicarious traumatization.* Unpublished paper.

Gowen, S. G., & Bartlett, C. (1997). Friends in the kitchen: Lessons from survivors. In G. Hull (Ed.), *Changing work, changing workers, critical perspectives on language, literacy and skills* (pp. 141–158). New York: State University Press.

Green, A. K. (1990). *Coming out of my shell*. St. John's, Newfoundland: Educational Planning and Design.

Green, L. (1992). *Ordinary wonders: living recovery from sexual abuse*. Toronto: Women's Press.

Griffiths, L. (1997, July 22). UK: Women face daily threat of violence—UNICEF. London: Reuters (wire service).

Hanh, T. N. (1991). *Peace is every step: The path of mindfulness in everyday life*. New York: Bantam Books.

Harvey, M., & Herman, J. L. (1994). Amnesia, partial amnesia and delayed recall among adult survivors of childhood trauma. *Consciousness and Cognition, 3*, 295–306.

Hawkins, C. (1984). *Family violence: Education for change*. Philadelphia: Lutheran Settlement House.

Heald, S. (1997). Events without witness: Living/teaching difference within the paternalist university. *Curriculum Studies, 5*(1), 39–48.

Helfield, I. G. (1996/1997). Rights of passage: From student to teacher. *Women's Education, 12*(4), 11–14.

Hellmut, K. (1992). *The filthy lie: Discovering and recovering from childhood abuse*. London: Hamish Hamilton.

Herman, J. (1992). *Trauma and recovery*. New York: Basic Books.

Herman, J. (1996). Crime and memory. In C. Strozier & M. Flynn (Eds.), *Trauma and self* (pp. 3–17). Maryland: Rowan & Littlefield.

Hewitt, P. (1988). Educating Priscilla. *Canadian Woman Studies, 9*(3&4), 12–14.

Hofer, J. (1999). Together we bloom: A video project on domestic violence. *Bright Ideas, 8*(4), 1, 10.

Hooks, B. (1994). *Teaching to transgress: Education as the practice of freedom*. New York: Routledge.

Horsman, J. (1988). The social dimension of literacy. *Canadian Woman Studies, 9*(3 & 4), 78–87.

Horsman, J. (1989a). *Something in my mind besides the everyday: Il/literacy in women's lives in a Nova Scotian county*. Unpublished Ed.D. thesis, University of Toronto.

Horsman, J. (1989b). From the learners' voice: Women's experience of il/literacy. In J. A. Draper & M. C. Taylor (Eds.), *Adult literacy perspectives* (pp. 365–374). Toronto: Culture Concepts.

Horsman, J. (1990). *Something in my mind besides the everyday: Women and literacy*. Toronto: Women's Press.

Horsman, J. (1994a). Working on memories of abuse. *Australian Journal of Adult and Community Education, 34*(1), 56–60.

Horsman, J. (1994b). The problem of illiteracy and the promise of literacy. In M. Hamilton, D. Barton, & R. Ivanic (Eds.), *Worlds of literacy* (pp. 169–181). Clevedon: Multilingual Matters.

Horsman, J. (1995, Spring). Violence and illiteracy in women's lives: Proposal for research and practice. *International Journal of Canadian Studies, 11*, 207–220.

Horsman, J. (1996). Responding to disclosures of abuse in women's lives. In Canadian Congress for Learning Opportunities for Women (CCLOW). *Making connections: Literacy and EAL curriculum from a feminist perspective* (pp. 15–30). Toronto: CCLOW/CCPEF.

Horsman, J. (1997). *But I'm not a therapist: Furthering discussion about literacy work with survivors of trauma*. Toronto: CCLOW (Discussion Paper).

Horsman, J. (in press). Why would they listen to me? Reflections on learner leadership activities. In B. Burnaby & P. Campbell (Eds.), *Participatory approaches in adult education*.
Mahwah, New Jersey: Lawrence Erlbaum Associates.

Hrubes, L. (1997, May). Flexible frame works: Opening the door beyond language. *The
Communication Link*, 2–10.

Jacobs, J. L. (1994). *Victimized daughters: Incest and the development of the female self*. New
York: Routledge.

Jones, A. (1994). *Next time, she'll be dead: Battering and how to stop it*. Boston: Beacon.

Joyce, V. M. (1993). *Singing for our lives. Women creating home through singing*. Master of
Arts Thesis: University of Toronto.

Joyce, M. (1995). Women of courage: Healing through wilderness adventure. In Canadian
Congress for Learning Opportunities for Women, *Isolating the Barriers and Strategies for
Prevention: A Kit About Violence and Women's Education for Adult Educators and Adult
Learners* (pp. 51–53). Toronto: CCLOW.

Joyce, M. (1996). Turn off the radio and sing for your lives! Women, singing, and experiential education. In K. Warren (Ed.), *Women's voices in experiential education* (pp.
253–256). Dubuque: Kendall Hunt.

Joyce, V. M. (in press). Bodies that sing: The formation of singing subjects. Proceedings
Sharing the Voices: The Phenomenon of Singing International Symposium II, July 2–5 1999.
St. John's, Newfoundland.: Memorial University.

Kadi, J. (1996). *Thinking class: Sketches from a cultural worker*. Boston, MA: South End
Press.

Katz, R., & St. Denis, V. (1991). Teacher as healer. *Journal of Indigenous Studies*, 2(2),
24–36.

Kelleher, S. A. (1997). *When women's touch turns to torture: The experience of women who
were sexually abused as children by a female perpetrator*. Unpublished doctoral dissertation,
University of Alberta.

Kroll, T. (1996, May 23). *The ladder*. Reprinted in Alphacom Digest, 248.

Landsberg, M. (1998, July 26). Women's legal victories were hard fought. *Toronto Star*, p.
A2.

Landsberg, M. (1997, July 19). Putting profits and tax ahead of kids. *Toronto Star*, p. L1.

Laub, D. (1995). Truth and testimony: The process and the struggle. In C. Caruth (Ed.),
Trauma: Explorations in memory (pp. 61–75). Baltimore, MD: Johns Hopkins University
Press.

Laub, D. (1992). Bearing witness, or the vicissitudes of listening. In S. Felman & D. Laub
(Eds.), *Testimony: Crises of witnessing in literature, psychoanalysis, and history* (pp. 57–74).
New York: Routledge.

Leroux, K. (1998a). We will not go backwards. *Groundwork*, 19(1), 5–7.

Leroux, K. (1998b). We will not go backwards (Part Two). *Groundwork*, 19(2), 13–15.

Leroux, K. (1998c). We will not go backwards (Part Three). *Groundwork*, 19(3), 11–13.

Lewis, T. I. (1998). *Weaving between the fragments: Performing "normal" after incest memory's
return*. Unpublished doctoral dissertation, University of Toronto.

Lewis, T. (1999). *Living beside: Performing normal after incest memories return*. Toronto:
McGilligan Books.

Literacy Project, The. (1998). *A guide to—Together we bloom: Women speaking out against
domestic violence*. Massachusetts: The Literacy Project Inc.

Littman, V. C. (1993). Navigating through: Reversing abusive and narrative. *Canadian
Woman Studies*, 13(4), 42–46.

Lloyd, B.-A., Ennis, F., & Atkinson, T. (1994a). *The power of woman-positive literacy work: Program based action research.* Toronto: CCLOW and Halifax: Fernwood.

Lloyd, B.-A., Ennis, F., & Atkinson, T. (1994b). *Women in literacy speak: The power of woman-positive literacy work.* Toronto: CCLOW and Halifax: Fernwood.

Lloyd, B.-A., Ennis, F., & Atkinson, T. (1994c). *Listen to women in literacy: The power of woman-positive literacy work.* Toronto: CCLOW and Halifax: Fernwood.

Lovell, M. (1993). *Amerasian domestic violence curriculum project.* Boston: International Institute. (Available through System for Adult Basic Education Support [SABES] Clearinghouse at World Education, 44 Farnsworth St., Boston 02210).

Lovell, D. (1996). In *MTML's Learner's Leadership Program* (p. 79). Toronto: Metro Toronto Movement for Literacy.

MacFarland, J. (1998, July 3). Jane Doe v. Toronto (Metropolitan) Commissioners of Police [On-line]. Available: www.blaney.com/janed.htm.

Makin, K. (1998, May 9). False memory's victims languish in jail. *Globe and Mail*, pp. A1, A2.

Markova, D. (1994). *No enemies within: A creative process for discovering what's right about what's wrong.* Berkeley, CA: Conari Press.

Martin, D. (1994, December). Can I talk to you for a minute? *LCA News and Views, 26–27.*

McBeth, S., & Stollmeyer, V. (1988). East End Literacy: A women's discussion group. *Canadian Woman Studies, 9*(3&4), 52–57.

McLeod, L., & Shin, M. (1990). *Isolated, afraid and forgotten: The service delivery needs and realities of immigrant and refugee women who are battered.* Ottawa: National Clearinghouse on Family Violence, Health and Welfare Canada.

Metro Toronto Movement for Literacy. (1996). *MTML's learner's leadership program.* Toronto: Author.

Miller, A. (1981). *The drama of the gifted child.* New York: HarperCollins.

Millward, M. (1992, March/April). Clean behind the ears? Micmac parents, Micmac children and the Shubenacadie Residential School. *New Maritimes, 7–15.*

Mitchell, A. (1985). Child sexual assault. In C. Guberman & M. Wolfe (Eds.), *No safe place: Violence against women & children* (pp. 87–110). Toronto: Women's Press.

Mitten, D., & Dutton, R. (1996). Outdoor leadership considerations with women survivors of sexual abuse. In K. Warren (Ed.), *Women's voices in experiential education* (pp. 130–140). Dubuque, IA: Kendall/Hunt (Boulder Colorado: Association of Experiential Education).

Moore, A. (1994). Taking space for woman-positive literacy work. In B.-A. Lloyd, F. Ennis, & T. Atkinson (Eds.), *Women in literacy speak: The power of woman-positive literacy work* (pp. 94–105). Toronto: CCLOW and Halifax: Fernwood.

Nadeau, D. (1996). Embodying feminist popular education under global restructuring. In S. Walters & L. Manicom (Eds.), *Gender in popular education: Methods for empowerment* (pp. 40–60). London: Zed Books.

Nonesuch, K., and others. (1994). *ABE fundamental level mathematics I.* Victoria, British Columbia: Centre for Curriculum and Professional Development and the Province of British Columbia Ministry of Skills, Training and Labour.

Nyquist, M. (1998). Struck dumb. *Canadian Woman Studies, 17*(4), 69–71.

Ontario Literacy Coalition. (1992). *The learner training institute: Resource package.* Ontario: Ontario Literacy Coalition.

Pearlman, L. A., & Saakvitne, K. W. (1995). *Trauma and the therapist, countertransference and vicarious traumatization in psychotherapy with incest survivors.* New York: Norton.

Potter, N. (1995). The severed head and existential dread: The classroom as epistemic community and student survivors of incest. *Hypatia, 10*(2), 69–92.

Roa, E., Jaber, B., & Ramirez, I. (n.d.), *I see a part of myself: Voices from the community.* Brooklyn, NY: The Open Book.

Rockhill, K. (1987). Literacy as threat/desire: Longing to be *somebody.* In J. Gaskell & A. McLaren (Eds.), *Women and education: A Canadian perspective* (pp. 315–331). Calgary: Detselig.

The Roeher Institute. (1986). *Vulnerable: Sexual abuse and people with an intellectual handicap.* North York, Ontario: Author.

Root, M. P. P. (1992). Reconstructing the impact of trauma on personality. In L. S. Brown & M. Ballou (Eds.), *Personality of psychopathology* (pp. 229–265). New York: Guilford.

Rosenberg, S. (1997). *Rupturing the "skin of memory": Bearing witness to the 1989 massacre of women in Montreal.* Unpublished doctoral dissertation, University of Toronto.

Rundle, L. B., & Ysabet-Scott, N. (1995). Violence: A barrier to education. *Women's Education, 11*(4), 5–11.

Russel, D. E. H. (1988). Incidence and prevalence rates of intra-familial and extra-familial sexual abuse of female children. In L. E. A. Walker (Ed.), *Handbook on child sexual abuse: Assessment and intervention* (pp. 19–36). New York: Springer.

Sapphire. (1996). *Push.* New York: Vintage Contemporaries/Vintage Books a Division of Random House Inc.

Shengold, L. (1989). *Soul murder.* New Haven, CT: Yale University Press.

Sobsey, D. (1988). Sexual offenses and disabled victims: Research and practical implications. *A National Newsletter on Family Violence, 6*(4), 1.

Spender, D. (1980). *Man made language.* London: Routledge & Kegan Paul.

Spivak, G. C. (1987). *In other worlds: Essays in cultural politics.* New York: Methuen.

Spring, J. (1987). *Cry hard and swim: The story of an incest survivor.* London: Virago.

Statistics Canada. (1998). *Family violence in Canada: A statistical profile.* Ottawa: Author.

Statistics Canada. Housing, Family and Social Statistics Division (1993). *Violence against women survey: Highlights 1993.* Ottawa: Author.

Steel, N. (Ed.). (n.d.). *Native women write now.* Fort McMurray, Alberta, CN, Keyano College.

Stimpson, L., & Best, M. (1991). *Courage above all: Sexual assault against women with disabilities.* Toronto, Ontario: DAWN Toronto.

Tal, K. (1996). *Worlds of hurt.* Cambridge, England: Cambridge University Press.

Terr, L. (1990). *Too scared to cry: How trauma affects children and ultimately us all.* New York: Basic Books.

Ticoll, M., & Panitch, M. (1993). Opening the doors: Addressing the sexual abuse of women with an intellectual disability. *Canadian Woman Studies, 13*(4), 84–87.

Toronto Star. (1993, November 18). "Survey reveals job-site violence," p. A14.

Transken, S. (1995). Reclaiming the body territory. In *Feminist perspectives.* Ottawa: CRIAW/ICREF.

Tynes, M. N. (1993). *The door of my heart.* Lawrencetown Beach, Nova Scotia: Pottersfield Press.

van der Kolk, B. A., McFarlane, A. C., & Weisaeth, L. (1996). *Traumatic stress: The effects of overwhelming experience on mind, body, and society.* New York: Guilford.

van der Kolk, B. A., van der Hart, O., & Marmar, C. R. (1996). Dissociation and information processing in posttraumatic stress disorder. In B. A. van der Kolk, A. C. McFarlane,

& L. Weisaeth (Eds.), *Traumatic stress: The effects of overwhelming experience on mind, body, and society* (pp. 303–327). New York: Guilford.

Walker, L. E. A. (1994). *Abused woman and survivor therapy.* Washington, DC: American Psychological Association.

War Against Women Report. (1991). *Standing Committee on Health, Welfare, Social Affairs, Seniors and the Status of Women War Against Women: Report* (Subcommittee on the Status of Women, Chair Barbara Greene). Canada, Parliament, House of Commons. Ottawa: Queens Printer.

Warland, B. (1993). *The bat had blue eyes.* Toronto: Women's Press.

Warren, K. (1996). *Women's voices in experiential education.* Dubuque, IA: Kendall/Hunt.

Weedon, C. (1987). *Feminist practice and post-structuralist theory.* Oxford: Blackwell.

Wente, M. (1994, November 26). A serious case of statistics abuse. *Globe and Mail,* p. A2.

Wente, M. (1997, February 1). Fraser, Freud and forgetting. *Globe and Mail,* p. D9.

Williamson, J. (1994). Writing aversion: The proliferation of contemporary Canadian women's child sexual abuse narratives. In W. Waring (Ed.), *By, for, and about feminist cultural politics* (pp. 197–233). Toronto: Women's Press.

Wisechild, L. (1988). *The Obsidian mirror: An adult healing from incest.* Seattle, WA: Seal Press.

Wittgenstein, L. (1969). *On certainty.* New York: Harper & Row.

Wolpow, R., & Askov, E. N. (1998). Strong in the broken places: Literacy instruction for survivors of pervasive trauma. *Journal of Adolescent & Adult Literacy, 42*(1), 50–57.

Women's Education. (1992). *Learning and Violence: Women Speak Out,* 9(14).

Women's Education. (1994). *Learning in a Toxic Environment,* 11(1).

Women's Network. (1998). *Beyond prescriptions- Meeting your health needs: A plain language workbook about health.* PEI: Women's Network Inc.

Women's Research Center. (1989). *Recollecting our lives: Women's experience of childhood sexual abuse.* Vancouver: Press Gang Publishers.

Author Index

Subject Index